THE MAKING OF
STAR WARS®

THE DEFINITIVE STORY BEHIND THE ORIGINAL FILM

THE MAKING OF

STAR WARS

BASED ON THE LOST INTERVIEWS FROM THE OFFICIAL LUCASFILM ARCHIVES

J. W. RINZLER

Ba................................York

Published in the United States by Del Rey Books, an imprint of The Random
House Publishing Group, a division of Random House, Inc., New York.

DEL REY is a registered trademark and the Del Rey colophon is a trademark
of Random House, Inc.

ISBN 978-0-345-47761-3

Printed in China through Palace Press International on acid-free paper

www.starwars.com
www.delreybooks.com

9 8 7 6 5 4 3 2 1

First Trade Paperback Edition

TO MY MOTHER AND FATHER, MARILYN AND ALAN

ACKNOWLEDGMENTS

At Lucasfilm present: This book could not have been completed without
the invaluable help of those in Lucasfilm's several archives. So tremendous
thanks to: in the Research Library, Jo Donaldson, Carol Wing, and Robyn
Stanley; in the Lucasfilm Archives, Laela French, Dinah Houghtaling,
Claudia Kishler, and Erika Abad; in the Film Archives, Sterling
Hedgpeth; and, last but far from least, a huge thanks to Image
Archives—that is, Tina Mills, Matthew Azeveda, and, in particular,
Michelle Jouan, who oversaw every last image and kept track of some
maniacal picture-gathering from obscure places. Also many thanks to,
in the chairman's office, Jane Bay and Anne Merrifield; at Lucas Licens-
ing, Howard Roffman and Amy Gary for overseeing the whole shebang;
Sue Rostoni for taking on the extra editing while shepherding along
the Expanded Universe, Troy Alders for his artistic acumen, and Leland
Chee and Nancy Frisch; in the legal department, David Anderman, Jann
Moorehead, Elaine Mederer, Chris Holm, and Sarah Garcia; and in the
marketing department, Steve Sansweet for the key tip and Lynne Hale
for the key assists; John Knoll at Industrial Light & Magic for his *Special
Edition* special knowledge; David Nakabayashi at the ILM art library; and
Lucy Wilson at George Lucas Books for providing pictures of life at Park
Way way back when.

And to Rick McCallum, without whom this would never have happened.

At Lucasfilm past: Many and sincere thanks to Charles Lippincott, whose
work three decades ago made this book possible—and for going beyond
the call in reading the manuscript and contributing essential information;
Ralph McQuarrie, for his great generosity and never-before-seen slides
and reference material; Lorne Peterson, for an afternoon of tireless image
identification and for letting us print a number of photographs from his
private collection; Fred Roos, for remembering who was the alternate Han
Solo and for sending some great pics; and Richard Tong, for digging up
valuable preproduction financial information.

Do-gooders at large: Many, many thanks to Tom Hunter, who took time
out to come up with incredibly important legal contracts and correspondence; Peter Jackson, for writing a fantastic foreword, and Matthew
Dravitzki, for facilitating that process; Iain Morris, for his design expertise; and F. Warren Hellman, whose memories of life on the board of
directors at Twentieth Century-Fox were a huge help.

At Tolleson Design: For putting together a beautiful book and making
sense of the hundreds of images, thanks to Craig Clark, Holly Hudson,
Charin Kidder, Said Osio, René Rosso, Boramee Seo, and Steve Tolleson.

At Ballantine: For making this happen and for understanding the point of
this book, thanks to Keith Clayton, Erich Schoeneweiss, Scott Shannon,
and Dave Stevenson.

And, of course, my heartfelt thanks to George Lucas, for what he did
thirty years ago and for the help given during the last year.

CONTENTS

FOREWORD BY PETER JACKSON

I regard myself as being very lucky, because *Star Wars* arrived in my life at an absolutely perfect time. I was sixteen years old. I loved visual effects, loved fantasy—and ever since the age of eight or nine had been harboring ambitions to make films. I was also a movie buff. I used to read *Famous Monsters of Filmland* magazine, and I remember *Starlog* magazine had started about a year earlier. I was just a fan like any other kid. But I was becoming a little bit disillusioned with science-fiction films around that time. There were films like *Logan's Run* and the remake of *King Kong*, and I remember feeling that the miniature shots looked just like miniatures, and the special effects looked like model work with dodgy bluescreen compositing. Nothing was really that impressive; certainly not since *2001* had anyone done anything really amazing in special effects. That was the frame of mind I was in.

Then *Star Wars* was released in the United States in May 1977. Can you imagine being a science-fiction fan, reading those magazines, reading all about *Star Wars*, reading about the phenomenon, about the queues around the block, how everyone was raving about it—but not being able to see it? Because the distribution thinking in those days was that they should hold the American summer movies until New Zealand had its summer. So *Star Wars* wasn't going to open here until our summer— December! And there weren't any entertainment channels on TV back then, no Internet; there really wasn't any way of hooking into it. You would just hear gossip about it—and it was immensely frustrating. It was a slow-brewing phenomenon that took months and months to make its way down here.

Once *Star Wars* came out in the United States, however, there was a whole new flood—a new culture—of science-fiction film magazines. I used to buy all of those that were packed with *Star Wars* photographs. All my friends and I could ever do was look at the still photos. I would look at the photos lying in bed at night, dreaming about what the actual film would be like. I remember being utterly familiar with the images of *Star Wars* months before I ever saw the film. I got the soundtrack album, too, so I heard the music a long time before I saw it.

Finally the summer came. Three or four school friends and I had bought tickets in advance for the first day, but we still had to queue up outside the Cinerama theater in Wellington. Inside the cinema had been equipped with Sensurround for films like *Earthquake* and *Rollercoaster.* It was all decked out with subwoofers. It had a good picture, a huge nice screen.

And as I watched the film, amazingly enough—even with all the hype and the expectations that I'd built up in my mind over the previous seven months—*Star Wars* delivered. My dreams didn't actually surpass the film. I remember standing and cheering and waving my arms around when Luke was flying toward the Death Star. I remember being incredibly overwrought at the excitement of it all. That sort of stuff didn't happen in films back then. It was probably the first time in my life I'd ever become that heavily engaged in a movie to the point of wanting to jump up and down and yell for the hero.

It connected. It was a movie that was incredibly successful at engaging us. Luke really was us. That was Luke's great contribution to the story of *Star Wars*. He was the character who you felt you could relate to—he wasn't outside of your reach. Luke was just a kid like us who was swept away in this adventure—and though incredible things were asked of him, he managed to find it within himself to deliver in the way that we all hoped, if we were flying that X-wing toward the Death Star. Certainly at the time, I don't think I'd ever seen a movie that was as successful at picking you up out of your seat and plunking you right down in the film.

Another real feature of its success was that *Star Wars* spoke to you in a truthful way. We were a generation used to seeing slightly removed, remote films that were made by an older generation of filmmakers who were slightly disconnected and old-fashioned in their relation to the genre. They weren't tapping into the youth culture and what it was like to be young in those days—but *Star Wars* did all that.

Obviously, the directing was a big part of this. The film felt like it was a world that didn't have anything to hide; it had a sense of its own reality; and it was very confident in the alternate reality it was showing. This was not 1977—it really was a place in a galaxy far, far away, a long, long time ago. *Star Wars* didn't feel self-conscious; it didn't feel gimmicky. I know what George means by "documentary camera," because the film had a truthfulness to it that was a big factor in helping you engage with the characters and forget the filmmaking very quickly. I think a lot of filmmakers fall into the trap of thinking, Well, if it's fantasy I can be more flamboyant. But the opposite is true. If you are bombarding the audience with images they've never seen before, you want to keep the camera as real and truthful as you can, as well as the performances of the actors. And George directed the actors in fairly naturalistic performances, considering the outrageous things that were happening on-screen. They all behaved and acted in ways that felt believable.

I think all of that came together to create an atmosphere in which the audience felt totally safe and familiar, and was able to empathize, while at the same time being totally blown away with the images on-screen.

I saw *Star Wars* several times that summer over Christmas and New Year's. I remember we went to a town called Hamilton, a couple of hundred miles north, to see relations, and *Star Wars* was screening in a little cinema, so I saw it there for the third or fourth time. I seemed to follow it around the country that summer as we went on our vacations. I remember buying a T-shirt with the photo of Han Solo and Chewbacca aiming their guns. I remember getting a poster of the Hildebrandt artwork, which went up on my bedroom wall. I definitely saw *The Making of Star Wars* on television, a week or two after it opened, so all sorts of new things were flooding into my brain—words that I'd never heard before, like motion control. Watching the TV documentary was in fact my first chance to glimpse the motion-control camera actually working, going over the surface of the Death Star. I also remember that it was incredibly frustrating because there was no way of recordings shows. I could only watch it once. That was my one shot to study how things were done.

I had my parents' Super-8 camera, and I'd been making little stop-motion animation films, little horror movies—but I remember after I saw *Star Wars* that I furiously started experimenting with spaceships. I read all the articles about how they kit-bashed them out of plastic model kits, so

I went out to the hobby store and got some various trucks and things, and I built the basic spaceship shape out of cardboard and tubes and pipes. Then I glued on all these model bits, and I put all the aging on them. I couldn't do motion control, obviously, but I set up a little dolly track and hung the spaceships in front of a black cloth in our living room. I tracked my camera toward and past the spaceships. I also figured out a way to rewind the Super-8 cartridge, so I could do a second pass where I superimposed a starfield on the background.

In New Zealand it wasn't really easy because there wasn't a film industry there, and no one really made films at that time. But concurrently with *Star Wars* coming out there were a couple of New Zealand feature films; Roger Donaldson made a movie called *Sleeping Dogs.* Certainly, I felt like everything that I wanted to do was just a little bit closer to being able to happen.

What *Star Wars* also did, which was terrific, and which definitely led into *The Lord of the Rings* much later on, was create a science-fiction/fantasy world that felt lived in, used. Things were scratched; there were oil marks, things broke down. That was a lesson I learned along with the whole world back in 1977. When you think of all the movies that have come out since that have created similarly used worlds, it seems to be so natural to everyone, and *The Lord of the Rings* falls into that category. We broke down all the costumes and made sure that the castles looked like they'd been repaired and patched up.

All of that work was done with the Weta Workshop, which I started partly through circumstance and partly because there weren't any of those sorts of facilities in New Zealand. I met other people who were interested in effects like I was, but we wanted to stay in New Zealand making films, so we had no choice but to set up our company—which in a sense is what happened to George as well. He had no choice really but to set up Industrial Light & Magic himself; they were inventing the technology as they were making the film. It's similar in that you're doing things that no one else is doing, so there is no alternative but to set it all up yourself. I've often thought that a lot of the stuff we've created in New Zealand—our own special effects company and our own mixing stages—all that down here, is almost like a Skywalker South.

When I met George many years later, I was not sure what to expect. I didn't know what to think because he'd spent a lot of time out of the limelight. The fact that he didn't direct a movie for twenty years after *Star Wars* meant that he wasn't doing a lot of publicity for the other films he was involved with. So he was a slightly mysterious figure, almost a mythic figure. But I was really delighted to find out just how friendly and funny he is. I wasn't expecting him to be as laid-back. George also has a great, healthy point of view about the world and filmmaking. He's got a very clever understanding of the entertainment industry, of both the pros and cons of the studio system. He's fantastic to talk to, and I just find that a lot of the things that he believes in, and a lot of the things that he says, I agree with a hundred percent. We both prize our independence, and we share a kindred spirit in that I've never had a desire to go to Hollywood and work there.

In the end, I just marvel at the way George used *Star Wars* to revo-

lutionize the way films are made. Not only do I admire the way he used profits from the movie to fuel the technology of making films, which obviously benefits everybody who comes after George, but he actually had this vision of what the technology should be. He wanted to edit movies on computers, which no one else was even thinking of in those days. He wanted to have digital sound; he wanted to push computers to a point where dinosaurs could be realistically rendered on them. The sheer vision! It's so easy, like everyone else, to say, Well, this is the technology that we have; this is the toolbox we have to work with, so we'll make the best film that we can with the tools that we have. But George throws away the toolbox and invents a new toolbox before he even starts making his film. So it's pretty extraordinary.

If you were to take *Star Wars* away, out of film history for a moment, and therefore all the technology that was generated by *Star Wars*, you would just be seeing a whole different landscape of entertainment over the last thirty years. Nowhere near as exciting. We'd all be in cinemas with terribly scratchy optical soundtracks watching celluloid disintegrate before our eyes. . . .

Wellington, New Zealand

Peter Jackson and George Lucas at the Letterman Digital Arts Center in 2006.

INTRODUCTION

The story of the making of *Star Wars* belongs to the 1970s, when independent filmmaking penetrated even the heart of corporate Hollywood. When Martin Scorsese, Francis Ford Coppola, William Friedkin, Brian De Palma, Robert Altman, Woody Allen, Stanley Kubrick, and others made a string of movies that shocked, energized, and entertained in ways that cinema never had up until then—the result of circumstances, cultural change, and artistry. Whether operating with next to no money or with a good-sized budget, these directors managed to make personal films that spoke to audiences everywhere: *The Godfather, A Clockwork Orange, The Exorcist, Taxi Driver, American Graffiti, Annie Hall* . . .

The particular story of how bearded iconoclast George Lucas transformed the joys of his childhood into a swashbuckling space-fantasy is a moviemaking tale wrapped around a fairy tale, and it has already been told many times in books, documentaries, magazine articles, and biographies.

So why tell it again?

Because the original story of the original film has never been told—because the original words have remained hidden, almost unknown and forgotten.

Lit by amber-colored lights and capped by a fabulous stained-glass dome, the jewel of Skywalker Ranch is its Research Library. It contains much of the Lucasfilm Archives. One day, after a tip from director of fan relations Steve Sansweet, I called library manager Jo Donaldson and asked if she knew of any old papers associated with Charles Lippincott, Lucasfilm's vice-president of marketing and merchandising in the mid-1970s. I'd heard he'd worked on a making-of *Star Wars* book that had never been completed, and I was curious.

A couple of days later, research librarian Robyn Stanley directed me to four boxes. As I went through the first box, which happened to be the least organized of the lot, I saw stacks of yellowed paper with the names "George Lucas, Harrison Ford, John Stears, Joe Johnston, Ben Burtt . . ." The next box had neatly filed folders marked with more names: "Carrie Fisher, Mark Hamill, John Dykstra, Gary Kurtz," and even "John Barry"—the fantastic production designer who is absent from nearly every account of the film's genesis, due to his untimely death in 1979.

After I'd examined the contents of all four boxes, it was clear that, over thirty years ago, Lippincott had gathered a huge quantity of material for a making-of book. He had conducted more than fifty interviews between 1975 and 1978, many of them over sixty transcribed pages long. I read through these thousands of pages during the next few months. The interviews were still fresh, sometimes quite candid, and—above all—more accurate than much of what has been written about the film since. Sixteen of the interviews—including conversations with writer-director George Lucas; producer Gary Kurtz; actors Harrison Ford, Mark Hamill, Carrie Fisher, and Anthony Daniels; and several key department heads—were completed a year or more *before* the film was released on May 25, 1977. They were particularly interesting because the speakers were unaware of the future impact of the movie. Even those interviewed after the film's release, in 1978, had no idea just how huge and lasting the effect of *Star Wars* would be, and their recollections of the previous years' events were still vibrant.

If ever there was a book wanting to be written, *The Making of Star Wars* was it—and strangely enough, while making-of books had been published on all the other Episodes, the original *Star Wars* film was without one.

Thanks to prequel trilogy producer Rick McCallum, I had spent the years 2002 to 2005 shadowing George Lucas as he and his team made *Star Wars*: Episode III *Revenge of the Sith*, which resulted in that film's making-of chronicle. When the thirtieth anniversary of *Star Wars* appeared on our publishing radar, I proposed a book about that one, too. It would have to be drawn from archival sources—but its writing ended up being as exciting as the process for *Revenge*, albeit in different ways.

Reading the Lost Interviews was the giant first step in the rediscovery of a fascinating story—and many half-forgotten stories: the front-projection dilemma, the earliest casting sessions, and how Lucas had to finance the preproduction of a film that *no one* wanted to make. Other key moments of research included asking Ralph McQuarrie if he had kept the original reference material Lucas had given him: he quickly found an old envelope from 1975 in his studio, still filled with interesting illustrations—including sketches Lucas had made of the first ships and the Wookiee planet from his rough draft. Internal notes from Industrial Light & Magic allowed me to re-create the chronology of its postproduction special effects, while a "diary" in the film archives department contained information on the trailer. E-mails to the law offices of what used to be Pollock, Rigrod and Bloom yielded, thanks to Tom Hunter, original letters written by Lucas's lawyers to Twentieth Century-Fox that revealed the real ebb and flow of a very difficult relationship.

Coincidentally, from 2005 to 2007, I was working on another book with George Lucas, which facilitated his patient answering of many questions. A visit to Park Way—where the offices and editing rooms of Lucasfilm were originally located—was very helpful, as was the reading of Lucas's bound versions of his various drafts, including the hard-to-find May 1, 1975, story synopsis and typed outline.

Since 1977, *Star Wars* has spawned two sequels and three prequels; countless books, comic books, and video games; television shows; and innumerable interviews. But its original creation, involving a relatively small group of gifted artists and craftspeople led by one inspired filmmaker, was recorded and transcribed many years ago in the Lost Interviews. Together, Lucas and his collaborators overcame health-shattering obstacles—storms, crises, an implacable studio, technical limitations, high stress, and bitter disappointment. In order to maintain the original points of view of the participants, nearly all of the quotes in this book are from the Lost Interviews recorded at that time. So, if someone is complaining about their career or explaining how little they know about special effects, these comments should be read as circa 1975 to 1978 (as should all dollar amounts). It may be that now they know more or have different opinions about what happened, but their words in this book are what they said back then. (The few exceptions are quotes from those—such as James Earl Jones and Peter Cushing—who were not interviewed until quite a few years later.)

To find out how it all came to be, read on. . . .

THE LOST INTERVIEWS

The interviews are listed in chronological order. Unless otherwise indicated, all interviews were conducted by Lucasfilm marketing and merchandising vice president Charles Lippincott. In fact, Lippincott already had in mind a quote to open his making-of *Star Wars* book, taken from Ralph Ellison's *Shadow and Act*: "That which we do is what we are. That which we remember is, more often than not, that which we would like to have been; or that which we hope to be. Thus our memory and our identity are ever at odds; our history ever a tall tale told by inattentive idealists."

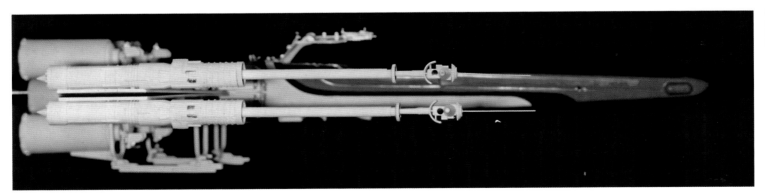

Concept sculpture of the X-wing starfighter by Colin Cantwell.

THE MAKING OF
STAR WARS®

TWO VISIONS

1968 TO AUGUST 1973

CHAPTER ONE

On the road while making Francis Ford Coppola's *The Rain People* during the days and evenings of fall 1968, production assistant George Lucas was also rising before dawn to work on his first feature film, *THX 1138*.

"George was writing the script," recalls Mona Skager, script supervisor on Coppola's movie. "He would write and I would type it up." During postproduction, while sitting with some of the crew in a dingy room, Lucas once spoke about another film he wanted to make. "We were all waiting in a motel room for Francis to come," Skager says, "and George was watching television—when all of a sudden he started talking about holograms, spaceships, and the wave of the future. Quite frankly, I didn't even know what a hologram was, but he had a vision of doing some kind of science-fiction film."

Skager is thus the first on record, but hardly the last, to be perplexed by Lucas's genre-bending ideas. Only a few years before, he had been a student in the University of Southern California's School of Cinema, making visual tone poems and abstract shorts with a professionalism that wowed his contemporaries; his last project had been *THX 1138.4EB*. Recipient of the Samuel Warner Memorial Scholarship, Lucas met Coppola on the Warner Bros. lot, where the slightly older UCLA film school graduate was making *Finian's Rainbow*. The two hit it off, with Coppola encouraging Lucas to write and make movies. Up until this time Lucas had figured he would work in the avant-garde documentary and animation fields. Instead, by 1968 he was scribbling out the plot and words for a feature-length version of his last student film while already contemplating a more fantastic, cinematic variation on a theme.

"I had thought about doing what became *Star Wars* long before *THX 1138*," Lucas says. "I've always been intrigued with Flash Gordon. It was

one of my favorite serials and comic books, along with Tommy Tomorrow and those kinds of things. I really loved adventures in outer space, and I wanted to do something in that genre, which is where *THX* partially came from. THX really is Buck Rogers in the twentieth century, rather than Buck Rogers in the future."

Lucas with camera, circa 1966.

improving anything, though they did succeed in completely alienating the film's director. They released *THX 1138* on March 11, 1971, without knowing what they were selling.

Though it found a small audience and some favorable reviews, the film was no *Easy Rider* at the box office. The film's tepid reception and its disastrous screening prompted Warner Bros. to withdraw funding from American Zoetrope; they also asked Coppola to pay back the $300,000 previously loaned for the development of six other films slated for production, among them *Apocalypse Now*, *The Conversation*, and *The Black Stallion*. Lucas's first film couldn't have been more disappointing from a commercial point of view—and would have aborted the career of a lesser talent. Personally, however, Lucas was happy with *THX 1138*, with its humor, its stylized visuals, its documentary-style storytelling, and its tale of an individual who steps outside his mental cage to a more liberated existence. Despite the fact that the creation of *THX 1138* left Lucas unemployed and penniless, it led to many positives—and, eventually, to *Star Wars*.

The young filmmaker at work on the documentary short subject *6.18.67* (1967)—a poetic look at the making of *Mackenna's Gold*, a Western starring Gregory Peck.

BLACK THURSDAY—AND BEYOND!

In 1969, following the release of *The Rain People*, Coppola and Lucas founded American Zoetrope, an independent film company, on Folsom Street in San Francisco. *THX 1138* became its first film. "When I met Francis and started working as his assistant, because he is very much the writer, he really started pushing me toward theatrical drama, acting—and writing," Lucas says. "He had to force me to write my first script. 'You want to do a film? You write it.' And I said, 'No, no, no, we ought to hire a writer to write it. I don't want to write it. I'm not a writer, I can't write.' But he said, 'You're never going to be a good director unless you learn how to write. Go and write, kid.'

"So I turned out my first script, *THX*, and it was terrible," Lucas continues. "I said, 'See! It's terrible. Let's hire a writer.' So he hired a writer—but that experience was worse than writing it myself. I may be a terrible writer, but at least I know what I want to say. So I went back and rewrote it with a friend of mine, Walter Murch, and it turned out being what it is."

Those familiar with the story of American Zoetrope know that what *THX 1138* was led to Black Thursday—the day which destroyed the fledgling company in its first incarnation and that could've permanently exiled both Coppola and Lucas from the industry.

On Thursday, November 19, 1970, in a screening room on the Warner Bros. lot, the lights went down and *THX 1138* was screened for the executives who had bankrolled the film to the tune of $777,777.77 (a tribute to Coppola's lucky number). After the lights came back up, it quickly became clear that Warner Bros. didn't understand the film, didn't like it, and certainly didn't have a clue as to how they were going to market it. Lucas had anticipated their reaction, and had even planned with his friends to escape with the negative should the executives try to seize it—and they did. Ultimately, Warner Bros. exercised its corporate mind-set by cutting the film by five minutes without really changing or

Lucas and driver Tony Dingman, while making Francis Ford Coppola's *The Rain People* in 1968; Coppola (below) gets a ride astride the vehicles of two motorcycle cops.

NIGHT OF THE DIRECTOR

While Lucas was at work on *THX 1138*, Coppola had delivered a second challenge: to make a happier kind of film. The young director took up the gauntlet, deciding to make a movie about his youth in Modesto, California, where teenagers cruised in beautiful hot rods and listened to great music while looking for girls and growing up. The film would be called *American Graffiti*, a wink to this vanished pastime. However, Coppola's first challenge—writing—was not something Lucas was eager to face again.

"When I was in college I took a creative writing class," Lucas says, "but I really didn't like it. My real thing was art, drawing, visuals. When I went to USC, my primary interest was camera and editing. That was what I really excelled in, so that was what I really liked. I was bored by scripts, and most of the films I did were abstract visual tone poems or documentaries—those were the things I really loved."

"So as I started out with *American Graffiti*, I said to myself, *I don't want to write this; I can't stand writing*, and I frantically went around trying to get a deal to develop the script."

His hope was that his friends Willard and Gloria Huyck (the Huycks) would write the script once he had funds to pay them. To raise the development money, Lucas spent more than six months chasing down possibilities, talking with lower- and upper-level studio executives, such as David Chasman, head of development at United Artists in Los Angeles. But he, like everyone else, declined, much to the frustration of an increasingly destitute Lucas.

Having heard that *THX 1138* had been chosen as one of the films to be featured in the Directors' Fortnight at the International Film Festival in Cannes, Lucas and his wife, Marcia, decided to spend their last few dollars on a vacation in Europe during the month of May 1971 (among the other films featured that year were Alain Tanner's *La Salamandre* and Volker Schlondorff's *The Sudden Wealth of the Poor People of Kombach*). At the time Walter Murch happened to be going with his wife, Aggie, to visit her mother in England. "I said, 'If you're going over there, we'll come, too—I've never been to Europe. I'll just get a backpack,'" remembers Lucas.

On the way he and Marcia stopped for about a week in New York City, where they stayed with Coppola, who was on location shooting *The Godfather*, partially to repay his debt to Warner Bros. While in Manhattan, Lucas took the opportunity to explore deal possibilities. Even though Chasman had turned him down, he was able to talk "directly" with David Picker, president of United Artists, about his ideas for *Graffiti*. "Picker said, 'Let me think about this. When are you leaving?' I said in a couple of days, on my birthday [May 14]. So he said, 'Why don't you call me at Cannes when you get to London, and I'll let you know.'"

On a previous visit with Coppola to New York, Lucas had checked out one avenue for his fantasy-space adventure. "I tried to buy the rights to Flash Gordon," Lucas recalls. "I'd been toying with the idea, and that's when I went, on a whim, to King Features. But I couldn't get the rights to it. They said they wanted Federico Fellini to direct it, and they wanted 80 percent of the gross, so I said forget it. I could never make any kind of studio deal with that."

But King Features' brush-off was key in the crystallization of Lucas's thinking—at that moment, his project went from being a licensed product to an original screenplay. "I realized that Flash Gordon is like anything you do that is established," he says. "That is, you start out being faithful to the original material, but eventually it gets in the way of the creativity. I realized that Flash Gordon wasn't the movie I wanted to do; if I had done it, I would've had to have Ming the Merciless in it—and I didn't want to have Ming the Merciless. I decided at that point to do something more original. I knew I could do something totally new. I wanted to take ancient mythological motifs and update them—I wanted to have something totally free and fun, the way I remembered space fantasy."

Those memories, of course, hark back to Lucas's 1950s childhood in Modesto, California. In what was then a rural town he, like millions of other children, had been able to dream along with the fantastic imagery of the tail end of the golden age of comic books and cinema. Artists such as Alex Raymond, Al Williamson, and Frank Frazetta illustrated fabulous

Lucas and Coppola in discussion at a restaurant, circa 1970.

worlds of the future and the past, while many of the swashbuckling films and 1930s serials were being broadcast on television for the first time.

Back with Francis and his wife, Eleanor, in their apartment, Lucas and Coppola no doubt compared notes on their prospective futures, neither of which looked too bright. "Francis was in the middle of severe trauma at the time, and Ellie was pregnant," Lucas says. "We had to leave at around 7 AM to catch the plane to London—but Francis and Ellie got up at four in the morning, running through the room on their way to the hospital, because she was in labor. She had Sofia that day. When we got to London and our tiny pension, because we were doing Europe literally on $5 a day, I found a pay phone and called David Picker, who said, 'I've thought about this and you can have some money and you can write it. I'm going to be at the Carlton. Come and visit me there and we'll talk about it.' So it was my birthday, it was Sofia's birthday, and I got *American Graffiti* all on the same day."

The "money" was $5,000 to develop the script, $5,000 upon delivery, and $15,000 more in the event the movie was actually made. "I immediately called the Huycks and said, 'I got the deal. We can write the script.'

But they said, 'Oh, gee, George, we just got a chance to direct our own movie.' So I said, 'Okay, look, that's a great opportunity; I'll think of something else.'"

Using his Eurailpass, Lucas took the train to Cannes, where he met up with Murch, who had bicycled there from England. Sticking to their budget, they stayed in a "beautiful" little hotel far off the beaten path in the hills above the town. "We even had to sneak in to see *THX* because we didn't have tickets," Lucas says. "There was also a press conference that we didn't go to, because nobody told us about it. But then I got to visit David Picker at the Carlton Hotel in one of those big suites—that was my first big-time movie experience. Before, I'd only been let into underling executive offices."

After confirming the details of the *Graffiti* deal, Picker asked Lucas if he had anything else that might interest United Artists. "I said, 'Well, I've been toying with this idea of a space-opera fantasy film in the vein of Flash Gordon,'" Lucas says. "And he said, 'Great, we'll make a deal for that, too.' And that was really the birth of *Star Wars*. It was only a notion up to then—at that point, it became an obligation [laughs]!"

Lucas didn't mention to Picker another film he'd been struggling to make for several years, *Apocalypse Now*, because it had already been turned down by United Artists, after having been rejected by Warner Bros. Born from the tumults of the 1960s, it existed as a script he'd worked on with John Milius and was going to be "*Dr. Strangelove* in Vietnam," according to Lucas, filmed in documentary style with hand-held 16mm cameras.

"I knew I could barely get off the ground a $500,000 cheap exploitation hot-rods-to-hell movie," Lucas explains, "so I figured, well at least I'll get that done. I'd continue to develop *Apocalypse Now*—it was all ready—but *Graffiti* would be cheap, it was quick, and I thought it was really commercial."

After traveling from the south of France to Italy, Lucas made another telephone call to the States—this time from Rome—to Gary Kurtz to discuss hiring Richard Walters to write *Graffiti*, since the Huycks were busy.

Years before, when Gary Kurtz had been drafted, he'd been one of the first conscientious objectors in the marines. Instead of being thrown into the brig, however, Kurtz had been assigned to the photographic unit. After serving his time, Kurtz worked with Coppola for the king of bargain-basement exploitation flicks, Roger Corman. Years later, when Coppola mentioned to Kurtz that Lucas was filming *THX 1138* in Techniscope—a cheap, grainy, but sometimes appropriate anamorphic wide-screen format—Kurtz traveled to Marin County to meet the director and watch a reel of his film, because he was thinking of doing a movie using the same technique.

"Later I came back to San Francisco to get an idea of what the dubbing room was like for *THX*," Kurtz says, "and at that time I talked with George at great length."

Returning from Europe to the United States a few weeks later, Lucas had lunch with Kurtz in the commissary on the Universal lot, across the street from where Monte Hellman was cutting his film *Two-Lane Blacktop* (1971), which Kurtz was line-producing. Kurtz had been hired in the

same capacity by Coppola for *Apocalypse Now*, which he was producing, but because that film was stalled Kurtz segued into the same position on *American Graffiti*. Lucas spent the summer of 1971 and most of the following year working on the *Graffiti* screenplay, first with Richard Walters, then by himself.

On December 28, 1971, the financing agreement between Lucasfilm and United Artists for the development of two films—*American Graffiti* and "a second picture"—was made legal. Oddly, even though United Artists had registered the title "The Star Wars" with the Motion Picture Association of America (MPAA) on August 3, 1971, it is not named as such in the agreement (perhaps because the studio's contract department wasn't talking with whatever department was responsible for the trademarking of titles).

Representing Lucas in the negotiations was the law office of Tom Pollock, Jake Bloom, and Andy Rigrod, which had helped the writer-director incorporate his own company, Lucasfilm, earlier that year. The trio had met years earlier during weekly poker games. They joined forces in 1970, eventually evolving their practice into one specializing in the entertainment field, with Rigrod handling contracts, Pollock studio negotiations, and Bloom merchandising—three areas that would be crucial for Lucas in the years to come.

"I worked as the lawyer for the American Film Institute for three years, as their business manager and putting together their new film school," Pollock says. "Many of my first clients were the filmmakers that I met there. Among them were two young writers named Matthew Robbins and Hal Barwood, and they had a friend who needed a lawyer, who was just in the process of making his first feature film, *THX 1138*. So they introduced me to George, and that's how we started our relationship."

Barwood, Robbins, and Lucas had met at USC. The former two had gone on to become filmmakers in their own right, and they all kept in touch. After collaborating with Lucas on the script for his student film, Robbins had even doubled for Robert Duvall when the actor was unavailable for the last shot of THX against the setting sun. Through Coppola, Lucas met Jeff Berg, who had seen *THX 1138* and been impressed. Berg became Lucas's agent—last of the key players brought to Lucas via his first film. The help of all parties was going to be needed to get *Graffiti* going, despite Picker's initial enthusiasm.

"I ended up writing *Graffiti*, and it wasn't that bad," Lucas says. "But UA read the script and said, 'No, it's not our movie.' So that meant another six months of taking it all over town trying to get it sold."

By this time, however, Coppola had recovered from his consecutive traumas. *The Godfather* had been released in March 1972 to critical and box-office mega-success, reversing the director's fortunes and elevating his deal-making clout to that of the divine. "Finally, Universal said they'd do *Graffiti* if I could get somebody like Francis involved," Lucas says. "So I brought Francis in as the producer."

The deal was for three pictures: *American Graffiti* and two future films. The "Lucas Option Contract" and "Inducement Letter" were signed on April 6, 1972. In addition to spelling out that *American Graffiti*'s production budget was not to exceed $775,000—even less than that of *THX*—it also stipulated that the two other pictures automatically had priority over any other projects Lucas might develop in the future.

"We were on our way," Lucas says. "I was starting to get into production,

George W. (Walton) Lucas Jr.'s signature on his agreement with the United Artists Corporation to write the script for *American Graffiti* and to eventually develop "a second picture."

Francis Ford Coppola's signature on Universal Pictures' "Inducement Letter," which enabled Lucas to make *American Graffiti* after United Artists passed on it, and which gave Universal an option on the "second picture."

but I still felt the script needed work. By this time the Huycks had finished their movie, so I said, 'Look, I'm going to start shooting in eight weeks, come and work on my script.'" Not really doing a rewrite, the Huycks worked primarily on the dialogue and the relationship between Steve and Laurie, two of the film's teenage protagonists.

Principal photography for *Graffiti* began on June 26 and wrapped on August 4, a twenty-nine-day schedule. It was a quick, grueling night shoot, with Lucas directing, Coppola producing, and Kurtz as the line producer/production manager. Harrison Ford, who plays Bob Falfa in the film, recalls his meetings with Kurtz: "He was the guy who told me no more drinking beer on the streets, and then no more drinking beer in the trailer, and then no more drinking beer. Those were my three basic contacts with him. He explained it was a matter of insurance. He was real nervous."

VIETNAM WARS IN SPACE

In November 1972, while Lucas was in postproduction on *Graffiti*, he sent Kurtz to scout locations in the Philippines and Hong Kong for what he hoped would be his next film, *Apocalypse Now*. Kurtz stayed on the road until Christmas. Columbia Pictures was showing renewed interest in the film, and Lucas, who had wanted to make *Apocalypse Now* after *THX 1138*, was even more intent on not being put off a second time.

Alas, after Lucas had turned over *Graffiti* to Universal in early 1973, but half a year before its release, Columbia dropped *Apocalypse Now*. Lucas doggedly took it to several other studios, but no one wanted it. The Vietnam War was just too controversial. Lucas was in a fix: He was desperately poor—and Universal, like United Artists before it, was confused by and pessimistic about the prospects of *American Graffiti*. It told several stories

that were intercut, which was revolutionary at the time, and it didn't seem to have a plot. Despite a particularly enthusiastic preview, Universal began toying with the idea of releasing it on television instead of in theaters.

It was at that moment of despair that Lucas turned back to the "unnamed science-fiction project"—because at least it had the remnants of interest back at United Artists, where he'd signed the original development deal.

"I was in debt," Lucas says. "I needed a job very badly, and I didn't know what was going to happen with *Graffiti*, so I started to work on *Star Wars* rather than continue with *Apocalypse Now*. I had worked on *Apocalypse Now* for about four years and I had very strong feelings about it. I wanted to do it, but could not get it off the ground. Columbia had just turned it down. It had started at Warner and then it went to Paramount, and it had been just about everywhere in town. Everybody had that script at least once, and the main studios had had it twice. I think everybody was just afraid of the Vietnam War and they were afraid that it was going to cost more than what we thought it was going to cost, and nobody wanted to go near it. So I figured what the heck, I've got to do something, I'll start developing *Star Wars*."

Throughout his life up to that point, Lucas had had a number of key interests, apart from cinema and art: anthropology—the interaction of politics, history, and people; mythology, as a representation of cultural conditioning; traditional adventure stories; and . . . speed. From hot rods to rocket ships. All three interests are present in *THX 1138*, which contains an ambiguous government, robot police, a judicial system ruled by a computer, and people who are persecuted for not taking drugs prescribed by the state; it opens with a clip from a Buck Rogers serial and ends with an

Lucas's love of fast machines began with his own Fiat Bianchina (left). It made the jump to cinema with THX (below), who roars away in a stolen Lola T70, and continued with the ethereal glow of John Milner's yellow hot rod cruising among other gleaming machines in *American Graffiti*.

"I grew up working on hot cars and I like hot cars," Lucas says. "It's something that I am personally drawn toward. Even before I was a teenager, I always wanted a hot car; when I got to be a teenager, I had a hot car and I worked on hot cars. That was my big drive in life—until I got into films. So it's carried over into film."

ultra-high-speed car and motorcycle chase. *Graffiti* also ends with a high-speed vehicular climax and a coda that mentions the Vietnam War—in fact, the whole film takes place within the shadow of that conflict and the impending social upheaval of the 1960s. But with *Apocalypse Now* on the sidelines, many of its particular political conceits were transferred to the front lines of Lucas's space-fantasy film.

"A lot of my interest in *Apocalypse Now* was carried over into *Star Wars*," Lucas says. "I figured that I couldn't make that film because it was about the Vietnam War, so I would essentially deal with some of the same interesting concepts that I was going to use and convert them into space fantasy, so you'd have essentially a large technological empire going after a small group of freedom fighters or human beings."

THE FORCE OF THE WILL

As George Lucas began to write, he moved in his mind from the large to the small, from big themes—such as those inherent in his thinking on conflict, governments, and Vietnam—to details, such as the names of characters and planets. He made lists that often read like streams of consciousness. Perhaps his first writing germane to *Star Wars* is a roster that dates from early 1973; the name at the top of the page is "Emperor Ford Xerxes XII" (Xerxes was a Persian king assassinated by one of his sons), followed by: "Xenos, Thorpe, Roland, Monroe, Lars, Kane, Hayden, Crispin, Leila, Zena, Owen, Mace, Wan, Star, Bail, Biggs, Bligh, Cain, Clegg, Fleet, Valorum."

Not long afterward, Lucas started combining first and last names, and assigned roles to them. Alexander Xerxes XII becomes "Emperor of Decarte." Owen Lars is an "Imperial General"; Han Solo is "leader of the Hubble people" (probably named for Edwin Hubble, the astronomer); Mace Windy is a "Jedi-Bendu"; C.2. Thorpe is a space pilot; Lord An-nakin Starkiller is "King of Bebers"; and Luke Skywalker is "Prince of Bebers."

Lucas used the same process for his locales, listing names, then giving them characteristics. "Yoshiro" and "Aquilae" are desert planets; "Brunhuld" and then "Alderaan" are city planets, capital of the "Border System." Others listed are: "Anchorhead, Bestine, Starbuck, Lundee, Yavin, Kissel, Herald Square." Aquilae is where the Hubble and Beber people live; Yavin becomes a jungle planet, whose natives are eight-foot-tall Wookies; Ophuchi is a gaseous cloud planet where lovely women can be found; Norton II is an ice planet; and a "Station Complex" is noted among the space cruisers.

From these lists Lucas moved on to a handwritten two-page idea fragment titled *Journal of the Whills, [Part] I,* which recounts "the story of Mace Windy, a revered Jedi-Bendu of Ophuchi, as related to us by C. J. Thorpe, padawaan learner to the famed Jedi."

The initials *C.J.* or *C.2.* (it switches back and forth) stand for "Chuiee Two Thorpe of Kissel. My father is Han Dardell Thorpe, chief pilot of the renown galactic cruiser *Tarnack.*" At the age of sixteen Chuiee enters the "exalted Intersystems Academy to train as a potential Jedi-Templer. It is here that I became padawaan learner to the great Mace Windy . . . at that time, Warlord to the Chairman of the Alliance of Independent Systems . . . Some felt he was even more powerful than the Imperial leader of the Galactic Empire . . . Ironically, it was his own comrades' fear . . . that led to his replacement . . . and expulsion from the royal forces."

After Windy's dismissal, Chuiee begs to stay in his service "until I had finished my education." *Part II* takes up the story: "It was four years later that our greatest adventure began. We were guardians on a shipment of fusion portables to Yavin, when we were summoned to the desolate second planet of Yoshiro by a mysterious courier from the Chairman of the Alliance." At this point Lucas's first space-fantasy narrative trails off . . .

Handwritten first page of Lucas's *Journal of the Whills.*

Journal of the Whills

I

this is the story of Mace Windy, a revered Jedi-bendu of Ophuchi, as related to us by C.J. Thorpe, padawaan learner to the famed Jedi.

Although light-years from what was to come, the two-page *Journal* has a number of elements that Lucas would recycle into subsequent drafts: the Jedi; the phonetics of *Chuiee;* a great pilot named Han; an academy; and the galactic Empire. "*Journal of the Whills* came from the fact that you 'will' things to happen," Lucas says. Much like the Disney films that opened and closed with the device of a storybook, "the introduction was meant to emphasize that whatever story followed came from a book."

No notes bear witness to the transition of Lucas's thinking from this fragment to his next effort, but he probably did what he would do again and again when creatively stuck: He started making new lists, with new plot points, before writing another tale. This time the plot points were hard coming—until he remembered a particular Akira Kurosawa movie he'd seen. Lucas had already been leaning in that direction, as the name *Yoshiro* in the *Journal* is a variation on *Toshiro,* the first name of the great Japanese actor Toshiro Mifune, who starred in many of Kurosawa's films, including *Yojimbo* (1961).

Lucas's ten-page handwritten treatment, titled "The Star Wars" and dated May 1973, relies for its structure on another Kurosawa classic, *Kakushi-toride no san-akunin* (*The Hidden Fortress,* 1958). Lucas had first encountered the work of the great Japanese director at USC, where he was impressed with *Shichinin no samurai* (*Seven Samurai,* 1954). Not only was its master-disciple relationship of interest to the young student, but Lucas also admired Kurosawa's fast edits.

"*Hidden Fortress* was an influence on *Star Wars* right from the very beginning," Lucas says. "I was searching around for a story. I had some scenes—the cantina scene and the space battle scene—but I couldn't think of a basic plot. Originally, the film was a good concept in search of a story. And then I thought of *Hidden Fortress,* which I'd seen again in 1972 or '73, and so the first plots were very much like it."

In Kurosawa's black-and-white masterpiece, two bickering peasants become entangled with a princess and a general (Mifune) who are hiding out during a civil war, and end up helping their social superiors in their adventures. Certain scenes in Lucas's treatment are reminiscent of *Hidden*

Fortress, notably where General Skywalker can't check his bird-steed in time and barrels into the camp of his enemies, much like Kurosawa's general who can't check his horse and gallops into a hostile camp. Skywalker's one noted mannerism—he scratches his head—is taken from Mifune's performance in several of Kurosawa's films. "Having the two bureaucrats or peasants is really like having two clowns—it goes back to Shakespeare," Lucas says, "which is probably where Kurosawa got it."

Lucas on the set of *THX 1138.*

(Continued on page 11)

Lucas's fourteen-page typed treatment begins with:

```
                DEEP SPACE.
The eerie blue-green planet of Aquilae slowly drifts
into view. A small speck, orbiting the planet, glints
in the light of a nearby star.

Suddenly a sleek fighter-type spacecraft settles omi-
nously into the foreground moving swiftly toward the
orbiting speck. Two more fighters silently maneuver
into battle formation behind the first and then three
more craft glide into view. The orbiting speck is
actually a gargantuan space fortress which dwarfs the
approaching fighters.
```

The fighters attack the space fortress, but the scene changes to a rebel princess who is fleeing across the galaxy with some loyal retainers and a treasure. It is the thirty-third century, during a period of civil wars. The sovereign of the Empire has posted a reward for her capture.

```
She is being guarded by one of her generals, (LUKE
SKYWALKER) and it is he who leads her on the long and
dangerous journey that follows.
```

Two terrified, bickering bureaucrats who have escaped the space fortress and landed on Aquilae are captured by Skywalker, who is disguised as a farmer. They meet the princess, who is also disguised. The small group travels "across the wastelands of Aquilae, headed for the spaceport city of Gordon, where they hope to get a spacecraft that will take them to the friendly planet of Ophuchi." They eventually arrive at a ruined religious temple where a rebel band of ten boys are hiding. After the boys defend the group against a large beast, they are admitted into the party.

```
The general, one of the bureaucrats, and one of the
boys, venture into a shabby cantina on the outskirts
of the space port, looking for the rebel contact who
will help them get a spacecraft. The murky little den
is filled with a startling array of weird and exotic
Aliens laughing and drinking at the bar. The bureau-
crat and the boy are both terrified as the general or-
ders two drinks and questions the bartender about the
rebel contact man. A group of bullies begin to taunt
and ridicule the boy. Skywalker attempts to avoid a
confrontation, but worse comes to worse, and he is
forced to fight. With a flash of light, his lazer sword
is out . . . One of the bullies lies double, slashed
from chin to groin and Skywalker, with quiet dignity,
replaces his sword in its sheath. The entire fight has
lasted a matter of seconds.
```

Deep Space.

The eerie blue-green planet of Aquilae slowly drifts into view. A small speck, orbiting the planet, glints in the light of a near by star.

Suddenly a sleek fighter-type space craft settles ominously into the foreground, moving swiftly toward the orbiting speck. Two more fighters silently maneuver into battle formation behind the first; and then three more craft glide into

the Star Wars.

by
George Lucas.

Lucasfilm Ltd
May, 1973

THE STAR WARS

The group makes contacts with the rebels but is reported on by a spy. At the space port the heroes are attacked but manage to escape in a stolen space fighter. A huge dogfight ensues and continues as they travel across the galaxy; Skywalker and his allies destroy many ships and avoid an asteroid, but have to crash-land on Yavin. On the planet surface, members of the group split up and are watched by a "giant furry alien." While some of the boys set up camp, another group heads for a city with the princess and the two bureaucrats; Skywalker then has to do battle with aliens riding giant bird-like creatures. He defeats them using his blaster, but cannot help riding into the aliens' camp. There the general does single combat with an alien leader, cutting him in half with his lazer sword. The frenzied aliens then throw Skywalker off a cliff, but he hangs on to a vine. Because of his miraculous return, the aliens worship him as a god.

The cover and first two pages of Lucas's treatment (above and left).

Tracking the captured princess, the chief alien leads Skywalker to a farm where he meets "a cantankerous old farmer who is married to an Alien" and finds the other group of boys. They attack the Imperial outpost where they think the princess is being held, but discover she has been taken to Alderaan. With their ships disguised as "Imperial rangers," Skywalker and the boys penetrate the Imperial prison. A fight erupts, but Skywalker escapes with the princess and wins a space dogfight.

```
The princess' arrival on Ophuchi is celebrated by a
huge parade, honoring the general and his small band.
The princess' uncle, ruler of Ophuchi, rewards the
bureaucrats, who for the first time see the princess
revealed as her true goddess-like self . . . . After the
ceremony is over, and the festivities have ended, the
drunken bureaucrats stagger down an empty street arm
in arm realizing that they have been adventuring with
demigods.
```

Note: Following each of Lucas's drafts, a running list will summarize those elements that will become permanent to the story. (Although not noted here, Lucas would also use certain material in subsequent films.) Spelling is consistent with that of the drafts. The elements are listed in the order they appear:

STAR WARS PROGRESSION

- Fighter-type spacecraft attack a space fortress
- Rebels on the run during a civil war
- A princess
- A Skywalker character (a general)
- Two bickering characters (bureaucrats, working for the Empire)
- A landspeeder going across wastelands in search of larger spacecraft for transport to a friendly planet
- A ruined temple
- Cantina confrontation
- A Jedi weapon ("lazer sword")
- After cantina, a spy
- The planet Yavin (jungle planet for the Wookees)
- A giant furry alien
- A cantankerous old farmer
- The planet Alderaan (capital of the Empire)
- Prison rescue and ensuing space dogfight
- Award ceremony

John Ford's 1956 film *The Searchers* was also an early influence. Its saloon scene partially inspired the treatment's cantina sequence. All in all Lucas's exotic creatures and aliens, space battles and bird-steeds come from a mind formed by the reading and viewing habits of a typical 1950s kid—but these influences were just beginning a long transformation. One can already see how the "lost" boys of *Peter Pan* have become, given the political sway of the writer's mind, jungle rebels with just a hint of the Vietcong. Lucas's idiosyncratic mental amalgam would continue to reformulate ideas and materials—while Lucas the deal maker would try to procure the necessary funds to create a cinematic venue for their expression.

A CLOCKWORK STUDIO

Having decided to develop the quasi-science-fiction film sometime early in the spring of 1973, Lucas approached United Artists again, and according to Lucas's agent Jeff Berg they talked about "an epic space fantasy." On May 7, 1973, Berg met with David Chasman, who was now vice president of production under David Picker, and gave him the fourteen-page typed treatment. On behalf of his client, Berg asked for a $20,000 development fee to transform the treatment into a screenplay. To give United Artists an idea of what kind of visuals he had in mind, Lucas had attached ten images to the treatment: four NASA photos (astronauts in space, satellites, spaceships with peculiarly shaped flat wings); a photo of US Army amphibious tanks; and five fantasy illustrations, consisting of a skull-faced, muscular man holding a dead woman, pietà-like; a sci-fi fantasy hero, crouching and holding a blaster; a swarm of warriors fighting a giant furry creature; another sci-fi hero standing next to a futuristic vehicle; and a goggle-faced alien staring out at the viewer.

Once again it was the time of the year for the International Film Festival, so Berg wired Chasman at Cannes on May 14, 1973. "I wrote something like, 'Hey, we're waiting [for] word from you on the science-fiction project—do you want to proceed with it or not?'" Berg says, "but they wound up passing on it." United Artists' official negative response came on May 29, 1973. "United Artists passed on it, and money was the main reason as I recall," Pollock adds. "We had told them from the beginning that it was going to cost $3 million. We wanted to go with UA, but we then had a contractual obligation to submit the project to Universal, because when they made *Graffiti* they made George sign a deal for two options."

In June 1973, however, Lucas was not enamored of Universal. In its continuing incomprehension of *American Graffiti*, the studio—in an almost exact replay of Warner Bros.' handling of *THX 1138*—had cut five minutes from the film. "We did not want to go with Universal," Pollock says. "At the time George was very unhappy with them, during the months of April and May, when the studio was recutting the movie."

Nevertheless, on May 30 or June 1, Lucas's treatment was duly submitted to studio executive Ned Tannen. Under the terms of the agreement, Universal had ten days to say whether or not they were interested. "We sent them a letter saying, this is the movie we want to make, it's going to cost $3 million. We want this fee, we want this percentage of the profits," Pollock recalls. "The only official word we ever heard was Ned calling back asking for more time. He couldn't make a decision in ten days. At the end of the ten-day period, we sent him a letter saying, 'Since you haven't said yes, the answer is no.' "

Later stories circulated that perhaps Tannen wanted it, but Lew Wasserman, the legendary éminence grise of Universal, had said, "We don't make science-fiction movies." Pollock's recollection, however, is that "Ned was in a waffling state because he was in a waffling state about *American Graffiti* at the time."

"The question becomes, *Did Universal screw up and let the letter go unnoticed—were they derelict in some kind of procedural area?*" Berg says. "The answer is no—Universal works like clockwork. They never screw up in that area. They have the most efficient notification follow-up department of any studio in town. They didn't proceed with the project because either they didn't believe in the idea, or they were not comfortable with George making a picture of that size, $3 million, which in 1973 was still regarded as an expensive picture. It was before the advent of the $8 to $10 million movies. Although Universal has a history of making expensive pictures, George had always presented himself as an underground, independent filmmaker. Psychologically, they weren't prepared."

Although this last rejection probably didn't hurt Lucas, the consistently pedestrian behavior of the studios almost certainly sharpened his distaste for Hollywood. "UA was very cool," Lucas says. "I just think they thought of it as a big, expensive movie and they didn't understand it. Universal was the same way." Maybe dreaming of a more ideal studio, Lucas adds, "I think Disney would have accepted this movie if Walt Disney were still alive. Walt Disney not only had vision, but he was also an extremely adventurous person. He wasn't afraid."

THE ADVENTURES OF FOX IN THE 20TH CENTURY

While Universal was still scratching its corporate head over *The Star Wars,* Jeff Berg had already started informal discussions with vice president for creative affairs Alan Ladd Jr. at Twentieth Century-Fox, which is located in Century City, Los Angeles, just west of Beverly Hills. "I'd been talking to Laddie about George Lucas. This was before *American Graffiti* came out, but Laddie had heard sensational things about it," Berg says.

Son of the well-known actor Alan Ladd (*The Blue Dahlia*, 1946; *Shane*, 1953), Alan Ladd Jr. had been recruited by Jere Henshaw only months before, in January. The result of a merger in 1935 between Fox Film Corporation and Twentieth Century Pictures, the studio in 1973 was operating under the presidency of Gordon Stulberg and the chairmanship of Dennis Stanfill. One of the old-guard Hollywood juggernauts, the studio's last few years had been rocky under the fading direction of longtime head Darryl Zanuck, who had finally left the company in 1971. According to Warren Hellman, who became one of the eleven directors on the board a few months later, the sole source of viable income in June 1973 was the television show *M*A*S*H,* which had started airing in 1972.

"Essentially Fox was going broke," Hellman says. "We were in violation of all the important bank covenants. We were in intense negotiations with Chase, who was the leading bank, and who was being very harsh on us."

New management was therefore looking for new ways to make hits, and the nearly incomprehensible Sean Connery vehicle *Zardoz* (1974) was Ladd's first project.

"I was having drinks one day with Jeff Berg, who was talking about what a fabulous picture *Graffiti* was," Alan Ladd Jr. says. "Universal was very unhappy with the picture, but Jeff thought it was a terrific film, so I said that I'd love to see it. Universal didn't want it off the lot, but I was able to arrange a screening. I saw it on the Fox lot at nine one morning—and it absolutely bowled me over. That's when I just said to Jeff that I'd like to meet George and hear about what ideas he's working on."

Berg arranged the meeting after making sure that Ladd understood that Universal still had right of first refusal. "George said he had this idea about *Star Wars,*" Ladd continues, "so I said, let's make the deal. Having met George, I felt that *Graffiti* was further from what he was really into than *Star Wars.*"

Moreover, at Fox, the science-fiction genre was currently hot. Their sequels to *Planet of the Apes* (1968) had been good business. The fifth and last film in the series, *Battle for the Planet of the Apes,* had just opened on June 15, 1973—and the "furry alien" in Lucas's treatment may have sparked dreams of a similar franchise. "When the *Planet of the Apes* series did so well for Fox, it's possible that people's interest was rejuvenated," Kurtz says. "I'm sure there were people there who felt that there were other things that could be done in science fiction that also would make money."

With Ladd's interest assured and Universal officially out of the picture, Tom Pollock sent Twentieth Century-Fox a letter on July 13, 1973, outlining the same terms they'd proposed to Universal. "It was a very lowball deal," he says, "with $15,000 for the development, $50,000 to write the script, and $100,000 to direct, some of which was even pledged to the completion of the movie. A $3 million budget and that's it. We had no negotiating power. They were the only ones that wanted it."

Pollock's letter to vice president of business affairs William Immerman also stipulated that the first-draft screenplay would be written by October 31; that Lucasfilm could hire a secretary at $175 per week; that Gary Kurtz would produce for $50,000; and that Marcia Lucas and Verna Fields were "preapproved as editors and Walter Murch is preapproved as postproduction supervisor"—a logical clause given that they'd all worked well together on *American Graffiti.* Forty percent of the net profits of the picture would go to Lucasfilm, and 60 to Fox. Another clause addressed the issue of power: "[Twentieth Century-Fox] shall not have the right to assign an executive producer or exercise any other production controls other than standard location auditors."

"I'm very, very adamant about my creative work," Lucas says. "Even when I was young I was not that willing to even listen to other people's ideas—I wanted everything to be my way. Over the years, starting in film school, I did start to work with others, because film is so collaborative, but I was still pretty closed-minded. I didn't mind getting input from the creative people around me—but not the executives. I grew up in the 1960s. I was very anti-corporation, and I was here in San Francisco, where anti-authority is even more extreme. On my first two movies I was really left alone. No one watched dailies, no one really read the script. And when the studios interfered at the end, I thought it was the end of the world. It

As the legal representative of Lucasfilm, Thomas Pollock signed William J. Immerman's return letter/deal memo of August 20, 1973, including it in his August 24 letter to Fox.

A letter of July 13 from the law offices of Pollock, Rigrod and Bloom became the basis for the deal memo between Lucasfilm and Twentieth Century-Fox Film Corporation for *The Star Wars*.

really wasn't, but I felt it was. So I fought for many years to make sure no one could tell me what to do.

"I'm realistic enough to know that you have to make compromises when filmmaking," he adds, "but if I can avoid them, I will."

On August 20 Immerman sent back modifications to Pollock's eight-page memo. On August 24 Pollock sent a letter with more amendments—including another preapproved *Graffiti* holdover, Fred Roos, as casting director—along with a note stating that United Artists had agreed to "waive its registration of the title [*Star Wars*] to any company designated by us." The "Memorandum Agreement" between Twentieth Century-Fox and Lucasfilm Ltd. was signed retroactively on August 20—just nineteen days after *Graffiti* was released to surprisingly strong box office—but based on the *pre-release* July terms. The timing illustrates another motivating factor for Fox: Besides having faith in Lucas, Ladd, by acting fast, was able to sign up the promising director for very little.

"I actually needed the money in May because I was so far in debt," Lucas says. "That's why I made the deal. In September, by the time they sent me a check, *Graffiti* was already a big hit and I was okay financially. It's ironic. If I'd just waited until *Graffiti* came out, I could have made the deal much better."

A month after signing, Lucas received $10,000; he would receive another $10,000 "upon delivery of the first draft screenplay," and $30,000 upon commencement of principal photography. The actual making of the film, however, was far—very far—from being assured at this point. The memo represented only an agreement to go to the next step; there was no formal production-distribution contract. The "Election to Proceed—Turnaround" clause made it clear that the studio could withdraw its

financial support at any time "until Fox's next Board of Directors meeting," at which time they could "elect either to go forward with the project or not go forward with the project." Lucas's own commitment, as stated in an additional clause, was subject to his previous three-picture deal with Universal. If that studio elected to proceed with his film *Radioland Murders*, which Lucas had also been developing with the Huycks simultaneously with *The Star Wars*, then the former film would take priority.

Fox had simply decided to go ahead with the first phase: the development of the screenplay. They could read it and bow out, or go ahead with a revised draft and then bow out, which is the way any studio deal works.

"As with most companies that go through a lot of problems, the board had become quite obstreperous," Warren Hellman says. "In theory Ladd reported to Stanfill, but he also had to bring his productions to the board—and it was always a moronic conversation. We were talking budgets and nobody knew anything about movies." The one semi-exception was real-life princess Grace Kelly, a board member and former mega-star—but from the world of 1950s movies, which meant she had little grasp of the intricate mechanics of large-scale modernized filmmaking. Nevertheless, the board of directors gave Ladd permission to proceed with the first step.

While Berg notified Universal that Lucasfilm had accepted the deal at Fox under the same terms proposed earlier to them, Lucas attended a screening of *American Graffiti* at USC. A young man named Joe Viskocil was in the audience, and he remembers that "somebody asked George what his next project was, and he said '*Star Wars*'—and bells started ringing in my head because I realized that this was going to be a big show. I just felt it was going to be something really big."

FIGHTING WORDS

AUGUST 1973 TO JANUARY 1975

CHAPTER TWO

While the story of *Star Wars* was still just a few key scenes in his mind's eye, Lucas's completed film *American Graffiti* was released on August 1, 1973—but only after Lucas had arranged additional screenings and strategies to garner support for his movie, all of which ultimately persuaded Universal to finally book it into theaters. Probably to the studio's great surprise, the seemingly disjointed film coalesced into one of the biggest moneymakers of all time—even more so in light of its profit-to-cost ratio, because the film was made for so little. For many kids, seeing *Graffiti* was a revelation: It was one of the first films to have humor that was *for kids,* while Lucas's and Murch's sound work made the music so alive that thousands of those same kids ran out and bought their first soundtrack ever. *American Graffiti* also sparked what has now become an American tradition of looking back on its immediate past—the 1950s, '60s, '70s—with fond recollections.

For Lucas the success of *Graffiti* meant many things, not least of which was the ability to pay off his many personal debts. He was also able to pay the mortgage on a home he'd bought in a burst of optimism just before the movie was released. Located in San Anselmo, a small town in Marin County (just north of San Francisco via the Golden Gate Bridge), it wasn't far from a second building he purchased in January 1974—a one-story Victorian house originally built in 1869, which Lucas began remodeling as offices, with its dilapidated carriage house eventually transformed into editing rooms.

The success of the film also led to various obligations and ceremonies, all of which slowed the transformation of the *Star Wars* treatment into a rough draft. "When I was writing *Star Wars,* for the first year, there was an infinite number of distractions," Lucas says. "*Graffiti* was a huge hit, plus I was restoring my office at the same time. Building a screening room kept me going for nine, ten months."

Lucas did not hire a writer to work on *The Star Wars,* despite the myriad preoccupations. It hadn't worked before, on *THX* and *Graffiti,* so there was no reason to try again. Instead, every day he'd walk up the stairs to his writing room at Medway—"it's like a little tower"—and plug away on a desk he'd built from three doors. "I grew up in a middle-class Midwest-style American town with the corresponding work ethic," Lucas explains. "So I sit at my desk for eight hours a day no matter what happens, even if I don't write anything. It's a terrible way to live. But I do it; I sit down and I do it. I can't get out of my chair until five o'clock or five thirty or whenever the news comes on. It's like being in school. It's the only way I can force myself to write."

Lucas's office in his former home in San Anselmo, as it appeared in 2006. Sitting at the desk he'd made from three doors (which is still there), Lucas could stare out of 180-degree wraparound windows while writing and suffering through the first drafts of *The Star Wars*.

in bed before I go to sleep, just thinking—or I'll wake up in the middle of the night sometimes, thinking of things, and I'll come up with ideas and I'll write them down. Even when I'm driving, I come up with ideas. I come up with a lot of ideas when I'm taking a shower in the morning."

Watching television also became part of the screenwriting process in the latter part of 1973, when Lucas began to collect real footage of flying planes in anticipation of creating his movie's aerial space battle. "Every time there was a war movie on television, like *The Bridges at Toko-Ri* [1954], I would watch it—and if there was a dogfight sequence, I would videotape it. Then we would transfer that to 16mm film, and I'd just edit it according to my story of *Star Wars*. It was really a way of getting a sense of the movement of the spaceships.

"Because one of the key visions I had of the film when I started was of a dogfight in outer space with spaceships—two ships flying through space shooting each other. That was my original idea. I said, 'I want to make that movie. I want to *see* that.' In *Star Trek* it was always one ship sitting here and another ship sitting there, and they shot these little lasers and one of them disappeared. It wasn't really a dogfight where they were racing around in space firing."

CHANGING BUREAUCRATS

On January 10, 1974, Lucas signed a necessary if somewhat surreal legal agreement with himself, whereby Lucasfilm Ltd. loaned out "George Lucas" as director to "The Star Wars Corporation," a subsidiary formed to facilitate the upcoming budget and legal dealings with Fox.

Perhaps to celebrate the release of *American Graffiti*, Lucas sat down with a group of friends at a restaurant in San Francisco's Chinatown in 1973: (from left to right) Gary Kurtz, USC professor Ken Miura, Mona Skager, Bob Hall, Aggie and Walter Murch, filmmaker Michael Ritchie, Lucas, and Kurtz's wife, Meredith.

"I work with a hard pencil and regular lined paper," he adds. "I put a big calendar on my wall. Tuesday I have to be on page twenty-five, Wednesday on page thirty, and so on. And every day I 'X' it off—*I did those five pages*. And if I do my five pages early, I get to quit. Never happens. I've always got about one page done by four o'clock in the afternoon, and during that next hour I usually write the rest. Sometimes I'll get up early and write a lot of pages, but that doesn't really happen much."

Like most writers, even when not at his desk, Lucas was working. "A writer is, every waking hour, constantly pondering scenes or structural problems. I carry my little notebook around and I can always sit down and write. That's the terrible part, because you can't get away from it. I'll lie

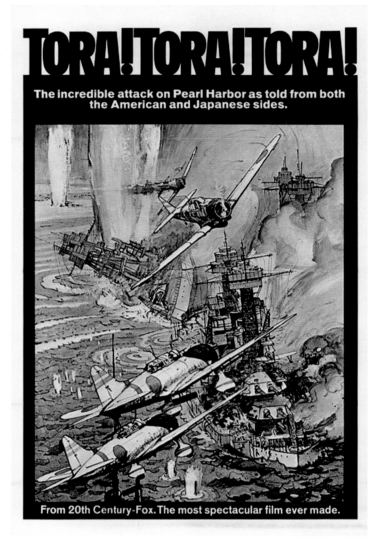

TORA!TORA!TORA!

The incredible attack on Pearl Harbor as told from both the American and Japanese sides.

From 20th Century-Fox. The most spectacular film ever made.

Throughout the winter of 1973–1974, Lucas worked on the script, writing and living most of the time alone, as Marcia was often in Los Angeles, where she was editing Martin Scorsese's *Alice Doesn't Live Here Anymore* (1974). Kurtz was busy trying to get *Apocalypse Now* off the ground and thinking about developing his own films. In the spring of 1974 Lucas sometimes traveled to Tucson, Arizona, when Marcia was on location cutting the same film. He would sit on the patio, perhaps with a book or two, and write during the day. "I've done a lot of reading for this picture. It's not really research so much as mythology and fantasy are taking over my life. I read everything from *John Carter of Mars* to *The Golden Bough*, so obviously all of that influences you in a certain way. I'm trying to make a

classic genre picture, a classic space opera—and there are certain concepts that have been developed by writers, primarily Edgar Rice Burroughs, that are traditional, and you keep those traditional aspects about the project."

"I remember George was writing *Star Wars* at the time," Martin Scorsese says. "He had all these books with him, like Isaac Asimov's *Guide to the Bible*, and he was envisioning this fantasy epic. He did explain that he wanted to tap into the collective unconscious of fairy tales. And he screened certain movies, like Howard Hawks's *Air Force* [1943] and Michael Curtiz's *Robin Hood* [1938]."

In enlarging the treatment to what became a nearly two-hundred-page rough draft, Lucas was continually aided by the transference of his *Apocalypse Now* ideas to the fantasy realm. Some of his notes scribbled on yellow legal pads are: "Theme: Aquilae is a small independent country like North Vietnam threatened by a neighbor or provincial rebellion, instigated by gangsters aided by empire. Fight to get rightful planet back. Half of system has been lost to gangsters . . . The empire is like America ten years from now, after gangsters assassinated the Emperor and were elevated to power in a rigged election . . . We are at a turning point: fascism or revolution."

While these ideas helped Lucas begin to form a plot that would go through several iterations, part of the tension inherent in his writing process stemmed from divided loyalties. On the one hand, he needed a solid structure on which to build his images: "The biggest thing was just finding a story that was interesting but not a gimmick," he says. "I had to find a story that would do all the things that I wanted it to do." On the other hand, Lucas's personal tastes tended toward more abstract storytelling, in the style of Jean-Luc Godard and other directors of the French nouvelle vague. Their filmmaking style, a big influence on Lucas's student shorts, was known as cinema verité, and it forsook much of what Hollywood had created in favor of a more emotional cinematic language. "I like Godard films. They excite me," Lucas explains. "In film school I tended away from storytelling; I just didn't like it—and it grew from a point of dislike to a point of real hatred. Then I forced my way back into storytelling. I thought that maybe I hated it so much because I couldn't do it. This is one of the reasons why with *Star Wars* I want to attempt a storytelling film."

Lucas's written records from that period bear witness to just how intent he was on plot and character development as he struggled to create a strong tale: "Notes on new beginning . . . for three main characters—the general, the princess, the boy (Starkiller)—make development chart . . . Put time-limit in children's packs . . . every scene must be set up and linked to next . . . make scene where Starkiller visits with old friend on Alderaan . . . Han very old (150 years) . . . Establish impossibility of attacking Death Star . . . Should threat be bigger, more sinister? . . . A conflict between freedom and conformity . . . Tell at least two stories: Starkiller becomes a man (not good enough); Valorum wakes up (morally speaking) . . . Valorum like a Green Beret who realizes wrong of Empire . . . Second thoughts about Plot . . . Make Owen Lars a geologist or something . . . The general addresses men . . . Skywalker leaps across (ramp being pulled away) . . . thundersaber . . ."

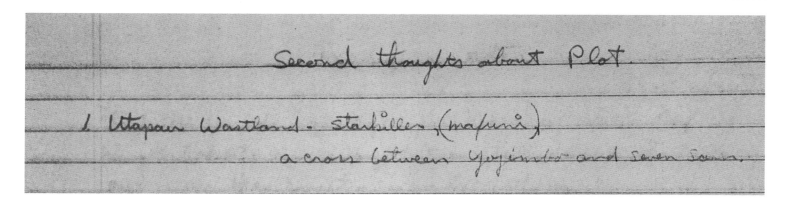

Second thoughts about Plot.

1. Utapau Wastland - Starkiller (mafuna)
    a cross between Yojimbo and Seven Samurai.

°the Empire is like america ten years from now; after: Nixonian gangsters assinated the emperor and were elected to power in a rigged election; created civil disorder by instigating race riots, aiding rebel groups, and allowing the crime rate to rise to the point where a "total control" police state was welcomed by the people. Then the people were exploited with high taxes, utility and transport costs gangsters a cartel made up of power companies, transport companies, & Crime organizations. Other Companies had to pay bribes to stay in business.

they increased the crime rate by slowing down the system of justice and punishment

When Lucas changed the two bureaucrats into robots, he was tapping into a long tradition of mechanical characters, including the Tin Man from *The Wizard of Oz*, *The Day the Earth Stood Still*, *Silent Running*, *Forbidden Planet*, and even Woody Allen's *Sleeper*.

He also made more lists of names and roles—"Kane Highsinger/Jedi friend; Leia Aquilae/princess; General Vader/Imperial Commander; Han Solo/friend . . ."—and for the first time two others are noted: "Seethreepio" and "Artwo Deetwo." They are both listed as "workmen." A later note contains a key transition from treatment to rough draft: "two workmen as robots? One dwarf/one Metropolis type." The latter reference is to the mechanical woman in Fritz Lang's silent film *Metropolis* (1926). The change of the treatment's bureaucrats into robots may have been a result of Lucas's sci-fi reading habits. "The law of robotics is obviously where the robots came from," Lucas says. "Isaac Asimov invented those robots. They may not have evolved very far at all from what Asimov's position was, or they may have evolved a great deal."

The idea must have been pleasing to Lucas, because soon the question mark of the first note was replaced by the enthusiasm of a still-later note:

"Make film more point-of-view of robots"—a thought that would have ramifications throughout the filmmaking process.

INTERREGNUM

Lucas completed the rough draft in May 1974. It is a sprawling story, though once again many elements that would make it into successive drafts are present—the Jedi versus the Sith, two bickering robots, Princess Leia, Han Solo—but as before, nothing is in its final form yet. Structurally, the story contains two motivating factors that push the characters from one scene to the next: "The princess and the general were going to a neutral planet," Lucas says, "which made it more of an escape movie, with them trapped in enemy territory and trying to get to safety. But I decided that didn't work and that it would be much better to have it be a rescue movie instead of an escape movie." This decision seems to have been made about halfway through the writing of the rough draft: In the first half Leia is part of the escape; once she is captured, her rescue, first on Yavin and then on the space fortress, becomes the plot's prime mover.

Although Lucas finished the first draft two months after the rough draft, in July 1974, their stories and dialogue are identical. Only the names have been changed for many of the characters and places; Lucas had originally intended those of the rough draft to be only placeholders. One element common to both drafts is "the force of others," which can be seen as an extension of the idea of "will" in the earlier *Journal of the Whills*. Lucas actually first wrote of this concept in a deleted scene from *THX 1138*, in which THX speaks with his friend SRT:

```
                          THX
        ...there must be something independent; a force, reality.


                          SRT
        You mean like OMM. [the state-sanctioned deity]


                          THX
        Not like OMM as we know him, but the reality behind the
        illusion of OMM.
```

From an early age, Lucas had been interested in the fact that all over the world religions and peoples had created different ideas of God and the spirit. "The 'Force of others' is what all basic religions are based on, especially the Eastern religions," he says, "which is, essentially, that there is a force, God, whatever you want to call it." It is the common denominator, a source of strength, and at this point in his writing process only the good guys seem to be aware of it. (In *Star Wars: The Annotated Screenplays*, Laurent Bouzereau points out that the expression is a variation on the Christian phrase *May the Lord be with you and your spirit*—in Latin, *Dominus vobiscum et cum spiritu tuo*, which was often written by Saint Paul at the end of his letters.)

A BEWILDERING JOURNEY

At the time only four copies of the first draft were made. Someone got hold of a government stamp and humorously marked the copy sent to Alan

(Continued on page 24)

THE STAR WARS

BY

GEORGE LUCAS

EYES ONLY!

Do Not Copy Under Any Circumstances

ROUGH DRAFT   LUCASFILM LTD.
                                    5/74

Lucas's bound copy of this draft has a mock-up cover with Flash Gordon–like characters blasting each other; one is on a jet hover-pad, while the other protects a girl. Interspersed in the pages are occasional illustrations pulled from comic books: Han Solo resembles a swamp creature, while "Captain Starkiller" (Annikin) is clearly a Buck Rogers type. In the rough draft, the first planet seen is Utapau, and, after five moons drift into view, a roll-up appears:

Until the recent GREAT REBELLION, the JEDI BENDU were the most feared warriors in the universe. For one hundred thousand years, generations of JEDI perfected their art as the personal bodyguards of the EMPEROR. They were the chief architects of the invincible IMPERIAL SPACE FORCE, which expanded the EMPIRE across the galaxy, from the celestial equator to the farthest reaches of the GREAT RIFT.

Now these legendary warriors are all but extinct. One by one they have been hunted down and destroyed as enemies of the NEW EMPIRE by a ferocious and sinister rival warrior sect, THE KNIGHTS OF SITH.

As a spaceship orbits the fourth moon of Utapau in the Kessil system, "Annikin Starkiller, a tall, heavy-set boy of eighteen . . . slowly makes his way across the canyon floor." On the surface, Annikin tells his father, Kane, who is a Jedi, and his ten-year-old brother, Deak, that they've been found. The two brothers watch with binoculars as their father explores the Sith ship after it's landed.

Suddenly, something huge moves in front of his field of view. Before either of the two young boys can react, a large, sinister SITH warrior in black robes and a face mask looms over them. He carries a long lazersword which cuts young Deak down before he or his brother are able to raise their weapons.

Annikin manages to fend off the seven-foot-tall Sith Knight till his father arrives—and cuts in half the face-masked warrior. After burying Deak, father and son set out for their home planet, Aquilae.

Meanwhile, on Alderaan, capital of the new Empire, the Emperor and his henchmen plot the final elimination of Aquilae and the last of the Jedi. "Governor Hoedaack has been appointed the First Lord of the Aquilaean System and Surrounding Territories." Clieg Whitsun watches the Emperor's speech and then goes to a nightclub where he meets Bail Antilles. During a surprise security check, Antilles is arrested.

Governor Hoedaack talks with "Darth Vader, a tall, grim-looking general," about the conquest of Aquilae; Vader thinks it will be a difficult fight because General Skywalker is leading the defenses. However, on Aquilae, Count Sandage, a corrupt noble, counsels King Kayos to give in to the Emperor. General Luke Skywalker, a large man in his sixties, interrupts the Senate meeting. They argue about the course of action, with Skywalker pushing for active resistance, and the Senators for capitulation or the status quo, including the Grande Mouff Tarkin, who "wears the long, black robes of the Aquilaean religion." The meeting is adjourned with the King saying, "May the force of others be with you all."

The King's sons, Biggs and Windy, run into the room, and the King invites Skywalker to say good-bye to his daughter, who idolizes Skywalker. They go outside to meet her just as "Princess Leia, about fourteen years old, possessing a soft beauty and iron will, is embracing her mother, Queen Breha." She bids her family farewell and goes off to Yuell to complete her studies.

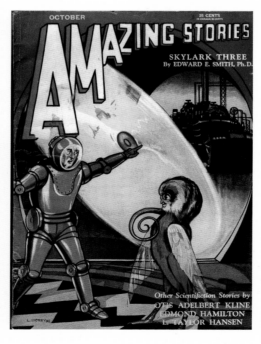

The title page for the rough draft (above left) with the government stamp humorously added. Comic-book inspiration came from such series as *Weird Fantasy, Weird Science, Shadow Comics,* and *Amazing Stories* (left).

In the war room, Skywalker tells his aide Montross to put everyone on alert, when Kane Starkiller and his son Annikin arrive. Kane asks Skywalker to take his son as his "Padawan Learner." When Skywalker asks why, Kane reveals that his arm and chest are mechanical. "There is nothing left but my head and right arm. I've lost too much, Luke. I'm dying." Suddenly Montross reports a giant asteroid or moon detaching itself from the Anchorhead system and heading their way. "It's as big as our third moon."

In the Palace of Lite the King and Queen watch two giant twin suns set in the green sky. Skywalker and Annikin arrive and report that Kane has gone to the spaceport of Gordon to meet an old friend, Han Solo, the Ureallian. Skywalker again pushes for war, but the king wants to get the approval of his allies first, and departs on a mission to Amsel to meet with the "full assembly."

General Skywalker receives word that Whitsun, who had disappeared, has just been admitted to Med Vac. They rush to the emergency room, where Whitsun says that the bad guys are just behind him—"A giant space fortress" is on its way, he explains. The general sends Annikin to pick up Princess Leia. At the Academy, Annikin retrieves Leia but not the hand-maidens, one of whom remains as a decoy.

The space fortress attacks Aquilae, and Skywalker has the starships scrambled. "Look at the size of that thing!" Devil Six remarks. A fierce firefight occurs in which the fortress is damaged; inside the space station, people scurry for cover . . .

```
Constant explosions rock the interior of the fortress.
Civilians, including women and children, scurry for
safety in the panic-ridden hallways. Two construction
robots, ARTWO DETWO (R2D2) and See Threepio (C3PO), are
blown, slipping and sliding across the hallway floor
into some freight canisters.
```

The former is "a short (three-foot) claw-armed tri-ped . . . Threepio is a tall, gleaming android of human proportions." The latter says, "This is madness . . . I'm still not accustomed to space travel." Artwo can talk, too, and tries to calm the other, but adds, "You're a mindless, useless philosopher." C3PO climbs into an emergency lifepod. R2D2 is persuaded to join him by increasingly violent explosions. The lifepod is ejected.

Only two starships are left in the attack. On the planet below, Skywalker is told that the King and his convoy have been destroyed and that the Senate has traitorously called an end to the war. He orders the two remaining starships to break off the attack. They do so—but are destroyed as they retreat. The last to die is Mace, the pilot leader. Vader orders the invasion of the planet.

Meanwhile, the two robots trek across Jundland, or "'No-Man's Land,' where the rugged desert mesas meet the foreboding dune sea." They argue and go opposite ways. R2D2 stumbles upon Annikin and the princess in their landspeeder. They take off and eventually find C3PO, too. The group travels back through the "hidden fortress canyon" entrance. Leia learns her father is dead, but her mother and two brothers are alive.

The Queen instructs Skywalker to flee to the Ophuchi system; the Chrome Companies will give him whatever he needs to get Leia on the throne. In exchange, Skywalker must bring, in tubes, the distillation of Aquilae's greatest scientific minds (which is what the evil Empire really wants). Annikin Starkiller, Skywalker, the robots, Captain Whitsun, the two young princes Biggs and Windy, and Leia all get into disguised landspeeders. Count Sandage arrives with troopers to prevent them from leaving, but Skywalker cuts him in two. They leave the canyon, as the fortress behind them self-destructs to make sure no one can betray them after the fact.

After traveling a bit, they espy the invasion army stretched out on the dune sea: "a convoy of giant tanks, troop carriers, giant dunebirds . . . Hundreds of troops ride one-man jetsticks." They have to wait until the giant army goes by. Meanwhile, back in the palace, General Vader meets with Prince Valorum, a Black Knight of the Sith whose goal is to track Skywalker.

As the heroes continue their trek, a romance develops between Annikin and Leia. "The speeders stop on a bluff overlooking a small cantina on the outskirts of Gordon. The spaceport can be seen in the distance." The general and Whitsun take one of the speeders to the cantina. A fight erupts there when the General is attacked by three creatures: He cuts the arm off one, cuts a rodent-creature in two, and slices a multi-eyed creature from chin to groin. An observer leaves the cantina, and Skywalker and

Whitsun, in an alley outside, meet Han Solo, "a huge green-skinned monster with no nose and large gills."

The others—princess, Annikin, et al.—join them. In the slum quarter they find Kane Starkiller. Whitsun takes the droids into another room to play "chess." Skywalker, Han, and Annikin meet with Datos and other rebels; they discuss the space fortress, or the "death star." They will have to flee on a freighter, with the two young princes put in hibernation; to do so they need an extra energy pack, so Kane rips one from his mechanical chest. "May the force of others be with you," he says just before dying.

Biggs and Windy are put to sleep, and are hidden in microcases. The next day they all go to the spaceport. But Annikin and Skywalker detect the Sith presence. They board the designated freighter; Han and the general are taken to see the captain, who turns out to be Valorum—it's a trap. They cut down his guards and the three face one another. However, the princess and the others have been gassed and are now prisoners—so the general has to surrender. As soon as they are taken to the prison, they overpower and kill their guards, and release the other captives. They escape and hijack a royal starship, which takes off, smashing through the hangar cover, but they are pursued by "hunter-destroyer spaceships."

As they are chased the princess confesses that she's in love with Annikin. He rebuffs her. Annikin and Whitsun man the lazercannons. They are being overwhelmed, so Skywalker directs them into an asteroid belt. The ship makes it through and enters one of the Forbidden Systems. Everyone ejects in lifepods—except Cliegg, who is accidentally killed. They land on Yavin, a jungle planet with enormous trees, an "eerie fog-laden purgatory."

The general and Han pull the two princes out of their micropacks. Annikin and Artwo go to look for Leia, and the former espies a group of Yourellian trappers who have trapped five Wookees—"huge gray and furry beasts." The trappers are "slimy, deformed hideous-looking creatures." In the fight that follows, six of the eight trappers are killed; one ventures too close to a Wookee, and is snapped in two; Annikin is left for dead. One of the trappers escapes with the princess aboard a "jungle crawler," so Chewbacca, the largest of the Wookees, takes Annikin to the Wookee camp.

The other group finds a small dwelling where they meet Owen Lars, "an aged and scruffy-looking anthropologist." His plump wife is named Beru. Back with the Wookees, Annikin meets Jommillia, a large, ferocious one. They fight, but eventually Annikin makes friends with the tribe. Riding jetsticks, Han and the general locate Annikin and Artwo. Han can speak Wookee, and confers with Chewbacca. They decide to assault the royal outpost, where Princess Leia is being held. Meanwhile, troopers arrive where the princes are holed up.

The general, Han, and the Wookees take over the Imperial outpost and learn that Leia has been taken back to Aquilae. R2D2 projects an image of the "death star fortress," which Skywalker and Annikin study. They have enough seized starships to attack, but not enough pilots. Skywalker decides to teach the Wookees to fly. Within the death star, Vader interrogates Princess Leia. Meanwhile, the stormtroopers return to the outpost with their captured princes, only to be captured themselves and have their prisoners released.

Alex Raymond's *Flash Gordon* comic strip was an early and important inspiration for the kind of hero Lucas envisaged. Here he battles Ming the Merciless.

Annikin goes undercover to the death star. R2D2 "punches his claw arm into the computer socket" and finds out where the princess is being held. Annikin disguises himself as a stormtrooper after punching one out. He fights with the others but is trapped and gassed. Vader tells Valorum to kill him.

Meanwhile, Skywalker leads nine starships in the attack on the death star; the ships have been painted in colorful Wookee designs. Within the death star, Valorum has a change of heart, realizing that the Jedi are nobler than the bureaucrats; he helps Annikin escape, and they rescue the princess together. The trio escapes via a chute into a trash compactor, but the walls close in on them. Fortunately, Skywalker's aerial attack knocks out the power, and they're able to get out. Vader wants to abandon ship, but Governor Hoedaack won't depart. Valorum, Annikin, the princess, and R2D2 climb into lifepods and escape. The couple kisses. The death star explodes.

```
In the throne room in the Palace of Lite, the heroes
gather...

Queen Leia, in all her grandeur, sits on the magnificent
throne of Aquilae. Starkiller and the general stand to
her right. Several old advisors stand to her left. Han
presents Chewbacca and a delegation of Wookees with a
treaty, gifts, and a medal of honor. They bow and exit.
Han moves to one side of the crowded court. Valorum
stands next to him. They watch as the two robots, Artwo
and Threepio, approach the queen, and bow.

                    QUEEN
Your service to Aquilae is greatly appreciated. You are
designated class A-4, and will serve Annikin Starkiller,
the new Lord Protector of Aquilae. Rise!

The robots rise and exit through the long entrance hall
to the throne. The queen turns and smiles at Starkiller
and the general. The general and Starkiller salute
their new queen.

                  FADE OUT
```

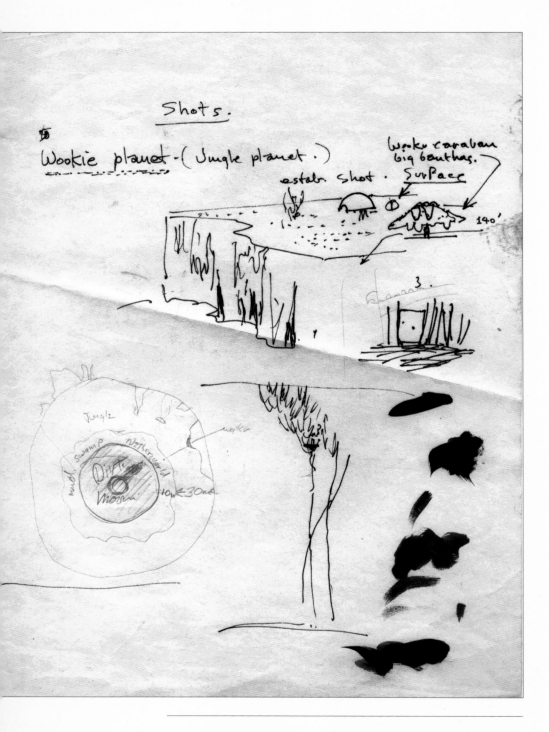

Lucas's sketch shows how he visualized the layout of the Wookie planet, Yavin. His notes indicate that certain shots were already forming in his mind in what is the only known visual representation of his rough draft.

STAR WARS PROGRESSION

- A roll-up (to begin the story)
- The Emperor
- The Knights of the Sith
- Seven-foot-tall Sith Knight
- Star destroyer (two-person size)
- A governor (who won't leave the space fortress when it is in danger)
- Darth Vader (a humanoid general)
- Darklighter and Biggs (as names: Seig Darklighter, a rebel leader; Biggs is a boy prince)
- The Senate
- Grande Mouff Tarkin (a corrupt religious Senator)
- The Force (of Others)
- "May the Force (of Others) be with you" (says King Kayos)
- Princess Leia
- Twin suns (watched by King Kayos and Queen Breha)
- Jedi in training
- The Kessil system
- Half-man/half-machine character (Kane Starkiller)
- Anchorhead
- Han Solo (an alien Ureallian, friend of Kane Starkiller)
- An Academy
- Space fortress attacks a planet (Aquilae)
- Two robots, R2D2 and C3PO
- Chewie (nickname of Devil Two, a hotshot pilot)
- Two robots trekking across dune sea
- Landspeeder picking up robots on the run
- Stormtroopers
- Droids playing chess
- Death Star (alternate name for space fortress)
- Prison break
- Space dogfight with good guys in gunports
- Chewbacca, a huge, furry Wookee, with whom Han Solo can communicate (they meet on the jungle planet Yavin)
- Owen Lars (an anthropologist)
- Artwo projects image of Death Star for planning purposes
- Darth Vader puts Leia in prison on the Death Star
- Artwo plugs into Death Star
- Hero (Annikin Starkiller) disguises himself to penetrate Death Star interior
- Two heroes (Annikin and Valorum) rescue Princess Leia from the Death Star detention area, escaping into a garbage chute
- Award ceremony

Although the rough draft and the first draft are exactly the same in terms of the story, many of the names have been changed in the later version. Lucas's notes from the period contain a list of "First Draft (rough draft)" name changes:

```
Ogana (Utapau)
Dai Nogas (Jedi Bendu)
Legion of Lettow (Knights of Sith)
Justin Valor (Annikin Starkiller)
Akira (father, Kane)
Binks (brother, Deak)
Townowi (Aquilae)
Granicus (Alderaan)
Son Hhut (Dashhat)
Dodonna (Valorum)
Jawas (Wookees)
Hu Tho (Owen Lars)
```

Also, Whitsun becomes Oxus, the princes Biggs and Windy become Oeta and Puck, Princess Leia becomes Princess Zara, and R2D2 and C3PO become A-2 and C-3. A Padawan Learner becomes a Juwo Learner, and so on. It's possible that Lucas contemplated changing the general's name from Skywalker to Starkiller, as one note reads, "Starkiller (Mifune)—a cross between *Yojimbo* and *Seven Samurai* . . ."—the name in parentheses again referring to Toshiro Mifune, the star of the two Akira Kurosawa films mentioned. Clearly, Kurosawa was on Lucas's mind, because Kane Starkiller does become Akira in the first draft.

STAR WARS PROGRESSION

- Dai Noga, as a name (for Jedi)
- A Hhut character (or "Son Hhat," ruler of the galactic kingdom)
- Jawas (huge gray and furry beasts)
- Dodonna, as a name (a Sith Knight)

One of Lucas's many lists of names, this one leads off with "Bink" and ends with "Oxus."

Ladd, who had been waiting for some time, EYES ONLY—DO NOT COPY UNDER ANY CIRCUMSTANCES.

"The first draft was a long time coming," Ladd says. "We had a number of conversations about it, and seemed to be in sync about certain things."

In addition to Ladd, Lucas gave his draft to several close friends for their feedback. His notes at the time include a list of readers—(1) Matthew Robbins and Hal Barwood; (2) Bill and Gloria Huyck; (3) John Milius; (4) Haskell Wexler; (5) Francis Ford Coppola; (6) Phil Kaufman—all filmmakers.

"I run around with a crowd of writers," Lucas says, "with the Huycks and with John Milius, and both the Huycks and John Milius are fabulous. John can just sit there and it comes out of him, without even trying. It's just magic. The Huycks are the same way. With the first draft, I showed it to a group of friends who I help; having been an editor for a long time, I usually help them on their editing and they help me on my scriptwriting. They give me all their ideas and comments and whatnot, then I go back and try to deal with it. All of us have crossover relationships, and we are constantly showing each other what we are doing and trying to help each other."

In a spiritual continuation of the temporarily defunct American Zoetrope, Lucas's converted Victorian house, now known as Park Way, became a haven for many of these same friends and colleagues. "I came up and started working at Park Way in 1974," recalls Lucy Wilson, Lucas's first hire (who still works for Lucas), whose office was on the main house's sunporch. "Hal Barwood and Matt Robbins shared an office there, and Michael Ritchie was there on and off. Matt and Hal were writing their movie *The Bingo Long Traveling All-Stars & Motor Kings* [1976]. Michael Ritchie had just done *The Candidate* [1972], and he was working on *Smile* [1975]. I think he had props down in the basement of the house. Anyway, that was fun because they were all very entertaining. George had invited these filmmakers basically to share his house with the same goal: that it would be a film community."

"George rented out rooms in his house to various filmmakers," Hal Barwood recalls. "And George of course had his offices there. He was living in another little house down in San Anselmo. And we would all stroll down the hill and walk off to various venues in San Anselmo and have lunch. And it was just a wonderful way, through enthusiastic conversa-

Lucy Wilson at Park Way (above). At Universal Studios, Lucas examines a script with friends Steven Spielberg and John Milius.

tion, to keep our interest in the movie business alive. Because the movie business is very difficult for most of us; we don't usually get a majority of our projects to completion. Most of our dreams turn into screenplays, but then stall out at about that stage. So it was a great way for us to encourage each other."

Although experienced filmmakers, Lucas's friends struggled to visualize his consecutive written drafts. "When people read *Star Wars* originally, they didn't have a clue really," Willard Huyck says. "It wasn't until George acted it out or told you what a Wookee was, and what it was going to look like, that it started to make sense. Because it was really a universe that nobody could understand from the scripts."

Nobody included Ladd, by all accounts. But by August 1974 Lucas was a well-known and respected director of a giant hit: *American Graffiti* had been nominated for five Academy Awards and had won several other awards, including a Golden Globe. "Fox had a very good deal," Jeff Berg says, "a hot new name in Hollywood for very little money, and it didn't matter too much what he wanted to do. I think that influenced Fox a great deal, because several times Laddie read the screenplay and said he just wasn't sure what George was trying to say."

"After *Graffiti* became a big hit, they couldn't refuse it," Lucas says. "They couldn't not do it. Just in terms of politics and the political intrigue of Hollywood. That's what it came down to in the end."

Not surprisingly then, Fox decided to go to the next step in the process of making *The Star Wars:* a second draft, which was actually Lucas's preference, because the movie he wanted to write into existence was proving elusive.

THE STUDIO STUTTER

"I find rewriting no more or less difficult than writing," says Lucas. "Because when you write, sometimes you rationalize away particular problems. You say, *I'll deal with that later.* So I struggled through the first draft and dealt with some of the problems. But now the next step is even more painful, because I have to confront the problems in a more serious way."

Even as he went through the headaches of writing a second draft during the summer and winter of 1974, another source of disquiet began to gnaw at Lucas: the contract. Although he had an agreement with Twentieth Century-Fox, they were hesitating before taking the next legal step. Standard practice at that time in Hollywood was for the production-distribution contract to follow two or three months after the initial agreement, as had been Lucas's experience with Universal on *American Graffiti.* But the question of how *The Star Wars* was going to get made, and how much that answer was going to cost, was causing anxiety at Fox. So in lieu of doing something decisive, they delayed doing anything.

"I got mad about a year after I had started working on it," Lucas says, "working and working and working, and they wouldn't give me a contract. They were saying, 'Well, he didn't really finish the script, either'—but writing a contract is different from writing a script. A script is a creative work that you are trying to eke out while coming up with something good." Or as Lucas's lawyer Tom Pollock puts it: "It was not until late 1974 that we even got a piece of paper out of Fox because they are so fucking slow."

Lucas used the law offices of Pollock, Rigrod and Bloom to translate his anger into what were to become harder- and harder-edged negotiations—if Fox was going to be nonresponsive, he was going to concede nothing. Pollock instigated several discussions with studio exec William Immerman, followed by a meeting with Immerman and Jeff Berg on August 23, 1974. The upshot was Pollock's summation letter dated September 4, with further amendments to the Memorandum Agreement (deal memo), some of which had long-ranging implications. Paragraph 1 states: "The Star Wars Corporation will own . . . all sequel rights [to] the screenplay 'The Star Wars.' " Paragraph 5 addresses "merchandising rights and commercial tie-ups," with 5.B stipulating that "Either party may license merchandising rights . . . subject to the other party's bettering the licensing deal." Item 5.D states "SWC shall have the sole and exclusive right to use . . . the name 'The Star Wars' in connection with wholesale or retail outlets for the sale of merchandising items."

Fox responded with another period of silence, followed by a second letter from Pollock, written on December 17, 1974: "It is very important to me and to George Lucas that these matters be settled at once." Immerman finally replied on December 27, optimistically writing, "I believe . . . we can therefore proceed with preparation of a formal contract."

But at that point, with nothing actually agreed upon, the correspondence petered out. Oddly, the rights being argued about were not considered potentially valuable, as the studio, with the exception of Ladd, had very little faith in the film or its director. Other forces were at work. "My perception is, there was a lack of respect for George," Warren Hellman says. "The movie industry is a very vituperative and petty industry most of the time—and part of the negotiations was just to see how much they could push George around because they felt like they could."

THE DARING DEVELOPMENT OF HEROES

Though Lucas was not pleased with how things were going with the contract department, he dutifully did his part in advising the studio's production department on his own progress. "George went off to write and the next draft was to be delivered twelve weeks later, according to the deal memo," Alan Ladd says. "In twelve weeks' time, George called to say he hadn't forgotten about it and that it would be here soon. Then some more time went by, but I always kept thinking to myself, *Well, next week it will be here . . .*"

While Marcia helped edit Scorsese's next film, *Taxi Driver* (1976), Lucas spent more time alone, making notes before committing to the second draft. "Sith knights look like Linda Blair in *Exorcist* [1973]," he wrote, as the bad guys are rechristened the Sith. "Vader—do something evil in prison to Deak," he wrote, as General Vader becomes a Dark Lord of the Sith, and Deak reappears as a brother, this time to Luke—the name of a boy, not a general, who replaces Annikin/Justin as the story's main character. "Luke reluctantly accepts the burden (artist, not a warrior, fear); establish Luke as a good pilot . . . farm boy: fulfills the legend of the son of the sons; pulls the sword from the stone. All he wants in life is to become a starpilot." Leia is also brought back from the rough draft, as Luke's cousin, a secondary character: "Leia: tomboy, bright, tough, really soft and afraid; loves Luke but not admitting it." Lastly, Solo metamorphoses from alien to humanoid in Lucas's notes: "Make Han in bar like Bogart—freelance tough guy for hire."

Other notes for the second draft contain pieces of scenes and ideas that didn't make it into the actual script: "Jabba in prison cell"; the love relationship between Leia and Luke Starkiller is divided into "seven stages/crucial scenes," with her being crowned queen at the end; "Han Solo a Wookiee? Wookiees talk to plants and animals." Lucas also analyzed and wrote notes on films he saw, such as John Ford's *They Were Expendable* (1945) and *Ben-Hur* (1959).

Lucas's habit of working and observing no matter where he was helped create and crystallize the character of Chewbacca the Wookiee. For many years, Lucas had an Alaskan malamute named Indiana, who would often sit in the passenger seat of his car. People driving by would sometimes express surprise that what they perceived from behind to be a person turned out to be an enormous canine. Amused, Lucas slowly combined Indiana, the Wookiees of Yavin, and the name *Chewbacca* into Han Solo's copilot: a great big, intelligent, friendly-but-fierce dog-creature sitting by his side.

As the weeks and months wore on, however, the difficulties of facing the blank page only increased for Lucas. "You go crazy writing. You get psychotic," he says. "You get yourself so psyched up and go in such strange directions in your mind that it's a wonder that all writers aren't put away someplace. You can just get so convoluted in what you're thinking about that you get depressed, unbearably depressed. Because there's just no guideline, you don't know if what you're doing is good or bad or

indifferent. It always seems bad when you're doing it. It seems terrible. It's the hardest thing to get through."

Still in a state of dissatisfaction, knowing it was still far from a shooting script, Lucas finished his second draft on January 28, 1975. A copy in the Lucasfilm Archives features a red cover with a Frank Frazetta–like illustration of a man holding a sword with an adoring, voluptuous woman wrapped around his leg.

A STARTLING SPACE FORTRESS

Lucas had clearly made major changes to the structure of his story between the first and second drafts. It's at this point that the well-known break occurred, when, having written something that was far too long for one movie in the first draft, he decided to begin the second draft in the middle of the first—at the moment the robots escape. In the first draft, they flee the Death Star; in the second, now on the side of the good guys, they flee a besieged rebel starship. One of his notes summarizes Lucas's thinking: "Whole film must be told from robots' point of view," a further development of the device of the two peasants in *Hidden Fortress*.

While at one time Lucas contemplated making two movies out of the first draft—ending the first with the escape from the Death Star, and having the second start with the crash landing on the jungle planet, and close with the attack on the space fortress—instead he combined and juxtaposed many of the more exciting scenes into a shorter, tighter single film. Another of his notes on structure reads, "time lock" to add suspense: "the empire has a terrible new weapon, a fortress station so powerful it can destroy a planet, possibly even a sun. It must be stopped before it can be put to use." By transforming the space fortress from a floating, somewhat meandering locale, in the first draft, into a horrific planet-destroying weapon, Lucas turned it into a character as well as an all-important structural element.

Though augmenting the role of the two robots, he jettisoned other *Hidden Fortress* elements. The general is no longer a major character, literally sleeping through some scenes, and the princess has disappeared completely; in their place, the character of Justin/Annikin, now Luke, has taken center stage. His adventures with the robots, while still picaresque, form the line that goes through the story. Indeed, the character of the young Jedi Annikin/Justin has been split in two: Han Solo takes on his womanizing ways and cavalier attitude, while Luke embodies his serious side, his metaphysical side. Both possess the attributes of the time-honored bildungsroman character—the one who comes of age before our eyes.

Luke's journey is told in part through his relationship with the Force, which in the second draft is more thoroughly analyzed. It now has a dark

Lucas struggled to meld many diverse influences into one story: swashbucklers, comic books, science fiction—and creature features, such as *The Wolfman* (1941). Tod Browning's *Freaks* (1932) had been banned in the U.K. for thirty years and in many cities and states in America, but was notably revived during the 1960s, when it played in the LA area at the Cinema Theatre.

(Continued on page 31)

Adventures of the Starkiller, Episode I: The Star
Wars, Second-Draft Summary, January 28, 1975

This time the story opens with a prophecy and a different roll-up.

> "...And in the time of greatest despair there shall
> come a savior, and he shall be known as: THE SON OF THE
> SUNS."—Journal of the Whills, 3:127

> The REPUBLIC GALACTICA is dead. Ruthless trader barons,
> driven by greed and the lust for power, have replaced
> enlightenment with oppression, and "rule by the people"
> with the FIRST GALACTIC EMPIRE.

> Until the tragic Holy rebellion of 06', the respected
> JEDI BENDU OF ASHLA were the most powerful warriors in
> the Universe. For a hundred thousand years, generations
> of Jedi Bendu knights learned the ways of the myste-
> rious FORCE OF OTHERS, and acted as the guardians of
> peace and justice in the REPUBLIC. Now these legendary
> warriors are all but extinct. One by one they have been
> hunted down and destroyed by a ferocious rival sect of
> mercenary warriors: THE BLACK KNIGHTS OF THE SITH.

> It is a period of civil wars. The EMPIRE is crumbling
> into lawless barbarism throughout the million worlds of
> the galaxy. From the celestial equator to the farthest
> reaches of the GREAT RIFT, seventy small solar sys-
> tems have united in a common war against the tyranny of
> the Empire. Under the command of a mighty Jedi warrior
> known as THE STARKILLER, the REBEL ALLIANCE has won a
> crushing victory over the deadly Imperial Star Fleet.
> The Empire knows that one more such defeat will bring a
> thousand more solar systems into the rebellion, and Im-
> perial control of the Outlands could be lost forever...

The story begins with a small rebel space fighter that is being overwhelmed
by four giant Imperial Star Destroyers. The smaller ship manages to destroy
one of them.

> The chaos of battle echoes through the narrow, main
> passageway of the starfighter. An explosion rocks the
> ship, and two construction robots, ARTOO DETOO (R2-D2)
> and SEE THREEPIO (C-3PO) struggle to make their way
> through the shaking, bouncing passageway.

The two robots are blown under a computer console; from there they see
only the legs of their captain, Deak Starkiller, when he arrives. R2-D2 now
communicates through beeps and whistles, which only another robot can
understand. Meanwhile, one of the Star Destroyers maneuvers above the
rebel ship close enough so that it can be reached through space.

> With fascist precision, ten stormtroopers wearing
> ominous armored spacesuits drop onto the top of the
> disabled rebel craft.

A fight ensues between the rebels and stormtroopers, with neither gaining
the advantage, until a mysterious stranger appears:

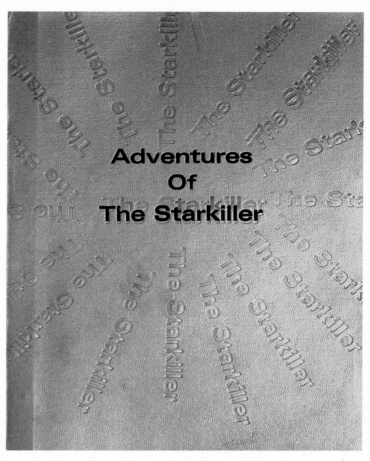

> At the far end of the passageway, a door swings wide
> revealing a rebel warrior wearing a breath mask and
> dressed in the distinctive uniform of an AQUILLIAN
> RANGER. A long, deadly laser sword glows in his right
> hand, while several chrome ping-pong sized balls magi-
> cally appear in his left. Tiny antennas project from
> the chrome balls, and before the stormtroopers can
> raise their weapons, the balls fly out of the ranger's
> hand. One of the balls stops in the middle of the
> troops and explodes. Three other balls shoot through
> the hole ripped in the side of the ship.

One of the balls blows up the hovering Star Destroyer—but the Ranger
falls in battle. Realizing his situation is desperate, Deak sends a number
of R2 robots from his starship to the surface of the nearby desert planet
Utapau to search for his brother Luke at the home of Owen Lars. R2-D2
is one of those sent, and he embarks with the ever-complaining C-3PO
in a lifepod. Back on the ship, Deak and his comrades do battle with the
stormtroopers, until . . .

> The remaining stormtroopers bow low toward the doorway.
> An awesome, seven-foot BLACK KNIGHT OF THE SITH makes

his way into the blinding light of the cockpit area. This is LORD DARTH VADER, right hand to the MASTER OF THE SITH. His sinister face is partially obscured by his flowing black robes and grotesque breath mask, which are in sharp contrast to the fascist white armored suits of the Imperial stormtroopers...Taking a deep breath, he raises his arms and every object that isn't bolted down is picked up by an invisible force and hurled at the young Jedi...Slowly Deak is forced to his knees as all his energy is drained from his being. Finally, he collapses in a heap. The sinister knight lets out a horrible, shrieking laugh...

Deak is taken prisoner by Lord Vader, who assumes that he is the son of the suns (Starkiller) and that they have altered the prophecy. On Utapau, R2-D2 and C-3PO argue and separate; the former is eventually captured by dwarf-like Jawas and put in a sandcrawler—where he discovers his companion, who had been found earlier. Other prisoners in the sandcrawler organize a break, and, in the confusion, the robots escape to a small settlement. A slimy mechanic directs them to the house of Owen Lars; however, he also reports their presence to a "gray Tusken."

The robots eventually find their way to a moisture ranch owned by Luke's uncle and aunt, Owen and Beru Lars. They meet there Luke's young twin brothers, Biggs and Windy, and his sixteen-year-old cousin, Leia, the daughter of Owen and Beru. The robots explain that they are looking for "Angel Blue," the code name for Luke. When they meet Luke Starkiller, he interrupts his laser sword training to introduce himself as "the Skywalker."

R2-D2 projects a hologrammic message from Deak, who asks Luke to take the Kiber Crystal (a plot device similar to the ring in J.R.R. Tolkien's trilogy) to their father, "The Starkiller," on Ogana Major. In council with Owen, Luke learns that their planet is under siege by the Imperial Legions of Alderaan, and that his brother is probably imprisoned on Alderaan itself. Owen has trained Luke, but he is not yet a Jedi, though he is a good pilot. Luke's feelings are divided: He'd like to stay and complete his archaeology studies, but he decides to accept the challenge. He visits his mother's grave as the twin suns of Utapau set. He then has a frank talk with his twin brothers:

> LUKE
> The time has come for me to tell you of your heritage, as Deak told it to me and as his older brother Cliegg told it to him. In another time, long before the Empire, and before the Republic had been formed, a holy man called the Skywalker became aware of a powerful energy field which he believed influenced the destiny of all living creatures...
>
> BIGGS
> The "FORCE OF OTHERS"!
>
> LUKE
> Yes, and after much study, he was able to know the force, and it communicated with him. He came to see things in a new way. His "aura" and powers grew very strong. The Skywalker brought a new life to the people of his system, and became one of the founders of the Republic Galactica.
>
> WINDY
> The "FORCE OF OTHERS" talked to him!?!
>
> LUKE
> In a manner different from the way we talk. As you know, the "FORCE OF OTHERS" has two halves: Ashla, the good, and Bogan, the paraforce or evil part. Fortunately, Skywalker came to know the good half and was able to resist the paraforce; but he realized that if he taught others the way of the Ashla, some, with less strength, might come to know Bogan, the dark side, and bring unthinkable suffering to the Universe. For this reason, the Skywalker entrusted the secret of THE FORCE only to his twelve children, and they in turn passed on the knowledge only to their children, who became known as the Jedi Bendu of the Ashla: "the servants of the force." For thousands of years, they brought peace and justice to the galaxy. At

Undated notes reveal Lucas's thinking about character and environment.

> ✶ Build characters
> Change programming on robots.
>
> ✶ Expand world = Behind every man must be a complete world,
> customs, friends, enemies, goals
> family, responsibilities, rules, religion (check anthropology)

one time there were several hundred Jedi families, but
now there are only two or three.

                    WINDY
What happened to them?

                    LUKE
As the Republic spread throughout the galaxy, encom-
passing over a million worlds, the GREAT SENATE grew
to such overwhelming proportions that it no longer
responded to the needs of its citizens. After a series
of assassinations and elaborately rigged elections, the
Great Senate became secretly controlled by the Power
and Transport guilds. When the Jedi discovered the
conspiracy and attempted to purge the Senate, they were
denounced as traitors. Several Jedi allowed themselves
to be tried and executed, but most of them fled into the
Outland systems and tried to tell people of the conspiracy. But the elders chose to remain behind, and the
Great Senate diverted them by creating civil disorder.
The Senate secretly instigated race wars, and aided
anti-government terrorists. They slowed down the system
of justice, which caused the crime rate to rise to the
point where a totally controlled and oppressive police
state was welcomed by the systems. The Empire was born.
The systems were exploited by a new economic policy
which raised the cost of power and transport to unbe-
lievable heights. Many worlds were destroyed this way.
Many people starved...

                    BIGGS
Why didn't the "FORCE OF OTHERS" help the Jedi to put
things right?

                    LUKE
Because a terrible thing happened. During one of his
lessons a young PADAWAN-JEDI, a boy named Darklighter,
came to know the evil half of the force, and fell vic-
tim to the spell of the dreaded Bogan. He ran away from
his instructor and taught the evil ways of the Bogan
Force to a clan of Sith pirates, who then spread untold
misery throughout the systems. They became the personal
bodyguards of the Emperor. The Jedi were hunted down by
these deadly Sith knights. With every Jedi death, contact with the Ashla grows weaker, and the force of the
Bogan grows more powerful.

                    WINDY
Where are the Jedi now?

                    LUKE
They're hidden; but many are still fighting to free the
systems from the grip of the Empire. Our father is a
Jedi. He is called "The Starkiller" and is said to be a
great and wise man, and tomorrow I am on my way to join
him and learn the ways of the "FORCE OF OTHERS."

He then takes the diamond-like Kiber Crystal from his uncle. He also loads
the robots into his speeder. On the way to the spaceport, he stops and uses

his binoculars to check if they're being followed—they are, by the Tusken
agent. At Mos Eisley, Luke meets two key characters . . .

Luke is standing next to HAN SOLO, a young Corellian
pirate only a few years older than himself. He is a
burly-bearded but ruggedly handsome boy dressed in a
gaudy array of flamboyant apparel...Han turns to his
companion, CHEWBACCA, an eight foot tall, savage-looking
creature resembling a huge gray bushbaby-monkey with fierce
"baboon"-like fangs. His large yellow eyes dominate a
fur-covered face and soften his otherwise awesome appearance. Over his matted, furry body, he wears two chrome
bandoliers, a flak jacket painted in a bizarre camouflage
pattern, brown cloth shorts, and little else. He is a
two-hundred-year-old "WOOKIEE," and a sight to behold.

The fight in the cantina, this time, has Solo ineffectively trying to defend
Luke, who then lights his "laser sword" and dispatches the bad guys. Solo
agrees to take Luke and the two robots to Ogana Major—if Luke's father
will pay him a million credits on arrival; for Han, it turns out, is in debt to
someone called Oxus, who is of "the grossest dimensions." Han does not,
however, have a ship of his own, so he fakes a reactor overload on a pirate
ship he serves on, causing the captain and other crew members—including
one Jabba the Hutt—to flee in terror. Han then steals the ship, maintaining
Chewbacca and science officer Montross Holdaack as his only crew. Holdaack is almost entirely robotic, with only his head and right arm organic.
Luke and the two robots climb aboard and the starship heads for Ogana
Major, making the jump to "hyper-skip."

But Ogana Major has mysteriously vanished—destroyed in an
enormous attack—so Luke asks Han to head instead for Alderaan, where
Deak is being held. Within a city suspended in a sea of cirrus methane,
Luke and Han steal the white uniforms of Imperial stormtroopers and,
with Chewbacca posing as their prisoner, they rescue the dying Deak. They
have a close encounter with vicious Dai Noga creatures in the bowels of
the city and almost get squashed, while fleeing two Sith Knights, in a huge
trash compactor. Back in their stolen ship, they are pursued by four fin-
winged Imperial TIE fighters, but they again make the jump to hyper-skip.
The Kiber Crystal keeps Deak alive on the journey to their next destination—the rebel stronghold on the fourth moon of Yavin—but they are
now being pursued by a giant space station.

Instead of landing—which the dense jungle terrain won't allow—the
heroes use lifepods to descend to the Massassi Outpost, where Luke and his
friends meet three Aquillian rangers, one of whom is Bail Antilles. During
a big meeting, General Dodana debriefs the rebels on the imminent attack
against the approaching Death Star . . .

The GRANDE MOUFF TARKIN, a thin, bird-like commander of
the outland Kesselian Dragoons, stands, and Dodana sits
down, revealing behind and to one side of him a wizened
old man with long silver hair—THE STARKILLER. He is
apparently asleep; but as the Grande Mouff rises, the
Starkiller's crystal-clear eyes open knowingly. An aura
of power radiates from the ancient Jedi that almost

knocks Tarkin over. The Starkiller is a large man, but
shriveled and bent by an incalculable number of years.
His face, cracked and weathered by exotic climates, is
set off by a long silver beard and penetrating gray-
blue eyes. Luke stares at him in awe. He's at once
proud, moved and slightly frightened...

The Kiber Crystal revitalizes Luke's father, who tells his son that he
intends to train him as a Jedi. Luke joins the combat mission to strike at
the exhaust port on the surface of the Death Star, which they learn was
responsible for the destruction of Ogana Major. Han receives eight million
in payment for his services, but refuses to join the rebels.

Luke flies toward the Death Star, with C-3PO, R2-D2, and Antilles aboard his ship. He keeps the Kiber Crystal in his pocket, as the rebels
concentrate their attack on the dual poles of the fortress. Darth Vader leads
the defense of the Death Star, ordering the men to their ships, but he soon
senses the presence of the Kiber Crystal. He and his cohorts blast away at
their enemies, and they nearly trap Luke's ship when Han, Chewbacca, and
Montross come to the rescue. Vader crashes into Han's ship, kamikaze-like,
killing himself and disabling the pirate craft. As Luke pilots his ship with
expert precision, aided by the robot's advice on the necessary angle for a
successful shot, Antilles and C-3PO fire the blasts that enter the exhaust
port and destroy the Death Star.

The small craft veers sharply away from the Death Star
as ominous rumbles and explosions can be heard coming from within the huge super fortress. The rebel ship
speeds past the small lifepod from the pirate ship
as it slowly drifts toward the green calm of Yavin's
Fourth Moon. Han, Montross and the furry Chewbacca
watch the ominous fortress grow smaller as they drift
further and further away. Suddenly, a great flash replaces the fortress and rubble streaks past the lifepod
and lone rebel starship. Several giant explosions follow, until there is only a smoke cloud where the mighty
fortress once orbited Yavin's Fourth Moon.

Back on the fourth moon of Yavin, the Starkiller tells his son:

THE STARKILLER
Your achievement will be sung through the ages. The
Kiber Crystal has stopped the onslaught of the Bogan
forces so that brave warriors can once again show their
merit...The revolution has begun.

A ROLL-UP TITLE appears:
...And a thousand new systems joined the rebellion,
causing a significant crack in the great wall of the
powerful Galactic Empire. The Starkiller would once
again spark fear in the hearts of the Sith knights, but
not before his sons were put to many tests...the most
daring of which was the kidnapping of the Lars family,
and the perilous search for:

"THE PRINCESS OF ONDOS."

STAR WARS PROGRESSION

- Opens with pursuit of rebel ship by Star Destroyers
- R2-D2 and C-3PO in service of rebels
- R2-D2 communicates with "electronic sounds"
- Stormtroopers blow open the door of the rebel ship's main passageway
- Darth Vader is a seven-foot-tall Sith Knight who appears as a terrifying figure
- Fight on rebel ship (between Deak Starkiller and Darth Vader)
- Lifepod with robots not destroyed because no life-forms are detected
- Robots sent to desert planet surface (Utapau) on a mission (to find Luke)
- Tuskens (special soldiers working for the Empire)
- Artoo captured by Jawas (three-foot-tall men) and taken to a sandcrawler (two stories high)
- Robots on homestead (who have escaped from Jawas, and received directions to Owen Lars's home)
- Homestead (several concrete buildings)
- Luke practices with a training ball (on Utapau)
- Artoo projects a 3-D hologram SOS (from Deak, Luke's brother)
- The word *droids* (used by Biggs, Luke's little brother, to refer to the robots)
- Evil or dark side to the Force (of Others, the Bogan)
- Luke goes to Mos Eisley
- Han Solo is now humanoid, teamed up with Chewbacca the Wookiee, and in debt (to an enormously fat character named Oxus)
- Jabba the Hutt character (a pirate)
- Luke, Han, et al., travel to a planet (Ogana Major), which has been destroyed
- Robots play chess-like game against Chewbacca
- Pirate ship makes jump to "hyper-skip"
- Money continually operates as motivating factor for Han Solo (who goes to Alderaan prison system in the hope of reward from Luke and Deak, whom he suspects are part of the royal family)
- Han, Luke, and company hide in lockers in their ship (which facilitates their sneaking into Alderaan)
- Han and Luke dress up as stormtroopers and pretend Chewbacca is a prisoner
- Han and Luke rescue prisoner (Deak)
- Dai Noga, a spider-like creature, tries to kill the heroes (on Alderaan)
- Imperial TIE ships
- Han and Luke in gunports fighting TIEs
- Rebel outpost on fourth moon of Yavin
- Debriefing of attack on Death Star by Dodana
- Han refuses to join the rebels
- Luke leads fight (making two passes on the exhaust port; C-3PO and Bail Antilles fire shot that destroys the Death Star)
- Darth Vader nearly destroys Luke, when Han and Chewbacca come to rescue

The cinematic swash-buckling element was represented by Errol Flynn in *Captain Blood* (far left) and *The Adventures of Robin Hood* (with Basil Rathbone), and by Stewart Granger in *Scaramouche*.

A photo of George Lucas taken in March 1973 (left).

On a rare snowy day in Marin County, Matthew Robbins and Hal Barwood pose for a photo taken by Lucy Wilson in front of Park Way house.

side, which the bad guys can use—thus enhancing their power to almost equal that of the good guys, conforming to Alfred Hitchcock's observation that the greatness of a hero is defined by the magnitude of the villain he or she must overcome.

LOOKING BACK

All in all, the second draft is a radical reworking of the first. "While I was writing the rough draft, they ended up in this cantina about halfway through; they walked in and there were all these monsters," Lucas says. "When I wrote the second draft about the only thing that remained was the cantina scene and the dogfight."

Not surprisingly, Alan Ladd was a bit perplexed. "In came another script and it had a lot of different scenes and a lot of character changes," he says. And though the script was more streamlined, Lucas's idea of the serial—crys-

tallized with the addition of *Episode I* to the title, and an end roll-up that promises more adventures—must have added to Ladd's confusion. For that matter, anyone reading through these drafts would be alternately amazed and thoroughly befuddled by the constant shifting of sands, the experience affording a glimpse into the mind-set that Lucas consistently describes as unsettling.

Even Coppola was startled: "My recollection was that George had a whole *Star Wars* script that I thought was fine," he says, "and then he chucked it and started again with these two robots lost in the wilderness. I remember thinking that the first script he showed me was really good and I was sort of curious as to why he was, you know, dumping that."

"It started off in horrible shape," Hal Barwood says. "It was difficult to discern there was a movie there. It did have Artoo and it did have Three-pio, but it was very hard for us to wrap our heads around the idea of a golden robot and this little beer can. We just didn't know what that meant. But George never gave up and he worked and worked and worked."

BOUNDARY BUSTERS

JANUARY 1975 TO AUGUST 1975

CHAPTER THREE

The delivery of the second draft in early 1975 didn't make a difference in The Star Wars Corporation's negotiations with Fox, which still declined to make a financial or legal commitment. The studio remained extremely dubious as to how much Lucas's ambitious scripts were going to cost to film, particularly because no official budget had yet been submitted. "For a couple of years after the initial negotiations," Andy Rigrod says, "there were no formal agreements and basically George was working out the script and working out the budget, which started at about $3 million."

©The Star Wars Corporation
1976

To remedy the situation, in addition to making notes for a third draft, Lucas employed Kurtz to formulate a more realistic budget. "After the second script, Gary really wanted to get started on something," Lucas says. "I had already taken a year and a half to write, and he wanted to get the production going."

The budget stall came from the fact that no one knew what anything was going to look like, so no one could calculate costs. The solution was to hire artists to create production illustrations and models that would provide something tangible on which to base estimates. Lucas had actually hired one of the artists back in November 1974, though he wasn't able to actually start a painting until late January, finishing it a couple of days later on January 31, 1975.

"I had been doing a stint as an animator at this little industrial film company [circa 1968]," Hal Barwood recalls. "One of the clients for the film company was the Boeing aircraft corporation, which at that time was designing the supersonic transport, the SST. I met a guy who was

doing concept paintings for it, and they were just stunning. It was this guy named Ralph McQuarrie.

"A few years later [circa 1973], Matt and I were working on our film *Star Dancing*," he continues, "so we tracked Ralph down in LA and he turned out these paintings. When we were ready to go see them, it just happened we were having lunch with George and he said, 'Hey, I'll tag along.' So we looked at these paintings and George said, 'You know, I'm gonna make a science-fiction movie someday. Maybe we'll get together.' And that was the beginning of the relationship with George and Ralph."

"George saw the work that I did for Hal Barwood and Matthew Robbins," Ralph McQuarrie says. "They had a real neat science-fiction script that they wanted to do, which a lot of people were interested in, though it never did get done. George talked about his idea for an intergalactic war picture. And I thought, 'Gee, that sounds ambitious.' And we said good-bye and I never expected to see him again. But a couple of years later [laughs] he comes back with the idea of me doing some illustrations like I did for Hal and Matt. I said, 'Great, I'd love to.' So George came over with the script one afternoon, and we arranged for a weekly salary.

"From what I understand," he adds, "Fox was all set to go, just on the strength of the basic idea, but they hadn't picked up their option. There might have been some slight hesitation. It seemed to me the paintings were of interest to them because they were concerned about how these things would look. I think they were done as a substitute for arm waving and verbal descriptions, and to start budget talks."

At their first meeting, Lucas showed McQuarrie the same illustrations he'd originally attached to his treatment, plus a couple of inspirational pieces pulled from comic books for Luke's landspeeder, and a drawing of a lemur for Chewbacca. He also made several sketches to demonstrate what he wanted.

Ralph McQuarrie at work on the CBS News Apollo coverage (far left), and posing for his *Winterhawk* poster (middle). His painting for *Star Dancing*, a Hal Barwood/Matthew Robbins film that never got off the ground (left), shows an astronaut on a planet covered with wheat. (The astronaut discovers an underground alien installation; later he meets the aliens themselves, who come back every year.)

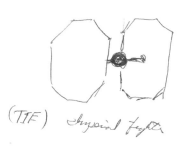

(TIF) Imperial fighter

During their first meeting in November 1974, Lucas drew three sketches—a TIE fighter, X-wing, and Death Star—to show Ralph McQuarrie what he had in mind, perhaps the first conceptual record of these designs (left).

A DREAMING EYE

Born in 1929, McQuarrie had attended Art Center from 1954 through 1956, studying advertising design. If he had answered *American Graffiti*'s question, "Where were you in '62?," his answer, according to a bio he wrote, would have been, "dropped out; read books; walked on beach; Zen; not sure what I want to do." The stopgap solution was to return to Boeing, where he had first worked in 1952 following two years of military service in Korea. As of 1968 he began working on the CBS News Apollo coverage, eventually segueing into freelance illustration work for filmmakers. For the somewhat itinerant artist who had been drawn to the fantastic since he was a child, the chance to do space-fantasy illustrations for *The Star Wars* was great fun. "I felt, *oh yes*—this is what I was meant to do."

"George would come into Universal Studios [to Kurtz's office] and go visit Ralph at his home in Los Angeles," remembers Kurtz's assistant, Bunny Alsup. "And basically, I felt that Ralph McQuarrie was very quiet.

He'd come in as if he weren't there and he would listen, and they would talk and they were all enthusiastic; they were all happily working, trying to tune in to the same finite idea."

Describing their collaboration, Lucas says: "I have a list of about ten scenes that I want to have painted. He does a rough sketch and then I correct the rough sketch, and then he does another rough sketch and I correct that, and we keep doing it until I feel we're close enough to where he can do a big drawing. So he does a big rough sketch just as big as the painting; I correct that and then he paints it. But Ralph also adds in an enormous amount of his own detail, his own textural and design elements, which are a great help. I just describe what I want and then he does it. I show him a lot of research material, a lot of things I've picked out, and he combines that with other things and invents a lot.

"That was the first step," he adds. "I really trusted him. Sometimes it was great, and sometimes we had to go back and change it and start over again."

Starting in November 1974, working from Lucas's verbal descriptions and visual references, and using Fritz Lang's *Metropolis* as a guide (with Alfred Abel, bottom left), McQuarrie drew his first sketches of R2-D2 and C-3PO (below). One sketch contains a tiny figure that recalls the alien from *The Day the Earth Stood Still* (bottom right).

"George wanted me to do sketches, and we did those in the course of getting straight between us both what the thing should look like," McQuarrie says. "He wanted the illustrations to look really nice and finished, and the way he wanted them to look on-screen—he wanted the ideal look. In other words, don't worry about how things are going to get done or how difficult it might be to produce them—just paint them as he would like them to be. So we approached it like that, and I finished four key moments that he felt he definitely wanted to see. So as much as I designed this, George really designed it, too."

Although often counted as four, McQuarrie actually painted five moments from the second draft (the reasons why only four are counted will become apparent later). One of those was the confrontation between Vader and Deak Starkiller.

"For Darth Vader, George just said he would like to have a very tall, dark fluttering figure that had a spooky feeling like it came in on the wind," McQuarrie says. "He mentioned the look of Arab costumes, all tied up in silk and rags. He liked the idea of Vader having a big hat, like a fisherman's hat, a big long metal thing that came down. George wanted him to have some sort of mask, because they were supposed to leap down from this big ship to a smaller ship that the rebels were in. The space suits began as being necessary for their survival in space, but the suits became part of their character. I made three or four little sketches, which he looked at and said, 'That's not right, I kind of like that hat, but maybe you should fool around with it a little bit more.' So I made some more sketches. He was going up to San Francisco to work on the script, and came down in another week and a half or two weeks to see what I was doing."

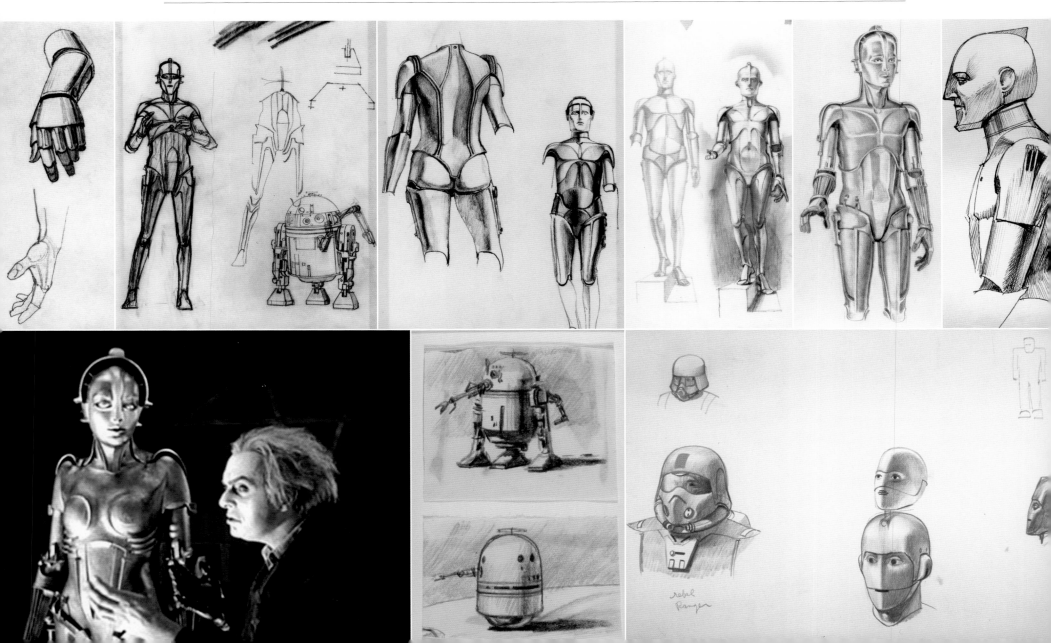

LAUNCH OF THE SPACESHIPS

Another artist hired was Colin J. Cantwell, whom McQuarrie says was on the production before him, but only by days or weeks; accounting records show that both began to be paid in November 1974. Once again Hal Barwood was instrumental, having recommended the model maker to Lucas. "I went out to see this thing he was doing for the San Diego planetarium space show," Lucas says, "and I hired him to help me with some models."

Like the production paintings, the models were being built to help formulate the budget—but they were also important to the film's special effects, which Lucas knew would make extensive use of miniatures. Cantwell was one of "the class of *2001*," having worked with Douglas Trumbull on Stanley Kubrick's classic 1968 film, as well as with Trumbull

again on *The Andromeda Strain* (1971). An experienced model maker, Cantwell also had a tremendous collection of space models and gadgets at his home, acting at times as a "space consultant."

Lucas worked with Cantwell as he did with McQuarrie, providing reference material, verbal descriptions, and his own sketches. Work with the model maker went more slowly, but as Lucas signed off on approved spacecraft, McQuarrie incorporated them into his paintings.

The third artist the director hired was Alex Tavoularis, who started in mid-February 1975 to draw out storyboards of the opening sequence to help calculate the costs of those special effects shots. Alex was part of Coppola's circle, the brother of production designer Dean Tavoularis, who had worked on *The Godfather*.

Although the trio's work was specifically designed to get the film made, Fox would not pay for any of them. And the $15,000 they'd given

McQuarrie's early sketches for Darth Vader. In one (top left), Vader brandishes what looks like an épée from a swashbuckling film.

for development was nothing near what was needed; Cantwell alone would cost $20,000. Lucas was thus obliged to pay them out of his *Graffiti* profits. If not for his cash, it's very possible that *The Star Wars* might have irretrievably stalled.

"There was basic apathy toward the project within Fox," Warren Hellman says. "The studio hoped a lot of times that it would just go away."

"It was the same thing with *American Graffiti,*" Lucas notes. "The only thing in the end that got *Graffiti* done was my persistent, dogmatic attitude that the movie was going to get made one way or the other. I was really in no position to get a movie made, but I knew that that movie was going to get made and I just did everything that I possibly could to have it happen. There was never a question in my mind that it wasn't going to be finished. *Star Wars* was a little more dubious . . ."

Or as Kurtz says, "Each step we dragged Fox along."

(Continued on page 40)

Perhaps the first concept model approved was Colin Cantwell's Y-wing—which the model maker showed in his studio to Lucas (top right). Like several artists who were hired for *The Star Wars,* Cantwell had worked on Stanley Kubrick's 1968 film *2001,* which also served as early inspiration for Lucas.

"In the first conversations George said that he wanted to do something very different from *2001,*" Cantwell says. "He wanted the movie to be as immersive and as new as *2001* but George wanted to make this action saga with a comic-book nobility."

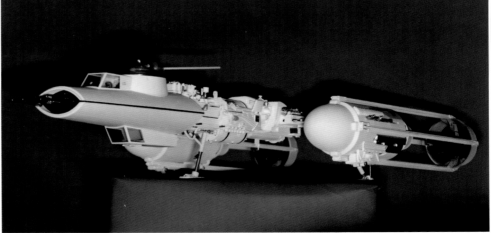

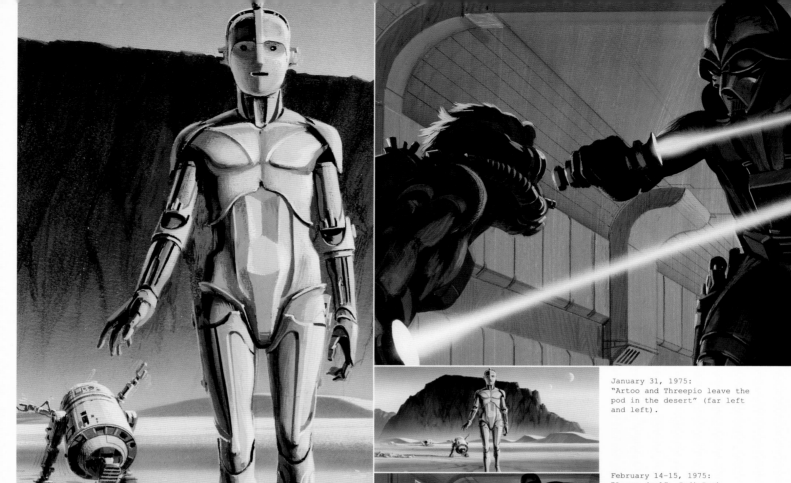

January 31, 1975:
"Artoo and Threepio leave the pod in the desert" (far left and left).

February 14-15, 1975:
"Laser duel": Jedi Deak Starkiller fights Darth Vader on the rebel ship as described in the second draft (above and left).

From Script to Concept Art

Ralph McQuarrie created about twenty-one production paintings, working mostly in gouache, opaque or semi-opaque watercolor, or a combination of gouache and acrylic. Following his meetings with George Lucas, he finished five key illustrations very quickly, taking a day or two for each, between the end of January and the first few days of March 1975. As model maker Colin Cantwell would finish approved concept vehicles, such as the Y-wing, McQuarrie would implement them into his paintings. (*Note:* All titles in quotes are from McQuarrie's notes.)

"The first one I did was Artoo-Detoo and See-Threepio walking across the sand. George had a picture of the little robot from *Silent Running* [1971]," McQuarrie says. "They were like square boxes with legs. So I

thought, *Well, if they're square, I'll make mine round,* which was like a garbage can with a dome on top. Instead of two legs, I gave Artoo three legs, figuring he'd throw himself forward like a person on crutches. That would be the way he would walk. I picked up some landscape from a photograph [of the Oregon coast] because I liked the cliff, and I just put the sand dunes in."

"I showed Ralph the *Metropolis* robot and the *Silent Running* robot, and I said I want something like this," Lucas adds. "And we're still putzing with it. I knew I wanted one via *Metropolis;* it's in the script, I wrote it that way. I wanted one to be a stubby little robot and I wanted one to be a kind of human robot. One is a public relations guy and one is just a standard robot robot."

February 22, 1975: "Battle for Death Star (fighters dive on sphere)."

In this early painting, based on Lucas's description (which was inspired by a John Berkey illustration), the Death Star is illustrated for the first time. Its size was still small enough for individual windows to be seen, as at that time it was just a floating weapon/space station—the big hole on the bottom being where the cannon would emerge, as shown in McQuarrie's sketches (above). "George wanted the Y-wing to be like a World War II TBF Torpedo Bomber," Cantwell says, "which had a gunner in the belly, facing back to cover the tail, and on top behind the pilot, and then the pilot facing forward. So the Y-wing could have that kind of interaction between three people on it."

February 20, 1975: "Imperial City, Alderaan—city floats in gray clouds."

This painting is usually not counted among McQuarrie's first for *The Star Wars,* for reasons that will become clear later.

March 6, 1975: "Cantina."

As per the second draft, Han Solo tries to outdraw an alien with Luke and the robots watching. "The fifth painting represents the inside of the cantina," McQuarrie says. "I had thought of it as being a central gallery over which would be a skylight; the bar was in that gallery, with daylight coming down. I thought of it first as a much more primitive place, with torn banners and regular archways. There wasn't much in it that would indicate that this was part of a society that had a lot of technical expertise. George

looked at it and liked the feeling of it (above left), but he had me put in a mechanical-looking thing." The technological device is similar to the "chrome ping-pong sized balls" that the Aquillian ranger uses to wreak havoc on the stormtroopers in the second draft (above right). "So I put in these little seekers. George envisioned them as seeking out a certain person—and when they would come to that person, they would kill him. It was like an automatic police force that could carry out a death sentence."

CALLING ALL CREW

April 1975 marked the beginning of what can only be described as a mind-boggling overlapping of activity for Lucas and company. If the first two years were marked by the horror of the blank page and the agony of writing, the next two years very likely left little time to feel anything. On or a few days after April 5, 1975, Kurtz traveled to London, taking all of McQuarrie's paintings with him to use as reference when interviewing potential department heads, because the next step was getting things going in England. Moreover, the more *The Star Wars* operated as a working production, the more likely Fox would begin to back them financially.

"Why England?" Kurtz asks rhetorically. "Because it was the solution to a multifaceted problem. There was the cost factor. Certain things are cheaper in certain parts of the world. We had investigated Spain, Yugoslavia, and several other countries, and we'd come up with what we thought was the best compromise. We also wanted locations for the desert planet to be in North Africa, and it's much closer to North Africa from England than from the United States. We could find deserts elsewhere—New Mexico, Arizona, or Old Mexico, Central America, either very good or spectacular—but we wanted slightly bizarre architecture that still looked real. Also we wanted an English cameraman, with a certain level of technological sophistication."

Lucas and his producer had done the math that showed the United States would cost almost twice as much as England in some below-the-line areas: that is, crew costs. With Fox already panicked about the budget, these savings were essential.

Before joining Kurtz in London, Lucas made a significant alteration to the second draft during the last couple of days in March 1975: He changed Luke into a girl. "The original treatment was about a princess and an old man," Lucas explains, "and then I wrote her out for a while, and the second draft didn't really have any girls in it at all. I was very disturbed about that. I didn't want to make a movie without any women in it. So I struggled with that, and at one point Luke was a girl. I just changed the main character from a guy to a girl."

Lucas then flew to England for a one-week stay. "We started interviewing cameramen and art directors first," he says. "Because those are the two key people you have to line up early. They are booked way in advance. First, I made a list of all the people in England whose work I admired and all the films I thought were well shot. I had certain ideas of a few guys that I was really high on. Then we interviewed lots and lots of people, practically everybody."

Among the cinematographer candidates were David Watkin, Gil Taylor, Anthony Richmond, Dick Bush, and Peter Suschitzky; among the

(Continued on page 42)

A McQuarrie sketch shows costume concepts for the Luke-as-girl character.

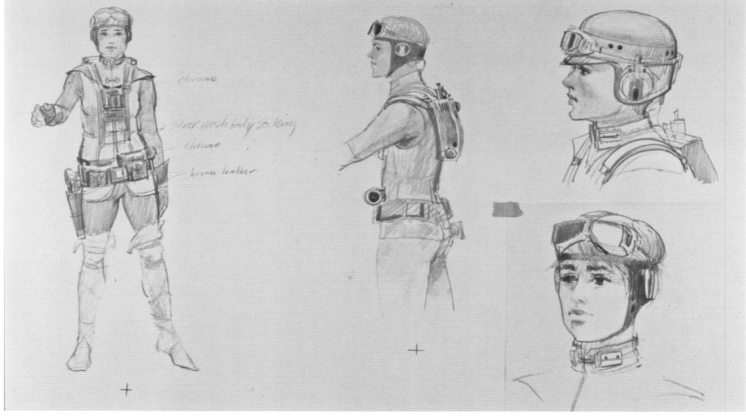

Ralph McQuarrie completed a second group of production paintings in late March and early April. Key interpretations, they are also notable in that some of them contain the only visual remnants of Lucas's transformation of Luke into a girl, when he revised his second draft script.

McQuarrie did several Chewbacca sketches, one of which features an early Han Solo, before getting approval from Lucas to start his paint-

ing. "Han Solo is in the blue cape," McQuarrie says. "It was simply an atmosphere sketch, a symbol for the film, a logo, which would capture the feeling of the film. It was almost like a one-sheet artwork, depicting the five main characters. And that was when Luke was a girl. George liked this Chewbacca, but I suppose he thought it could be a little more weird, and he decided to take off the flak jacket."

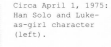

Circa April 1, 1975: Han Solo and Luke-as-girl character (left).

Another logo-poster concept also featured a bearded Han Solo with light-saber, the Death Star, and the girl-with-no-name (bottom left).

April 1, 1975: "The fantastic five painting (Luke is a girl at this time)" (far left).

art directors, Michael Stringer and Brian Eatwell. At the time, Lucas was trying to decide between going with younger, less experienced people, who would perhaps have more enthusiasm, or choosing more experienced but perhaps less flexible veterans.

"I talked with them to find out what their personality was like and about their philosophy of film," says Lucas, who had dinner with at least one. "Then we narrowed it down to two or three people of each. Some of them couldn't do it because they already had other commitments."

Separately, Kurtz saw production supervisor candidates and surveyed all the London studios during a "whirlwind" trip, compiling a list of sound stage sizes and investigating postproduction facilities. To help with budget estimates and hiring, Fox hired a local consultant for two weeks: production designer Elliot Scott, who began by reading the revised second draft. One of his first recommendations was special mechanical effects supervisor John Stears.

"Scott called me," Stears says, "and said he had a picture with a certain amount of problems effects-wise in it, and would I like to go and talk to him, which I did. I read the script as it was then, and I started a feasibility study for Fox. It was a question of talking to the director: long talks about the feel of the movie, and what's physically, technically, and financially possible within the budget."

A former matte painter who also had a license to work with explosives—essential to his work on several James Bond films of the 1960s—Stears began by talking with electronics and engineer specialists, along with camera mechanics.

"Stears had actually gotten on the movie before I even got to England," Lucas says. "He had been brought in by Fox to do some preliminary estimates, so when I got over there to look at it, they had done a preliminary budget; he and Elliot Scott had worked on it, and Stears stayed on because he had such a good reputation. Everybody said he was one of the best and there weren't a lot of other guys of the same caliber available."

But even with the aid of concept art and consultants, Kurtz found it difficult to pin down a realistic budget. "I came up with a $15 million and a $6 million and $10 million budget," he says. "And it was totally arbitrary. You have to design the sets before you know how much things are going to cost."

AN OLD MAN ON THE SIDE OF THE ROAD

Between the second and third drafts, Lucas wrote a six-page story synopsis. Dated May 1, 1975, it served as a primer for Fox executives short of time who needed to understand what the movie was about. Not long afterward Lucas, uncharacteristically, typed out a new outline in four single-spaced pages as he continued to fight his way toward a story. The combined efforts contain key developments. About a month after changing the main character into a girl, Lucas changed her back into Luke, while at the same time resuscitating the princess.

"It was at that moment," says the writer, "that I came up with the idea that Luke and the princess are twins. I simply divided the character in two."

(Continued on page 46)

Circa April 1, 1975:
Luke as girl overlooking Mos Eisley

"The landspeeder was based on a lot of ideas and drawings I had seen," Lucas says. "I described what it was and I showed Ralph a lot of pictures of things that were close to what I wanted, from comic books and science-fiction novels, and strange things out of *National Geographic* or some industrial magazines of an interesting design—say, a door handle that looks like a spaceship."

The landspeeder went through several iterations before coalescing in the painting; McQuarrie did sketches, and Cantwell built a concept model (below). "This is a shot that George wanted," McQuarrie says. "He wanted them on this cliff where they first view Mos Eisley. We knew it was going to be a matte painting, that it was to have two suns. George also wanted the car floating, so I took this point of view and thought it would be kind of interesting if you didn't actually see the ground. Luke was a girl here, and she's carrying that big long rifle which George wanted. It was one of the things he liked."

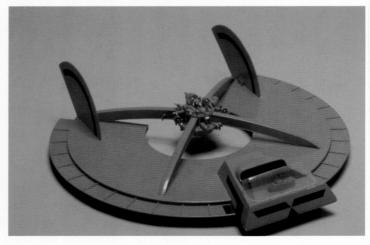

March 28, 1975: "Imperial troopers in Death Star corridor."

By this time Colin Cantwell had finished his prototype for the pirate ship, which can be seen in the background. As described in the second draft, Chewbacca is carrying the wounded Deak on his shoulder. A bearded Han Solo wears a blue cape and holds a lightsaber, with Luke standing behind him; at this point in the creative process, storm-troopers could also use lightsabers.

Circa March 31, 1975: Pirate ship in Alderaan docking bay.

A McQuarrie painting also features the Cantwell pirate ship parked in the cloud city/prison.

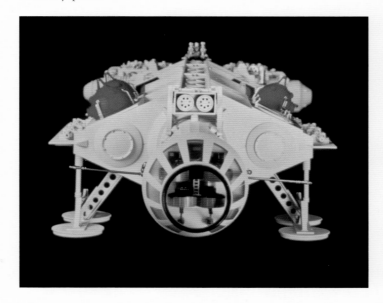

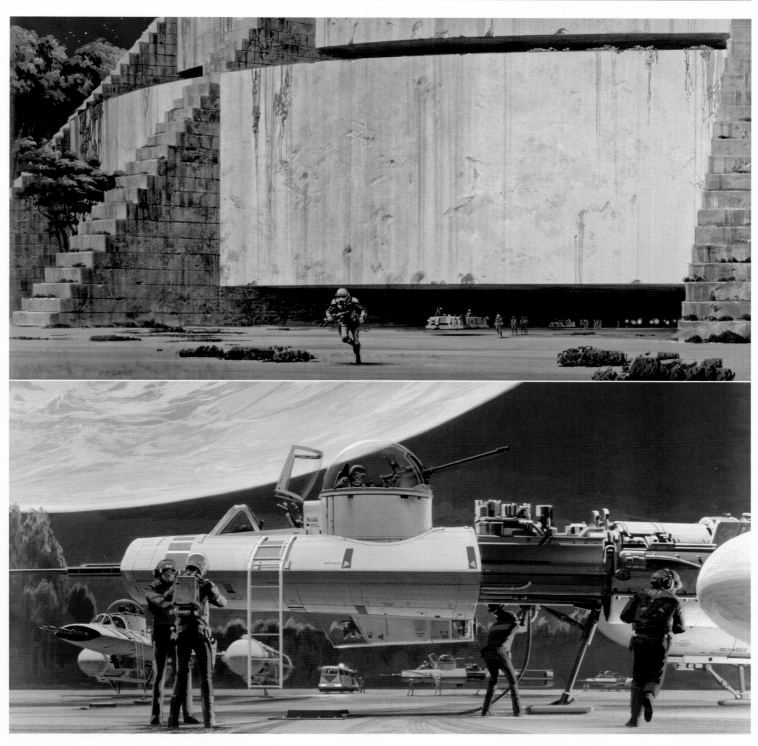

April 3, 1975: Temple on Yavin and "Rebel space base (fighters on fourth moon, outside temple hideout)." "George wished to have the fighter squad come running out of this Aztec-like ruin," McQuarrie says, "which was their headquarters (top), and the fighters were parked out on the field (bottom). We had quite a thorough idea of what it was like. To me it was really one of these seven wonders of the galaxy, a pile of giant disks that were so dense that you almost had the feeling that there was less gravity inside this thing. It wasn't a fully real place."

A sketch by Alex Tavoularis is one of the first to show Princess Leia (below left). A sketch by perhaps Colin Cantwell shows her rebel ship, with notes indicating which action takes place where (below right).

An early character-costume sketch (opposite) reveals how closely linked visually Luke and Leia were; though not explicitly stated as being twins, the idea was present in Lucas's mind and may have been communicated as such to McQuarrie.

The concept had already been germinating in his mind: Biggs and Windy began as twin-like princes in the rough draft, becoming actual twins in the second draft. The desert planet also has twin suns. No doubt in his readings Lucas had come to appreciate the mythological significance of twins, which have been regarded as sacred by many cultures since the beginning of recorded history. Their use as a literary device for defining characters in relation to each other was also helpful: "The princess is everything Luke wants to be," Lucas says. "She is socially conscious, whereas he is thrown into things; intellectually, she is a strong leader, and he is just a kid."

Indeed, her character is so strong, even in the abbreviated synopses, that she eclipses Deak, who nearly disappears from these notes, surviving only as an unnamed "Captain." On the other hand, an unnamed older Jedi appears for the first time. This elderly man is, quite literally, the wizard on the side of the road, whom the hero meets on his journey.

In exchange for his teachings, the old man requests payment in the form of food, which recalls Kurosawa's seven samurai who are paid with rice by farmers to protect their village.

In the outline Lucas refers to the old man's mystical powers as being like those of "Don Juan"—a reference to *The Teachings of Don Juan: A Yaqui Way of Knowledge* by Carlos Castaneda, which was first published in 1968, with sequels in 1971 and 1972, followed by *Tales of Power* in 1975. Castaneda's fictional Don Juan Matus is like a shaman, with the ability to shape-shift, who teaches the mastery of awareness—to the point where one may keep it beyond death. His mystical influence seems to have been key in transforming Lucas's concept of the Jedi from a samurai warrior into a more mystical warrior.

"I spent about a year reading lots of fairy tales—and that's when it starts to move away from Kurosawa and toward Joe Campbell," Lucas says. "About the time I was doing the third draft I read *The Hero with*

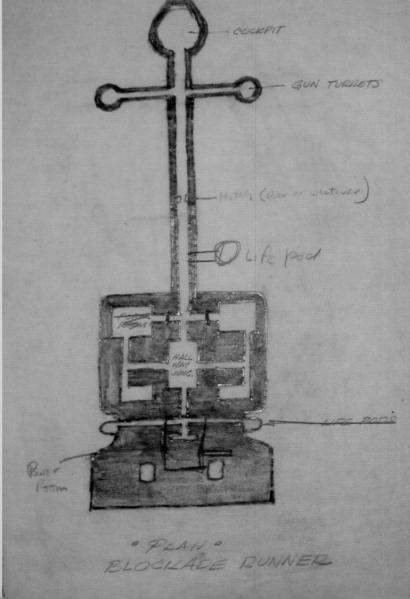

a Thousand Faces, and I started to realize I was following those rules unconsciously. So I said, *I'll make it fit more into that classic mold.*"

More scholarly and perhaps as mystical as Castaneda, Joseph Campbell wrote that all mythical stories of the hero—cross-culturally and across history—contain the same elements, which can be classified as a monomyth. Although there are variations, essentially the hero receives a "call to adventure," undergoes adventures and trials, and eventually surpasses his mentor and achieves an apotheosis.

The influence of these two writers, and others, can be felt not only in the philosophy but also in the developing structure of Lucas's story, to which he made several changes: The Kiber Crystal moves from the moisture farm to Alderaan, where the old man has to *search* for it; instead of Deak it is the princess, a character more integral to Luke's heroic journey, who is rescued; and the attack on the Death Star is supplemented, perhaps because Lucas was searching for a more physical confrontation, with a duel between Luke and Darth Vader, who fight on its surface.

(Continued on page 50)

The Adventures of Luke Starkiller (episode one) "The Star Wars," Story Synopsis and Typed Outline Summary, May 1, 1975

The story synopsis includes an introduction written for the benefit of the Fox executives, which explains the genre they are about to enter: "In the grand tradition of Edgar Rice Burroughs's *John Carter of Mars,* and Alex Raymond's *Flash Gordon, The Adventures of Luke Starkiller* is an engaging human drama set in a fantasy world that paralyzes the imagination."

> The REPUBLIC GALACTICA is dead! Ruthless trader barons, driven by greed and the lust for power, have replaced enlightenment with oppression, and "rule by the people" with the FIRST GALACTIC EMPIRE.
>
> It is a period of civil wars. Throughout the million worlds of the galaxy, scores of independent solar systems are battling for their freedom against the tyranny of the EMPIRE.
>
> For over a thousand years, generations of JEDI KNIGHTS were the guardians of peace and justice in the galaxy. Now these legendary warriors are all but extinct. One by one they have been hunted down and destroyed by the sinister agents of the Empire: the DARK LORDS OF THE SITH.

Much as in the second draft, two Star Destroyers pursue a tiny silver spacecraft above the planet Organa. Two robots scurry for cover. Stormtroopers pour into the smaller ship; two rebel warriors charge, one with a "laser sword," another with a laser pistol. Darth Vader enters. The robots escape in a lifepod to the surface of Organa and are captured by "vile little Jawa Metal Trappers." They are sold to a moisture farmer and then meet "Luke Starkiller, who dreams of someday becoming a mighty Jedi warrior and thereby learning the mystical ways of the 'force of others.'"

He learns from one of the robots that a rebel princess has been captured and taken to "the dreaded cloud city of Alderaan." Luke runs away from home with the two robots to rescue the princess.

At this point the synopsis moves into more general descriptions: It is a "story not only for children, but for anyone who likes the action-adventure genre to which it belongs: the Heroic Quest." It then describes the ending, a climactic space battle where outnumbered rebel starships "attack an awesome space station known as the 'Death Star.'"

An additional four undated pages, written as notes, supplement the same story, retelling it and adding to it.

The Imperial starpilots let the robots' lifepod go because they don't detect life-forms inside it. The robots argue when they land and split up: "Threepio gets picked up and Artoo gets chased/shot by Jawas." Instead of being directed to Owen Lars, the robots are bought by Owen Lars and his nephew at Anchorhead, and transported home.

At their moisture farm Luke talks with the robots about his dreams; at dinner Owen tells him he can't go to the Academy—they argue and Owen strikes the boy, who is protected by Beru. Cleaning the robots later, Luke stumbles on a message from the "Captain" saying the princess has been

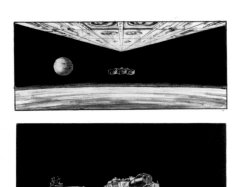

Lucas employed artist Alex Tavoularis to storyboard scenes from the second and third drafts, as well as the synopses.

taken prisoner and sent to Alderaan. Enclosed in R2 is a signal device to locate the princess. Luke rushes outside, then returns to kiss his aunt good night while she's sleeping. He then leaves home with the robots.

On his way to the spaceport, he passes a "poor old man." He picks him up, and the old man talks about his adventures as a Jedi. Luke is "in awe" and wants to become his apprentice; the old man agrees and will train him "for food." When they stop for water, the old man gives Luke a lesson about the "force of others . . . Old man can do magic, read minds, talk to things like Don Juan."

They arrive the next day at the cantina, and the old man talks to Chewbacca. "Bugs molest Luke, start fight. Old man cuts them down." Chewbacca leads them to Han, who is a captain. They persuade Chewbacca and Han, after negotiating the fee, to take them to Alderaan, where R2's signal device is leading them. There they hide in the ship as TIE fighters escort it into the docking bay. Darth Vader and other Sith Knights sense the presence of a Jedi, but they find only the robots.

While the old man looks for the Kiber Crystal, the others rescue the princess, which doesn't go smoothly. "She's a tough babe; doesn't appreciate their help—a trap? Han punches her in the face and Chewbacca carries her out." They then have to face the Dia Noga and have various adventures, while the old man gets the crystal, at which point the Sith Knights "become ill." They nevertheless confront the old man and wound him, but he's rescued by the others, and they all blast off. Vader "lets them go," but still sends some TIEs after them; these quickly give up. The old man tells them they're being followed, but the princess needs to go to her "hidden fortress anyway."

They crash-land on Yavin, but are located by loyal troops. Han receives his money, after they arrive at the base, and leaves the group, which saddens Luke. In the Control War Room, they "spot something very big." The old man knows it's the Death Star—and the only way to destroy it is by putting a "bomb in its exhaust system."

Most of the rebels are skeptical, but Luke lands on the Death Star with the bomb—"runs into Vader; sword fight—Han to the rescue. Artoo shot . . . End scene—all come together, cheer. Make Luke a Jedi knight."

STAR WARS PROGRESSION

- Robots sold to Owen Lars by Jawas
- Owen Lars, a farmer, antagonistic toward Luke
- An old man/Jedi, whom Luke meets (on the road to Mos Eisley), tells Luke about the mystical ways of the Force of Others
- Han Solo captain of his ship
- Old man Jedi goes on his own mission (in Alderaan, to find the Kiber Crystal)
- The heroes (Luke, Han, et al.) rescue the princess from her detention cell (on Alderaan)
- Princess at odds with Han, attracted to Luke
- Luke blows up Death Star (with bomb)

VALIANT VAN NUYS

Although Lucas had made the decision to shoot in England and North Africa, he decided to create his own special effects house in Northern California. The two primary reasons for doing so were cost and control. By having his own facility, Lucas could authorize the making of specialized equipment, hire his own people, and keep an eye on production. If a film frame had to sit three days in an optical printer, his effects house would have that luxury. "Once we added up the cost, it was just cheaper and easier to control the elements by doing it ourselves," Kurtz says.

Lucas had talked with others, doing due diligence. He had discussed the project with the few specialists in the area, Howard Anderson and Linwood Dunn, as well as Jim Danforth and Phil Taylor. Douglas Trumbull, who had supervised the effects on *2001*, might have been a candidate for special effects supervisor, but he was more interested in directing, having recently completed *Silent Running*.

"I learned everything I could about special effects in school," Lucas says. "I got the books and read everybody. But I hadn't worked very extensively with special effects and optical problems, and there aren't that many people around who know this kind of stuff anymore."

In April 1975 the director met with John Dykstra, who had assisted Douglas Trumbull on *2001, Silent Running,* and many commercials. "I was working for Doug at a special effects company called Future General," Dykstra says. "We'd finished up a couple of projects for Paramount, who owned that corporation, and we were on a hiatus situation. Gary Kurtz called one day and asked me to come and interview with him and George, to talk about some special effects on a movie called *Star Wars.* I didn't know what the movie was then. As I remember, I just went in and we discussed it. George outlined the concept of the film primarily with regard to what the special effects would be—what he wanted to do and what he wanted to have happen. More than anything else, he wanted to get fluidity of motion, the ability to move the camera around so that you could create the illusion of actually photographing spaceships from a camera platform in space."

To get his visual points across, Lucas was armed with the project he'd begun two years ago: the aerial battle short created from films on television. "At one point I had twenty to twenty-five hours' worth of videotape," he says. "I condensed that down to four or five hours, then I looked through that and condensed it down, shot by shot, to about an hour. We transferred about an hour to 16 mm film, and then I cut that down to about eight minutes. I would have the plane going from right to left, and a plane coming toward us and flying away from us, to see if the movement would generate excitement.

"We showed the film to John Dykstra when he started," Lucas adds. "I described what I was going to do, and then I showed him the film and said this is what it's going to look like."

Two or three weeks after the interview Dykstra made a verbal commitment to do the film.

It was the meeting of two people whose goals overlapped: Lucas wanted to see his vision of a dogfight in space come to life, while Dykstra had the theoretical technical means to do it—if he was allowed to build a motion-control camera. "We had already gone over several problems," Lucas says, "but I think the camera came out of the fact that John had wanted to build

Richard (Dick) Alexander at work in the ILM machine shop (above right); John Dykstra reflects, sitting on the floor of the motion-control stage (below right). "We've got milling machines, lathes, welders, everything you'd need in a general workshop," Alexander says. On the floor of the shop and all over the ground floor were skid marks left over from when Dykstra took his dirt bike and tore around the vacant warehouse before the walls were up (inset).

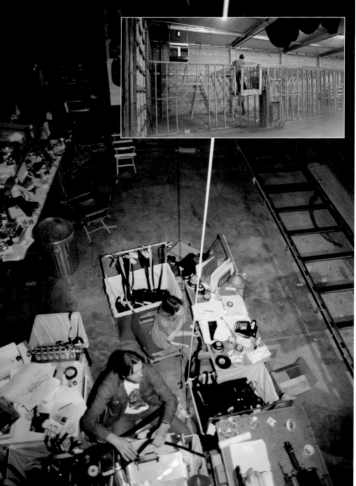

one. He had been playing around with it up here in San Francisco before, and he had played around with it at Trumbull's for a while. He was anxious to actually build one, because it was an idea that John had had for quite a while and this seemed like the perfect opportunity to exploit that."

Given Dykstra's previous work in the Bay Area, Lucas had originally hoped to create the effects house in or near San Francisco. In late May 1975, however, Dykstra found what he considered the ideal location: an empty warehouse renting for $2,300 per month at 6842 Valjean Avenue in Van Nuys, a suburb just north of Los Angeles. He then persuaded Lucas that their technical needs forced them to be closer to the film development and color processing houses of Hollywood. Lucas reluctantly agreed, none too thrilled about being stretched even farther from his home base.

Richard Alexander, one of Dykstra's colleagues from *Silent Running,* was one of the first people to come out and look at the place. Alexander brought with him Richard Edlund, a colleague from Bob Abel's commercial house. "I came out and looked around," Edlund says. "There wasn't anything to see: It was an empty building. John asked me how much responsibility I wanted, and I said, 'I don't know. How about director of photography for the special effects? He said, 'Fine. That's the deal.'"

Edlund had already heard rumors about the project, which was scheduled to come out in two years' time. "There were an estimated 350 shots, and it ended up being taken all around town before we got to it," he says. By comparison, *2001* had about three years to do 205 shots—with eighteen months dedicated almost exclusively to those shots.

"Everybody said, 'It just *can't be done* in the time allotted,'" Edlund adds. "But John had sold George on the idea that we could build the system that could do it. So John arranged to get a studio together out in the valley and build the system, which started with a camera that would be able to photograph something repeatedly through programming and motors—that is, once you have the shot programmed, you can repeat that program over and over, as many times as you want, and then correlate information so that the shot can be done on a background for stars or a matte. So we proceeded to go ahead and build our systems. We were hideouts, in a way; we were not known people."

Others had balked not only because of the time constraints, but also because of the very limited special effects budget. "John seemed to be the only one who was qualified and who was also interested in taking on the challenge," Lucas says. "A lot of the people who were qualified didn't want to have anything to do with it. They didn't think it could be done. They thought it was impossible for the kind of money we were talking about."

The situation hadn't been helped when the studio had taken photos of the models Cantwell had built and authorized an independent special effects budget estimate. "I think they budgeted on the outside," Lucas adds. "Fox went to Van Der Veer [a special effects house] and a few of those places, and asked them, given 350 shots and the storyboards, how much do you think this would cost? The estimates came in and averaged out to around $7 million. We were saying at that time that we would do it for $2.3 million, but then Twentieth Century-Fox cut it down to $1.5 million. They just assumed that it would all get done somehow. They just figured that we could do it for a million and a half, and that it was our problem, not theirs—because they didn't think we could even build the models for a million and a half, *let alone* all the special effects."

Again, a comparison with *2001* is useful: Its 205 special effects shots cost $6.5 million out of a total budget of $10.5 million, in 1967 dollars. Given the intervening eight years of inflation, it's no wonder that nearly no one would go anywhere near what had to resemble an impending train wreck of a film. Moreover, in Hollywood at that time, special effects films were considered expensive without being guaranteed box office. Fox was thus still dragging its feet, given the ever-present lack of a contract, and, after slashing its budget, committed funds to Lucas's special effects start-up only theoretically.

"When it came down to the real crunch," Lucas says, "when we needed the half million dollars to get going, because we'd already committed the money, they delayed for about four or five weeks. So I had to put up the cash."

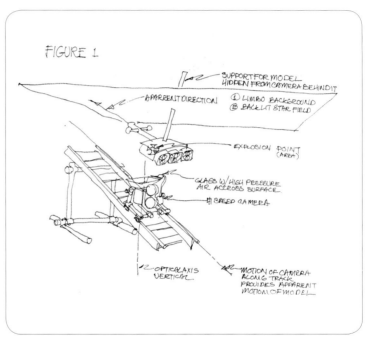

FIGURE 1

Before ILM was up and running, the special effects house created estimates for the opening sequence. In this drawing Cantwell's rebel ship is placed on a rented high-speed camera for shot 3. It was calculated that these four seconds of screen time would take one and a half weeks to rig and three days to shoot, with two camera passes, for a total of two weeks and $15,017. (Note that the rebel ship has front gun turrets, unlike the pirate ship.)

A NEW LEGION

At the moment of incorporating his special effects company, Lucas needed a name. "It just popped into my head," he says. "We were sitting in an industrial park and using light to create magic. That's what they were going to do." Industrial Light & Magic was born.

But before any work could occur at the newly christened establishment, the right people had to be hired and the warehouse had to be converted into shops and offices. Dykstra worked out of a little back office he had at Universal and made phone calls. One of the first went to model builder Grant McCune. "I decided to do it," McCune recalls, "and we started out with almost no experience in building models in this quantity or this type."

Graduating with a degree in biology and then training as a laboratory technician, McCune changed careers and met Dykstra in 1969. Later they

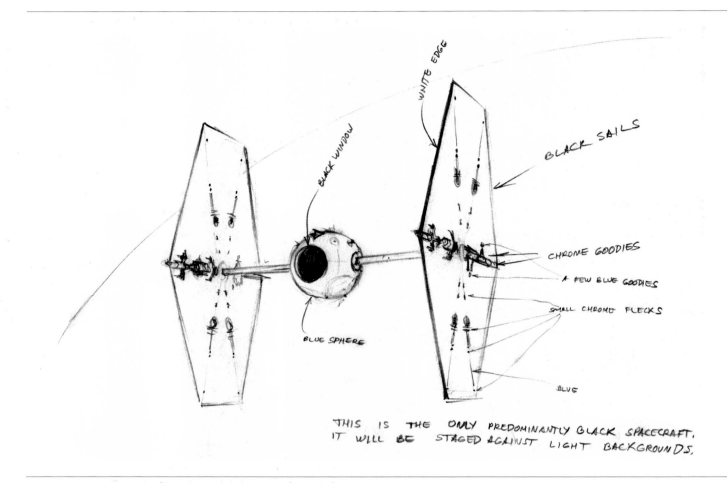

WHITE EDGE

BLACK WINDOW

BLACK SAILS

CHROME GOODIES

A FEW BLUE GOODIES

SMALL CHROME FLECKS

BLUE SPHERE

BLUE

THIS IS THE ONLY PREDOMINANTLY BLACK SPACECRAFT. IT WILL BE STAGED AGAINST LIGHT BACKGROUNDS.

worked on the television movie *Strange New World* (1975), while their mutual interest in miniatures meant they flew gliders, sailed model boats, and raced model cars together. "I started on day one. It was June 1 of '75," McCune says.

Other key technicians hired that month were Jerry Greenwood, who would help build the special mechanical equipment; Richard Alexander, who began the machine work, having apprenticed seven years in England at an optical instrument company; Bob Shepherd as the facility's production manager; Al Miller, the electronics designer; Don Trumbull, father of Doug Trumbull, who commenced work on the camera system, drafting the blueprints; Bill Shourt and Jamie Shourt, who joined McCune in the model shop, specializing in mechanical design; and Edlund, who started the camera department. They all knew one another and had worked together before: Richard (Dick) Alexander had once shared an apartment with John Dykstra for six months; Shepherd and Dykstra had worked on *Silent Running;* the Shourts, Edlund, and Alexander had all worked for Bob Abel.

"All of us had worked with each other and were pretty good friends," McCune says, "and we talked to each other on a weekly basis just as

friends. When John put the crew together, he put it together instantaneously, at least the nucleus of it."

Robbie Blalack and Adam Beckett were the last two of the initial crew hired, in July 1975. "John called me up and said, 'I've got the effects on *Star Wars,* I want to talk to you about putting together the optical department,'" Blalack says. He started immediately. Beckett began the animation and rotoscope setup shortly thereafter.

While the project alone was interesting, even at that time Lucas already had a reputation as an innovative filmmaker. "The idea of working with George Lucas was the most exciting thing to me," Edlund says. "Because I'd really liked *THX 1138.* I loved his approach and his attitude." Edlund had worked mostly in 1960s television up till then: *The Outer Limits, The Twilight Zone,* and *Star Trek.* "I teleported hundreds of guys." A number of times he even played Thing—a disembodied human hand—on *The Addams Family.*

Under the aegis of this skeleton crew, the downstairs of the Van Nuys warehouse was quickly transformed into an optical department big enough for two optical printers, a rotoscope department, two shooting stages, a model shop, a machine shop, a wood shop, and offices—Dykstra's

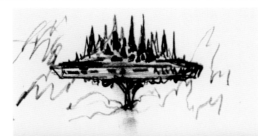

"We've got twelve thousand square feet divided between the two stages," Dykstra adds, "but we ended up having to modify the building incredibly. Jim Hanna is an amazingly nice landlord. He said, 'Well, whatever you want to change, you've got to put it back eventually, but that's okay.' He was really loose about us hanging fixtures back there or cutting something in half or taking the floors up."

"As soon as we got the physical plant built so that we could do work, which took about six weeks, to actually get some walls up, there was a whole big move-in period," Shepherd says. "Everybody was new to their job and they were setting up their own departments. We tried to give everybody what they wanted: desks, tables, a chair, their own pencil sharpener. Then three main things got going simultaneously. One was the generation of the models, the second was the camera system, and third was the optical compositing system."

It was up to the small band to figure out what equipment was required for these three main areas, to estimate how much time it would take to build new equipment or modify preexisting equipment, and to hire the additional people required to do it all. "It was really overwhelming," Dykstra concludes, "because I sat at a little desk and figured out how to spend $1.28 million."

"We were all sitting down arguing about what had to be done," Richard Alexander says, "and Don Trumbull would wheel out his sheets of brown paper and we'd all start scribbling on them, and writing this and that. There was no real one person deciding anything, which was kind of nice."

During these embryonic brainstorming sessions, while all contributed, each was aware of everyone else's specialties. "Don answers all the mechanical problems," McCune says. "While John dreams about 8-perf with 4 pins to pull it across at 50 frames per second with perfect registration."

"There's a significant difference between coming up with a good idea," Dykstra agrees, "and executing it."

"We had a lot of conferences about optical and camera equipment," McCune adds. "But it was only six weeks before we were starting to produce models and the machine shop was starting to produce mechanical devices. We had a lot of conferences with George; a lot of them went through John from George and back to me. He knew what he wanted."

Industrial Light & Magic, or ILM, at its birth seemed to have the two elements necessary for creativity: a certain amount of chaos and a certain amount of money. After their first three weeks of existence in June, Lucas had already shelled out $87,921. While those same two elements, in differing quantities, would combine to create other situations, at the beginning everyone was enthusiastic. "I thought that at some point, things have got to change—the people who have ideas to do things should be allowed to do them," Edlund says. "It was providential to me that *Star Wars* came along, because it was the response to that dream. We all got together, in a highly unorthodox way, in this little warehouse out in Van Nuys."

TRAVELING THE WORLD

In the spring of 1975, simultaneous with the beginnings of ILM, Gary Kurtz flew with Francis Ford Coppola to the Florida Everglades, the former scouting for a suitable jungle planet, the latter a suitable Vietnam for *Apocalypse Now,* which was beginning anew to attract

sitting opposite Shepherd's. "We just walked around putting tape on the floors and figuring out general areas," Shepherd says. "Next we made drawings for the spaces that were required and started building them."

Upstairs on the smaller second floor were the animation, editorial, and art departments, along with a screening room—though at the beginning these rooms were empty. "My original vision of this place included a swimming pool," Dykstra says, laughing. "Seriously, it had to have high ceilings and it had to be far enough out of the central Hollywood complex; otherwise you end up with people constantly dropping in. People find out that you're doing special effects, and they want a job or to build models, so you end up with a guard at the door, which makes it really a crummy situation. So we wanted a nondescript location, while still being close enough to the freeway and the lab processors in downtown Los Angeles. And we do have high ceilings, twenty-four feet to the bay, which means that we can put lights up real high to get particular angles, or we can put the camera up on the ceiling to get a wide shot looking down."

studio interest. Kurtz then traveled alone to Olympic National Forest in Washington and "trudged around for three weeks looking at the rain forest." The national park was soon rejected, though, because it had too many inherent restrictions. He then went to Toronto to look at the IMAX system. "They were willing to pick up the tab between that and regular 35 millimeter," he explains, "which could have been half a million dollars. But converting theaters is difficult, and optical effects were next to impossible in that format. Special equipment would have had to be built. It was just beyond us to seriously consider it." Not having a production designer yet, Kurtz then flew to Calgary, Canada, to talk with Anthony Masters, who was working on Robert Altman's *Buffalo Bill and the Indians* (1976).

Kurtz then rejoined Lucas, and the two traveled to Mexico City during the July 4 weekend. This was actually their second trip, having been to Guaymas, Mexico, the previous spring. Lucas's friends the Huycks had been and were still on location down south working on *Lucky Lady* (1975)—another Fox film, which would remain strangely tangential to *The Star Wars* throughout its production.

Lucas went primarily to see how a big-budget movie was being made and to talk to potential department heads. He had toured the sets on the previous visit and had probably witnessed some of the film's problems: Location shooting on boats had caused many complications; many of the cast and crew had become ill, including the film's star, Liza Minnelli; and one person had died. By July they were just finishing, so Lucas was able to renew talks with *Lucky Lady*'s cameraman Geoffrey Unsworth, and spent Sunday morning chatting with its veteran production designer John Barry.

Barry had worked as a draftsman on *Cleopatra* (1963). Kubrick had offered Barry the production designer job on *Napoleon,* which he worked on for one whole week (the film was never made). Barry moved on to become production designer on *Kelly's Heroes* (1970) before collaborating again with Kubrick on *A Clockwork Orange* (1971). Years before, he'd been on the TV series *Danger Man* (1964–1966), where he'd met its art director, Elliot Scott, who afterward took on Barry as his assistant—and who had suggested Barry to Lucas back in England.

"George came to see me in Mexico," John Barry says, "and decided that perhaps I'd be the one to do it. I have just enough experience to be able to cope with the problems, and just enough inexperience so I should take it on. I think anybody with more experience would have just said, 'I don't think I can do it in that amount of time.' "

Indeed, the clock was ticking, with principal photography tentatively planned for February 1976, less than a year away. Having read the script, Barry said that he would need "seven months minimum"—exactly the time remaining—to design and build the sets.

"I knew we were going to have an incredibly difficult job," Lucas says. "Just the sheer size of the thing was going to be difficult, and I wanted somebody who I felt was really down to earth and solid and could get the job done—without costing me ten times what I thought it was going to cost me. He was doing a good job on *Lucky Lady,* and just talking with him I got an impression. You look at the films he's done and you listen to people who have worked with him. Based on those things, you make your decision."

Conversations went well with Unsworth, too, as he understood the look Lucas was after. "Geoffrey Unsworth was very flexible," Lucas adds. "His style was so much different on every movie, so I thought he would be great, easy to work with, and I really liked what he had done. Also I wanted to give the film a very diffused look, similar to what he had done on *Murder on the Orient Express* [1974]. It had that fairy-tale quality about it.

"So I decided I wanted to go with Geoffrey Unsworth. He said, 'Okay.' And I wanted John Barry to be the art director, and he said, 'Okay,' and then we got going."

One of those who had fallen ill during the *Lucky Lady* shoot was set decorator Roger Christian, but he became the third person of that production team hired by Lucas for *The Star Wars.* After Lucas and Kurtz returned home, on his way back to London, John Barry flew up to San Francisco for more talks on how to do the necessary within the $1 million budget that had been allocated for the sets.

THE *JAWS* CONNECTION

Lucas never acquired an office on the Fox lot "because he believed politically, and he was right, that you don't want to be on the same lot as the studio, because they can invade your space and give you a hard time," explains Charles Lippincott, who had been hired to handle the film's marketing and merchandising. "And Fox did give me a hard time because I was the major person working out of that office, and they really put the screws to me. But they couldn't do anything, 'cause George was at Universal—it was a very smart idea."

Instead Lucas would occasionally make use of Kurtz's office on the Universal lot, where Steven Spielberg also had an office in one of the bungalows (Kurtz's bungalow was 426). Lucas and Spielberg had met back in the late 1960s, when the latter had been amazed by the former's *THX 1138.4EB.* They had since become good friends, so when Spielberg was back from Martha's Vineyard and in postproduction on *Jaws* (1975), Lucas naturally went around from time to time to see how things were developing. Unusually for most directors, but standard for Lucas, he had already been thinking about the soundtrack for *The Star Wars,* and was leaning toward a classical, romantic one. Spielberg suggested the fellow who had just finished composing the soundtrack for *Jaws;* Lucas got to hear some of it and was impressed.

"Steven said, 'I worked with this guy and he's great!' " Lucas remembers.

Thus in the spring of 1975 Lucas met with perhaps the most key member of his team: composer John Williams. "Steven Spielberg introduced me to George," Williams says, "and told me about *Star Wars* and George Lucas, and how much he admired him."

Williams proceeded to read the script, but wouldn't start actually composing for more than a year, as he had prior commitments to Alfred Hitchcock's *Family Plot* (1976), *Black Sunday* (1977), and his own violin concerto.

Not only did Lucas start thinking about the music early on, he was also eager to start work on the sound effects and sound design of his film—to continue his tradition of innovative sound use as established by *THX 1138* and *American Graffiti,* which had one of the first soundtracks specifically

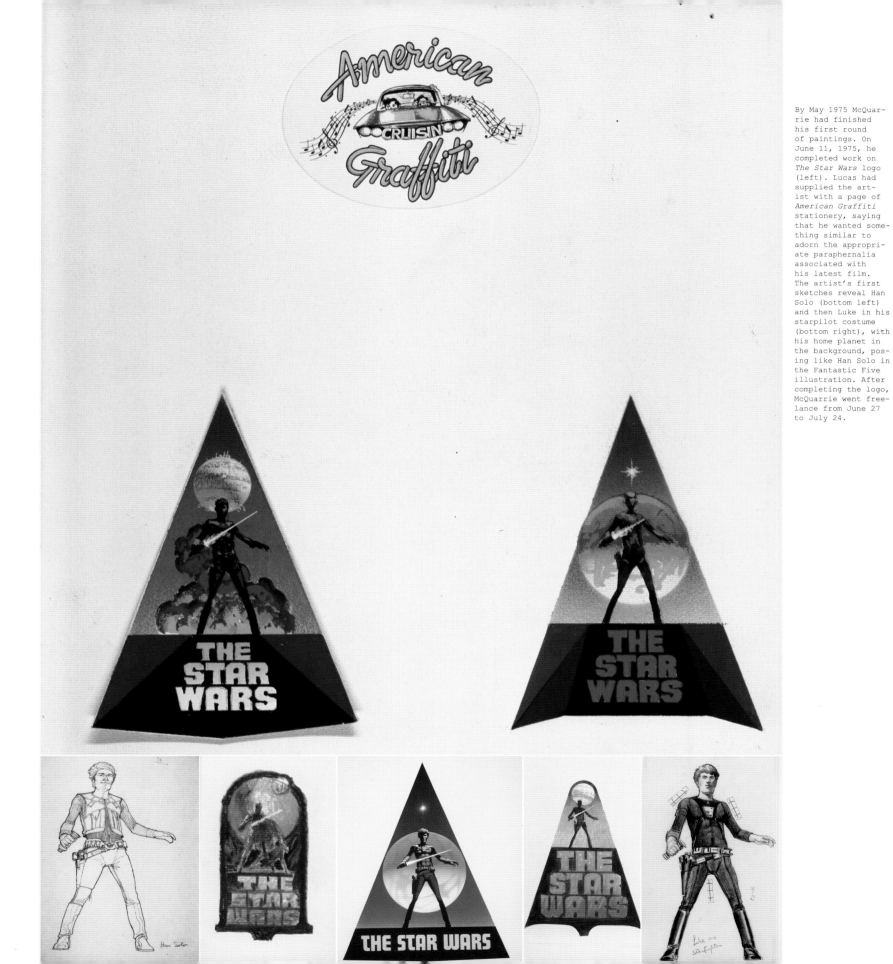

By May 1975 McQuarrie had finished his first round of paintings. On June 11, 1975, he completed work on *The Star Wars* logo (left). Lucas had supplied the artist with a page of *American Graffiti* stationery, saying that he wanted something similar to adorn the appropriate paraphernalia associated with his latest film. The artist's first sketches reveal Han Solo (bottom left) and then Luke in his starpilot costume (bottom right), with his home planet in the background, posing like Han Solo in the Fantastic Five illustration. After completing the logo, McQuarrie went freelance from June 27 to July 24.

In Mexico, DP Geoffrey Unsworth (left), Willard Huyck (middle), and Lucas talk while on a boat, as much of *Lucky Lady*—the production they were visiting—was being shot on the water. Another movie shot on the water was *Jaws,* whose production offices were at Universal Studios (opposite top), where Lucas and friends visited Spielberg: (from left) Hal Barwood, Gloria Huyck, Lucas, Kurtz, Colin Cantwell, Willard Huyck.

made for stereo. "Usually Walter Murch worked with me," Lucas says. "He is a genius who I went to school with who had done the sound work in all my movies." Murch had been preapproved in the deal memo—but as of July 1975 he was occupied elsewhere on a number of projects, including *Julia* (1977), and had committed to do *The Black Stallion* (1979). "So we decided to go to USC. We called the sound department and we asked Ken Miura, who is a friend of ours, 'Who's the next Walter Murch?' And they sent us Ben Burtt."

"I've always collected sound effects," Burtt says. "Since I was about seven years old, off the TV. As a teenager I used to go to the drive-in movies and reconnect the wires from the speaker to make direct recordings."

Burtt's professional career began the day Ken Miura called him. "I met with Gary and saw some of the paintings for *Star Wars,*" Burtt continues. "They wanted someone to come up with a voice for a creature called a Wookiee. Apparently a Wookiee was going to be an important character and they were concerned about getting some kind of voice for him before they started shooting. Gary said, 'We've got this big sidekick, like a giant teddy bear, but he can be ferocious if he's coming to the rescue; the rest

of the time he's like a big dog.' The problem they had was that he didn't speak English. He wasn't going to speak an intelligible language; he had to sound like an animal, but we had to understand his emotions. I got a look at the script after a month and met with George in August, and at that point it became evident that they really wanted someone to build a whole library of material."

"Ben started collecting sounds before we even started shooting the film," Lucas says. "I described what I wanted the spaceships to sound like and what I wanted from the laser swords, and I said, 'Collect weird, strange sounds. Go to the zoo, collect all the animal sounds. Go to transportation places.' We had several categories that I wanted him to do. One was animals; another was all kinds of dialects and dialogues. And one was just to collect any kind of sound that could be used for a laser gun—weird zaps and cracks and things like that."

"They sent me down some equipment from Zoetrope," says Burtt, picking up the story. "A Nagra and some microphones, and I just started gathering sounds. George thought that bear sounds might be the right direction to take for the Wookiee, so that initiated the search for all kinds of bear material. I also broke down the script in terms of every possible

"I recorded the original sounds on the Nagra IV-S, their only stereo model [released in 1971]," Ben Burtt says (far left, recording a bear named Pooh), "and I played with it on $1/4$-inch tape-that is, I played it into an ARP synthesizer that Coppola happened to have. I also had the use of a Moog and a Harmonizer, which is an Eventide piece of equipment, a device with which you can play a sound, and then raise or lower the pitch without changing the time reference. So I could play a voice, and I could play it high-pitched or low-pitched while retaining the same rapidity of speed. I had a Urei dip filter, which is just a fancy filter for taking out unwanted material, and I had a graphic equalizer."

Lucas works with McQuarrie (left).

thing that might make sound: laser guns, laser swords, the landspeeder, the various spaceships. I went through and saw how many different sets were in the film. So I made a big notebook with that stuff divided up, and I kept a record of ideas that might apply to any one of those areas, and then I'd go out and look for them.

"In the early stages I spent a lot of time hunting down animal recordings. I listened to all the various material I could get out of libraries in town, and all the various studios. Occidental College has a huge collection of bird sounds from around the world. I went there and spent several days listening to everything they had. But we wanted the sounds to be original, so I also rented animals; I went to people that trained animals for movies, who have ranches, who have bears and elephants and camels. I'd go out in the desert where it was quiet and stand around with the recorders."

THE ARRIVAL OF GENERAL BEN KENOBI

Presumably during short stints at Medway and on the road, Lucas developed his third draft from the May 1 Story Synopsis and notes. At Park Way, Bunny Alsup had joined the group in the restored Victorian house. "The environment was great fun because we were a small, intimate group and were all young fledgling filmmakers," she says. "George was writing *Star Wars*. He'd turn the pages over to me and I'd type them. *Star Wars* was a much more difficult script for me to type [than *American Graffiti*] because it was like a foreign language. Science fiction was

foreign to me and he had many words I'd never heard of in my life. Spelling the names was also a challenge, because he was inconsistent in how he spelled them."

The pages Lucas handed off were as usual prefigured by his notes: "Robots and rebel troops listen as the weird sounds of stormtroopers are heard on the top of the ship . . . Sith rips rebel's arm off at end of battle . . . only seven Sith—one in each sector . . . small ships avoid deflector shields/tractor beams."

Another note falls under the title, "New scenes: Luke sees space battle." Luke's emergence as the hero of the film was one reason Lucas made a decision to write additional scenes on Utapau, which show Luke observing the opening battle in the sky and then talking with friends. It was Lucas's own friends Matt Robbins and Hal Barwood who had provided another reason: They thought that Luke needed to appear earlier in the film, to establish a link with impatient audiences. "Francis had read the script and given me his ideas," Lucas says. "Steven Spielberg had read the script. All of my friends had read the script. Everybody who had read the script gave their input about what they thought was good, or bad, or indifferent; what worked, what didn't work—and what was confusing. I would do the same on their scripts. Matt and Hal thought the first half hour of the film would be better if Luke was intercut with the robots, so I did that."

And while some characters were cut out completely, two who were absent from the second draft return. Leia replaces Deak, becoming the

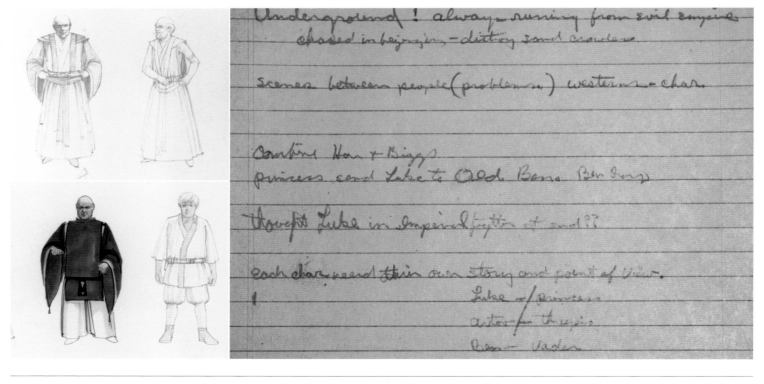

In late July and early August, McQuarrie returned to work on *The Star Wars,* doing costume designs. One of them is a first look at General Ben Kenobi. The sleeveless shirt recalls the garb of a samurai from one of Kurosawa's films (top right). Lucas's notes from the time indicate major plot revisions—"princess send Luke to Old Ben"—and ideas that didn't quite make it into the third draft: "combine Han and Biggs."

unnamed princess of the Story Synopsis. She is reintroduced at the film's outset, as she was in the treatment, instead of halfway through on Alderaan. The old man also acquires a name: General Ben Kenobi, who becomes the wizened old man/Jedi and occupies the role of mentor, originally filled by General Skywalker in the rough and first draft. He trains Luke in the ways of the Force, becoming an important foil in the student's voyage of self-discovery. Perhaps due to Lucas's appreciation of Campbell's analysis of mythology, Luke is more of a loner; he is stripped of his brothers and cousins—and now his father is a dead Jedi.

Luke's voyage is also more defined in the third-draft notes, as it becomes more related to the Force, which he learns about in specific stages: "1) Luke learns about Force (in desert); 2) Luke tries to experience Force (in ship); 3) Luke becomes a man of the Force (Alderaan); 4) Ben explains Luke's experience (in ship); 5) Luke with crystal struggles with Force (on Yavin)."

"I have come to the conclusion that there is a force larger than the individual," Lucas says. "It is controlled by the individuals, and it controls them. All I'm saying is that the pure soul is connected to a larger energy field that you would begin to understand if you went all the way back and saw yourself in your purest sense."

Another note reads, "Learn about the Force—all around us in every living creature." It is defined in similar terms by Kenobi in the third draft. As the hero's journey becomes more linked to the Force, the Kiber Crystal's importance naturally fades. Primarily a "MacGuffin"—a plot element that Alfred Hitchcock defined as an item of no emotional significance, but which keeps the story moving—the crystal also has a new rival in the plans to the Death Star. It thus moves far into the background, as the third draft has little space for two MacGuffins.

The crystal, however, is still part of the aerial attack on the Death Star—the last element to undergo structural alterations. "Between the second and third drafts, Luke stopped on the surface on the Death Star," Lucas says. "He and Artoo had to go and take the bomb by hand, open up the little hatch, and drop the bomb in it—then they had fifteen seconds or something to get off the surface before the thing blew up—but as they were going back to the ship, Darth Vader arrived. So Luke and Vader had a big swordfight. Luke finally overcame Vader and then jumped in the ship and took off. But in trying to intercut the dogfight with the old-fashioned swordfight, I realized that the film would have just stopped dead. It was too risky.

"I feel that I'm fairly decent at construction, not necessarily plot, but construction," Lucas says of these changes. "Neither *Graffiti* nor *THX* had plots. I'm not really interested in plots. That's one of the problems I've had with this movie—it's a plotted movie, and I find plots boring because they're so mechanical. You go from here to there, and once you know what's going to happen, that's it. And I just am not enthralled with that kind of action. I'm much more into the scenes and the nuances of what's going on. I find that fascinating."

(Continued on page 63)

Lucas wrote notes on Luke's cognitive progression in relation to the Force, followed by a list of words formulating key ideas for the film.

The Star Wars: From the Adventures of Luke Starkiller,
Third-Draft Summary, August 1975

The REPUBLIC GALACTICA is dead. Ruthless trader barons,
driven by greed and the lust for power, have replaced
enlightenment with oppression, and "rule by the people"
with the FIRST GALACTIC EMPIRE.

For over a thousand years, generations of JEDI KNIGHTS
were the guardians of peace and justice in the galaxy.
Now these legendary warriors are all but extinct. One by
one they have been hunted down and destroyed by the sinister agents of the Emperor: the DARK LORDS OF THE SITH.

It is a period of civil wars. Rebel Armies, striking from fortresses hidden deep within the Great Rift,
have won a crushing victory over the powerful Imperial
Starfleet. The Emperor knows that one more such defeat
will bring a thousand more solar systems into the
rebellion, and Imperial control of the Outland systems
could be lost forever. To crush the rebellion once and
for all, the Emperor has sent one of his most ferocious
Dark Lords to find the secret rebel strongholds and
destroy them...

In the third draft only one Star Destroyer pursues the rebel ship above
Utapau. Time is more condensed now: The exterior shot segues immediately into a pitched interior battle with the stormtroopers, who blast
their way through the smaller ship's front door. On the planet below, while
checking a mechanical rig that resembles a "Christmas tree," Luke Starkiller
notices bright lights in the sky, so he travels to the power station to tell his
friends—Fixer, Camie, Deak, and Windy. When he arrives he meets his old
pal, Biggs, who has just returned from the military academy.

Back on the ship, we're introduced to Princess Leia Organa:

A beautiful young girl about sixteen years old huddles
in a small alcove as the stormtroopers search through
the ship. She is LEIA ORGANA, a rebel princess. The
fear in her eyes slowly gives way to anger as the muted
crushing sounds of the approaching stormtroopers grow
louder. She steps from her hiding place and blasts two
troopers with her laser pistol, but she is greatly outnumbered and quickly captured.

She is brought to Darth Vader, who tells her the information she intercepted will soon be recovered. The robots escape and are eventually bought
by Owen Lars, who is Luke's uncle.

Back on the planet surface, Biggs tells Luke about the Academy.
Meanwhile, Vader tortures Leia in the Alderaan prison; he wants to
know where he can find the stolen information—and the rebel base.

During dinner, Owen confesses that he has used Luke's education
money to buy the robots, so Luke will have to save up again to attend the
Academy. Luke is dismayed, but shortly thereafter is intrigued to discover
that the robots have been involved in the "Counter Wars" against the

Alex Tavoularis's third-draft storyboards reveal Princess
Leia Organa as she is captured aboard her rebel ship.

Empire. He tells them that he wants to be a "startrooper" and fight like his father, who was a Jedi. Accidentally, he triggers a message in R2:

> The fragment breaks loose with a snap, sending Luke tumbling head over heels. He sits up and sees a small (15 inch) 3-D hologram of Leia Organa, the rebel princess, being projected from the face of little Artoo. The image is a rainbow of colors as it flickers and jiggles in the dimly lit garage. Luke's mouth hangs open in awe.
>
> LEIA
> Whoever finds this message, I beg you see this R-2 unit delivered safely to the authorities on Organa Major. It is of the most vital importance to all free systems. I guarantee in the name of the United Assembly that you will be richly rewarded for your efforts...My Commanders, use fix Arra Code...X loc tan too nine, I am lost. The Sith Lord will surely take me to Alderaan. You must continue alone...

After deliberating over the risks presented by this haphazard quest, Luke leaves a "video-slate" message that says:

> LUKE
> Aunt Beru, Uncle Owen, I don't mean to hurt you and I know you've been good to me, but I'm leaving. There are important things I must do. I've taken my speeder and the "droids" which you bought with my savings. I've also taken my father's lightsaber. You can keep everything else. I am grateful for all you've done. I'll miss you, Aunt Beru. I love you both...

Luke and the robots take the landspeeder and head out to find an old friend of Luke's father: "General Kenobi was my father's commander, and he is probably the greatest of all the Jedi knights . . . or at least my father thought so." Following a skirmish with aggressive desert nomads called Tusken Raiders, who loom up in front of his electrobinoculars, Luke is tied up and left dangling, rotating in the air, when . . .

> A huge menacing shadow on the canyon wall gives way to a shabby old desert rat of a man, who appears to be at least seventy years old. His ancient leathery face, cracked and weathered by exotic climates, is set off by dark, penetrating eyes, and a scraggly white beard. BEN KENOBI squints his eyes as he scrutinizes Luke in his predicament.

"You're General Kenobi?!? The Jedi Knight? The commander of the White Legions?" asks a disbelieving Luke, who introduces himself as the son of Annikin Starkiller, and says he knows Ben's *Diary of the Clone Wars* by heart. But Ben is hesitant to join Luke on a new adventure; he is old and, as he illustrates by breaking open his arm, now partly mechanical. Ben fixes his arm, but admits he has little of the Force left in him . . .

> BEN
> Let's just say the Force is something a Jedi Warrior deals with. It is an energy field in oneself, a power that controls one's acts, yet obeys one's commands. It is nothing, yet it makes marvels appear before your very eyes. All living things generate this Force field, even you...It surrounds you and radiates from you. A Jedi can feel it flowing from him...
> (patting his stomach)
> ...from here!...When a creature dies, the force it generated remains. The Force is all around us. It can be collected and transmitted through the use of a Kiber Crystal. It's the only way to amplify the power of the Force within you.

Ben explains that his Kiber Crystal was taken at the Battle of Condawn—during which Luke's father was killed. One of Ben's disciples took the crystal and became a Sith Lord. The few crystals that remain are in the possession of the Sith Lords on Alderaan.

Across the galaxy these same Sith Lords, in a crystal chamber on Alderaan, feel that Ben Kenobi has joined the fight against them.

> VADER
> Something old has been awakened. The Force has suddenly grown stronger. We must travel future paths with caution.

Ben and Luke go to the Mos Eisley cantina, where Kenobi cuts down bullies who attack Luke. They then meet Chewbacca, who leads them to Docking Bay 23 and Captain Han Solo. "She's been to Terminus and back," he says of his ship. Luke and Ben leave to raise money for their passage, while Solo fends off Jabba the Hutt, who comes to collect a debt; apparently Solo has built his own vehicle, but Jabba paid for it. Solo triggers a fake reactor problem, which causes Jabba and his cohorts to flee—all except Montross. Solo outdraws him and tells him to get lost.

Soon afterward, they all blast off in the ship, when Ben suddenly feels that the planet Organa Major has been destroyed. On Alderaan, Vader tells Princess Leia, in her cell, that the Death Star is operational:

> VADER
> It would be much easier if you were to tell us where the outposts are...Otherwise we'll be forced to destroy every suspicious system...What a waste...
>
> Vader starts to leave.
>
> LEIA
> You'll never stop them...No matter how many machines you build.
>
> The door slides closed behind Vader, leaving Leia alone in the darkness.

Ben tells Han to go instead to Alderaan so they can rescue the princess, using money to motivate him. The old Jedi is confident that Leia won't submit to mind control, due to the fact that she is "a swan sensana." On the journey, Ben begins teaching Luke the ways of the Force, using a lightsaber and training remote; Solo is unconvinced and blasts the remote with his pistol.

As in previous drafts, they play possum to penetrate the Alderaan defenses. When the ship touches down, Ben leaves to find the Kiber

The pirate ship is escorted by TIE fighters into the Imperial prison floating city of Alderaan in these Tavoularis story-boards.

Crystal, telling Luke, "May the Force be with you." Han and Luke disguise themselves as stormtroopers, but it is Solo and Chewbacca who open her cell door and find the princess: "Suspended inside the cell by invisible rays, a bloody and mutilated Leia Organa hangs upside down. A strange yellow glow radiates from her eyes." Chewbacca flings her across his shoulders. Meanwhile Ben looks for the Kiber Crystal, accidentally going into Class-room 96:

> Ben finds himself in a small conference room filled
> with about a dozen or so bureaucrats listening to
> an instructor who is explaining a type of technical
> philosophy. The class turns and stares at the old man.
> Ben raises his hands and all the bureaucrats, including
> the instructor, begin coughing and grabbing at their
> throats. They are unable to breathe and eventually
> collapse on the floor.

The others penetrate the bowels of the city, which now have a slimy, liquid ground cover. Ben eventually finds the pedestal on which the Kiber Crystal rests and gains renewed strength from its presence. Luke and company encounter a vicious Dia Nogu creature, but the resourceful Leia regains consciousness and takes charge, bantering with Han. They have various close shaves before Leia makes them slide down a garbage chute. Han declares: "I've got a very bad feeling about all this."

Ben is intercepted by Darth Vader, who tells the old man:

> VADER
> I've been waiting...At last we meet again...It could
> only have been you...
>
> BEN
> The Force of the Bogan has grown strong with you. I
> expected your master...
>
> VADER
> You were once my master, but I am the master now...the
> Crystal will be of little use to you...Your powers are
> weak...Old man, you should never have come back.

Their lightsabers clash, but stormtroopers enter the fray and manage to wound Ben—just before Luke returns with his friends and helps him back aboard. The pirate ship takes off, and the crew defend themselves from marauding fighters. Leia then reveals that R2-D2 is carrying the plans for a giant battle station—the Death Star.

The fourth moon of Yavin is still their destination, and they take lifepods to travel there from the ship. Ben gives Luke the glowing Kiber Crystal; Tarkin debriefs the rebel pilots, instead of Dodona (the two have switched roles, with Dodona being the cowardly general); and the attack on the Death Star commences. As in the second draft, the Death Star is seen for the first time as it approaches Yavin. Only R2 accompanies Luke this time, as the starfighter is much smaller and the astromech droid is now part of the outer shell. During the raid, Luke grasps the Kiber Crystal, and Vader and Luke seem to sense each other. Luke again makes two runs on the exhaust port, and Han makes a surprise return to save Luke from the pursuing Darth Vader. It is Luke who fires the shot that destroys the Death Star, but the Sith survives . . .

> Vader's starship with a bent solar fin limps into the vast darkness of space attempting to make it back to the relative safety of Alderaan.

Back on Yavin 4, Princess Leia hands out medals to the new heroes:

> Old Ben is sitting to the right of the Princess, while the Grand Mouff Tarkin sits on her left. Leia is dressed in a long, white dress and is staggeringly beautiful. She rises and places a gold medallion around Han's neck, then repeats the ceremony with Chewbacca, the robots and finally Luke. They turn and face the assembled troops, who all bow before them.

STAR WARS PROGRESSION

- Windy and Biggs are no longer twins, each becoming a friend of Luke's; Deak, Luke's brother in the second draft, is replaced by Princess Leia aboard the rebel ship (Deak and Windy are "two tough boys")
- Vader kills rebel officer (rips arm off; throws objects with Force)
- Princess Leia places the Death Star plans into R2-D2 (and sends him to "whoever" on planet surface)
- R2-D2 is Owen's second choice (bought when Luke notices a bad motivator on his first choice)
- Vader uses torture robot on Leia (in Alderaan prison)
- Biggs Darklighter, a cadet, friends with Luke
- C-3PO has oil bath
- Luke watches twin suns
- General Ben Kenobi (name added to old man/Jedi, half-man/half-machine)
- Tusken Raiders, savage desert nomads who ride banthas, attack Luke
- Ben Kenobi rescues Luke
- "Lasersword" now a "lightsaber"
- At his house, Ben explains the Force to Luke, and one character must convince the other to deliver valuable information
- Han Solo owes Jabba the Hutt money (for construction of ship)
- Kenobi senses the destruction of planet (Organa Major)
- Kenobi tells Luke to feel the Force, with training remote
- "May the Force be with you," Ben says
- General Kenobi can walk around unnoticed thanks to the Force
- Heroes flee into an area (on Alderaan) covered with slimy liquid and encounter a Dia Nogu, which yanks Luke underwater
- Princess finds access to the garbage chute
- Luke fires shot that destroys the Death Star

THE RETURN OF *APOCALYPSE NOW*

"I had worked on *Star Wars* for about two years," Lucas says, "and we were starting preproduction. Francis had finished *The Godfather II* (1974) and he was saying, 'I'm going to finance movies myself—we don't have to worry about anybody, so come and do this movie.' I had a choice: I had put four years into *Apocalypse Now*, and two years into *Star Wars*—but something inside said, 'Do *Star Wars* and then try to do *Apocalypse Now*.' So I said that to Francis, and he said, 'We really have to do it right now; I've got the money, and I think this is the time for this film to come out.' So I said, 'Why don't you do it then?' So he went off and did it."

What must have been a difficult choice was made somewhat easier by the reaction Lucas was still experiencing to *American Graffiti*. "Part of my decision was based on the fan mail I had gotten from *Graffiti*," he says. "I seemed to have struck a chord with kids; I had found something they were missing. After the 1960s, it was the end of the protest movement and the whole phenomenon. The drugs were really getting bad, kids were dying, and there was nothing left to protest. But *Graffiti* just said, *Get into your car and go chase some girls. That's all you have to do.* A lot of kids didn't even know that, so we kept getting all these letters from all over the country saying, 'Wow, this is great, I really found myself.' It seemed to straighten a lot of them out.

"I also realized that, whereas *THX* had a very pessimistic point of view, *American Graffiti* said essentially that we were all very good. *Apocalypse Now* was very much like *THX*, and *Star Wars* was very much like *American Graffiti*, so I thought it'd be more beneficial for kids," he adds. "When I started the film, ten- and twelve-year-olds didn't really have the fantasy life that we'd had. I'd been around kids and they talked about *Kojak* and *The Six Million Dollar Man*, but they didn't have any real vision of all the incredible and crazy and wonderful things that we had when we were young—pirate movies and Westerns and all that. When I mentioned to kids, like Francis's sons who are eleven and eight, that I was doing a space film, they went crazy. In a way I was using Francis's kids as models, because I'm around them the most. They're the ones who I talked to about the story. I know what they like."

Optical department supervisor Robbie Blalack poses within an optical printer at ILM.

FRENZY

AUGUST 1975 TO SEPTEMBER 1975

CHAPTER FOUR

August 1975 saw action in England, with Lucas and Kurtz flying over from the States for the first of many brief preproduction stays. The latter arrived first and continued to review studios; at this point Pinewood was the front-runner. On August 1 production designer John Barry officially started, renting space at Lee Electrics in London. His first assignments were to build a landspeeder and to work on the robots with John Stears. They began by making a cardboard mock-up of R2-D2 based on the McQuarrie paintings. Kenny Baker was hired to be the man inside the droid.

"I got the job right away," says Baker, who came to the interview with his longtime cabaret partner, Jack Purvis. "I said, 'I can't just walk into a movie and leave my partner stranded.' They said, 'Well, we have plenty of work for Jack,' and they made him head Jawa."

"We had to start with a tiny man to go in Artoo," Barry says. "He's only forty inches, Kenny, and very strong, fortunately, because it's very hard to move. So we figured out where it was going to hurt him, and all the techniques around the boots. He's got these specially made little boots that lace up tightly and hold his—the robot's—boot firmly to his leg so that it moves as one. Then the harness that holds the body onto Kenny was quite important."

"It just wasn't very comfortable," Baker says. "They had screws going through the robot's head that stuck into *my* head."

"When George came back to England around the middle of August, I said, 'Look! What about that?'" Barry says. "And little Kenny—he's a wonderful little man, I must say, marvelous—he came around the corner in the studio in this little wooden dust bin, a sort of mock-out trash can. He's waddling across the floor, and George says at once, 'That'll work.'"

"We met Kenny and he was a good possibility for one of the robots," John Stears says. "Working with Kenny in the early days, we made up mock-ups, and we could see exactly what he could do and what he couldn't do, how fast he could move, and so on. Therefore we got into a mechanical situation, because this thing has to do things that Kenny was not physically capable of doing."

Once a mechanical R2-D2 was deemed necessary for some shots, Stears spent a lot of time at a hospital where limbs were made for amputees; he visited atomic research facilities to study how the mechanical arms worked, even talking with a robotics professor "who thought I was crazy," Stears admits. "With that knowledge, I once again worked out what was possible, spoke to George about it, and we tailored the actual mechanical answer."

"Maybe it's only over lunch, but all the time you're talking about, 'How about if we do this, how about if we do that?'" Barry says. "The outside of the robot we conceived of with lots of little panels, doors, all over it—so we know that if ever we need another arm or another antenna, we can say it is right behind that panel."

As the workload increased, the production art department slowly staffed up and soon had about twenty-five to thirty people. Among them, John Barry supervised the efforts of Harry Lange, another of the class of *2001*, who was designing control panels. "He's got a tremendous eye for that sort of thing," Barry says. "He really produces amazing things out of some amazing materials. The trick of it all was to come back with an eggbeater and half a vacuum cleaner, and suddenly whip up the most amazing control panels." Another new hire, Liz Moore, concentrated on the landspeeder and C-3PO fabrication.

Back in 1973 Kurtz had spoken to a local production supervisor named Robert Watts, who was preparing *The Wilby Conspiracy* (1975) for location shooting in Kenya, and had asked him to send over his résumé. In April 1975 Watts had received a call from Peter Beale, the Fox representa-

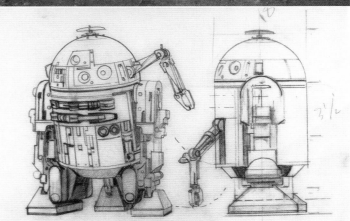

tive in London, who asked Watts to meet Kurtz in Soho Square on May 1. Kurtz then contacted him in June to speak further about the project—and now Watts was undergoing the last part of his lengthy interview process by meeting with Lucas.

"I reckon I was about ten years old when I first went on a film set," Watts says, "and it was about that age that I decided it was the life for me." His grandfather had worked as a script writer at Ealing Studios, where Watts obtained his first job as assistant office boy in 1960, afterward working his way up to third assistant director and then production manager on films such as Roman Polanski's *Repulsion* (1965), *Thunderball* (1965), and *You Only Live Twice* (1967).

In addition to interviewing more potential department heads, Lucas had important conversations with John Barry, who says, "I talked with George very much. He showed tremendous interest in the sets, so we knew

very much what he wanted to do and where he wanted to be. George really wants to be involved in everything on the movie, whereas sometimes with a director you have the opposite problem. My personal taste leans more toward *Barbarella* [campy sci-fi film, 1968], which George didn't want to do. He wants to make *The Star Wars* look like it's shot on location on your average, everyday Death Star or Mos Eisley spaceport—which I think is a very valid point.

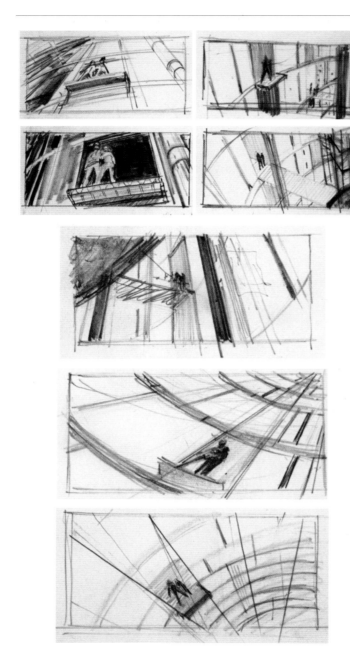

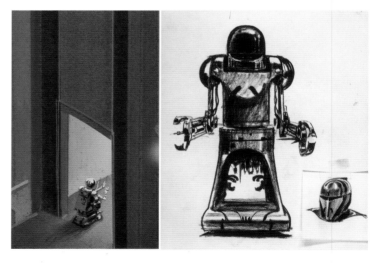

"Lash La Rue scene—Luke vaults over space left by retractable bridge" was McQuarrie's title for his November 21, 1975, painting that visualized John Barry's idea of late August (top right; preparatory sketches, above left). Around the same time McQuarrie finished the Alderaan interior (middle right; his sketch of a robot was for a detail—below right—in the bottom left-hand corner of the painting).

"The eighth illustration is the elevator scene, which was just the result of a little pencil sketch I did," McQuarrie says. "We didn't talk very much about how the elevator should be; George just said there would be a row of elevators and Luke, Han, and Chewbacca would have to come to them and stand there. So I decided to make them individual tubes rather than just open doors, just so they would be different. This big canyon wall was part of that Lash La Rue scene, where Luke has to jump across."

THE MAKING OF STAR WARS

"The thing is to design the sets simultaneously," he adds, "knowing how you're going to turn one into the next, because another area of responsibility is the budget—which, in this case, is a large percentage of the overall budget, in that there's not a large number of very expensive actors."

After talks in England, Barry flew to the States at roughly the same time as Lucas, who was preparing for the casting sessions. According to Ralph McQuarrie's handwritten notes, John Barry arrived on August 20, 1975. The two met with Lucas to go over the artist's paintings and discuss the sets in even more detail. "I had worked with Ralph McQuarrie while I was writing the script," Lucas says, "and we designed certain things, but John was very willing to step in and say, 'Yeah, these are good designs, let's use those.' He wasn't hung up on the idea that everything would have to be his; he was very open to suggestions and he was very easy to work with. He also had a lot of good ideas of his own, adding creatively onto things without making it cost an enormous amount of money."

One idea that Barry came up with at the time involved Luke and Leia escaping on Alderaan. "This was John Barry's idea," McQuarrie says, "to have this cliffhanger scene where the bridge retracts and Luke throws the little hook and swings her across. They call it the 'Lash La Rue' scene. This was after we had about three days of talks with John Barry, to introduce him to the project. I sat in because George thought I could do some sketches maybe while we were talking, but it was definitely established at that point that I was a sketch artist and not the art director, because John was going to be the art director."

A CAST OF THOUSANDS

While Barry returned to England to supervise the burgeoning full-scale sets, and while ILM was still being set up as they built cameras and equipment, and while a contract with Fox was still outstanding, and while he was working on the fourth draft, Lucas began interviewing actors for *The Star Wars* in late August.

Having earned the director's high opinion by casting *American Graffiti*, Fred Roos helped Lucas organize what was going to be a long process. "I was brought in to do some tests and give my opinion from time to time," says Roos, who had built up his expertise by casting around forty low-budget movies.

"Fred didn't get paid or anything," Lucas says. "Fred is just a friend who is also a very good casting director who helped out as best he could. I asked his advice because I trust Fred's opinion quite a bit; he's very sharp about talent and casting. He's a producer now and he really doesn't cast anymore, but he got interested because I was working out of the American Zoetrope office in Los Angeles. Our offices were next door to each other, so he helped us. When I was in England, I could trust him to do tests and things, so he took some time out to do it. He really just did it as a friend."

Like the two before it, Lucas's third feature film was not a star vehicle, so he was going to have to devote enormous attention to the choice of his relatively unknown leads. "Deciding to cast unknowns was not a controversial decision," Roos says, "because nobody cared at the time."

Roos called casting director Dianne Crittenden in August 1975, and she eventually hired two assistants as the interviews multiplied. Crittenden may also have been recommended by the Huycks, who had worked with her on *Lucky Lady*, and she knew Coppola because they had attended Hofstra University at the same time. "I hadn't read the script and I didn't talk to George until right before we were ready to start," Crittenden says. "It was just: 'We need two young guys and a girl for this thing, and George will be here for three weeks.' And I felt, *Well, that will be fine.* Then I read the script and found it fascinating, but I really didn't know what it was about. I think I read it eight times before I finally got into it. But George knew what he wanted. He wanted Han to be a cowboy, the 'James Dean' character, but instead of a horse, he's got a spaceship. Luke was a farmer. I said, 'What do you mean, a farmer?' And he said, 'It's a moon-farm or an interplanetary farm.' George's concept of the princess was an independent, strong one. Someone who was capable of leading her people, as opposed to some fragile fairy-tale kind of princess."

With everyone ready, three weeks of casting began within the Zoetrope offices at the Goldwyn Studios in late August—and it was relentless, from 8 or 9 AM to 6 or 8:30 PM, as quickly as two people every five minutes, around 250 actors per day.

"I saw thousands of kids," Lucas says. "I would see them for one minute, three minutes, five minutes. It gave me a physical idea of who they are, because you know about a person in one minute when you first meet them and they sit down. Your first impression of them is the same impression more or less as the audience's when they meet them. The illusions can be much greater in theater because, with lighting and the distance, you are farther from the actor. You can fake things much easier. But with film, in a close-up, you are looking into somebody's eyes—you are not only looking at the person as an actor, you are also looking at them as a human being. So I have to rely half on the human being and half on the actor. That's been a prime requisite of anybody I use—I've hired very good actors who I've also felt could be that character in real life."

An envelope (left) was sent to McQuarrie from Kurtz's Universal Studios office in September 1975 and was used by the artist to store reference material given to him by Lucas.

Francis Ford Coppola and Fred Roos (right, with initialed bag, "F. R.") in the Dominican Republic shooting the Cuban sequence during the making of *Godfather Part II*, circa 1973.

Though the speed of the interviews made perfect sense to the low-key director, many of the young actors rolling through the doors were somewhat perplexed. "Generally, George would ask, 'What have you been doing?'" Crittenden says. "And they would respond, 'You mean, today, or with my life?' George would say 'Either.' And you could see people start to squirm. They'd ask, 'What's this about anyway?' And he'd say, 'Well, we're doing a science-fiction movie.' I received hundreds of phone calls later with people asking, 'What was I doing there? What happened?'

"George was looking for something very *visual*."

DOUBLE JEOPARDY

"Brian De Palma called me to do *Carrie* [1976]," Crittenden says. "So I said, 'I can't because I'm working with George.' And he said, 'You're working with George? He's my friend and we're looking for the same thing, so I'll just sit in on this.' So that's what happened. But it added confusion to the process, since Brian is the one whose name more people knew. They'd sit there and they would say, 'Oh, I just loved *Hi, Mom!* [1970].' Which didn't bother George; in fact it seemed to make him feel more comfortable, because it became easier for him to watch the performances. Afterward, the actor would leave and George would say, 'A definite three,' and Brian would say, 'I'd give them a four,' and it would go on like that."

A mutual friend of De Palma and Lucas, editor Paul Hirsch heard about the casting sessions, which began as somewhat notorious—and have become legendary. "Brian was terrifying these new actors and actresses," Hirsch says. "Brian told me George had the opening speech and he had the closing speech, and vice versa. They were seeing so many people that they got it down to less than a minute. If they knew they weren't interested in the person they were seeing, no sooner had George finished the opening speech than Brian would launch into the closing speech."

McQuarrie's early sketches of Han Solo may reflect Lucas's changing idea of his appearance and costume, from a more savage pirate to a more debonair James Bond or gunslinger type (left). Another McQuarrie sketch (right) perhaps reflects Lucas's fixed pursuit of Alec Guinness for the role of Ben Kenobi—the drawing, which is markedly different from earlier depictions, has the hairdo and look of Guinness. Written by Lucas in the corner are the words "Ben Kenobi."

"During that time, I called Brian and he said, 'Listen just a second. George wants to speak to you.' And George said he liked my work and maybe we'd work someday together," Hirsch adds. "I remember saying, 'Gee that's really terrific.' I had heard things about *Star Wars* and if there was really one film I wanted to work on, it was that one. Brian would go over and see the miniatures at ILM, and he would tell me that he was envious of George. Brian was doing this movie with girls slamming doors and George was having all this fun making models and building things."

"Brian and I are very good friends," Lucas says, "and when I started casting, which is a laborious job that goes on for ten hours a day, with a person coming into your office every two minutes, you try to be pleasant and sharp and to have your analytical eye attuned—but it gets to be very, very difficult day in and day out, week after week. So Brian asked if he could sit in on my sessions and I said, 'Sure,' because it's great to have company, somebody to compare notes with and somebody to keep you alive, so you don't become completely blotto toward the end of the day."

THE GAUNTLET

"In the beginning we were very open," Lucas says. "We had two male characters, so I wanted the farm boy to be shorter than Han Solo, so they didn't conflict visually; I didn't want two guys looking exactly alike. I also made a decision in the casting to lower the age considerably from what I'd had in mind, because I wanted to make a movie about kids for kids, though, in a way, it's an adult kid's movie."

"We talked about Jodie Foster," Crittenden says of the actress, who was about fifteen at the time. "We were down to that age. The princess was supposed to be about sixteen, Luke was about eighteen, and Han was in his early twenties. He was the old guy. But for purposes of shooting and having a full eight-hour day, people had to be over eighteen. It was incredible, the varied types of people that were brought in. We went so far as to send every school letters and we met people who had never acted before. We really wanted to cover everything.

"During the first week, by the third day, we'd seen nearly everybody—John Travolta, Nick Nolte, Tommy Lee Jones," Crittenden adds. "Mark came in the second day."

Twenty-four-year-old Mark Hamill was actually a little dubious about the test, according to Crittenden, because he already had a recurring role in *The Texas Wheelers*. "I think the TV series almost kept Mark from doing it," she says. "When we saw him the first time, he wasn't even sure whether he would be available. I really did have to persuade his agent [Nancy Hudson] that it would be beneficial at his age to do a feature film rather than to just keep his career stagnating in television."

"My agent said that there was going to be a general meeting at Goldwyn," Hamill says, "and that there was no script. The only thing she knew about the kid was that he's from a farm. At that time, to show you how much I knew about the film, I started practicing a midwestern accent. So we were scheduled one every fifteen minutes—it was one of those. Thousands of people sitting on the floor; you wait two and a half hours, and then you go in and talk. And I talked to Brian De Palma. I think he introduced me, but George didn't say anything all the way through it. I told them about my brothers and sisters, and how we moved around, living in Japan."

His brief interview over, Hamill left knowing little more than before, and was immediately replaced by the next in line. While Lucas wasn't making any decisions just yet about those he was seeing, De Palma hired John Travolta and Bill Katt, as well as Sissy Spacek and Amy Irving.

RETURN OF THE LADYKILLER

"By the second week, we were into the dregs already," Crittenden says. "By the third week, we were just pulling people from colleges. But George wanted to see *everybody*. After a while Brian got tired and he dropped out."

Consistent with his rethinking of each draft after finishing it, as the sessions drew to a close, Lucas flirted with the idea of casting only African-Americans in key parts. He talked with Lawrence Hilton Jacobs, who was playing Freddie "Boom Boom" Washington in the hit TV comedy *Welcome Back, Kotter*. Lucas also considered doing the whole film in Japanese with subtitles. While this last idea might seem to have grown from the drudgery of the casting sessions, it was actually related to his love of Kurosawa and a desire to re-create the feeling of disorientation he'd felt as a student watching films from different cultures. Lucas imagined what it would be like to watch a foreign film as if it had just washed up on the shore—all of its customs, history, language, and mannerisms strangely exotic, somewhat familiar, but not explained—an idea that would inform much of the style of the completed *Star Wars* as it had *THX 1138*.

"There was talk at one point about having the princess and Ben Kenobi be Japanese," Crittenden recalls, "which led George into thinking Han Solo might be black."

"This was actually when I was looking for Ben Kenobi," Lucas says. "I was going to use Toshiro Mifune; we even made a preliminary inquiry. If I'd gotten Mifune, I would've also used a Japanese princess, and then I would probably have cast a black Han Solo. At the same time, I was investigating Alec Guinness."

He entrusted Crittenden with the first step of that process, and she was able to put a copy of the script into the hands of the famed English actor in September. "I had a friend working on the film *Murder by Death* [1976] and I just said, 'I would like to come over and see Alec Guinness,'" Crittenden says. "I went over and talked to him, and he said, 'Let me see your script.' George had cleverly attached to the script a whole set of sketches for the film, so I hand-delivered the script to Alec Guinness—who called me about two hours later and said, 'I love this; I'm very interested in it.' So I set up a lunch for George to meet him. It all happened without a middleman or an agent or a lawyer."

In fact, Guinness almost turned down the picture when he realized what genre it was tapping. "I was in Hollywood making a movie, and on my second to last day a script arrived on my dressing room table," he says. "I saw it was going to be directed by George Lucas, and George Lucas I knew about because of *American Graffiti*, which I admired very much. So I was immediately excited, but when I opened the script and saw it was science fiction, I said, 'Oh lord.' I've never done a science fiction [film]; I've seen one or two of them and enjoyed them, but I always thought they were sort of cardboard, from an actor's point of view. But because of Lucas, I started reading it—and I found myself involved. There was an excitement in the script. I wanted to turn each page to know what happened next. I wanted to know how each little incident was concluded. It had a touch of

Tolkien's *Lord of the Rings*. It was a rather simple outline of a good man who had some magical powers. It was an adventure story about the passing of knowledge and the sword from one generation to the next."

Lucas's lunch with Guinness went well, with the actor being "impressed" by the "new breed of filmmaker." But they were far from a contract.

A BAG OF TRICKS

Simultaneous with the three-week casting session in August and September, the ILM model shop had increased its output. Cantwell had by this time built a Star Destroyer, X-wing, Y-wing, Skyhopper (originally a good-guy fighter), a landspeeder, a small Death Star sphere, a TIE ship, and a sandcrawler. The last was a truncated pyramid with tiny "gravity grippers" that would search for things, according to McCune. "It had two little tanks that pulled it around and it looked more like a barge for picking kelp." McCune and his team—at this point Bill and Jamie Shourt—realized that these concept models, while fanciful and ornate, were by the same token impossible to photograph. The models were consequently "heavied up" so they would work with mattes, and made large enough so they'd have room for essential motors, lights, and other equipment.

"The X-wing just kept getting fatter and fatter," McCune says. "But the basic ideas for the pirate ship, Star Destroyer, X-wings, and Y-wings were all nailed down tight within the first thirty days. The TIE ship came right after that."

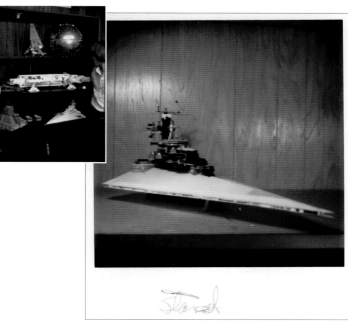

"I asked George whether the Death Star was always going to be near a planet," Cantwell says. "He said it was, so I explored a very risky thing with a prototype model: I tried making it silver [far left, on top shelf], so you can set scenes where it would show in space."

In John Dykstra's office at ILM (left), Joe Johnston stands next to shelves exhibiting Cantwell's concept models, from the top: Skyhopper, Death Star sphere, landspeeder, pirate ship, sandcrawler with tanks, Star Destroyer. Lucas took a Polaroid of the last ship, penciled in its name, and gave it to McQuarrie for reference (right, "star d").

Models were a priority for two reasons. First, cockpits and ship interiors were going to be built in England based on the miniatures, but production couldn't start until the models had been approved. Second—and crucially—they were planning on using front projection on the set for the escape from Alderaan battle with the TIE fighters, which meant that ILM had to have plates ready by early 1976. John Dykstra had used front projection on *Silent Running*, and one of the pieces of equipment he'd had Don Trumbull build was a front projection rig, with four-by-five plates and motors in it for rotating the image.

To help complete all the models in the allotted time, McCune hired David Beasley, whom Bob Shepherd had found in the "Unemployment Department." To help with the redesign of the concept models and to create storyboards for the front projection sequences based on the third draft, Joe Johnston was hired to start the art department in August 1975. Earlier that summer Johnston had been working at Magic Camera on an aborted Paramount project, *The War of the Worlds*.

"Bob Shepherd knew about me and called me up," Johnston says. "I was going to the beach every day and really enjoying the summer, and he ruined it! [laughs] He said, 'We're doing another space movie and we want you to come up and see what you think.' My first thought was, *Oh no. I don't want to work*. I changed my mind, though, after I got there. It looked like a fun job. It looked like a good project."

Johnston needed somebody to translate his concept drawings into orthographic schematics for the model shop as a basis for building, so Steve Gawley was hired (he soon segued into the model shop).

"John Dykstra and I sat down with Joe Johnston," Lucas says. "John took the models and said that we had to change them, for his technical needs more than anything else. The wings had to be fatter or they wouldn't show up in bluescreen, and we had to fatten the bodies up so we could fit the suspension bars in. Joe was the one who added all the aesthetics in terms of detailing."

"George wanted all the rebel ships to look secondhand, old and beat up," Johnston says. "He wanted them to look like they weren't as well

Richard Edlund, Rose Duignan, John Dykstra, Lucas, and Joe Johnston consult together (right). The ILM model shop as it got up to speed (opposite): In the foreground are David Grell, Steve Gawley, and Joe Johnston. The door led to the optical department, while the wood shop was to the left of the model shop, and the motion-control stage to the right.

THE MAKING OF STAR WARS

built or well designed as the Imperial ships. If he didn't like a ship, he'd say, 'Do more sketches.'"

"Joe was the only one who could draw from inside him," Shepherd says. "He could really make images that you understood. So Joe would do a drawing, and it would get kicked around at that conceptual level. At some point it would be okayed, the drawing would be handed to Grant, and they'd say, 'Build it.' And he'd ask, 'Well, how big is it?' And they'd answer, 'Well, it's got to be this big for photographic reasons,' or 'We're going to put a light in it.' After the scale was established, the guys in the model shop looked at the thing and embellished it from their own head—they are artists in their own right—and that's why they have to be able to *think*."

THE DEMISE OF THE LOCKED-OFF SHOT

From the beginning there was no question that new and valuable creative thinking was taking place on Van Nuys Boulevard. Complicated negotia-

tions took place with the special effects hires. "We were involved in some new patent processes," Andy Rigrod says. "We had to get licenses for them. There was [going to be] a huge staff, and every one of them had to be employed under agreement so they would promise to not give away the secrets that were involved in the processes."

One of the most important processes was the creation of the motion-control camera John Dykstra had proposed. To understand why this camera was needed, one has to appreciate where special effects were at the time. If a director wanted a shot of several starships flying through space, his team would have to combine various pieces of film, all shot separately: a starfield, each spaceship, lasers, perhaps a planet, and so on. The different pieces of film would then be combined with an optical printer, which would enable the compositor to arrange the several pieces into one. This was a very expensive and tricky process, for a number of reasons. The miniature set would have to be left standing until the film came back—it was a "hot" set—because they'd have to use it again if any mistake had been made. Moreover, the process was so complicated that nearly all shots

(Continued on page 74)

Pirate Ship

"I went by Colin's place quite a bit," McQuarrie says, "and would take photographs of the models as they produced them from casts. I was putting them in the paintings and some of the paintings I updated as Colin would get further into developing them."

After about two weeks of talks with Lucas, Cantwell finished his concept models several months later, in May. "It took a long time," Lucas says. "By the time he was done, ILM had been set up."

Johnston's early sketch was based on Cantwell's model for the rebel ship (below right); an alternate Cantwell prototype had more rocket boosters (below left), and those were incorporated into a later sketch by Johnston of the pirate ship (bottom right), and into a painting by McQuarrie (opposite, below).

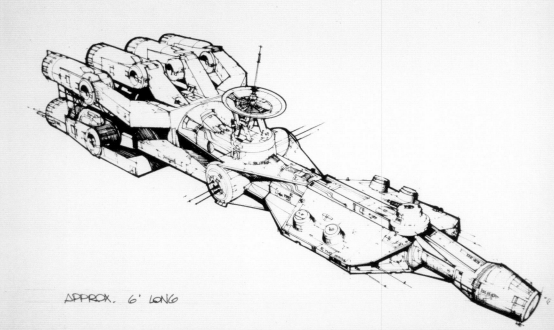

APPROX. 6' LONG

With Lucas's approval at each stage, John Dykstra drew additional sketches of the pirate ship, which Joe Johnston turned into more concept designs that Steve Gawley translated into orthographic drawings; then the Shourts and Grant McCune started construction (below left, Jamie Shourt and McCune; in the background is the "spray booth"). "It's really an amazing acrylic sculpture," McCune says. "It was like a six-inch tube with four-inch tubes stuck out at the ends, and wings of eight-inch Plexiglas. Jamie Shourt is an incredible mathematician and he figured out every piece of it on paper with his little mini computer—all the three-plane geometry problems. It weighed about 125 pounds" (below right, the nearly complete model).

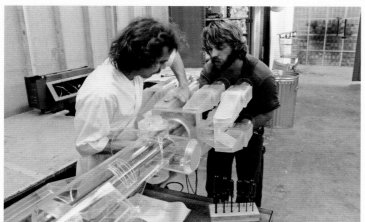

R. M°QUARRIE

had to be static—the camera couldn't move because it could never success-fully and repeatedly film all the needed elements if it did.

"In many cases you are using all kinds of flimsy stuff that doesn't nec-essarily want to repeat its motions exactly," Dykstra explains. "So if you shoot a very complex move and send it in, you have to cross your fingers and hope everything will work right. You can't tear that rig down and go on because if it comes back from the lab and it's bad, you can't duplicate that rig again. You can proceed to shoot the next element only after each of the elements had been viewed."

The Star Wars had an estimated 350 shots, each with as many as seven or eight elements—which represented a staggering amount of time and money doing it the contemporary way. "So we had to create systems that would allow us to shoot a shot, tear down the rig, then set up and shoot another shot—with the certainty that it would be okay one way or another," Dykstra continues. "We needed to be able to record the information using the latest techniques to ensure that we were going to get something good to start out with—but also, if we didn't get the shot the first day, a camera that would enable us to go back and do it again."

Lucas's short film of aerial action had also made it clear to everyone at ILM that the status quo of science fiction—static spaceships flying on rails—wasn't going to be satisfactory. The X-wings and TIE fighters were going to have to dive, weave, and bank. "Before we developed the equip-ment for *Star Wars*, those moves could be made," Dykstra says. "But it was a very complex problem to get them combined into one shot. You could make a zoom or a pan or a tilt during a shot, but to zoom, pan, and tilt in the same shot and maintain matte integrity was really difficult. So the moves were primarily linear in the films [of that time]." Complex moves had been created for commercials that had maybe one shot, but they'd never been attempted on such an ambitious scale, because it was too risky and expensive. "They weren't viable in terms of achieving that effect over and over in a variety of situations."

Not only would elements within the shot have to maneuver more freely but, to fit the director's vision, the camera would also have to be able to move as if it were a handheld device in a cinema verité film—that way, people would feel like the space battle was real. Nearly every other film up until then had used what was referred to as a "locked-off shot," in which the camera wouldn't move during the special effects shot. To audiences, this was a telltale sign that they were about to see something fake. Nice, perhaps—but fake, because up until that moment in the film, the actors and objects, as well as the camera, would move about in a familiar way, and then suddenly everything would become still. Consciously or unconsciously, this would be a signal to the audience that something not occupying the same space as the actors was about to appear. But Lucas was adamant that he wanted his effects to occupy the same reality as his protagonists.

"It really means making the viewer feel as though it's a real situa-tion," Dykstra says. "You can move the camera—you can watch a ship come from a distance and pan and follow him and watch him go away, covering a 180-degree field of view. In the old shots you saw a very narrow cone of vision. Everybody knows that you can line up *one* shot and have it look right, if you don't move the camera. But if you start moving the camera, that is the subliminal cue to the person watching it, even if he knows nothing about film, that he's watching real live-action photography. Because the moving camera puts him in a space. Instead of viewing a postcard, he's seeing a three-dimensional reality."

FANTASTIC MOVING MACHINES OF THE FUTURE

The motion-control camera would solve many of these special effects puzzles, because it could be programmed to repeat its actions exactly, an idea that had been around for several years. In fact, the camera would be the combination of three machines that already existed in differ-ent forms: a specialized camera, a specialized mechanical rig, and a

(Continued on page 77)

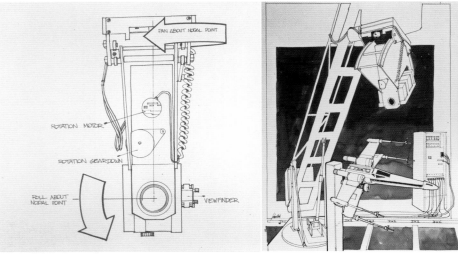

Technical drawings indicate how the motion-control camera would work and how it would photograph the models, which would be placed on blue pylons (left) to hide the armatures holding them up—one of Dykstra's innovations. Joe Johnston, Steve Gawley, and others upstairs in the bare-bones ILM art department (above right).

Sandcrawler

Circa April 5, 1975, McQuarrie revised Cantwell's sandcrawler design and illustrated the escape of the robots from the vehicle as described in the second draft (below). The sandcrawler has stalled because of falling rocks from the cliffs, and the Jawas are trying to figure out how to put the track back on the wheels. The vehicle the Jawas use for storing their wares had originally been inspired by photographs of a NASA-designed rover built for exploring the terrain of alien planets (perhaps more like Cantwell's model, top right). The Jawas themselves are outgrowths of the "shell-dwellers" in Lucas's *THX 1138*.

"It was supposed to be a very large, old, rusty, and tracked vehicle," McQuarrie says. "You had to climb up all the stairs to get in, and there were a lot of rooms in it, storage places. I envisioned this thing on the front with teeth to be part of a scoop that comes down with a hydraulic arrangement to pick up things, like a garbage truck."

"Ralph had done a painting of the sandcrawler," Johnston says. "He had done side views, and it was real long and streamlined. I thought that it could be higher and more awkward and rustier, kind of clumsy looking, so that influenced my redesign of same" (below right).

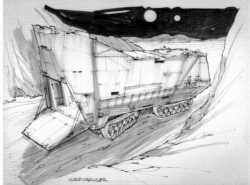

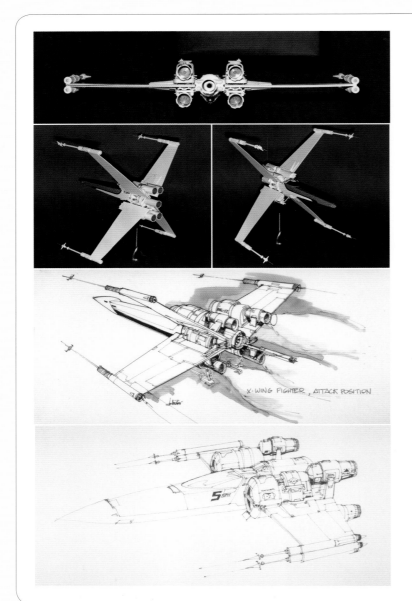

X-WING FIGHTER, ATTACK POSITION

X-Wing

"The X-wing had a box inside of it, with gears made of rubber bands, pipes, and motors, and it was continually evolving," McCune says (top right, with surgical tubes for circulating air to cool the engines; below right, McCune holds an X-wing model by its armature). "I wanted a dragster," Lucas says, "with a long narrow front and a guy sitting on the back. Then Colin came up with the split-wing thing."

"Out in space it had to be able to draw its guns like in a Western," Cantwell says. "So that was the equivalent" (prototype concept models, top left).

"Cantwell's was a little bit too sleek and slender," Johnston says. "In fact

he used a dragster body from one of Revel's ¹⁄₁₆-scale model kits; he just took that and added some engines and a little cockpit over it. Fortunately, Grant, John, and I were able to keep an eye on the model-builders and supervise them all the way through so that if something started getting out of hand, as it did several times on the X-wing, we could step in and handle it [middle right, Dave Jones in model shop]. The X-wing went through six or seven body changes [middle and below left]. We had a lot of trouble with the nose. From the front, you need that little lip on there; we worked with that a long time, getting it into a shape that didn't look obscene."

specialized electronic-control device, all of which came to be called the "Dykstraflex."

"All three of the aspects of that camera system were developed at some point, partially, in the past," Dykstra says. "Doug Trumbull deserves a lot of credit, because a lot of the people who worked on *Star Wars* were people that he nurtured. The name *Dykstraflex* was really a joke. The Dykstraflex is not my camera; it's not a *new* concept. It's been around for years, from the days of the RKO General Pictures [in the 1950s]. The name of the camera is not indicative of its designer so much as it's indicative of the joke that was going around. There was a Trumbullflex, and the same people that made the Dykstraflex had made the Trumbullflex."

These same people were Dykstra, Don Trumbull, Richard Alexander, and Al Miller. "When we worked with Doug [at Future General], we had a camera that was similar but not quite as sophisticated," Dykstra continues. "We had an electronic-control system that was far more sophisticated, but not nearly as useful. We had a mechanical drive system that was also more sophisticated but not nearly as versatile. Those elements were designed by somebody else; we went in and tried to figure out how to use them. *Star Wars* was our first opportunity to take those devices and make a device that incorporated all of their best aspects, plus any good aspects that we could come up with, and eliminate the problems.

"Al Miller and I sat on the floor in my house in Marina Del Rey, drank two bottles of wine, and came up with the outline for what the functions of the electronics were. At the same time, we figured out how the mechanics would have to work and a lot of the basic parameters for the camera. Then we went into the drawing stage and Bill Shourt and Richard Edlund and Dick Alexander and Don Trumbull—everybody had some input to that device."

"The entire camera system was designed for *Star Wars*," Edlund says. "Any trade-offs that we had to make were in relation to the film that George gave us—the 16mm edit of World War II clips that showed all of the dynamics, the cutting sequence, and the way the ships would move. We knew the kind of shots that he wanted; it was a tremendous help in preventing what could have been an arbitrary mishmash.

"John had been working with Doug Freeze [an engineer in Hollywood] and Don Trumbull a little bit before I got involved," Edlund adds. "My main desire was to keep the camera as small as possible so that it could get as close as possible to whatever it was photographing, without depth of field becoming a problem—depth of field being the worst problem in miniatures, because if anything is at all soft, it ruins the shot. Everything was going to have to be absolutely crisp. One fuzzy shot in the whole movie and you've lost your credibility. So I redesigned all the lenses to some degree, adding extra f-stops to the lenses and things like that. Also, we made the camera head narrower than the camera, so that the models could fly above to the right, above to the left, and you could just miss them on the bottom; the fact that you could do that makes the shots much more exciting. It gives you the illusion that the camera is much smaller than it is—the smaller the camera, the greater the illusion."

Most of the machine work was done in the warehouse on Van Nuys. They welded the tracks, which took about a month, bought war-surplus drives and stepping motors, and converted equipment. The hardware cost around $60,000.

"I'd say that the major construction took about six months [June to December 1975]," Dykstra says. "We had portions of it functioning before that, but there was a lot of lag time because of the unavailability of electronic parts. It's a totally modular system, compatible with every other device in the shop. We used consistent plugs and connectors. We used the same power-drive systems. All of the track systems use pipe clamps, which means you can bolt pipes together to make whatever fantastic shape you need, and then disassemble them and re-form them into some other shape. They are very sturdy and give you supports for the ships or for the cameras or any oddball thing, which is real useful. It's a workhorse device; it's not a computer and that's really important. It's a calculator. It's nowhere near as sophisticated as we could have made it with microcomputers."

VISTAVISION STRIKES BACK

The VistaVision system had been developed in the 1950s by Paramount and Technicolor, but was short-lived. The idea behind it was to give the public an image whose size and quality absolutely dwarfed the black-and-white gizmo in the living room. "When television came out, the producers scrambled to come up with some way of enticing the people back into the theaters," Edlund says. "As it turned out, VistaVision got shelved after a while. But a tremendous amount of money had been spent on cameras and equipment, which was just sitting around. A movement [inner-camera mechanism] that had perhaps cost $25,000 or $30,000 to build, we could get for a thousand bucks. So we amassed all of this stuff."

Not only was the high-end equipment a bargain, VistaVision film was also the ideal format for special effects that were going to involve a considerable amount of duping. Instead of vertical 4-perforation film frames, VistaVision used horizontal 8-perforation frames, literally twice the real estate as standard 35mm film, which would still be used for all the regular live-action photography. "It gave us double the quality up front," Edlund says.

"It's like anything else," Dykstra says. "The more area you use to record the information, the more information is recorded, the more detail. What that boils down to in motion picture terms is: You start with a large 70mm negative, and when you reduce it for 35mm projection, even though some elements have been duped, you end up with very nearly the original quality. You can go through one generation and still come out right about the same place. Plus, VistaVision allowed us to use every single film stock known to Kodak; everybody processes it, so it's just easier to work with."

While the motion-control camera was being built and VistaVision had been decided upon, the next step was to find the right optical printer, the job of Robbie Blalack. Having started doing theater at Pomona College, then migrating to nonlinear film and editing at Cal Arts in 1970, Blalack had founded his own two-person optical printing company in a basement after buying a 35mm machine from his school. "I brought my own optical printer to ILM," Blalack says, "and we went out and found a second printer at Howard Anderson's. We went to Anderson because nobody was manufacturing the movements, but he had the equipment and he had no use for it. He's not into VistaVision."

Anderson's optical printer hadn't been used since 1963, according to Blalack, having been built originally for *The Ten Commandments* in 1956. "That printer got totally reworked from the ground up, really," he says. "After we bought it, we began a very long, difficult, and interesting period

(Continued on page 80)

Star Destroyer

"Colin Cantwell's Star Destroyer had antennas and guns sticking out the sides, which wouldn't have matted well," Johnston says (below). So ILM gave it a lower profile and built it about twice as high. "We made it look like a fortress, while his looked more like a naval ship or an aircraft carrier." After Johnston sketched it and Steve Gawley did orthographic drawings

(middle), Dave Beasley and Gawley started on the actual model (bottom right).

"Dreadnoughts were sent out [circa] 1907 by Teddy Roosevelt to announce to the rest of the world that this new country was a military power," Cantwell says. "So you have this fleet of painted white battleships going around. So the shape then came partly from the battleships—and the shape of a paper airplane."

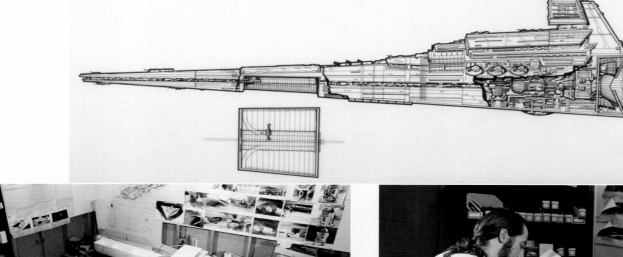

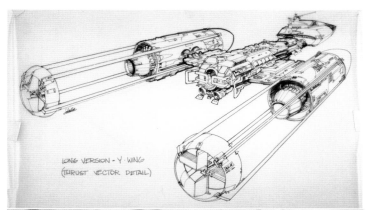

LONG VERSION - Y-WING
(THRUST VECTOR DETAIL)

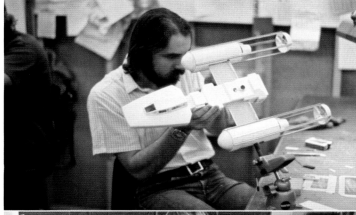

Y-Wing

A Joe Johnston revised sketch (top), which was then sculpted by the model shop, including Dave Beasley (middle), and painted by Johnston (bottom). "I described it and we worked on that together," Lucas says, "but I would say that's about 70 or 80 percent Ralph's design."

"It was supposed to seem like an old, stock space fighter that was just barely flying," Johnston says. "They'd taken everything off of it."

TIE Fighter

"In World War II the super dive-bombers had an artificially created siren wail created by air ducts," Johnston says. "They didn't serve any purpose except to create this noise, which would terrify people. It was intended that the TIE should achieve the same effect with just a menacing appearance. It was supposed to look terrifying even though it wasn't necessary that all that stuff have a specific function."

The acronym *TIE* was created by Lucas but not defined. "I came up with 'twin ion engine fighter,'" Johnston adds. "There were other ideas, like 'Third Intergalactic Empire,' but I thought 'twin-I engine' made more sense." Later the wail would be added by Ben Burtt.

Of the TIE fighters, Lucas says, "they were influenced by some paintings by John Berkey." (Below, a Johnston sketch—and the same sketch—bottom— pinned up in the model shop.)

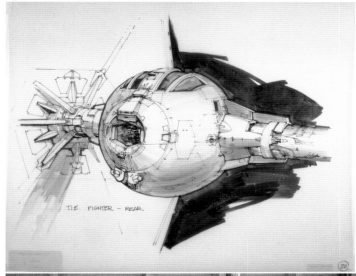

TIE FIGHTER - REAR

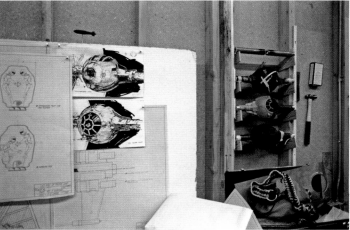

of updating VistaVision as a printing format. We used the existing movements and the existing bases, and built the take-ups; electronic motors were put on it, along with new optics, new lamphouses, new lenses—the whole works. That project lasted a good ten months, possibly even a year. We started with myself and Paul Roth, a friend of mine from Cal Arts, and we just kept adding people as we needed them and testing. There were no experts to help us, so we had the fun—or the nightmare—of doing that."

From Anderson they also purchased a matte camera, whose parts were eventually recycled into a contact printer by Rich Peccarella. Another Blalack buy was a densitometer, to measure brightness, among other things. Many of the cameras put on the compositor and optical printer were old Bell & Howells from 1925, a testament to their durability. The equipment and upgrades for the optical department were essential in order to process the VistaVision film in an assembly-line fashion.

The last element in the VistaVision equation was a specially built editing table, or "motion-viewing system," as Dykstra calls it. "We didn't have the right editing device for VistaVision, so we had to make our own. We figured out how to do it so we could run six pieces of film in it—but it took us six to eight months to generate the technology."

In the summer and fall of 1975—apart from building the printers, motion-control camera, models, and other complex equipment—ILM personnel also had to negotiate with the unions of Hollywood. "ILM was easy to set up," Tom Pollock says. "We just rented the building. The tough part was the union problems."

"The primary conflict was that the unions, when we first started on the project, were upset because we were bringing in people from the outside to do the special effects," Dykstra says. "And their primary bone of contention [as they described it] was they had people who had been in the industry for years and years and years, who knew what they're doing— and if we couldn't find someone amongst their roster of people to satisfy our needs, then we wouldn't find them anywhere. But I had to find people who were well versed in a variety of things. I interviewed their people and, quite frankly, didn't find anybody that I wanted. So we continued to develop a shop without the union's approval—in fact, negotiations were broken off by the union, not by us."

"Fox was real scared," Pollock says, "because they don't like to cause any waves. They wanted us to use their sixty-five-year-old matte painters and miniature people who were over on the lot. But George was absolutely adamant that we wanted to set up our own shop with our own people. That was one of the control things that we'd been fighting about from the beginning."

Part of Lucas's independent streak came from necessity, but another part came from experience. "George learned a lot from Francis Ford Coppola," says Matthew Robbins. "In his histrionic and flamboyant way, Francis would go out and hurl himself against the realities of filmmaking and film distribution, while George very quietly absorbed these lessons and built his own version of an alternate Hollywood. Not only was he very apart from the system, George was a rebel and was grateful to not be in Southern California. The whole culture of the studios and business managers, agents and lawyers, to him, was enormously distasteful and threatening. He felt that the Hollywood enterprise was corrupt. That it wasn't really about creativity, it was about making money. I think American Zoetrope and a great deal of Lucasfilm was in reaction to Hollywood."

"This is a business where hustlers come to town to make the quick buck," says Charles Lippincott. "You lease the car, you lease that house and everything else possible, up to that mistress you may be living with; you make token payments to writers and pay everybody else with promises, and you sit out that year and see if you can make that one big killing. There's a lotta guys that die here. It's the valley of the quick kill."

"George was shrewd. He understood Hollywood immediately," Willard Huyck observes. "He was the same way in film school. After about two weeks, he said, 'Oh, I see how it works.' He figured out how to do his own thing, and it was the same thing in Hollywood. He understood it right away and said, 'Yeah, I don't like the way it works, I'm going to move to San Francisco and do my own thing from there.'"

When negotiations broke off between the unions and ILM, both parties were content to see how things developed.

PRODUCTION NEEDS POWER!

In September 1975 Lucas and Kurtz headed back to London for one week. At this time production supervisor Robert Watts officially started, as did set decorator Roger Christian and art director Les Dilley. Watts immediately launched into the hiring of the English crew, preparing in conjunction with Peter Beale short lists from which Lucas made final choices.

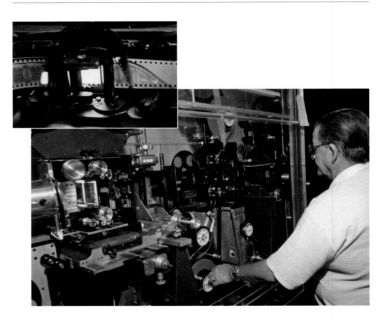

The Anderson optical printer (above, with Don Trumbull) was one part of a complex special effects system that also required particular celluloid considerations. "We had steadiness problems based on the perforations, so Kodak would send people out from Rochester [New York] to help us work this out," Richard Edlund says. "They took pictures of my setup; they took us very seriously and were very helpful. I would order special films [laughs] that hadn't been made since the Second World War because they had certain qualities that we needed for testing or whatever. So they would make up special batches of film for us and put it on ESTAR Base [ESTAR Base is coated on thin 0.0048-inch (120-micrometer) ESTAR (polyethylene terephthalate) base], which is like polyester but much harder and thinner."

Because Lucas had elected to film in England, it was only natural that local actors be cast in many of the supporting roles. "My agent rang up and she said there was this man called George Lucas making a 'space film,' do you want to go and see him?" says Anthony Daniels. "She said they were very interested because I'm good at mime. She talked a lot about the film and said the only trouble is, the part is a robot. So I said, 'Oh come on, I'm a serious actor. We've got to get on with my career, don't we?' But I went to Fox and met George, and I must say that I did immediately like him. We greeted each other and then there was silence. Fortunately for both of us, the production paintings were on the wall facing George. So I turned to the pictures and asked him about them, and he opened up and became quite dynamic. His excitement spilled over, and it was about an hour later when my meeting ended. A couple of days later, I picked up a script and read it for the first time—and it took me a long time to read, so I thought I'd better read it again. After reading it three times, I wrote out the story in sections and when I got to understand vaguely what it was about, I became very excited about the character See-Threepio. I realized he was not an ordinary robot and began to forget all of my original ideas about playing a robot."

That robot's costume dollars, however, were part of an overall special effects budget that John Stears had long since completed—but which was not forthcoming from Twentieth Century-Fox. "We had John Stears and about two or three special effects guys, but we needed to actually start construction on the robots," Lucas says, "which meant a commitment of money. It meant hiring many more people and actually starting to build those robots. But Fox wouldn't commit—and we needed them to commit in September."

Elliot Scott had long since completed a set cost budget (moving on afterward to a prior commitment)—but as there was no green light from the studio, there was no money for that department, either. "I had meetings with Fox," Kurtz says, "and they came up with certain budget estimates on set construction, wardrobe, and special effects—that's one of the things that made the studio nervous: the special effects area. Between the first and second and third drafts, the story changed considerably. We redid the budget over and over again. One of the budgets I did was $13.5 million direct, without overhead."

Lucas and Kurtz returned to the States for more budget talks, while Robert Watts and John Barry departed to location-scout in North Africa. Back at the source of Fox's worries, ILM was indeed running up quite a bill—$241,026 by August 8—with operating costs of about $25,000 per week. "They had built a lot of equipment and were spending money right and left," Kurtz says, "and we hadn't seen anything yet. But we weren't supposed to see anything until Christmastime at the earliest."

"Fox didn't know whether we were on schedule or ahead of schedule or behind schedule—or even if there was a schedule," Shepherd says. "It was a new type of picture."

An aerial view of EMI (Elstree) Studios in England, which became one of two studios for the *Star Wars* production.

"I'd rather have a nasty person who's good at his job than a nice person who's lousy," notes Watts.

Of course that crew would have to have a studio to work in. While Pinewood had been the front-runner, Barry had told Kurtz back in August that, given the size of the production, just one studio would not be enough. "When I got to the very first meeting, we sat down and I asked, 'Where should we go: to EMI and Pinewood, or Pinewood and Bray Studios, or Bray and Shepperton, or Shepperton and EMI? It won't fit into one studio, will it?'" Barry says. "Because, as I'd read through the script, I'd done a sketch plan of each set, and the size of that set. I then explained that if you are lucky enough to get up a big set, you shoot it in two days—and it takes another month to get up another set on that stage—which means you can only use a big stage twice in your schedule. So there was a shuffling of feet and looking around . . ."

Subsequent to Barry's revealing ratio of sets needed versus stages available, Kurtz did more research. By fall the combination of EMI and Shepperton Studios had won out. Just a few miles north of London, EMI (also known as Elstree) was selected as the main studio because they had no scheduling conflicts; could offer Stages 1 through 9, except Stage 5, which they'd leased to Paul McCartney; and had the best facilities. The two largest sets would be built on Shepperton's enormous H Stage. EMI would also allow them to maintain their own departments. "You can come in here and work completely independently of them," Watts says. "You just rent the studio—four walls, if you like, which is a good system."

"We took over completely: lock, stock, and barrel," Barry adds. "We have a freelance crew here, and freelance people tend to be more on their toes."

Production designer John Barry (holding rolled-up blueprints), art director Norman Reynolds, Kurtz, and Lucas inspect the second studio, Shepperton Studios, standing in its enormous H Stage.

PURGATORY

SEPTEMBER 1975 TO DECEMBER 1975

CHAPTER FIVE

On October 1, 1975, Bunny Alsup traveled to England to set up house for Kurtz and his family, who followed on October 6, 1975. Lucas settled overseas shortly thereafter, as preproduction hit full speed in preparation for a March start to principal photography—at least, that's what was supposed to have happened. Everything changed when, in mid-October, Fox's worries mushroomed into full-blown panic.

Like nearly all the major studios during the 1970s, Twentieth Century-Fox was having good days and bad days, and many of its corporate decisions were based on transitory moods generated from the latest box-office or production reports. The fate of *The Star Wars* wasn't being helped by Fox's most recent big-budget experience: *Lucky Lady,* which was about to be released with much justifiable hand-wringing. "*Lucky Lady* was a fiasco," Kurtz says. "And it had been in the same position that we were: *Lucky Lady* had started as an independent picture. Stanley Donen was controlling everything himself. They were leaving him alone— but halfway through production he got into serious trouble. The studio had to keep flying down there and they eventually took over the entire production. That experience was very fresh in their minds when we were making our picture."

In other words, Fox thought they could see the handwriting on the wall—and pulled the plug.

As of the middle of October, the studio imposed a "moratorium" on *The Star Wars* production. People were paid their salaries, but Fox refused to finance any further development until the board of directors meeting scheduled for December 13. At that time, the fate of the film would be decided.

"There was a bit of hysteria around here at that point," Alan Ladd says, "because we'd just come off *Lucky Lady,* and the company was getting very bad press about it being the most expensive picture Fox had made since 1969. And *Lucky Lady*'s cost had at least been covered in guarantees, while the budget for *Star Wars* kept escalating and escalating [with no such assurances]. We kept setting certain budgets and it kept increasing and increasing and increasing. There was concern because the research and development kept going on and on, and nothing was being seen. A couple of people came in and said, 'Look, it's never going to stop unless you just say, *That's it.*'"

Even with the paintings and concept models as visual aids, Fox was not clear about the goals of the film and the corresponding crucial role special effects would play. ILM's investments in developmental technology "confused" them, according to Ladd, while John Stears's feasibility study on the other side of the Atlantic didn't please them.

"I just don't think they were as aware as they should have been about how a film like this gets made and the fact that things have to be done way ahead of time," Lucas says. "It takes six months to design a robot and build it. They just figured you could do it in six weeks, because they're used to making television movies where you come in and three weeks later, everything is ready to go. This isn't that kind of a movie, and the more time and money that's spent up front, the less time and money you have to spend actually making the movie. You save money."

"Fox's position was no contracts, no approved budgets, no money," Pollock says. "And they were all over in England preparing to shoot. The special effects unit had started. George was already $400,000 of his own money into the movie. Not yet reimbursed. He had advanced that much money, the bulk of which went to get ILM started, because Fox just wouldn't pay for it until they had a budget approved by their board."

Lucas's accounting records reveal that he began making personal loans to the Star Wars Corporation in October 1973, for salaries and other expenses—and given Fox's reticence he would have to continue subsidizing the film through the fiscal year 1975–76 for a grand total of $473,368. Though the trajectory of the film's budget estimates is difficult to plot precisely, the basic upswing was from $3 million at the time of the treatment to about $6 million to $8.2 million; yet, strangely and somewhat irrationally— given that at one point the budget had ballooned to $15 million—Fox's panic ensued after the budget had been brought back down. "My final realistic budget was $8.2 million direct [without overhead]," Kurtz says. "But they insisted we cut back. They stopped work on everything, and insisted that we cut the budget back to $7.5 million. So we went through the exercise of doing it. Laddie kept asking me if this was going to be realistic, and I said, 'I doubt it. If you want to present it to the board that way, it's up to you.'"

"George made the comment that it's really a $15 million movie being made for half its budget," recalls Lippincott.

"Ladd just couldn't go to the board and say it was going to cost more than a certain amount," Lucas says. But at the time, the director was unaware of Ladd's relationship with the board and the intrigues at Fox, and could only stand by looking on in anger at what was happening to a film he'd worked on intensely for more than two years. Not surprisingly, on October 22, 1975, *Variety* noted the presence of Lucas and Kurtz "in town working on budgeting of their multi-million dollar sci-fi epic, 'Adventure of Star Killer' [sic]."

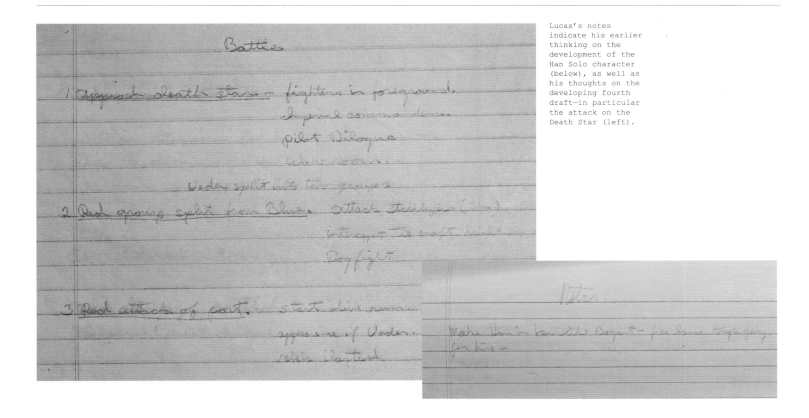

Lucas's notes indicate his earlier thinking on the development of the Han Solo character (below), as well as his thoughts on the developing fourth draft—in particular the attack on the Death Star (left).

As October crept into November, stress levels rose and the clock kept ticking. A March 28, 1976, start date had been agreed upon, which was key because of the location shooting in the desert. There was a certainty that if they went beyond that date, the actors in the robot suits would not be able to survive in the heat. So after feverishly reworking the numbers and making changes that would have a long-lasting impact on the film, Lucas and company turned in a revised budget for the amount specified, thinking it was done and approved—when Fox insisted that the $7.5 million include overhead, which meant that another $600,000 had to be shed to lower the budget to $6.9 million direct.

At this nadir, Lucas—because he still had no contract, was earning a pre-*Graffiti* salary as writer-director, and had invested a large percentage of his savings—saw little hope for success. "I thought *Star Wars* was going to make anywhere from $16 to $25 million," he says, "which would have been successful. But when the price got way up there, I became very pessimistic. I could rely on a low-end box office of $16 million, but if it cost $8.2 million, after you put the advertising and all the costs on it, we'd barely break even. And when Fox took away six weeks of our preproduction time, I knew it was going to cost us three or four weeks of shooting time; as a result, those three or four weeks were probably going to cost ten times as much as the six weeks in preproduction, because there are so many more people involved."

"George always described it to me as a kids' picture, a little Disney film, that he didn't think anyone would want to see, but he wanted to see it," Steven Spielberg says. "He would get excited about it, telling me the story and showing me Ralph McQuarrie's concept paintings, which were phenomenal, but in the next breath he would be putting down its commercial chances."

"In the end," Lucas sums up, "I really didn't think we were going to make any money at all on *Star Wars*."

Besides creating a dim view of the long term, the studio-sanctioned delay was wreaking havoc from Los Angeles to London.

ONCE MORE INTO THE BREACH

"We cut back 10 percent of John Barry's art department budget, across the board, without even consulting him," Kurtz says.

In a series of what must have been painful conversations back in London, Lucas and Barry went through the script, which Lucas was busy transforming into a fourth draft, and tried to find areas where they could decrease costs. "If we had a scene that involved a lot of extras that was tied in to another scene," Lucas says, "we would either eliminate the scene with all the extras or plan on shooting them at one time. Part of it had to do with camera angles: If I wanted to shoot certain angles, we'd have to build

Lucas and John Barry look over set design maquettes, with Lucas checking out the available camera angles (right and above).

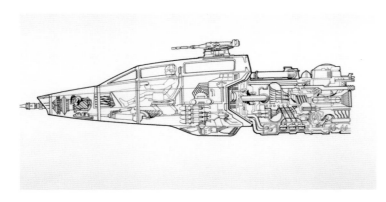 

Budget cuts led to McQuarrie's circa January 1976 painting (right, with redesigned Y-wing, left), as the rebel starfighters were moved inside on Yavin to save money. "I saw a navy pilot that was running across a flight deck with a clipboard in a World War II photograph," McQuarrie says. "I took him, and repeated the same gesture, but changed the uniform and put a helmet on him. The ships of course were Joe Johnston's design. The

fighters were lined up in these long rows and were towed down to the launching platform, which had doors that opened, so the fighters would come shooting out. George liked that basic idea; at least he thought it was fine to have the fighters inside, because it solved some problems of shooting them, too, because the overhead would just be black [instead of jungle]."

more sets, so I would eliminate those angles. I cut out scenes. The compromises had started, and it was difficult—because we had already cut it down to the bone and then we were faced with the fact that we had to cut it even further."

Cost-cutting measures went from the small—the Mos Eisley hangar was originally supposed to have a sliding concrete slab overhead—to the big: Alderaan was cut out of the picture, and all of its scenes were transferred to the Death Star. The rebel base, originally located outside in the jungle, was moved to a less technically challenging and cheaper set inside a temple; Ben Kenobi's house was also scaled down from a multilevel structure to a one-story home with windows to make it easier to light. "Ben's house was originally a very bizarre three-story cave, all carved out of rock, much bigger than it is now. Budget cuts forced us to change that," Lucas says.

The delays affected personnel as well. Director of photography Geoffrey Unsworth had to back out, so Lucas replaced him with Gilbert Taylor. "*A Hard Day's Night* [1964] and *Dr. Strangelove* [1964] were two of my favorite movies. I loved their style, and then I had seen *Macbeth* [1971] and had seen Gil worked well with color, too. But I was really more intrigued with the documentary style of *A Hard Day's Night* and *Strangelove*. I wanted the film to look like those; that was really why I hired him," says Lucas.

"When George asked me to do *Star Wars* I was delighted," says Taylor, who had been impressed by *American Graffiti*. "It fitted in with our finishing time, which meant a large number of the crew on *The Omen* [1976] could also join the team. Many of my crew had been associated with me for over twelve years and worked efficiently and fast."

Decreasing dollars also meant bringing in a local editor, John Jympson, rather than Northern California resident Richard Chew. Lucas had been talking with Chew, a San Anselmo acquaintance who had edited *The Conversation* (1974) and *One Flew Over the Cuckoo's Nest* (1975). But Chew was expensive and, at that time, tired from his latest editing gig, whereas Jympson meant less money, no travel expenses, and no work

permit problems. "I had never really worked with an editor before," Lucas says. "I had cut my own movies, so I didn't really have a relationship with a regular editor and it was very difficult to come up with somebody. We tried to get one editor first and we didn't get him, John Victor-Smith. But Jympson had cut *A Hard Day's Night*, so I talked to him, I liked him, and he seemed like he was going to work out."

A DOUBLE-EDGED SWORD

Some of the changes engendered by budget cuts actually provoked sighs of relief at Industrial Light & Magic. "We were going to have to make Alderaan, which I wasn't looking forward to," Dykstra says. "All of those clouds." Which also allowed them to scrap the idea of renting a Learjet to film billowing formations. News of fewer scenes on the jungle planet was also welcomed.

The much larger and extremely long-term effect, however, was to make it pretty much impossible for the special effects crew to deliver quality front projection plates in time for the live-action shoot.

"I guarantee you a week of no nourishment from the umbilical cord to a fetus is going to do a lot more than just make him a week younger when he comes out," Dykstra says, angrily. "We ended up in a situation that we could not compensate for, and nobody from the studio came out here and said, 'Oh, I understand the problem.' They just said, 'Well, there's no money, but we want the stuff on the same day.' That's bullshit. It isn't ever going to happen—but it doesn't do any good to make excuses, because what's important is getting it done. But that really hurt us badly—and it was really a morale loser, too, because it was obvious that we weren't going to make it."

"What we were faced with then," Robbie Blalack says, "was a delivery schedule in England. I believe, starting in April of '76, we were to deliver a series of process plates, and the first sequence that was to be photographed was the gunport sequence. Actually, the first part of it was to be the pirate ship cockpit, distinctly different from the gunport."

In an effort to manage the worsening situation, Joe Johnston was hard at work on the special effects storyboards for the front projection sequences, taking over from Alex Tavoularis, whose work had finished in mid-June. Johnston's storyboards had been submitted to Lucas and revised on October 10 and 22, 1975. "The first job that ILM had was to take that 16mm film, with the script that described everything, and draw a storyboard for each frame of film," Lucas recalls. "Because you can't do it intellectually, though even storyboarding it is difficult."

"George, John, and I would sit down and we'd have three- or four-hour meetings," Johnston says. "George would talk, I would draw, John would sometimes suggest how the shot could be done more easily, and that's really how they were done. It was just a matter of George saying, 'This is what I want to see, or I want to see two ships drop into frame and come right at us.' I would sketch it out real quickly, and they'd look at it and say, 'Yeah, that'll work.' I'd put a number on it and put a description underneath, and we'd do another one. It was a really slow process."

Not only was it tedious, it was a process that somewhat troubled the film's director at the time. "I've got a tremendous storyboard for the action sequences," Lucas says. "I haven't really done that much storyboarding in the past. I like to do it, but when you bring in a storyboard artist, they bring a lot to it. You tell him what to do, but they end up bringing in their graphic designs. In a lot of movies, I've seen scenes that looked like story-boarded scenes—you can see the way it was done—and I've always been much more loose about how things come together while shooting it. That's something I've always enjoyed. I like to be able to think about things on the set, because things happen slightly more randomly that way. It's more interesting."

VOYAGE TO THE SANDS

In November 1975, leaving the robot designs and the few sets that had already been started in limbo, Robert Watts and John Barry left for their second North African scouting trip, to Morocco and Tunisia, which Barry knew well thanks to his location shoot there on *The Little Prince* (1974) as well as a more recent solo trip for *The Star Wars*. The candidates had been narrowed down to those two countries from a list that had originally included Iran, Libya, Turkey, Spain, and Algeria; Lucas had wanted to film in the latter country on the same location Michelangelo Antonioni had shot the scene in which the Land Rover breaks down in *The Passenger* (released in the United States on April 9, 1975). However, Algeria and Libya were too politically volatile for Fox, while Iran was too far away for efficient transportation. Moreover, Lucas had been intrigued by the photos Barry had taken on his previous recce. "I did quite a big trip around Tunisia looking for interesting things," Barry says. "Djerba had this white architecture, and George liked the look of that from the photographs; he also liked Matmata, where people live in these holes in the ground."

Barry traveled with a list of logistical and artistic prerequisites, the gist of which was that the locales had to meet the environmental and stylistic needs of the script while not overwhelming any scene, which might take audiences out of the story.

"John and I went to Morocco to see how it compared to Tunisia," Watts says. "We went down to the south where we found sand dunes and a bit of

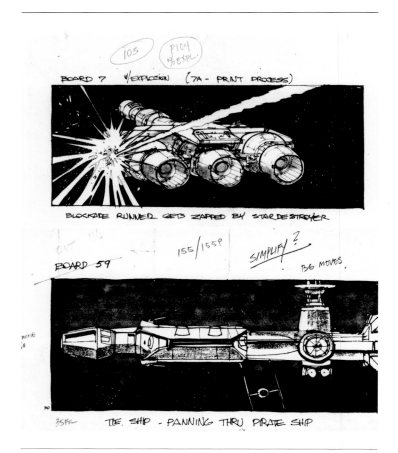

BOARD 7   w/EXPLOSION   (7A - PRINT PROCESS)

BLOCKADE RUNNER GETS ZAPPED BY STAR DESTROYER

BOARD 59   155/155P   SIMPLIFY? B/G MOVES.

TIE SHIP - PANNING THRU PIRATE SHIP

canyon. But the architecture was very Arab; everything looked like *Beau Geste*. After about a week, we called George from Casablanca and said, 'It isn't as good as Tunisia.' John and I then went from Casablanca to Djerba, where we met up with George and Gary. And the minute George saw the island of Djerba, he made the decision to film there, which really keyed from the architecture, because it is strange and it was right. Having got the architectural key to it, we went to the south, where the sand dunes were sufficient, and then we visited the salt flat and the strange hole in the ground."

As they were led from location to location by a Tunisian guide, Lucas began to form in his mind the various locales into physical spaces that made sense within the story. "I loved the architecture in Djerba and I loved the salt flat and that hole—I was real excited about that," he says. "But I had to fit them together, so I came up with the idea of having the homestead out on the flat, in one location, with the hole in the ground in Matmata. It would be very bizarre and I thought that would be a great idea—but everybody was very upset about that. It meant we had to shoot two locations instead of one, which meant another day shooting and more money. But I thought it'd work out very well—it was one of the really rewarding finds."

Another location they visited was a "fabulous series of old grain stores that we were going to use as a street in Mos Eisley," Barry says. "We didn't get to use it, but you'll notice George used its name in the script, Tatooine—one of the planets is called that." Lucas integrated that name into the work-in-progress fourth draft; the Mos Eisley scene never made it into the draft, but would've featured the Jawas.

"We found these great things in Tunisia, little grain houses that were four stories high but with little tiny doors, little tiny windows, it was a hobbit village," Lucas says. "We had a whole sequence with these little hobbit-world slum dwellers but we had to cut it out."

In addition to its artistic advantages, Tunisia won out over Morocco because it was logistically superior. "Its locations change very quickly in a very short distance," Barry says. "The sand dunes, the big ravine, and the salt flat location—they are all within thirty minutes of one another, which is amazing. And the sand dunes were accessible by truck. It's dreadful, isn't it, to think that that's what moviemaking revolves around? Instead of ideas, it revolves around, 'Can you get hotel rooms or can you get there on a plane?'"

In fact, Fox's delays were forcing them to overlap with something truly horrifying: tourist season. "Packaged tours to us are dreadful," Watts sighs. "They book so far in advance, taking all the rooms, and they get a better rate—because film productions never have the ability to book a year in advance, ever. I've suffered this in many countries in the world recently, because this is a recent innovation. Cheap packaged tours."

THE STARFIGHTERS HAVE LANDED

On their way back to California in mid-November 1975, Lucas and Kurtz stopped in New York City for an East Coast casting session. Lucas interviewed Jodie Foster for the part of Leia and Christopher Walken for Han, the latter, according to Kurtz, becoming a favorite in the eyes of Fred Roos. By the end of November they had returned to Los Angeles. While Kurtz departed once again for England after the first week of December, Lucas continued work on the script, supervised efforts at ILM, and gave new assignments to Ralph McQuarrie, who had gone freelance during the months of September and October (working on *The Adventures of the Wilderness Family*, 1975; and *The Winds of Autumn*, 1976).

McQuarrie would occasionally work at the new ILM premises, in order to study and then incorporate Joe Johnston's latest vehicle modifications into his illustrations. An early ILM hire, who had been a student of Jamie Shourt when Shourt was a university professor in Colorado, Paul Huston remembers a late-November visit: "There were maybe ten people in the little warehouse. Joe Johnston and I were upstairs in the art department, where we had these wooden tables on sawhorses on the plywood floor, and we were just drawing X-wings all day with our tracing paper and Rapidographs. But when Ralph McQuarrie would come in, Bob Shepherd would let the word get out that Ralph was there. Everybody would go to the front office and there'd be one of Ralph's illustrations on a piece of illustration board with tissue paper over it. One time Ralph folded the tissue paper back to reveal this painting of a TIE fighter over the Death Star with an

BOARD 21

BOARD 27A

Johnston storyboarded with Rapidograph pens and gray felt markers in black-and-white and shades of gray on Canson Vidalon tracing vellum. Early boards incorporated McQuarrie's early take on Chewbacca (left), which he subsequently revised (above); Johnston's Leia is drawn from Tavoularis's interpretations of the princess (bottom left). Early storyboards also made use of Cantwell's rebel ship (opposite above) and pirate ship (opposite below), and reveal Richard Edlund's technical notations.

Hundreds of location shots were taken during the recces to Tunisia (right), which then served as inspiration for John Barry's production design sketches (opposite), one of which reads, "Djerba Hotel, Tatanouine," which became "Tatooine" (above right).

Opposite: The homestead sketch is identified as being on the Salt Lake, Tozeur, Tunisia (below left). Barry's sketch of the bones, with a tiny R2, is dated 1975 (below right), and his sketch of the city of Chebika (above left) is marked "alternative town to Ajim near Salt Flat location."

X-wing—just this incredibly detailed, beautiful painting. I'd never seen such a high quality of skill. I was just knocked out by that vision.

"Ralph's illustrations became a focus for everyone involved in the visual work," he adds. "There was no question that we were trying to achieve some part of the direction that Ralph was showing there in his illustrations. It unified the whole facility. And then he's such a nice, gentle man, it was just really a revelation to meet him."

"He's real quiet, but he's really fun underneath," Dykstra says. "There's a whole bunch of stuff going on in Ralph's mind all of the time."

"I think McQuarrie's paintings are why the movie's taken the shape it has," John Stears also remarked in England, "because those sketches are so specific. They're beautiful."

Lucas's return from London also gave renewed urgency to ILM's model shop. Three key ships had to be finalized so that full-scale sets could be built based on certain portions of the miniatures: An interior and partial exterior were to be constructed for the sandcrawler; hallways had to be built for the rebel ship; for the pirate vessel, a cockpit, a central area, gunports, and a partial but massive exterior were in the works. "ILM would do a sketch and then they would do a preliminary blueprint," Lucas says. "Then they'd build a little model, which we'd look at later in England while we were doing the big blueprints, which were for the construction people. At each stage, I would have to look at it first and approve it."

As they soldiered on despite Fox's moratorium, the situation had become even more complex because Han Solo needed new "wheels." A television series called *Space: 1999* had debuted earlier that year, and Lucas found that its main ship looked too much like the first pirate ship—which the model makers had finished literally the weekend before they heard.

"They were all very upset that I changed the design, 'cause they had just finished building the other pirate starship," Lucas says. "They had spent an enormous amount of money and time building that other ship, and I threw it out. It's one of those decisions that was very costly, but I felt that we really needed the individuality and personality of a better ship."

The exact cost of the first pirate ship is difficult to ascertain, because, according to McCune, "it got billed for everything," but a rough estimate would be around $25,000—about a third of the total budget for the models. "It was seven feet long and had four hundred cycles of electronics going through it," he says. So instead of scrapping it completely, that ship became the rebel ship, which was only in a couple of shots, while the vessel with more screen time was redesigned. "Joe, George, and John worked up this new idea for what they called the round 'Porkburger,' " McCune laughs.

"The flying hamburger was my favorite design," Lucas says. "I thought that the other design was too close to *Space: 1999* and too conventional looking. I wanted something really off the wall, since it was the key ship in the movie; I wanted something with a lot more personality. I thought of the design on the airplane, flying back from London: a hamburger. I didn't want it to be a flying saucer, but I wanted to have something with a radial shape that would be completely different from anything else."

The ship, by necessity, quickly took form. "The pirate ship was a highly modified smuggler's freighter," Johnston says. "George wanted it to look like it'd been hot-rodded, so we put bigger engines on it and stripped things off of it. He also liked the idea of having a double inverted saucer shape. So I did a series of saucer shapes, freighters, spaceships—and one of them was very similar to how the ship ended up.

I think mine had the cockpit in the center on the top instead of being on the side.

"The second pirate ship was probably the ship we designed the fastest," he adds. "It probably took less than a week."

So speedily was the design approved and building started that, because Lucas liked the look of the first pirate ship's cockpit, it was simply transferred to the new pirate ship, creating an aesthetically pleasing nonsymmetrical design. "We didn't have time to generate a new fancy cockpit for the pirate ship so we just sawed it off the first ship and stuck it on there," McCune says.

The rebel ship was now without a cockpit, "so George and Joe came up real quick with this hammerhead shark idea. That was simply two cardboard buckets filled with Styrofoam and paper peeled off and dug out and covered with styrene and model parts, just to solve the problem right away," McCune adds.

SPECIAL FORCES

All this activity at ILM meant that the facility had to again hire more people. Some were art or industrial design students (many from Long Beach State University), some were "high school or college dropouts or burnouts who knew how to run an electric drill," according to Shepherd, while a couple were hired thanks to their unique skills. Jon Erland and Lorne Peterson, who started on December 8, were known to be experts at making very complex rubber molds. "I hired those guys," Shepherd says. "In fact, almost all the people in the model shop, with the exception of Grant McCune, were people that I scrounged up wherever we could find them. People who knew how to build miniatures, who understood new processes and new plastics. Grant wanted people with 'mental chutz-pah.' He wanted them to be able to think a problem through and also be very good with their hands."

"Bob Shepherd and I knew each other from living in Seal Beach," Lorne Peterson says. "He asked, 'Do you wanna help out?' It was a science-fiction film, but I had no idea what kind of science-fiction film . . . I think when I started there were thirty-some people."

"Jon and Lorne came on just about the time we were starting to make the Death Star molds," Grant McCune says. "They both had a lot of experience—and they're the ones who saved our asses, because we were still at a point where we were experimenting with materials. When Jon and Lorne came, they knew the latest ways of mold making and pattern making; that's when we got the vacuum former and the injection molder. That's how we were able to produce the number of models that they needed for the explosions and things like that. I would say that those two guys really saved it."

"The rest of the crew developed in strange ways," Richard Edlund adds. "Doug Smith, who turned out to be my right-hand man, started out sweeping the floors."

(Continued on page 93)

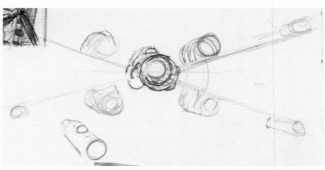

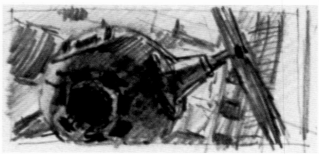

November 25, 1975: "Fighters low over Death Star" and "One of the fighters dashing down trench." In this early McQuarrie concept of the Death Star surface, its walls are smooth and the cannons low to the canyon floor (opposite top). "George just wanted an atmosphere sketch of the action and the hail of laserfire," McQuarrie says (the painting that so impressed Paul Huston and others at ILM, opposite bottom).

December 5, 1975: "Throne room scene—princess receives heroes." McQuarrie's painting was based on his consultations with Lucas after the latter returned from England. "George went back and described it to Ralph," John Barry says, "who then did the painting from the concept we knew we could handle. It's such an enormous set that we were going to have to build in such a short time, so it had to be something that had those wing effects that keep disappearing. That way, we wouldn't have to keep building the part 'round the corner."

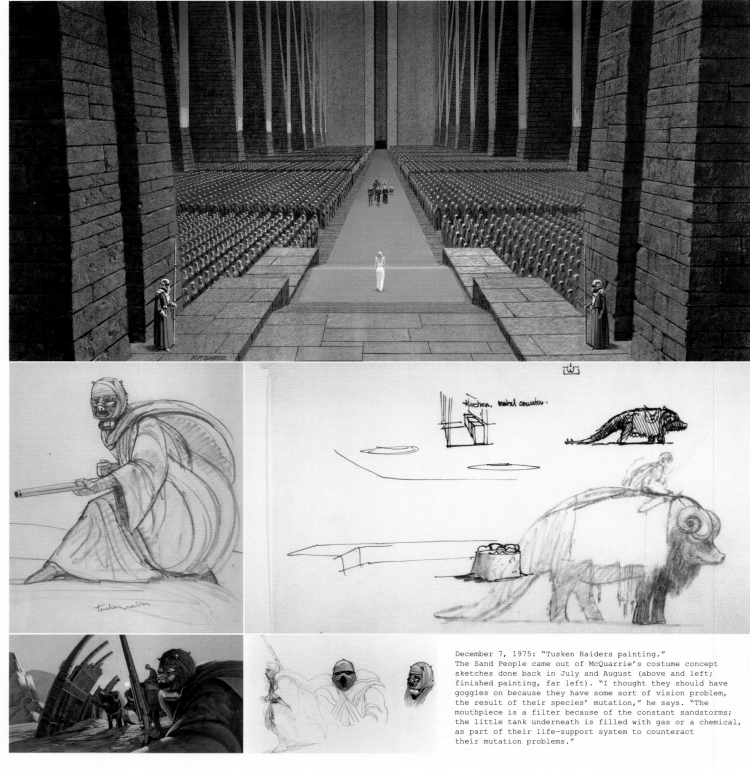

December 7, 1975: "Tusken Raiders painting." The Sand People came out of McQuarrie's costume concept sketches done back in July and August (above and left; finished painting, far left). "I thought they should have goggles on because they have some sort of vision problem, the result of their species' mutation," he says. "The mouthpiece is a filter because of the constant sandstorms; the little tank underneath is filled with gas or a chemical, as part of their life-support system to counteract their mutation problems."

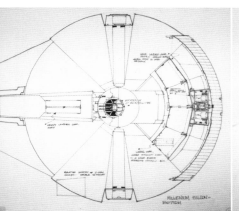
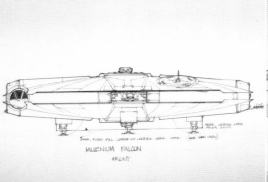
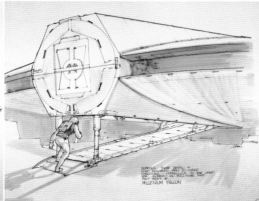

GREEN LIGHT, GO!

On December 13, 1975, Fox had its long-awaited board of directors meeting. The fate of *The Star Wars* hung in the balance—at least for the studio. Lucas was fully prepared to take his project elsewhere if necessary. A participant at the crucial meeting, Warren Hellman says, "To the best of my recollection, Laddie came in and said, 'I'm a believer in this—we've gotta go ahead with this project. Now's the time we really have to get behind this.' Dennis Stanfill was being neutral, and finally went along with it. But the board never had enthusiasm for the project."

It was decided to give the film the green light. Though each board member had been given a portfolio made by Lippincott containing artwork by Ralph McQuarrie and Joe Johnston, according to Hellman, Ladd's backing was the key. At least one letter written by Pollock makes it clear that the Star Wars Corporation was aware of this: "George Lucas is extremely pleased with his relationship with Alan Ladd Jr."

"I would have loved to have been at that meeting with Laddie's board of directors," says Michael Gruskoff, one of the producers of *Lucky Lady*, "when he presented *Star Wars* as a $7 million movie with a small furry animal and two robots, with the budget constantly going up and just a few sketches to show—and he needed an answer *right then*."

"If at any time, Laddie would have left, the project would have died. There is no doubt," Pollock adds.

"Kubrick's *2001* didn't break even until late 1975—and that was the most successful science-fiction film of all time," Lippincott says of the 1968 release. "You had to be crazy to make a science-fiction film when we wanted to."

Another letter, written shortly after the board meeting, expressed concern over a possible management change—Fox was still on treacherous financial ground—asking for assurances that if Ladd were to leave the company, Lucas would have final cut. "Unfortunately, after some negative experiences in the past at other studios, George does not feel that he can entrust the product of four years of his life to an unknown person," Pollock wrote to Immerman on January 5, 1976. "George feels very strongly about this point—as strongly as about anything else we have ever discussed." The reply was that, as a publicly held company, Fox could not grant final cut.

But Lucas's space fantasy was a go-project and the purse strings began to loosen. From then on, everything from casting to set building to special effects jolted back to life and quickly took up a truly frenetic pace. On December 17 Lucas was interviewed by Lippincott, perhaps to mark the occasion of the critical point that had been reached after two and a half years of work:

George Lucas (Lucas): I'll talk about anything.

Charles Lippincott (Chas): Why did you write this story, The Star Wars?

Lucas: Well, I read a lot of books, including Flash Gordon. I loved it when it was a movie serial on television; the original Universal serial was on television at 6:15 PM every day, and I was just crazy about it. I've always had a fascination for space adventure, romantic adventures. And after I finished *Graffiti*, I came to realize that there were very few films being made for young people between the ages of twelve and twenty. When I was that age, practically all the movies were made for that age. I realized that since the Western had died, there hadn't been any mythological fantasy movies available to young people like the ones I grew up on: Westerns and pirate movies, Errol Flynn, all that. They just sort of petered out to the point where they don't do them anymore, and then it petered out on television. Now all you get is cops and hard drama. So instead of making important, gripping, isn't-it-terrible-what's-happening-to-mankind movies, which is what I started out doing, I decided it would be much more useful for me to make movies that made kids have a fantasy life and feel good, so they could go ahead and have a more productive life.

Chas: The Star Wars *has been through quite a few conceptual changes, there's been several scripts—what was the evolution?*

Lucas: Well, the problem is what happens in a lot of movies. It started as a concept. So I want to make a movie in outer space,

Joe Johnston did several sketches of the second pirate ship. Because a hamburger or saucer doesn't really have a front, mandibles were added to give the new vessel orientation. "We justified the mandibles by saying that they could be a freight-loading area where your cargo goes in," Johnston says. "Something comes out and grabs the freight and takes it back into the ship."

The cockpit (above right) was lifted off the first pirate ship.

let's say an action-adventure movie just like Flash Gordon used to be. People running around in spaceships, shooting each other, and exotic people and exotic locations, and an Empire. I knew I wanted to have a big battle in outer space, a dogfight, so that's what I started with. Then I asked myself, *What story can I tell?* So I was looking for a story for a long time. I went through several stories, trying to find the one that was right, that would have enough personality, tell the story I wanted to tell, be entertaining, and, at the same time, include all the action-adventure aspects that I wanted. That's really where the evolution came from: Each story was a totally different story about totally different characters before I finally landed on *the* story. A lot of the scripts have the same scenes in them. On the second script I pilfered some of the scenes from the first script, and I kept doing it until I finally got the final script—which is the one I'm working on now—which has everything from all the other scripts that I wanted. Now what I'm doing in this rewrite is I'm slowly shaving down the plot so it seems to work within the context of everything I wanted to include. After that, I'll go through and do another rewrite, which will develop the dialogue and the characters.

Chas: Do you conceive of a scene you would like to do in a certain setting and then . . .

Lucas: This film has been murder. It's very easy to write about something you know about and you've lived through—it's very hard to write about something you make up from scratch. And the problem was that there was so much I could include—it was like being in a candy store, and it was hard to not get a stomachache from the whole experience. But there were things I knew I didn't want to have, like exposition. I wanted the story to be very natural. I wanted it to be more of a straight adventure movie rather than something that had such complex technology that most of the film was spent dealing with the technology.

And I didn't want to make it so obscure that you didn't understand what was going on at any given point—which is very hard to do in a science-fiction/fantasy movie, because everything is unfamiliar and therefore, by definition, needs to be explained.

Chas: How did you conceive of the characters?

Lucas: My original idea was to make a movie about an old man and a kid, who have a teacher-student relationship [treatment, rough, and first drafts]. And I knew I wanted the old man to be a real old man, but also a warrior. In the original script the old man was the hero. I wanted to have a seventy-five-year-old Clint Eastwood. I liked that idea. Then I wrote another script without the old man. I decided I wanted to do it about kids. I found the kid character more interesting than the old man. I don't know that much about old people and it was very hard for me to cope with it. So I ended up writing the kid better than the old man. Then I had a story about the kid and his brother, where the kid developed— and a pirate character developed out of the brother [second draft]. As I kept writing scripts, more characters evolved. Over the two-year period of rewriting, rewriting, rewriting, all the characters evolved. I pulled one character from one script and another character from another script, and pretty soon they got into the dirty half dozen that they are today. It was a long, painful struggle, and I'm still doing it, still struggling to get them to come alive.

Chas: What point have you been trying to reach with them now?

Lucas: Essentially, I'm trying to knock out all the plot loopholes and I'm trying to smooth it out and add more intensity to the film, make it work better. I'm trying to make the characters more interesting, more enjoyable.

Chas: Your films, even when you were working as a student, always have been strongly oriented toward design, a strong visual sense.

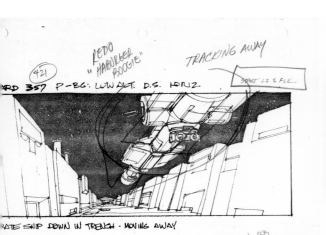

BOARD # 364 BACKGROUND Stars and Yavin FRAME COUNT:

SHOT # 427 LAZER START / STOP DUPE SHOT

LOCATION: Yavin atmosphere TRENCH #

CAMERA MOVE Tracking wi

DESCRIPTION LONG SHOT YAVIN. Several X-wing, Y-wing and the pirate ship race over the camera toward Yavin in the distance.

PROCESS PLATE #

SCRIPT # 268

DIALOGUE

How did you conceive of the visuals in this film?

Lucas: I'm trying to make a film that looks very real, with a nitty-gritty feel, which is hard to do in a film that is essentially a fantasy. Photographically, I'm working on a filtered look, nostalgic, a looking-back quality. I'm using a lighting style that is very dramatic, in the style of Greg Toland [the cinematographer on *Citizen Kane*, 1941; and *My Darling Clementine*, 1946], using strong shadows. Framing-wise, I'm going to try for a semi-documentary, loose frame that will give it a nervous "now" quality, a sense of being captured, which will look real but at the same time be slightly fantastic. Binding all those things together will create, hopefully, a fantasy-documentary look.

Chas: You've had a strong orientation toward documentary. Your first two features used documentary cameramen. Why?

Lucas: I have a strong feeling about it. I like cinema verité; it's one of my real loves. Cinema verité films are challenging, and that whole genre is in my blood. *Apocalypse Now* was going to be a real Peter Watkins [famed BBC documentarian and Academy Award winner], you-are-there, newsreel-type movie. Ultimately, the genre of the movie you're making determines the style that you have to use, and I'm a strong believer in style. *Graffiti* had a real Sam Katzman, AIP [American International Pictures], hot-rod movie style, and everything was sitting there center frame. *THX* was a totally two-dimensional drawn-on, surreal style, with very eccentric graphics and framing—but it also had that documentary quality, which I achieved mainly through the lighting. In this film I'm going to use a documentary frame but with theatrical lighting. I like to have that edge of reality because I want the movies to make you believe they are real. I try to do it with the acting, too.

Chas: What is happening with the acting?

Lucas: It's more improvisational and linked to the style I use in directing, which is to have more than one camera and lead back away from the people, so that the actors essentially play the scenes themselves. The cameras are onlookers, and you aren't right in there. People aren't acting to cameras, people are acting to each other. I won't really demand that they get the lines right. They can play as much as they want with what they've got, which makes for a much more casual, sometimes much more intense interaction between actors rather than just having every little piece be perfect and done to the camera.

Chas: What do you look for when casting?

Lucas: I look for magic. What else can I say? Besides being solid actors, I'm looking for somebody who has the personal and physical qualities that I want that character to have.

Chas: You were talking the other day about having two concepts of the characters . . .

Lucas: I'm essentially thinking of casting in two different directions. One is a little more serious, a little more realistic; the other is a little more fun, more goofy. Right now my first choice is to make it fairly serious, because I think it'll be more fun that way. Because I think you have to have a very strong reality in a movie for people to really enjoy it, and the more serious characters will give it the stronger reality.

Chas: Have you had any luck with Alec Guinness?

Lucas: We're negotiating.

Johnston's story-boards with Edlund's notes reflect the pirate ship design revision. An earlier shot of the ship approaching Yavin (above middle) is replaced with the second vessel (above right), while one storyboard showing the first pirate ship moving along the Death Star trench is marked, "Re-do 'Hamburger Boogie'"—a notation referring to the second pirate ship, which had been inspired by the form of a hamburger

Revised Paintings

"When new spaceships were designed, I would put them in and paint out the one I had," says Ralph McQuarrie. Once the second pirate ship had been approved, the artist launched into a series of paintings so all concerned could see what the new vessel looked like in the context of the film's burgeoning sets and special effects.

An early sketch (top) led to a painting of Ben and the others arriving in the Mos Eisley docking bay with the first pirate ship (middle). The crane at the top of the picture was considered too old-fashioned and not included in the film, according to McQuarrie. A later painting (above) features the revised pirate ship design. Han Solo's clothes also reflect a redesign: Instead of being in blue and with a cape, he wears a vest and sweater, light trousers, and dark boots. The beard has been shaved, too, so that he looks more like Buck Rogers.

Chas: Will you have the studio putting any weight on you?

Lucas: I hope not. It's not likely. The big issue usually comes down to whether you have movie stars or not, and since I'm not having movie stars, I don't think they would know one actor from another.

Chas: How did you get them to agree to that?

Lucas: It's just something that was a given at the very beginning. I said, "I am not going to put movie stars in this movie." It wouldn't do me any good, because the film is a fantasy. If it's a Robert Redford movie, it's no longer a fantasy; it's a Robert Redford movie and you lose the whole quality of the fantasy, which is the only commercial aspect of the film in the first place. In order to create a fantasy, you have to have unknowns. I'm a strong believer in that. Part of the charm of *Graffiti* was that you'd never seen any of those people before, except Ronnie Howard, and I sort of slipped by with that. But essentially it was all fresh talent who you'd never seen in the movies before. It has a quality of making it not be a movie where players are acting a part; it has a tendency to make you believe that these are the real characters.

Chas: How are you going about choosing the various personnel, like your cameraman?

Lucas: I keep track of whose work I like as I go to the movies. So I interviewed thirty or forty cameramen, whose work I admired, to see how I get along with them. It's especially hard for me in picking a camera [director of photography], because I never had a camera before. I've more or less shot my own movies. On *Graffiti*, Haskell Wexler came in, and he's a very close friend of mine. It was really just him helping me out; it wasn't like having a DP on the picture. I've never really had that to contend with, so on this picture it's been tricky. I've been trying to find somebody who will essentially work with me and do more or less what I want to do, the way I want to do it. I like to take a lot of chances, do a lot of very eccentric things—and finding somebody who is open-minded enough to take chances and not worry about whether it's going to look good is very difficult. And this picture is going to be difficult, technically: It has a lot of front projection, a lot of huge sets lit with backdrops and paintings, and challenging stuff that a lot of younger men can't handle because they've never done it. They shoot on location and they know a certain kind of lighting, but they don't know the old-style giant-set-on-a-sound-stage lighting with backdrops and tricky cutouts.

Chas: What's cameraman Gilbert Taylor like?

Lucas: He's very free-thinking, very talented, will do anything. That's originally what I was looking for. He's very similar to Geoffrey Unsworth. I think he's the best black-and-white cameraman in England. I've only had about two meetings with him; I don't think he's even read the script yet, quite frankly. Matter of fact, I'm sure he hasn't. What it comes down to is: I have a

tendency to want a lot of the control over it. A lot of the decisions will be made for him, and I will expect him to build on those decisions and make them come out the way I want them.

Chas: Are you open to suggestion?

Lucas: Yeah, more or less; less than more, I'm afraid. Up till now the movies I've made have been my own movies; they've been very small and I've been able to handle everything. This is the first time I'm going to have to deal with a real crew in a real movie in a real professional situation. I want to be able to call all the shots, but I'm going to have to be slightly removed from a lot of what's happening. That'll be interesting. But I think I'm ready for it. I've loosened up a little bit. As you get older, you get tired more quickly. It's more fun to have other people make suggestions, so you don't have to do all the work.

Chas: Considering that this is a film that takes place in another galaxy, possibly in another time, where there's been no contact with Earth, how are you going about designing things as simple as eating utensils?

Lucas: I'm trying to make props that don't stand out. I'm trying to make everything look very natural, a casual almost I've-seen-this-before look. You see it in the paintings we've had done, especially the one that Ralph McQuarrie did of the banthas. You look at that painting of the Tusken Raiders and the banthas, and you say, 'Oh yeah, Bedouins . . .' Then you look at it some more and say, 'Wait a minute, that's not right. Those aren't Bedouins, and what are those creatures back there?' Like the X-wing and TIE fighter battle, you say, 'I've seen that, it's World War II—but wait a minute—that isn't any kind of jet I've ever seen before.' I want the whole film to have that quality! It's a very hard thing to come by, because it should look very familiar but at the same time not be familiar at all.

Chas: How are you going about that with the various people you work with?

Lucas: I keep saying, 'Keep it nondescript.' I say that every time, every place I can. It can be a computer, but it's got to be a nondescript computer. I don't want anything to stand out. I don't want any of the costumes, any of the spaceships, any sets, any animals—I don't want anything in the movie to stand out. I want you to walk out of the movie and if somebody asks you what were they wearing, I want you to say, 'I can't remember what they were wearing. I can't remember what the sets were like.' If they ask, 'What did the ray guns look like?' You'd say, 'I don't know—they just looked like ray guns.' If the whole movie looks like that, it'll be terrific. It'll be absolutely the opposite of what all the science-fiction movies are. With every other science-fiction movie, you remember what every set looks like, you know exactly the costumes they were wearing—because it all stands out and it all looks like it's been designed. I'm working very hard to keep everything nonsymmetrical. Nothing looks like it belongs with anything else. You walk

A series of images show how elastic a certain shot could be: (from top down) what started as a McQuarrie sketch of an Imperial pilot tracking another ship became a Tavoularis storyboard of the same pilot approaching the cloud city of Alderaan, which became a McQuarrie painting of a Y-wing as it flew toward a planet (possibly Yavin), which became the Colin Cantwell Death Star, which finally became another revised McQuarrie painting of the same pilot following the redesigned pirate ship approaching a redesigned Death Star.

After Alderaan's scenes had been moved to the Death Star, and following the pirate ship redo, McQuarrie updated his paintings to include the new vessel and starfields instead of clouds outside the docking bay.

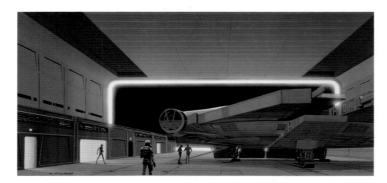

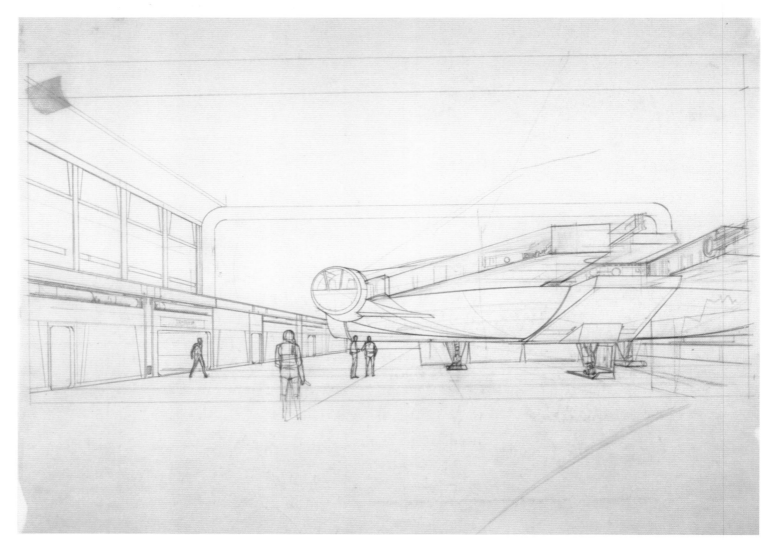

Early storyboards by Joe Johnston show Imperial officers in helmets firing at the second pirate ship as it tries to leave Alderaan/the Death Star (the model has changed, but the sky, instead of stars, can still be seen outside); rebel pilot Biggs wears a helmet with an Egyptian-style all-seeing-eye emblem in a storyboard intended as a guide for front projection "Process Plate #14A."

SHOT # 129P
LOCATION:
LAZER START / STOP
from soldiers
DUPE SHOT
TRENCH #
CAMERA MOVE Locked off

DESCRIPTION Two people in foreground firing at retreating (backing out) Pirate Ship. *Note Shot here.

PROCESS PLATE #
SCRIPT #

into a set and there's lots of different influences, not just one influence. It's a very common thing in science fiction to see a set that has one influence. Everything matches. The chairs match the table, match the rug, match the design of the doors, match the door handle, match the lamps. I want it to look like one thing came from one part of the galaxy and another thing came from another part of the galaxy.

Chas: How'd you go about choosing your composer, John Williams?

Lucas: I'd heard that he was a very good classical composer, very easy to work with. I liked what he had done with Steve [Spielberg], who recommended him very highly and he thought I should talk to him. So I did and we got along very well, so I decided to hire him. I really knew the kind of sound I wanted. I knew I wanted an old-fashioned, romantic movie score, and I knew he was very good with large orchestras.

Chas: Any particular scores you've liked by him?

Lucas: I liked *Jaws* [which had been released on June 20, 1975, and become a mega-hit].

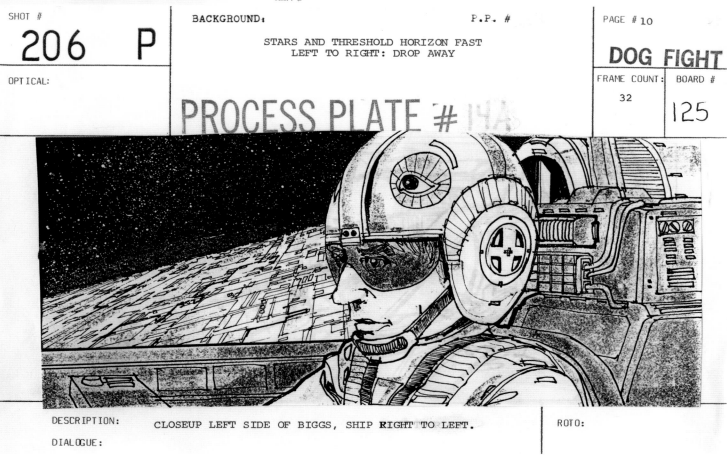

SHOT # 206 P
OPTICAL:

BACKGROUND:
STARS AND THRESHOLD HORIZON FAST
LEFT TO RIGHT: DROP AWAY

P.P. #

PAGE # 10
DOG FIGHT
FRAME COUNT: 32
BOARD # 125

PROCESS PLATE # 14A

DESCRIPTION: CLOSEUP LEFT SIDE OF BIGGS, SHIP **RIGHT** TO LEFT.
DIALOGUE:
ROTO:

Chas: How are you treating the musicians in the cantina? You've talked about a different type of music for that . . .

Lucas: It will be a very bizarre, kind of primitive rock. I'm toying with the idea of adding a country-and-western influence to the film, combining country and western with classical. If I can get away with it, I might do it.

THE BIG BATTLE BEGINS

Just before and after Fox's decision, Lucas attended casting sessions while in Los Angeles. Between sessions, ILM needed more attention—but before showing up at Goldwyn Studios *or* at Van Nuys, rising before dawn as he had while writing *THX 1138*, Lucas was busy hammering out the fourth draft. In particular, he was honing the end battle, which ILM needed to get a jump on.

"It wasn't until the fourth draft that I described the dogfight in detail," Lucas says. "What I did each time before that, as I finished the draft, was think to myself, *This is not the final script*, and then write, 'There is this big battle and Luke wins.' But now I had to really work it all out. Some of the details had been sketched in, so I took those and expanded them. I would also consult the World War II footage I'd cut together, and the storyboards that had been made in conjunction with the edited film, and just write the story and then restructure it like an editor would. It was almost like making a documentary film, in that I cut it and wrote it at exactly the same time. That seven minutes of film time, when it was translated shot by shot, became about fifty pages of the script, because each shot was described in detail."

On December 17 Lucas explained to Lippincott: "I have to do twenty-five boards [shot descriptions] a day, so I'm getting up at three o'clock in the morning to start the twenty-five—but I have to get them done by nine

Lucas inspects the second pirate ship construction at ILM with Bill Shourt (right, next to the core of the vessel) and with Bill Shourt and Jamie Shourt (opposite, left); later Joe Johnston works on the ship's paint job, inside the spray booth (opposite, right).

o'clock in the morning. The casting and testing I can't show up late for, but every time I go out to ILM, I end up going out there at nine o'clock instead of eight o'clock because of the fact that I *can't leave* until I finish my twenty-five boards."

Handwritten notes reveal that one of the rebel pilots, "Chewie"—a leftover from previous drafts—was going to be one of the few to survive: "Chewie: 'Here we go again . . . I've got a malfunction, Luke . . . I can't stay with you . . . You did it! You did it! They went right in!'" But with *Chewie* becoming the nickname of Chewbacca, Solo's copilot in the fourth draft, rebel pilot Chewie became rebel pilot Wedge. Solo's end heroics were also solidified in Lucas's notes: "Full shot of wingman POV. Out of the sun charges Han Solo, in his pirate manta-ship heading right for the TIE ships."

Rushing to ILM with his pages in hand, Lucas would then consult with Dykstra and Johnston on the impending front projection plates, after which he'd review the model makers' progress on the essential miniatures. Immediately upon Lucas's approval of Johnston's new pirate ship sketch, Steve Gawley had done the orthographic drawings, and the model-building crew had started work that continued through Christmas and New Year's, coming in Sunday nights at four in the morning to take pieces out of molds so that they would be ready for Monday-morning revisions.

"Joe Johnston and I actually carpooled from Long Beach to Van Nuys every day," Gawley says. "It was like 124 miles round-trip every day, but we were thrilled as can be to be working on something this cool. Though the distance sometimes did get in the way—you know, you'd be working late so that it wouldn't pay to drive home, so we'd sleep over in the screening room."

That excitement must have carried over into the creation of the new pirate ship, building a palpable sense of pride in the work, because all eleven artists who had a part in it signed their names on the finished model.

AMAZING STORIES

Lucas arrived, on time, for at least three casting sessions—December 12, 15, and 30—as videotape still exists for those meetings. Among the tested were, on the first day, Kurt Russell, Patti d'Arbanville, Richard Doran, and Terri Nunn; on the second day, Kurt Russell (again), Chris Moe, Forest Williams, Amy Irving, Christopher Allport, Terri Nunn (again), and Will Seltzer; and on the third day, Terri Nunn (for the third time), Lisa Eilbacher, Robby Benson, Eddie Benton, Linda Purl, Andy Stevens, Mark Hamill, and Carrie Fisher.

Newcomer Harrison Ford was present all three days. While most tests were for the Luke and Leia parts, with Nunn clearly the front-runner for the latter, Ford was called upon to read Han Solo's lines for each tryout. According to Ford, he was asked to read with the others thanks to Fred Roos, who had helped persuade Lucas to amend his policy of not considering any actors who'd appeared in *American Graffiti*. The long and inconclusive first casting session had also changed matters, as both Cindy Williams and Charles Martin Smith—like Ford, *Graffiti* veterans—were also allowed to test.

Roos also went so far as to "cast" Ford in a staged performance for Lucas's benefit, which happened to include another *Graffiti* stalwart, Richard Dreyfuss. Roos had long ago cast Ford in one of his first parts—a political activist in *Zabriskie Point* (1970), a role that was eventually cut from the film—and he seems to have had an ongoing concern for the struggling actor's welfare.

"I left acting to become a carpenter because our second baby was coming and we like to eat," Ford says. "I wasn't making it as an actor."

Because the sessions were being held at the American Zoetrope offices, Roos "hired" Ford, who was also a skilled carpenter, to install a door there—precisely when he knew Lucas would be coming by. "Getting George to consider Harrison took some working around," Roos says.

"I was out there kneeling down in the hall, putting up this elaborate doorway," Ford says. "Dreyfuss, the big movie star, came in to see George for the picture, and there I was cast as the blue-collar worker. That was the only time I saw George, not more than three or four weeks before they were set to make a decision."

The ploy worked, according to Roos: "It just kind of clicked for George at that point."

The test was offered, pretty much, without explanation. Many times, I was asked to explain to the testees what the story was about, or George would offer a very simple explanation—that there was this farm boy sent off to the big city, who got involved in this adventure. Then we'd read the scene. But there were not very many people who were not hung up on that level of it. It was a very difficult situation for most of them."

The cursory summaries were the result of Lucas's desire simply to see these candidates on-screen; their understanding of the situation mattered little compared with their performance's unpredictable chemical reaction to the video and film stocks on which they were being recorded.

"I have them do readings, then videotape tests, then film tests," Lucas says. "Each time, I weed people out. By the time I get down to an actual film test, I've really gotten to know that person. I've gotten to know their acting ability and all the ramifications of their personality. Because you have one impression when you meet somebody for five minutes and another impression when you call them back and talk to them for half an hour—and then you have another impression when they've played the scene on tape and you can sit back in a room and study it on television."

In addition to the actors, calls had gone out for "little people and giants," according to Dianne Crittenden, whose assistants used "breakdown services" to send letters to every agent in town; she also put ads in the trade papers. As he had during the first casting sessions, Lucas was contemplating a different tack, this time playing with the idea of doing the film almost entirely with little people—according to Lippincott, "rewriting the whole film for midgets."

"When I was in New York, I had also done some screen tests for little people," Lucas says. "I explored all kinds of ideas of making it exotic. I think that idea was a little influenced by *Lord of the Rings*."

While that concept was ultimately short-lived, Lucas had not forgotten his idea of casting a black Han Solo, Ford notwithstanding. As all these ideas fought for dominance in his mind, two dark-horse actors arrived for their videotape tests on December 30: Mark Hamill and Carrie Fisher.

LUKE STARKILLER

The dialogue chosen for those trying out for the Luke Starkiller role was originally written for Ben Kenobi. In the third draft he explains to Han Solo the financial situation after they've discovered that Organa Major has been destroyed, coercing him into helping rescue Princess Leia:

```
                    HAN
        Why?

                    LUKE
        Well, for one reason, we don't have your other five
        thousand.

                    HAN
        Who's going to pay me then?

                    LUKE
        I think there are some things we should talk about.

                    HAN
        I'm beginning not to like you.
```

Lucas during the second casting session in December 1975.

"I thought, *Here's a possibility*," Lucas says. "Harrison was right for the part, so Fred suggested he read with everybody, which I thought was a great idea—but I wasn't going to commit. I wanted someone just like Harrison, but not Harrison, because he was in *Graffiti* and I didn't want people thinking of another film while watching *Star Wars*—I wanted it to be new. But Fred liked to help actors survive and was giving him work, and was pushing for him for that part. But I had to go through the whole process. I wasn't going to take anyone just because I knew them, or I knew they could act well—I really wanted to see all the diverse possibilities and come at it fresh. Plus, I wasn't going to choose anyone until I'd tested the whole cast together."

"I think I did fifty or sixty tests for them—testing other people," says Ford, continuing the story. "I was asked to help them test other people.

Video excerpts from the taped auditions: Lisa Eilbacher, Linda Purl, Eddie Benton, Cindy Williams, Carrie Fisher, Amy Irving, Perry King and Charles Martin Smith, Robby Benson, Mark Hamill, Kurt Russell, Frederic Forrest, Harrison Ford, Andrew Stevens, William Katt, and Will Seltzer.

Mark Hamill, though he'd made it this far, was anything but a shoo-in for the part. "George was open to re-seeing some of the people, like Mark, who he'd dismissed early on," Crittenden says. "This is one place where Fred Roos came in, because Fred had worked with George before, so George respected him."

"There was that one meeting," Hamill recalls, "and then Christmas rolled around and I had forgotten about it completely. The next thing I heard, Nancy had gotten me a test with George, way out of nowhere. Four pages of dialogue. There was one great line, though, and it was the hardest piece of dialogue I'd ever memorized. I came about a half hour early to the test, memorizing this line the way you memorize 'she sells sea shells by the seashore.' And it was, 'We can't turn back. Fear is their greatest defense. I doubt if the actual security there is any greater than it was on Aquilae or Sullust. What there is, is most likely directed toward a large-scale assault.' Who talks like that? But you're selling it."

Although perplexed by his lines, Hamill had actually followed the progress of the production since its beginning, reading about it in the "Films in Preparation" section of *Variety*. The young actor had even contacted his agent way back when to see if she could perhaps get him a walk-on role, because he was curious to learn how science-fiction films were made, such was their rarity.

"I was sitting in the outer offices with Harrison," Hamill continues. "And he's Harrison. And I was thinking, *He seems real calm and everything*. I asked him what he'd done, and he told me about *Graffiti*. So he knew George a little bit. We went in and sat down, and Harrison said, 'Hi,

George!' and was so loose with him it made me feel good. I asked, 'Is there anything you want to tell me about the scene?' And George said, 'No. Let's just run through it.' We did, and I asked, 'Is there anything you want me to do differently?' And George said, 'No. Let's shoot it.' He was so unenthusiastic, I thought, *Oh, well, it's probably hopeless*. We ran through it again with no stops, and he said, 'Cut. Okay. Thank you. Harrison, can you stay a couple of minutes?' And I thought, *That's it*. I didn't feel bad or disappointed. It was just a clean no-go."

PRINCESS LEIA ORGANA

The daughter of Hollywood icons Debbie Reynolds and Eddie Fisher, Carrie Fisher was attending the Central School of Speech and Drama in London when she was first contacted in early December. "Carrie Fisher was a social friend of mine," Fred Roos says. "George was about to cast another actress, but I kept urging him to meet Carrie and test her."

"They called me in London to test with the first block of girls," says Fisher, who had recently played a minor but notorious role in *Shampoo* (1975). "They wanted me to come home, but you can't leave that school in the middle because it's like doing a play, and we were just into final production." Fisher took a rain check. "I thought I'd totally missed testing for it."

Circumstances favored Fisher, however, and she was contacted again while at home in Los Angeles during her Christmas break. Like Hamill, she received her pages in advance. "Leia was unconscious a lot," she says. "And I wanted to be unconscious; I have an affinity for unconsciousness. I thought I could play that very well. But I also wanted to be involved in all of it, with Wookiees, with the monsters in the cantina. I was caught by my mother and some of my family rehearsing it in my underwear. I would come out of the bathroom and say, 'General Kenobi!' My family thought I was crazy, because the dialogue was, 'A battle station with enough fire-power to destroy an entire system.'"

Her designated scene was the one in which Leia reveals the importance of what R2-D2 is carrying. "When we finally tested Carrie, we had the opportunity to soften her a little bit because she wore her hair pulled back straight and was dressed rather severely," Crittenden says. "We added some makeup and had her wear something that was a little more feminine and younger looking. Carrie was very unique in that she was formidable for an eighteen-year-old. She had a tremendous

amount of sophistication, so in fact the hardest thing to do was to get her to be young."

"It was like they were doing an assembly line," remembers Fisher, who had been told by Brian De Palma that Jodie Foster had the inside track. "That day I think they had ten or fifteen people. They had me do it a couple of different ways: conversational and then arch. They taped a rehearsal and they taped another one, and there was very little direction—and I thought, *There is no way that I have it*. I didn't hear anything for about three weeks, so I thought, *Well, I'm not going to get to have lunch with monsters*."

HAN SOLO

While Hamill and Fisher were counting themselves out, Harrison Ford was feeling optimistic. "It would come to me in different ways," he notes. "Fred Roos would say, 'Wow, you're lookin' real good.' And Roos's

Lucas and Hamill, with his "sides."

girlfriend would come over and squeeze my hand as I was leaving. That kind of thing. But not a word from George."

Perhaps because Ford did so many tests, the film made more sense to him. "There are certain key lines with the characters: 'Look, kid, I've been from one side of this galaxy to another and I've seen a lot of strange stuff—but nothing to make me believe that one all-powerful Force controls everything,'" says Ford. "Is that easy enough? It's real easy the way George has it set up."

The tests completed, Lucas prepared for a few last meetings at ILM and a long stay in England, while the actors went their separate ways.

"I saw Terri Nunn at the unemployment office a month later," Hamill says. "She asked me, 'Did you get it?' I said, 'No. Did you?' She said, 'No,' and we embraced and that was the last I saw of her. Because I still didn't know; I'd heard it was 80 percent sure someone else . . ."

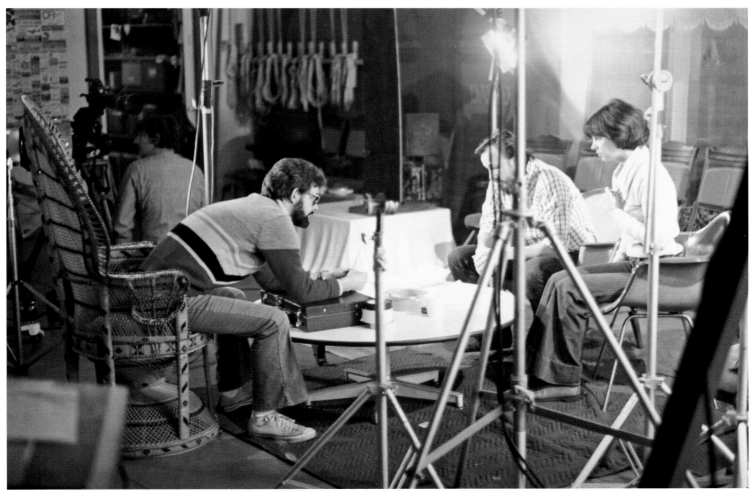

Frederic Forrest and Cindy Williams (left); Harrison Ford and Terri Nunn (above).

RISE OF THE POETIC STATE

DECEMBER 1975 TO MARCH 1976

CHAPTER SIX

Budget cuts obliged Lucas to change the story considerably. The elimination of Alderaan and the moving of its scenes to the Death Star had the fortuitous effect of giving the bad guys a single location, eliminating many scenes, and concentrating the action into a more quickly moving story. However, the combined stresses of dealing with Fox, ILM, the art departments, and casting took their toll on the writer-director. "Essentially you are doing two jobs," Lucas says. "If a director works ten hours a day, then a writer-director ends up working twenty hours a day. Because when he isn't directing operations, every spare moment he's sitting down and rewriting. So you're constantly working. It was hard for me the first couple years; I was all movies. It was literally seven days a week—every waking hour, I was thinking about my movie."

While his notes reveal thoughts, like "Change Death Star name . . . Luke doesn't know father Jedi; Ben tells Luke about father," a December 29, 1975, conversation with Alan Dean Foster, who was preparing to write the novelization of the film, reveals much more of Lucas's mind-set as he wrote the fourth draft. Also in attendance were Charles Lippincott and John Dykstra, as the meeting was in the latter's office.

Fairy tales: "I put this little thing on it: 'A long, long time ago in a galaxy far, far away, an incredible adventure took place.' Basically it's a fairy tale now. *Star Wars* is built on top of many things that came before. This film is a compilation of all those dreams, using them as history to create a new dream."

The Kiber Crystal: "I think I'm taking the Kiber Crystal out. I thought it really detracted from Luke and Vader; it made them too much like supermen, and it's hard to root for supermen."

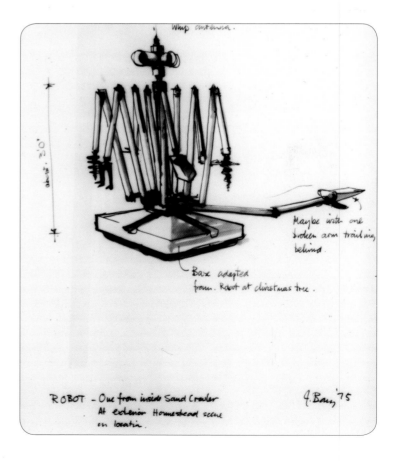

Whip antenna.

Maybe with one broken arm trailing behind.

Base adapted from Robot at christmas tree.

ROBOT - One from inside Sand Crawler. At exterior Homestead scene on location.

J. Barry '75

2nd. TYPE B. based on YAK + Manatee head. Head only to move.

J. Barry.

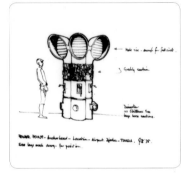 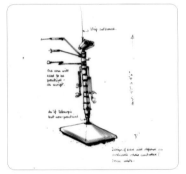

The Force: "I'm dealing with the Force a little more subtly now. It's a force field that has a good side and a bad side, and every person has this force field around them; and when you die, your aura doesn't die with you, it joins the rest of the life force. It's a big idea—I could write a whole movie just about the Force of Others. Now it really comes down to that scene in the movie where Ben tries to get Luke to swordfight with the chrome baseball when he's blindfolded. He has to trust his feelings rather than his senses and his logic—that's essentially what the Force of Others comes down to.

"It's also in the end now during the trench run where they have to shoot a torpedo into a little hole. They're using this computer readout, and there are four runs on this thing: one guy makes his run and he fails; the second guy makes his run, and he fails; Luke makes his run, and he fails. When he comes around the last time, Vader is getting closer, destroying everything, Luke's ship is damaged and he's really in trouble—but at the last moment, he just pushes the computer aside. Ben, in the end, says, 'Luke, trust your feelings.' "

Darth Vader: "Vader runs off in the end, shaking his fist: 'I'll get you yet!' In a one-to-one fight Vader could probably destroy Luke."

Luke's father: "I'm going to have his father leave him his laser sword. I have to have a scene where Luke pulls out the laser sword and turns it on, to give audiences a sense of what laser swords are all about. Otherwise there is no way in the world to explain what happens in the cantina. It happens so quickly that unless you know that it's a laser sword, you'll be lost."

Uncle Owen: "His uncle isn't a son of a bitch anymore; because he gets killed, I have to make him sympathetic, so you'll hate the Empire."

Ben Kenobi: "When this cranky old man pulls out his laser sword and cuts down three guys in a second—that's when you realize the old man is a master. This guy is a lot more than you think he is."

Tusken Raiders versus Luke: "I changed it because that electric windmill they put him on was a huge special effect that was going to cost an enormous amount of money. Now they just beat him up."

Sequels: "I want to have Luke kiss the princess in the second book. The second book will be *Gone with the Wind in Outer Space*. She likes Luke, but Han is Clark Gable. Well, she may appear to get Luke, because in the end I want Han to leave. Han splits at the end of the second book and we learn who Darth Vader is . . . In the third book, I want the story to be just about the soap opera of the Skywalker family, which ends with the destruction of the Empire.

"Then someday I want to do the backstory of Kenobi as a young man—a story of the Jedi and how the Emperor eventually takes over and turns the whole thing from a Republic into an Empire, and tricks all the Jedi and kills them. The whole battle where Luke's father gets killed. That would be impossible to do, but it's great to dream about."

The "little thing" that Lucas added to introduce and establish his story's genre was a direct result of his choice of reading between drafts. Bruno Bettelheim's *The Uses of Enchantment: The Meaning and Importance of Fairy Tales* was published officially in 1976, but copies must have made their way into bookstores earlier, because Lucas says, "I read Bettelheim, and it all began to inform the story and the characters." Fairy-tale Princess Leia, for example, becomes much more prominent in the fourth draft, particularly in its beginning.

An area that seems to have given Lucas difficulty throughout the many drafts is the period of time between the cantina scene and the moment in which the pirate ship blasts out of Mos Eisley. In different contexts with a variety of foils, Solo's character is searching for a way to define himself, and Lucas is never quite satisfied. In the fourth draft, still searching, Lucas has replaced Jabba the Hutt with Imperial bureaucrat Montross, whom Solo has to outfox in order to take off.

Lucas also further defines the character of Luke, altering his motivation. Whereas in the third draft Luke makes the decision to seek adventure himself, in the fourth his actions and reactions are more varied—he is less sure of himself.

"Usually, the hero has come to a decision on his own by observing and realizing the position he's in and moving forward," Lucas says. "This time the hero avoids that position. But then I have the position thrust upon him—because it's inevitable. I'm taking the existential view and putting a slight determinist slant on it. I believe in a certain amount of determinism, from an ecological point of view. It's that things essentially reach their own equilibrium. If you don't live a certain way, ecologically speaking, you will be forced into a position that will level it. What I would call an 'unpoetic state' will eventually become a 'poetic state,' because an unpoetic state will not last. It can't. It's like economics. It's like life, it's like animals, it's like everything. You can set up an artificial reality, but eventually it will equalize itself, and become real.

"When the challenge comes with Ben at his home after he gets Leia's message, Luke immediately rejects it," Lucas explains. "He wants to go fight the Empire, you can tell that he wants to, but he doesn't feel that he can take on the responsibility. As a result, destiny comes into play. Because if you don't do anything about the Empire, the Empire will eventually crush you. There is a scene where his friend Biggs explains that you can't avoid the issue forever. Eventually it will catch up with you, and then you will suffer the consequences.

"To not make a decision is a decision. It happens in all countries when a certain force, which everybody thinks is wrong, begins to take over and nobody decides to stand up against it, or the people who stand up against it can't rally enough support. What usually happens is a small minority stands up against it, and the major portion are a lot of indifferent people who aren't doing anything one way or the other. And by not accepting the responsibility, those people eventually have to confront the issue in a more painful way, which is essentially what happened in the United States with the Vietnam War."

Lucas and Barry study a set maquette.

(Continued on page 111)

The Adventures of Luke Starkiller as Taken from the "Journal of the Whills" (Saga I) Star Wars, Fourth-Draft Summary, January 1, 1976

FADE IN...
A long, long time ago in a galaxy far, far away an incredible adventure took place...

FADE OUT
...War drums echo through the heavens, as a ROLLUP slowly crawls into infinity...

It is a period of civil wars in the galaxy. A brave alliance of underground freedom fighters has challenged the iron fisted oppression of the powerful GALACTIC EMPIRE.

Striking from a fortress hidden among the billion suns of the galaxy, rebel spaceships have won a crushing victory over the awesome Imperial Starfleet. The EMPIRE knows that one more such defeat could bring a thousand more solar systems into the rebellion, and Imperial control over the galaxy could be lost forever.

To crush the rebellion once and for all, the EMPIRE has constructed a sinister new weapon: THE DEATH STAR. Powerful enough to destroy an entire planet, it spells certain doom for the champions of freedom...

"The awesome yellow planet of Tatooine emerges from a total eclipse," and the adventure begins. This time C-3PO spots R2-D2 receiving the plans from a mysterious young female—and the astromech droid is given a "mission." The shootout has been omitted (perhaps for budgetary reasons), and the script simply cuts to Vader standing in the rebel ship's hallway. The young girl is stunned by stormtroopers, but Vader no longer mentions the Bogan Force when later threatening the girl, who turns out to be Senator Leia.

Down on the planet, Biggs and Luke talk about the latter's fear of leaving to join the Alliance.

BIGGS
...Deak and Windy are going away, why don't you just tell me you're afraid to go.

LUKE
I'm not afraid...

BIGGS
Luke, you're going to be stuck here the rest of your life. If you want things to change you're going to have to make them change. Ahh, I don't know why I waste my time, you'll never break away...

Back on the Death Star, which appears much earlier in this draft, Imperial Senators and generals "sit around a black conference room." Governor Moff Tarkin is now on the side of the Empire.

MOTTI
It won't be long before the Death Star is completely operational, then we will easily be able to destroy

Man-Machine Progression

The identity of the man-machine character changes from draft to draft. The first to reveal his inner wiring is Akira, in the first draft; then it is Montross, in the second; then Ben Kenobi in the third—but ultimately it is Darth Vader who comes to embody the script's ambivalence toward technology or, more accurately, toward humanity. Although it is not explicitly stated, Vader made the jump to man-machine in Lucas's mind while he was at work on this latest version.

"The thing about Vader wasn't really developed until the fourth draft, when I was sorting out Vader's real character and who he was," Lucas says. "The backstory is about Ben and Luke's father and Vader, when they are young Jedi Knights. Vader kills Luke's father, then Ben and Vader have a confrontation, just like they have in *Star Wars,* and Ben almost kills Vader. As a matter of fact, he falls into a volcanic pit and gets fried and is one destroyed being. That's why he has to wear the suit with a mask, because it's a breathing mask. It's like a walking iron lung. His face is all horrible inside. I was going to have a close-up of Vader where you could see the inside of his face, but then we said, 'No, no, it would destroy the mystique of the whole thing.'

"A machine is only as bad as the man that sits behind it," he adds. "It's an extension of mankind, and if it develops bad technology, it's because the mind behind it was bad. Man's relationship to machines is a theme that I have used in all my films, whether it's a boy in a car or the robots in *THX.*"

HE'S GONE TO LONDON TO MAKE A MOVIE

In early January 1976, armed with the fourth draft and a go-project, Lucas arrived in England, joining a production house now advancing at full throttle. He settled into a house in the Hampstead area, and the business of preparing *The Star Wars* for location shooting in Tunisia in late March began in earnest. The small production offices at EMI were now fully staffed: "There's Gary Kurtz, the producer, his assistant, Bunny," Robert Watts says, mentally running down the corridor. "Then there's me and Pat Carr in the production office, with Bruce Sharman, who's the production manager. Go to the accounts department, you'll find Brian Gibbs, the production accountant; he has three assistants and a secretary, and then there's Ralph Leo, the Fox auditor who's with us, and Graham Henderson, who is in charge of controlling set costs. Andrew Mitchell is the managing director of EMI."

Two new department heads had also moved in: costume designer John Mollo and makeup artist Stuart Freeborn, both of whom had actually been hired the previous month, but whose work really started in the new year. "I had been working on another Twentieth Century film, *The Omen,*" Freeborn says, "and we were making some false dogs for the close-ups; otherwise we'd have some bitten artists. George Lucas popped in to see what we were doing, and it all happened from there. He said, 'If you can make these dogs that all work, then have a go at making the animals for this picture.' "

Stuart Freeborn had started his career working with the late Sir Alexander Korda in 1936. He labored under contract with various companies until 1947, and then went freelance, enlisting the aid of his wife, Kay, and son, Graham. "They're usually with me because they know the routine, and they're both very good at certain things."

"I knew of Stuart from *2001,*" Lucas says. "He was the guy I wanted, because I really liked the apes in that film. It was a fantastic job."

On *The Star Wars,* Freeborn was faced with a multitude of creatures instead of just one. "Once we got the prototype on *2001,* they were all designed on the same principle," he says. "For this film, of course, every one's different; each one's got his own problem—every one of them is a prototype."

For his first three or four weeks, Freeborn worked alone on the movie's most important prototype, Chewbacca, creating concepts and masks based on McQuarrie's design. He was joined by his family and assistants as the load increased week by week.

The route to John Mollo was slightly more circuitous. "We were in talks with Milena Canonero, who had worked on *Barry Lyndon* [1975] and *A Clockwork Orange,*" Lucas says. "But she was about to do a documentary on Fellini, so she recommended her assistant on *Barry Lyndon,* John Mollo. I met him and he seemed very good. I wanted somebody that really knew armor, somebody who was more into military hardware, rather than somebody who knew how to design for the stage. I wanted designs that wouldn't stand out, which would blend in and look like they belonged there."

In Mollo, who had written with his brother Andrew several books on military fashion, Lucas found a good match. For *The Charge of the Light Brigade* (1968), Mollo had supervised the creation of three thousand military costumes, and he had worked on *Napoleon* in a similar capacity.

One of the earlier man-machine characters was Montross, but by this point in the production, he had been recast as a background pirate (left, in a Mollo sketch), standing to the right of Jabba the Hutt.

John Mollo

"Milena Canonero rang me up and asked if I was doing anything for the next six months," Mollo says. "And that's how it happened, really. The first few days that I was working, they weren't quite sure if the film was coming off, so I sat around reading the scripts and looking at the deal with a certain amount of horror. Immediately after Christmas, Ron Beck joined and we started setting up a fashion showing for George.

"We got hold of an acting model and a Polaroid camera, and we went along to the costumers where we tried to find items in stock that approximated the drawings. For Darth Vader, we put on a black motorcycle suit, a Nazi helmet, a gas mask, and a monk's cloak we found in the Middle Ages department. We got things from every department and put them all together, and then we Polaroided them. When George came back to England in January, we repeated the performance at Berman's; it was a live fashion show. George would say, 'I don't like that; I do like this.' We did very little drawing; it was more of a practical make-do amend, because there was already an established style."

The style had been meticulously worked out by Lucas and McQuarrie, who had dedicated himself to that task from July 24 to August 29 of the year before. "Ralph and I have already drawn out many of the designs, so it's often a matter of pulling it together," Lucas says. "For the stormtroopers and Darth Vader, Ralph had a very strong influence. Essentially they are his designs. The other characters, such as the princess, Mollo actually did."

Mollo also used paper dolls to try out ideas and, together with Lucas, consulted many reference books in his office at Elstree, often checking with Barry to see how the costumes would fit into the sets. "We're quite

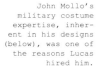

John Mollo's military costume expertise, inherent in his designs (below), was one of the reasons Lucas hired him.

close together," John Barry says. "John is just down the corridor, so we see each other often and he looks at what I'm doing and I look at what he's doing, and we talk about it all the time."

The need for instantaneous communication among all the department heads and Lucas was all the more necessary given their now incredibly accelerated schedule—and as expected, costs began to soar, particularly those related to the building of the sets. "We were very, very stretched at that point. Normally, this sort of picture you'd expect to prepare for twenty-six weeks, or sixteen certainly," Barry adds. "But because it's twelve weeks, it really is frighteningly busy. It really is quite a nightmare."

"We could have had a reasonable number of people working at reasonable hours," Lucas says. "But because Fox waited until the last minute, we had to hire twice as many people and we had to have them working on golden time, twenty-four hours a day, in order to get the sets finished—and that cost us a lot more than it normally would have cost us. The creatures were a big problem, too, because they wouldn't let us start the makeup people. They were six weeks short. Everybody was six weeks short, so, to get all their work done on time, they just cut six weeks off the schedule. It was therefore impossible for everybody, and there was a lot that never got finished. The monsters were part of it, the sets were part of it, the special effects were part of it, transportation costs were part of it—the ramifications go all the way through the picture."

"That's why we've burned the midnight oil for a long while now," John Stears says.

"The overriding thing for me really at that stage was the amount of work that we had to do and the amount of stuff there was to achieve," says art director Norman Reynolds. "We had grave doubts about getting it done in time."

"The most amazing thing about it all is that it's down to Bill Welch, the construction manager, who is making an enormous contribution to the movie," Barry notes.

Lucas would often pop in to see how Stuart Freeborn was doing on his first project, Chewbacca the Wookiee, which he was making from straight yak hair (below, Freeborn's sketches, which bear some resemblance to the man, also below). "I would go in there every day and push the nose around a little bit and push the chin up," Lucas says. "I kept pulling the nose out and pushing it back. It was difficult, because we were trying to do a combination of a monkey, a dog, and a cat. I really wanted it to be cat-like more than anything else, but we were trying to conform to that combination."

"Chewbacca was a fascinating one," Freeborn says, "because he had to look nice, though he could be very ferocious when he wanted to be. It was fun making a monster that looked friendly and nice for a change, instead of being menacing. I had seen a sketch [by Ralph McQuarrie] and I based it on that because it was very good, and it looked just right to me."

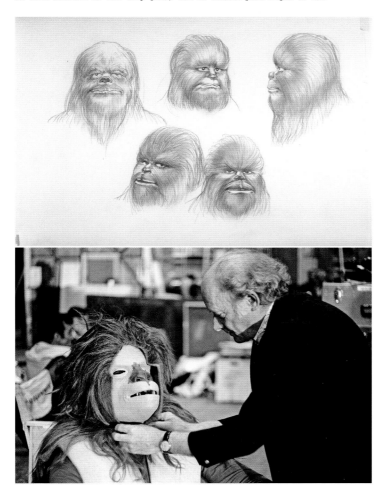

FIRST OF THE FINAL CAST

To rally and coordinate his troops, Lucas held Friday production meetings. To communicate his visual dictates, he had McQuarrie's and Johnston's paintings and drawings, and his World War II footage, but he occasionally screened films to make a point. "George knows what he wants on the screen," Watts says. "I think it first became apparent to me when, about three months before we started shooting, George ran pictures, usually on Wednesday evenings, including *Forbidden Planet* [1956], Leone's *Once Upon a Time in the West* [1968], and Fellini's *Satyricon* [1969]. Tunisia was like the landscape of the Leone film, which was indicative of the feel George wanted to inject into the space age. My own personal feeling about George is that he is an instinctive director; he is communicating through film."

Lucas was also studying how his potential cast communicated through film, reviewing their tests. "You get a completely different impression when they are actually photographed," he says. "How the film reacts to them can be altogether different, too. Sometimes I'm surprised in various ways. Somebody would be really terrific in person, but when you finally get them down on film, they don't work at all; or somebody else might be nondescript in person, but when they get on film, they photograph completely differently—they come alive. It's even quite different going from videotape to film. Some people who work on videotape, don't work on film."

One actor who did not need to be tested for his chemical relationship to film was Anthony Daniels, who had already been cast as the person inside the robot C-3PO, signing his contract on December 5, 1975. "When I went back for the second interview, Pat Carr, the production secretary, asked when could I go to the studios to be cast," Daniels says. "She meant 'cast in plaster,' so I said I hadn't been *cast* in the part yet. She seemed slightly embarrassed and so did Robert Watts. I thought that was a bit strange. But I went in and talked to George again for about an hour, and I asked him, 'Can't I play it, because I'd really like to.' And he said yes. It was just a gas. It was like winning a prize. But I later found out that Lucas had cast me the first time—and my agent hadn't wanted to tell me about it in case I hated the whole idea! So I was excited about the whole thing and started going to the studios to have the costume made."

Following the green light, in early January, negotiations were also concluded with Alec Guinness, who agreed to play the part of Ben Kenobi for £15,000 per week and 2 percent of the film's net profits. "I suddenly thought that I'd like to make two or three more films," Guinness told *The Sunday Times*. "I feel there's a new kind of filmmaker about. The days of the big cigar are over. They live more simply. I find them easier to work with."

"I can see how the story would have appealed to Guinness," Harrison Ford says. "It's a real American story and it has a mythological quality to it; for him it probably has the cowboy-and-Indian concept of America. I think that Guinness thought this was a picture about America."

With Guinness cast, the other roles would have to work around him, as an ensemble. Though nothing else was definite, Christopher Walken was an option for Han Solo, with Charley Martin Smith a Luke Starkiller possibility, along with Will Seltzer and Mark Hamill, who was still in the running despite his own misgivings. "I think if George had chosen Walken, the princess would have been Jodie Foster," Ford says. However, Foster wasn't yet eighteen years old, which was also true for Terri Nunn. Their status as minors would've been a big drawback to the compressed schedule, as they could have worked only a limited number of hours per day.

A CONVERSATION

On January 10 George Lucas debriefed Gary Kurtz on the changes to the film represented by the fourth draft. During their conversation, Lucas mentions new scenes or reworkings of scenes that never made it to the film or any of the drafts, while Kurtz's preoccupations are largely logistical.

George Lucas: . . . We go back to the planet Tatooine and we have Luke and his friends, and he sees Biggs and they go outside. We cut back to a confrontation between Vader and the princess, then we cut back to Luke and Biggs at the Anchorhead power station. The scene is now inside, but we'll probably move it to the outside, or half and half.

Gary Kurtz: The discussion is now later in the film?

Lucas: Yeah. Then Artoo and Threepio are wandering around in the desert. They have an argument, and they split up. Then we go to the power station; we have Luke and Han Solo in that scene, which is the one that may be changed . . . Luke is going to have a scene where he works with the robots to find out where they're going; all that is a little bit different. He says he'll help them; he'll take them to Ben Kenobi, but that's the only place he's going to take them.

Kurtz: They don't think they could make it on their own?

Lucas: Well, they're not having very much success; they'd probably get picked up by Jawas again, so he takes them.

Kurtz: In the crossing-the-desert process [front projection] scene, they're watched by the Tusken Raiders; they make camp and they're attacked by the Raiders?

Lucas: Right. Now, in this attack they don't put him up on the windmill, they just drag him into the clearing and start looting the car; then Ben comes and scares them off. Then Ben takes Luke back to his house, and Luke and Ben get into various discussions about the robots, they see the message, and Ben talks Luke into taking him to Mos Eisley [. . .] So they go, they see Mos Eisley, and they drive through and ask some Jawas for directions, and . . .

Kurtz: You're eliminating the crystal chamber scene, where Darth Vader talks to the Sith knights?

Lucas: The crystal chamber is cut. It might be replaced by another scene with Vader. I'm not sure. I know the crystal chamber part is out, but there might be a scene with Darth Vader in the prison with Leia and a torture robot.

Kurtz: I'm just worried about which scenes are shot with which actors . . .

Lucas: Well, I may be moving this scene earlier.

Kurtz: Let's see, they go into Mos Eisley . . .

Lucas: Right. In the cantina, they have the fight with the rodents, and they meet Chewbacca and Han Solo, who's sitting at one of the tables. Now, here is the tricky part: After the cantina scene, we've faded out or dissolved or cut, and it's morning. We cut to Luke or Han—doesn't make any difference because they're going to be intercut later—say we cut to

Luke first. Luke and a man walking down the alley. Cut to them outside of a speeder lot selling the speeder—

Kurtz: Seen from across the street.

Lucas: —seen from across the street in a long shot. Intercut with that is Han and Chewbacca getting the spaceship ready in the docking bay. And some Imperial troops come in. They want to search the ship . . . I think I'll switch that. Luke and the group arrive at the spaceship. They all get on board and Han starts making ready for the trip, then the Imperial troops arrive. They get into a gunfight with the troops. Really Han does, nobody else does, and they take off just in the nick of time.

Kurtz: It's going to be harder to make that alley scene and the used-speeder dealer work during the daytime than it is at dusk.

George: Well, I can do it in early morning.

Kurtz: Okay, so they sound the alarm. Then we cut inside the pirate ship?

Lucas: Right. Then we go into a kind of warp drive, and they go faster than the speed of light, and there is that scene where they are playing the game and Luke is learning the Force—

Kurtz: Now is that going to be during the time warp?

Lucas: Yes [. . .] And they get drawn in to the Death Star. Then you intercut that with Darth Vader finding out that they've arrived, that they're there, they've caught 'em.

Kurtz: He knows at that time that they're the right ones?

Lucas: Yes. Cut and the troops board the pirate ship in the docking bay, except no one's aboard. So they go out to get some scanners. Cut and it's empty. Bottom panels get kicked out of the floorboards, and our group emerges. They start trying to figure a way of taking off and go into the main living area of the spaceship—and Darth Vader's there. But Ben has mysteriously disappeared. Instantly, in cutting, all of a sudden he's not in the group anymore. Darth Vader says, 'Nice try,' and he marches them off the ship, which is the first time you realize that Ben isn't there anymore. Darth Vader puts them down in a cell. Everybody goes in the cell except Artoo, and they start taking Artoo down the hallway—except when they get down to the end of the hallway, Ben attacks the troops. I haven't quite figured out if Vader's still there . . . No, Vader won't be with this group. The troops march little Artoo down the hallway—and get wiped out by Ben in a very slick way. Then you cut into the prison cell, and all the guys are there, and Ben opens the door and they all escape. They run down the hallway and go into the princess's cell.

Kurtz: How does Ben find out that she's there?

Lucas: He has a way of knowing these things, because he has the Force of Others. It might get mentioned earlier. Maybe he just senses her presence. Afterward, they all go down into the underground dungeon and fight with the Dia Noga. The robots are now in that sequence.

Kurtz: Artoo goes along under the water . . .

Lucas: . . . with the light on, the little periscope—

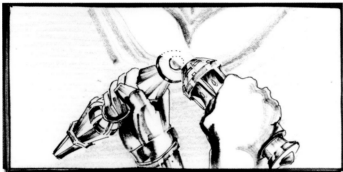

Kurtz: Periscope?

Lucas: The little antenna, something that pokes out of the water. We'll have a skin diver play that part.

Kurtz: Let's back up. When they get put in the cell, what are they wearing?

Lucas: Just their regular clothes.

Kurtz: They don't get changed into prison garb or anything?

Lucas: No. I thought about that. I decided we won't do it. They don't stay in there long enough.

Kurtz: So Ben shows up and helps them escape, but there's no big fight in the control room of the prison?

Lucas: No. Except for the fight with Ben.

Kurtz: Do we see how Ben gets in there?

Lucas: No, we don't see how he gets in.

Kurtz: So they get out of the garbage room and they're across from the starship . . .

Lucas: . . . and they see the starship. This is all very complex. It's going to have to be worked out in detail; I don't know whether I can just sit here and tell it. Ben will split off because Vader will have shown up in one of the hallways, and they will have this confrontation just like they did before. Before they fought over the Kiber Crystal, but now the Kiber Crystal's gone.

Kurtz: What about Ben being wounded, and all that stuff aboard the pirate ship after the end of the fight?

Lucas: Ben is going to be wounded, but not as bad, so there's no big scene afterward. [At one point Kenobi was budgeted for a hospital "smock."]

Kurtz: All right, so you have an exterior shot and the pirate starship arrives and you see the fourth moon of Yavin, and the two lifepods jettison away. This is all in miniature . . .

Lucas: No, you don't see the lifepods jettison away. You're in orbit, and she says, 'The Death Star is behind us, so nothing's going to be here too long.' They're in orbit, and you just cut down to the jungle. You have these shots across the steaming jungle. You cut to the shot of the temple, that one in the drawing, and the troops run out and greet them. They're in a little car and come riding up . . .

Kurtz: A couple of long shots . . .

Lucas: Yeah, it moves right along. You cut inside—

Kurtz: Now, the discussion of where the vulnerable part of the Death Star is—that's in a little side room, in one of the war rooms?

Lucas: In that briefing room, which is connected to the war room; it's all one big room. Half of it is briefing room and half of it is war room.

Kurtz: So then they have the big fight, then Luke comes back and lands, and we have the scene where everybody runs up and greets him, and then we go to the throne room scene. That happens the same way as before.

In England, Ivor Beddoes took over storyboarding for principal photography, while Joe Johnston continued in the States doing them for the VFX, concentrating on Ben Kenobi battling Darth Vader and a group of stormtroopers.

Lucas: Yes. Two points: the Crystal Chamber is now out, and the docking bay control room is now out. I've got to tell John Dykstra about that.

Kurtz: Before Vader and the TIE ships take off, is there anything of them in preparation?

George: Yeah. He can be in a hallway. I think I'm going to have a big control room on the Death Star, because I want to try to develop something where they're approaching the green fourth moon. Truth of the matter, I have much more script than I need . . .

GETTING DOWN TO SETS

The main work at EMI was always building the sets, and Lucas and Barry recommended their intense consultations that had been interrupted by Fox's six-week delay. "For three or four weeks George and I were both sitting on the same stool in front of the drawing board," Barry says. "George has quite a good grasp of it all; he's a mechanically minded person and he understands the blueprints. The most important thing about a set is how it works: What can you see from the doorway? So we talked about that for quite some time, both of us drawing at the same time, and George saying, 'I don't need that. I will need that corridor.' It's up to the art department to try and find out what it is he wants, and then make suggestions which he'll accept or otherwise, but he has an idea in his mind about all these things."

"Barry brought a lot of knowledge about building sets," Lucas says. "How you maneuver things around, use forced perspective, or build a false wall. He did a lot of the set designs, because I had never worked on a set before. I learned a lot from John."

One of the ongoing challenges was coordinating production in England with the special effects in Van Nuys. "They sent me very good photographs of the model—the exterior of the pirate starship— as they were building it," Barry says. "At that time we were building our exterior, too. With the X- and the Y-fighters, they just made two extra models when they cast them. Now the two companies building the full-sized ones have the models in their place, and they're working from them."

"It would be a lot easier if ILM were on the next-door stage," Watts notes, "so we could just dash in and out, and there wasn't an eight-hour time shift, and a shipping situation, and a communication problem. So the director could actually pop over there and say, 'Yeah, that looks great,' or whatever. This is the first time I've worked on a picture where the two powers of the show, as it were, are on different sides of the Atlantic: live action here and models on the other side. It'll be interesting to see the end result . . . "

One of the side effects of working with ILM was to inspire Barry to go into the junk business. "ILM was basically using the same premise that

had been used on *2001*," he says. "They used model kit parts to make their models look interesting. But I had to build full-scale seventy-feet-across versions of these things—but then it dawned on me that, of course, the actual kit parts represent *real* things, like crank shafts, so I could go back to the originals. So one of the first things we did on the picture was to buy thousands of pounds' worth of junk from drain companies and the like—we have a buyer who's a very eccentric and amusing man—and we invested £10,000 in a big machine that had previously been making dinghies and boats. The comlink is in fact part of a faucet. The handle of the lightsaber is a very old photographic flash unit, though we never just picked them up and used them. They were repainted, sign writing was put on, and sometimes they were cast again in plastic. Luke's binoculars are an old Ronoflex.

"I took George to all the fun places," Barry adds. "We went to one of the big weapon-hire companies that had endless rows of arms and armor. We found the gaffi sticks there; we just picked them off the wall, and took something off and whacked them a bit. George and the dresser, Roger Christian, and I got together a lot on those things. Rather than have your slick streamlined ray guns, we took actual World War II machine guns and cannibalized one into another. George likes what he calls the 'visceral' quality that real weapons have, so there are really quite large chunks of real weapons with additional things fixed onto them. It's just so much nicer than anything you can make from scratch; it stops them from having that homemade look."

Reference photos of interesting junk (above), some of which became interesting props through the intermediary of John Barry's art department (left, a blaster).

One of the first special effects tests at EMI concerned R2-D2, which became the model for several other robots in the film (far right, a blueprint for R2, dated January 20, 1976, drawn by P. Childs; a note indicates that the "top section of leg" has been modified).

VOYAGE TO THE UNKNOWN

Following the first special effects tests on January 14 with "laser swords, R2-D2 model, and illuminated control boards," a second test took place on January 23 with "laser swords and Jawa 'eyes.'" Between the two, Lucas sat down on January 20 with Kurtz and director of photography Gil Taylor, who at this point was quite new to the production and clearly coming to grips with many of its technical challenges.

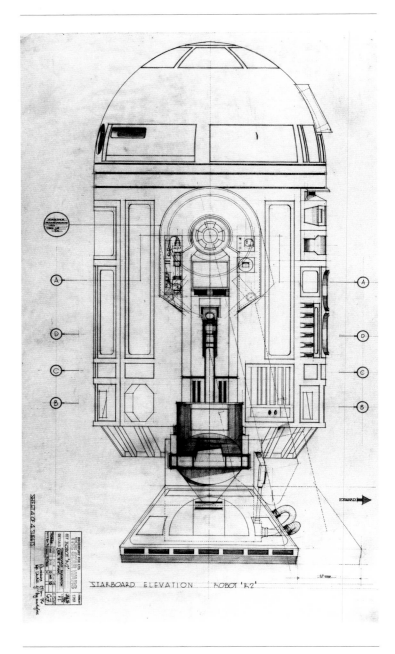

STARBOARD ELEVATION   ROBOT 'R2'

LASER SWORD

George Lucas: As it stands now, we've got three scenes with the light sword. The first scene shows what it is: Luke just turns it on. The next one is a very quick scene in the cantina—it'll just be a flash. In both those cases, it's just one sword. The last is the final battle between Ben and the warlord. That's going to be a tricky one where they actually fight, but at least now it's down to a very controlled setup.

Gil Taylor: Are the laser sword and the laser gun one and the same thing?

Lucas: No. Laser guns are going to be essentially real guns that fire a blank that makes a big flame. We'll make it into a nice laser-gun sound later; then we will optically, in cases where it is necessary, animate the blasts, so you'll see the bolts ricochet around. But you'll never actually have to deal with it photographically.

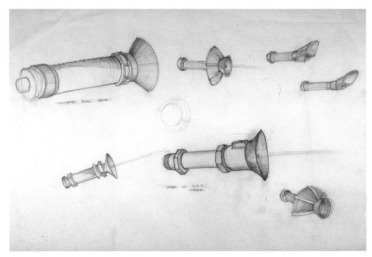

LANDSPEEDER

Lucas: The speeder is very low to the ground, like a hovercraft. It runs maybe a foot or two off the ground.

Taylor: I know it sounds outrageous, but if it was doing a lot of speed and you were shooting down like a railway track, you wouldn't see much at all except a lot of things going by. Of course, I'm going back many years to a Hitchcock film, Number 17, in the 1930s—we had people fighting on railway carriages . . . [Taylor was a clapper loader on that film.]

Lucas: In a car on the salt flat you could go pretty fast.

Gary Kurtz: The ideal way to do it is a Wescam hanging from a helicopter, because it flies at fifty to sixty feet and it's not affected by air pockets. The camera's hanging down as close to the ground as you dare put it, and even if there's a severe jolt the only thing that hits the ground is the camera and it's in a bubble. It's gyroscopic—have you ever seen one of these things in use?

Taylor: The thing is to get the right angle . . .

Lucas: If we had mirrors, or pieces of shiny metal, in front of the wheels, little plates tilted down, it would reflect the ground right underneath it and would help mask the wheels themselves.

Taylor: That sounds like it could work.

Kurtz: I hope we can find a stretch of road that meets the requirement—

Lucas: We found it. I don't know what it's like now—it's rained there a lot—but it was fairly decent. It was a hard, scraped road; it wasn't dusty. There was a problem with telephone poles, but we could mask those out. We don't need that much, about twelve to fifteen seconds' worth, a side view, a front plate going forward, and two side plates. The way the story is written now, there's only one scene like this, and a couple of long shots.

Taylor: Is it an open cockpit?

Lucas: No, it's closed.

Taylor: Oh, it's all closed. So when you've got dialogue, where are you? Are you outside?

Lucas: We'd be outside.

John Stears (top left)

McQuarrie's early concepts for the laser sword (middle left), and production's reference photos of early prototypes (bottom strip).

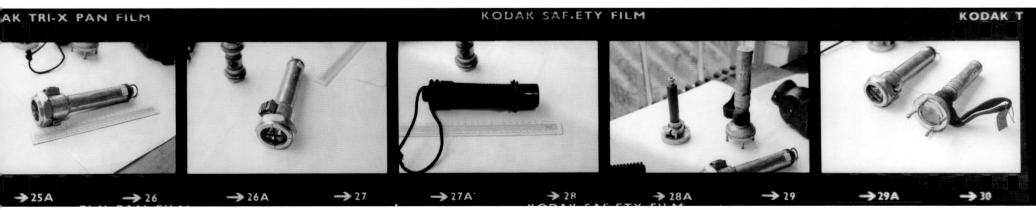

Taylor: I see. Then there would be no wind as such and they would be completely air-conditioned inside.

Lucas: Yes. I want to be outside the ships, the fighters, as well, so we can see the reflections of light on their windshields, and use that as a device to create a sense of speed. I think we'll probably do it on the speeder, too, because then we could have a really quick strobing, and shoot with a slightly long lens—not a real long lens, but long enough to lose a lot of the glass. We can shoot right through the glass. The thing of it is, no matter how fast you're going along, clouds don't move very fast. They won't give you a sense of speed; whereas if we do it in the studio, we could fake something up that looked like it was going much faster. We have a whole lot of process shots with these ships, so we wanted to make some kind of rig that would change the key light drastically—it would zip all the way around, go from one side to the other side in a very short amount of time.

Kurtz: If the key light represents the sun, and the ship is flying along and suddenly turns, then the key light moves over here very quickly—if you've got some sort of a rig to move a single source of light across it. The other possibility that we came up with was to mount a whole raft of lights and have some sort of rheostat mechanism that would allow you to change from one to the other. The problem with incandescent lights is that they don't heat up and die down quickly enough.

Lucas: I've discovered that the one thing that creates the illusion of movement is light. We cut the end battle scene out of all kinds of old war movies, everything from *The Dam Busters* and *Battle of Britain* [1969] to documentaries and *Tora! Tora! Tora!* And the one thing in the footage that makes it real is that the key lights change all the time. Even when they're

just flying along in a straight line, the light is never sitting there; it's always rotating and moving. It's really a nice feeling, even if it's illogical. Even when you can't figure out what's going on, it's nice to see that light dancing across the cockpit glass—there's even a shot in one of those films where half the dashboard is all lit up and half is in dark shadow, and the shadow slowly moves up the dashboard. That's a shot I want to get, where you play with the light inside of the ship as it flies around. Because this dogfight is going to be, hopefully, extremely quick. When we get into it, I want lots of flashing, strobing, and moving light, so the excitement continues from the exterior to the interior.

THE REBEL BASE

Lucas: I want to rely on source lighting as much as we possibly can in the hangar, and design the source lighting into the sets. Things won't be perfectly lit—we'll have very hot spots and very dark spots, combined with the fact that I do want to get a soft edge. I want the film to be slightly filtered to give it a romantic quality. We have to find the simplest and easiest way of accomplishing everything, because we've got so many things to do. If we spend a lot of time trying to do something really complex, it's going to bog us down.

Taylor: Are there going to be practical lamps in the big hangar?

Lucas: There are fluorescents or something. The main thing is that we want it to be very dark. We may want to rig a triangle light with a floodlight in the front. So you'd have a ship sitting there with a ring of these lights around it, shining up at it, these little floodlights that sit on the floor. We could use those on a couple of sets.

John Barry sketches for the "second" and "third" background landspeeders, along with their blueprints.

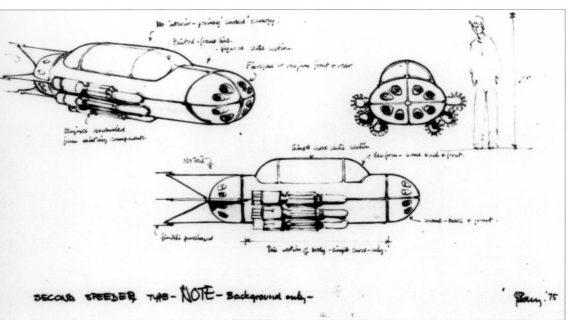

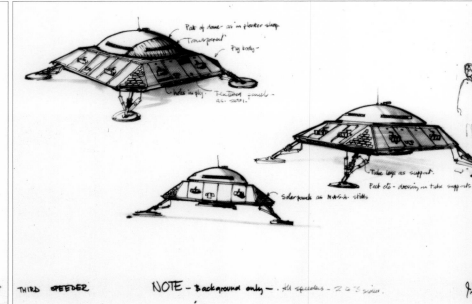

Taylor: But if that's a painted cutout ship and I've got yellow lights, it's going to make all this yellow, which we don't want.

Lucas: We have a real ship. The circle lights will be cold, and the work lights will be very warm, so they'll contrast. I'd like to have lots of lights, because that will work if we're using a slightly filtered look—it'll flare out and make everything look very complex. Combined with realistic source lighting and a slightly longer-than-normal lens, our backgrounds will be out of focus; I think, in a lot of cases, that will save us.

Kurtz: In this particular case, we're going to move the extras around and shoot without touching the camera. Just shoot sectional pieces and have it matted together. The seven or eight matte shots will be filmed with the VistaVision camera locked down; all the rest will be shot normally.

Taylor: I wouldn't have thought there was any studio big enough. Even the sound stage at Shepperton wouldn't accommodate that.

Lucas: Well, we're going to do it in this airplane hangar, so we have the length; we just don't have the height. We're going to try to double-expose the people, so that we have a whole lot of people, and then cover what's left with a matte.

Taylor: We would have to—we can't put in any big lamps, we'd probably have to accommodate that with the CSI-type lamp.

Lucas: Well, the scene can be much darker than it is in Ralph's painting. The only thing that needs to be illuminated brightly would be this strip down the center, and if some of it kicked off onto the first and second rows . . . because if all of this goes dark, it saves us a lot of problems.

Taylor: Would that be a day scene?

Lucas: I don't know. We were trying to decide whether we should do it day-for-night.

THE CONTRACT, PART II

"Right around the end of 1975, all of a sudden this became a go-project," Andy Rigrod remembers. "Then we started doing serious negotiations."

The nine-page deal memo had to be transformed into a production-distribution contract, "which is a monstrous forty- to sixty-page document that formalizes the agreement by which a studio finances a motion picture, obtains certain rights in it, distributes the picture, and shares the profits with the filmmaker," Rigrod explains. "From the very beginning there were tremendous amounts of negotiations with the studio."

Although Twentieth Century-Fox was still calling the financial shots, by waiting so long the studio had actually managed to bargain itself into a corner. Thanks to *American Graffiti,* which by now had grossed more than $100 million and was one of the top ten moneymakers of all time, Lucas was a director to be reckoned with, who would normally receive greater pay. Fox had also antagonized the production by refusing to fund key elements of preproduction and by postponing negotiations—to the point where it was now the weaker party.

"The longer it took, the tougher we got," Lucas says. "Because the longer they dillydallied, the more our stock went up—and the more it looked like we could make the film somewhere else if we really had to. We were willing to take it from them. It was at least two years after we got the deal memo that they finally drew up a contract, and during those two years things

(Continued on page 124)

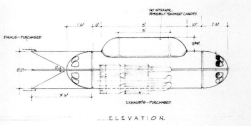

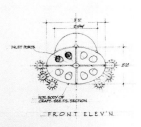

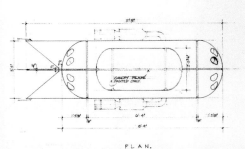

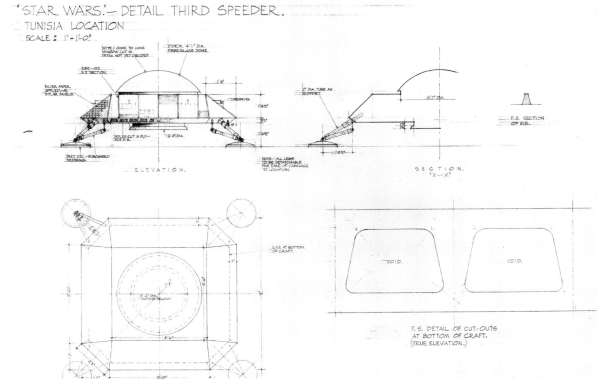

Originally inspired by images from comic books, Luke Starkiller's land-speeder went through many stages, the first back in October 1975. "I terrified George, the poor thing," Barry says. "I can think how awful he must have felt, too. The first thing we did, we built it so that four people could get in, which made it enormous—a great, comfortable seat for four people."

Lucas instructed them to make it smaller, a directive reinforced by their visit to Tunisia. "When George saw the locations, the roads were much narrower than he would have wished," Barry adds. "So we had to find the smallest vehicle there was and make it half as small again. There's a little thing called a 'Bomb Bug,' which is a trike; it has three wheels. We shortened it and squeezed it. I think in the end we made it a little bit too small—there was the problem of getting the chassis into the tiny exterior, and we still had to get the four characters in."

"We may have gotten it a little bit too small," Lucas agrees, "but I wanted it to be a small vehicle, especially since it was Luke's speeder. He wouldn't really be able to afford the big job. We did little clay sculptures of the landspeeder and we had it all designed out, and then we turned it over to a car company in England that actually built it."

Designed by Les Dilley and John Stears, a carousel was built, with a sixty-foot diameter, to propel the full-scale vehicle in circles and make it look like it was hovering when in close-up. How they would create the illusion of a fast-moving hover vehicle in long shots was still a conundrum. "They considered hanging it from a helicopter," Barry recalls. "One of Stears's ideas was a little cable on an underground monorail, with a rod sticking out, which would be easy to matte out by moving the sand around."

The landspeeder went through many modifications. One build had the driver almost lying down in the three-wheeled "trike" with his head at the rear (right). A blueprint (opposite, top) has him in a more conventional sitting position. A John Barry sketch dated early 1976 (opposite, below) shows the speeder traversing the Tunisian grainery location where at one time a scene with Jawas was planned.

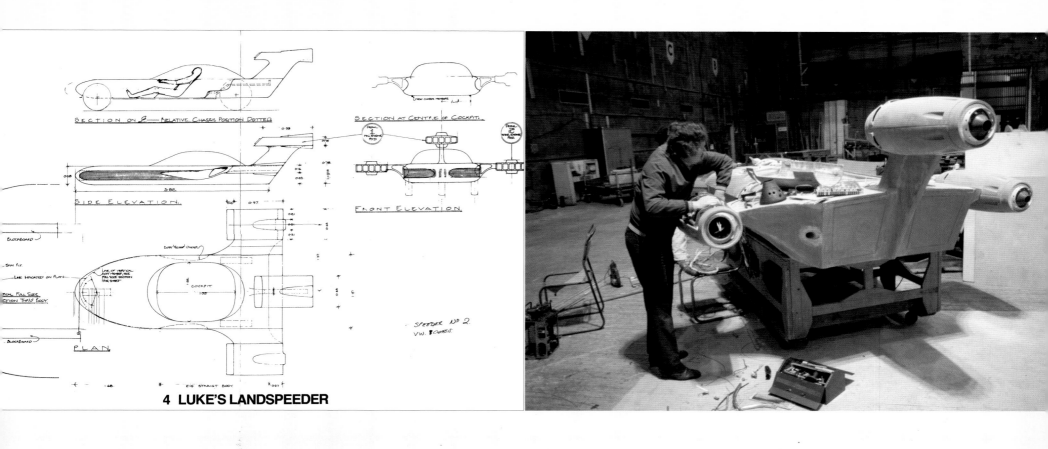

4 LUKE'S LANDSPEEDER

SECTION ON B — RELATIVE CHASSIS POSITION DOTTED

SIDE ELEVATION.

SECTION AT CENTRE OF COCKPIT.

FRONT ELEVATION.

PLAN.

COCKPIT

SPEEDER Nº 2.
VW. CHASSIS

FOUME   TATAHOUINE.   GHORFA.   HOTEL.   ①

had changed. And I had written four scripts—they had only paid me for one—while the least they could have done in that time was crank out one contract. But I didn't go back and say, *I want to get paid for a rewrite; I want to get paid for each script.* We left the deal memo intact. I left the money, I left the points, I left everything that was in the deal memo. But we did say, 'You want to negotiate the contract now? We'll negotiate the *whole* contract.' "

"Bill Immerman, who is the head of business affairs at Fox, and I handled the negotiations," Pollock says. "But we did not renegotiate George's money, which is what they had expected us to do. They had expected us to come back and say, *If this movie is made, George should get $250,000 or $300,000 as a director, instead of $85,000, and he should get more points, and this, that, and the other.* But George didn't need the money anymore, so we went after all the things we wanted in the beginning but never had any chance of getting, because the studio never gives them up. Which is control—control over the making of the picture and control over the exploitation of all the ancillary rights."

"Fox had been working on the assumption that we would accept their standard contract, while we had been working on the assumption that we weren't going to accept anything," Lucas adds. "We said, 'This point isn't right, and we don't want this . . .'—and they were shocked because nobody had ever done that before."

On February 1, 1976, the most formal budget so far was drawn up. The below-the-line budget was $6,568,932, with the total projected budget as $8,228,228; every last expense was itemized, and its cost projected into the future. Lucas was assigned $72,700 to direct and $50,000 to write, while his several trips to Los Angeles and London, his "Living Costs," were reimbursed, totaling $8,210. His out-of-pocket costs were also covered by early 1976. The past was refunded, but the future was wide open. (Proof that things were happening in a somewhat chaotic manner, this budget still had remnants of items from previous drafts. For example, the Kiber Crystal had been budgeted for £300; two Sith Lords had costumes for £500 each; forty Aquillian rangers had costumes totaling £6,000; a Montross pirate outfit would cost £150—while an early address list notes that Bill Bailey had been cast as Montross, and Jay Benedict was to play Deak Starkiller—but only as an extra still carrying the name, as an in-joke, from the second draft.)

"You have to prepare for contingencies that may never happen," Pollock continues. "What happens if the film goes $4 million over budget and Fox decides they want to take it over? You've got to fight that out now, otherwise you'll have no rights later. What if they want to take it away from George and recut it? What are our rights? Everything is negotiated out, every possible contingency—and it takes forever. Andy Rigrod is really brilliant at that—that's his strength in the firm."

"There was an open area in the deal that was always more or less ambiguous," Jeff Berg says, "that had to do with the notions of sequels and television, and publishing and merchandising and soundtrack: areas that were important to George because he knew the life of *Star Wars* would exist beyond the making of the first theatrical motion picture. So those were additional points that continued to be negotiated throughout the complete development phase of the project."

"It was hard for Fox, at the time, to forecast two years down the line and say we shouldn't give something up now if someone came in and offered a buck," Jake Bloom says. "They had a historic way of merchandising films and it was hard for them to understand our client's position. We weren't interested in a buck—we were interested in preserving whatever rights we could and in making merchandising deals, if the upfront money justified the deal. We weren't interested in making a blanket across-the-board merchandising deal, because we felt that if the picture was successful we would be selling out—and in the long run it would cost our client a fortune." Within the film business, more prescient words may never have been spoken.

THE THRILLING THREE

While hard-core negotiations began in the States, by late January, Lucas had decided on his final cast. After getting Guinness, Lucas chose Harrison Ford to play Han Solo, Mark Hamill to be Luke Starkiller, and Carrie Fisher as Princess Leia Organa.

"Harrison's test was very good," Lucas says. "I think he always had the edge because I liked him a lot in *Graffiti;* he had a quality. The Han Solo part wasn't written for him, but I'd had him in my mind when I was writing it—even though I'd decided at one point that I wasn't going to use anybody from the past. And I auditioned other people for that part. I had a black actor [Glynn Turman] who was one of the finalists and more heroic, and I had an older actor [Walken], who was the more maniacal of the group; Harrison was the funnier, goofier one—but he could also play mean. When I went younger with Mark, I decided I would also go younger with Han. The fact that I had Harrison in mind when I did the tests was helpful; he really worked well with Carrie and Mark—the combination was very good."

Turman had also been recommended by Fred Roos, who had been "impressed" by his performance in *Cooley High* (1975), but Ford won out. "I've always had the feeling that I was hired for the job because I did the right thing for that character," Ford says. "Acting is a matter of mechanics, and it was presumed I had sufficient capacity as an actor to handle the material, or was as close as George could get for the part."

Although giving it a different chronology, Ford agrees that Luke and Han were cast as a duo. "I think George cast the relationship between Han and Luke," he says. "That's where George is a real student of human nature, 'cause he picked the kid automatically as soon as he picked me. I found it very easy to assume that relationship with Mark."

"I try to cast it as a very good ensemble," Lucas explains. "You think of it not only in terms of very good personalities who are going to work well on the screen, as good actors who are going to really be at the top of their craft, but also in terms of how all the actors interrelate as a group."

The choice of Hamill also jibed well with the script. "If you read the original description of Luke, it's almost exactly the way Mark is," Lucas says. "In the end, it was between Mark and an actor who was a little bit older and a little bit more collegiate. He wore glasses; he was a little bit more intellectual. He was more like Kurt in *American Graffiti*, and Mark was a little younger, more idealistic, naïve, and hopeful; a little more Disney-esque."

"My agent took me to lunch, and she was going down a list of business matters, like a grocery list," Hamill says, "when in the very middle she said, 'You have the part in *Star Wars,*' and then she went on with the next item. 'Wait a minute—back up!' I interrupted.

"George chooses you for your personality," adds Hamill, who was

understandably shocked when he heard the news. "I mean, as a person, the actor is already so close to being the character. I'm not saying that's true all of the time, but one phase of them is that character. I think if George would have had five more meetings with me, I wouldn't have gotten the part."

The last lead to be cast was Leia. "I had another girl who was much younger, who looked like what you might envision as a princess [Terri Nunn]," Lucas says. "She was very pretty and petite, but she also had an edge to her. Whereas Carrie is a very warm person; she's a fun-loving, goofy kid who can also play a very hard, sophisticated, tough leader. This other girl couldn't play sweet and goofy. Whereas with Carrie, if she played a tough person, somehow underneath it you knew that she really had a warm heart. So I cast it that way. The princess is one of the main characters, so the actress was going to have to be able to generate a lot of strength very quickly with limited resources available—and I thought Carrie could do it."

"I ran outside in excitement," says Fisher, "because I'd seen *American Graffiti* three times and liked it a lot."

The budget benefited from the casting of unknowns. While Guinness's long career and reputation earned him a substantial sum, Hamill's weekly salary was $1,000, Fisher's $850, and Ford's $750. Another veteran English actor to receive more than his American counterparts was Peter Cushing, who was cast as Governor Tarkin and paid £2,000 per day. Apart from starring in dozens of Hammer horror films of varying quality during the 1960s, Cushing had started by playing bit parts in Hollywood films, such as James Whale's *The Man in the Iron Mask* (1939) as well as Laurel and Hardy's *A Chump at Oxford* (1940), later returning to England to play Osiric in Laurence Olivier's *Hamlet* (1948).

"The character of Tarkin, as I kept rewriting the script, kept evolving into a bigger and bigger part," Lucas says. "And after we'd started designing the costumes, and I saw what Darth Vader looked like, I felt I really needed a human villain, too, because you can't see Darth Vader's face. I got a little nervous about it, so I wanted somebody really strong, a really good villain—and actually Peter Cushing was my first choice on that, once I'd decided we were really going to spend some money to go with a really good actor rather than just some stock day-player villain."

"When you get to be my age and you're still wanted, it gives you an awfully nice feeling," Peter Cushing would tell *Starlog* magazine. "The older you get, the lonelier you feel. When you're over sixty, you think you're on the shelf."

The last hurdle to the final cast was the United Kingdom itself, which had to be persuaded to let the American leads into the country. "The only problem that came up was the original equity problem about getting all three of the young actors into England," Kurtz says. "We solved that through the Film Producers Association, saying, in effect, that we need a waiver on this because we have three hundred jobs at stake in England, and we have a lot of other actors that are locally hired. That was just a casual thing. They were willing to listen to reason."

(Continued on page 128)

Uncanny Cans

In early 1976, under the watchful eyes of Lucas and Barry, blueprints began to be generated by the art department's five draftsmen: Ted Ambrose, Rich Greene, Peter Childs, Allan R. Jones, and Peter Shields. The group had a scant twelve weeks to get finalized dozens of complex sets, two very demanding robots, weapons, and armor. "Designing pictures is so difficult," Barry says. "And paradoxically, its contribution to the movie is less than its difficulty, because one wants to make only a subliminal contribution. In a novel, a character's apartment might get three or four pages of description. But the way the audience sees a set, it can make a strong comment immediately on the characters, which is very dangerous in that sense."

Pirate ship interior: A John Barry sketch from November 1975 shows a pirate ship interior consistent with Colin Cantwell's design (opposite, top left—note that only the robots are playing chess), which featured a single long corridor. When that design had to be scrapped, maquettes were made of the new exterior (top right). Blueprints were drawn up on February 17, 1976, of the rear undercarriage assembly; the huge set was quickly constructed (below left); and the interior redesigned (right column).

"It had to appear to fit the exterior, so it had to have a curved design,

a circular corridor." Barry says. "George wanted it to look like a spaceship from *2001* that had aged two hundred years. The hold had the sequence where Luke is training with the remote, so we had to have a wide area, which gave us the foreground part. Then we had to have removable panels, so that John Stears could fit in the controls to the remote robot. The curved corridor had to be built with panels, so we could take them off and get lighting in. The ramp had to match exactly the exterior ship, which we'd already built. So gradually, to a great extent, the design evolved out of all those problems."

Death Star blueprints: The biggest challenge facing production was to build, as cheaply and as quickly as possible, several Death Star sets: a control room, conference room, prison sets, hangar, war room, hallways, elevators, and so on. The art department rapidly generated blueprints for the "garbage room" on February 23; the "cells corridor" on March 1; and the "conference room" on March 12. "The inside corridors we had to build on the stage concentrically, one inside the other, in order to get them all to fit," John Barry says. "Ralph did some more drawings, which were the navy-blue Death Star, based on this concentric concept of the corridors running around. I figured that although the Death Star is enormous, you have to always build it on the curve to remind yourself that you are in a round shape."

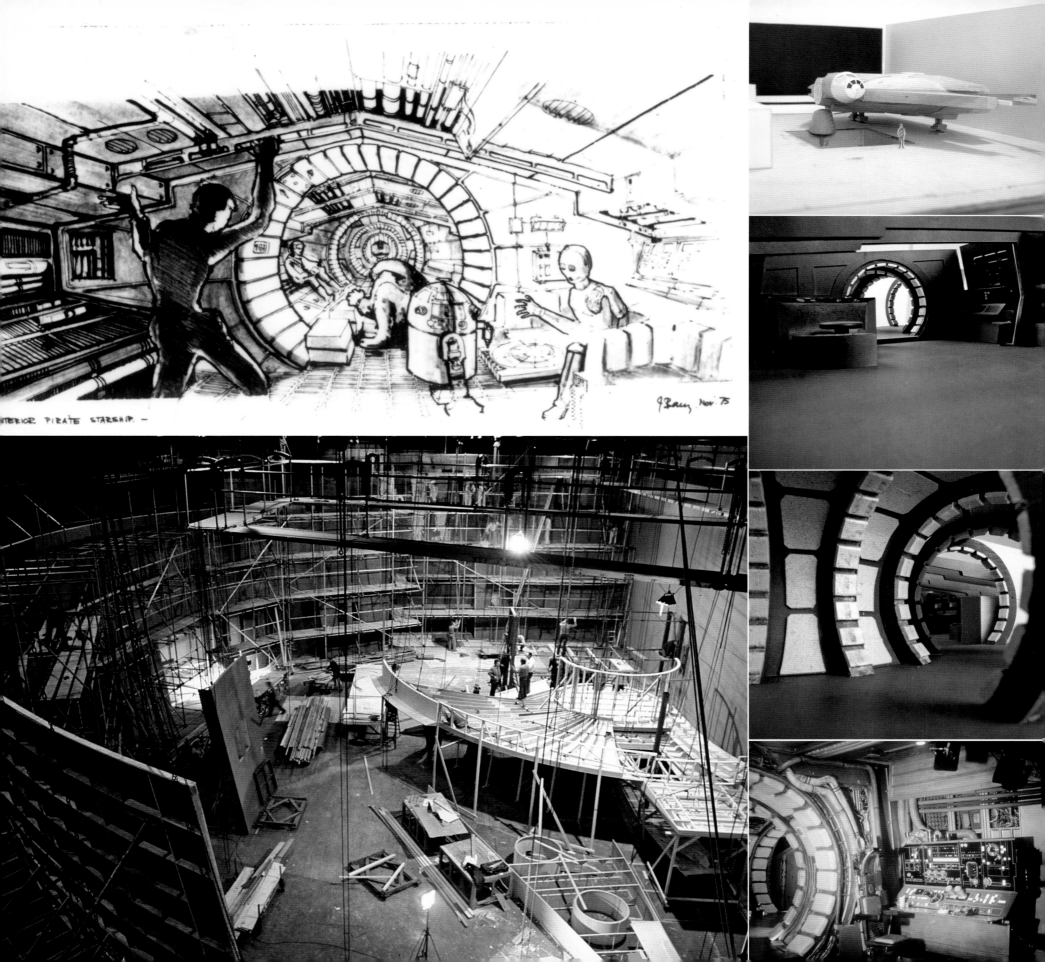

INTERIOR PIRATE STARSHIP. —

J. Barry Nov. 75

PT1145

On the other side of the pond, ILM was making its first attempts at blowing up models. But the explosions were not looking good on film. One errant Y-wing even slid down a wire, detonated, and put a hole in John Dykstra's leg. ILM's predicament was not improved by the possible addition of the jungle planet Yavin to their list of imminently due front projection plates.

Another principal-photography-driven deadline involved computer graphics. "Gary and George had just left, and I was working with Jim Nelson, who was the only authority around here," Ben Burtt recalls. "At this point my assignment was still rather vague. George and Gary gave me no goal, no quota, they didn't need anything by a certain date. They more or less wanted something to listen to when they got back from England. So in the meantime I started working on other things—specifically, they needed computer graphics sent to England to run on those little screens on the sets and on the dashboards of the spaceships. So I was handling that for about three months at ILM; I had to find some animators to do it. Eventually, Dan O'Bannon took over, but Robbie Blalack and I found Larry Cuba."

Ben Burtt records Petulia in the drained walrus pool at Marineland.

A Cal Arts graduate and already a pioneer in the use of computers to create animation, Cuba was awarded the contract in February and began work in March, with a June 1 deadline. His main task was to give the stolen Death Star plans a computer-graphics form for the big debriefing scene. "George knew enough about computer animation to specify the kind of things that he wanted," Larry Cuba says. "He wanted the computer to look like it was really drawing the graphics. They also needed background screens moving all the time, and general computer activity."

The key element of the plans was the trench run that led to the exhaust port, into which the rebels were to fire their torpedoes. "I visualized it as one continuous shot: coming upon the Death Star, flying toward the surface, entering the trench, going straight down the trench, and dropping the bomb at the end into the target," Cuba says. "It turned out, for very technical reasons, to not be a trivial task to make all those continuous linkages from the different ways of rendering things."

Before Cuba left for Chicago, where his equipment and setup were located, he went down to ILM for reference material. "I said, 'Okay, where's the trench that I've got to simulate on the computer?'" he recalls. "And someone said, 'Over there,' and pointed to a stack of boxes where pieces of the modules were just lying there. So I took one each of the modules."

"I designed the Death Star modules," Joe Johnston explains. "They represented, initially, the three trench stages. The theory was that at one end of the trench, where you first enter, there's not much detail: the buildings are all low, and the trench is shallow and wide. But then as you get closer to the exhaust port, the trench becomes deeper and narrower, and the buildings higher and more detailed."

"During the process a trench seemed to be forming at ILM," Cuba says, "so Ben Burtt mailed me photographs that he'd taken to give me an idea of what the trench looked like. But there was no reason to match their design precisely." In Chicago, Cuba set to work using his PT1145 "basic digital computer," which was connected to a Mitchell camera with an animation motor. It would take two minutes to do a frame, for about two thousand frames, or three days of continual computer processing, to end up with ninety seconds of animation.

Ben Burtt was also busy doing his other job: collecting sounds. "George did not want anything in the picture to sound electronic, except maybe the robot language," he says. "Electronic sounds had been in a sense a cliché in science-fiction movies. They wanted to avoid that and have as many organic sounds as possible—real sounds that existed and could be recorded in the world. You can't beat the reality of sound like that. So I went to Marineland and spent some time recording the dolphins, seals, and sea lions. They were in the middle of draining the walrus pool one Saturday, so I went down there and recorded Petulia, a big walrus. A lot of her sounds became part of the Wookiee. Basically, the Wookiee ended up being a combination of Petulia and a young cinnamon bear by the name of Pooh, owned by a trainer in Tehachapi, California.

"The most interesting stuff came from a place here in Burbank called Pacific Airmotive," Burtt continues. "It's a company that builds and tests jet

Several of the nine C-3PO faces sculpted by Liz Moore, with a variety of eye and mouth shapes, were photographed (far left). Following the creation of the mold made from Anthony Daniels's body (middle left), pieces were individually constructed, which the actor then tried on—testing, among other things, his ability to actually walk wearing his costume (middle and below left, with Liz Moore and Norman Reynolds observing). Later Lucas and Barry (top left) puzzled as to how to attach the approved head design to the body.

engines. You've got four isolated engines sitting in a wind tunnel, and they run up the engine and go into a lot of different maneuvers. I would bring the microphones in their test chambers and get everything from 747s down to helicopter and turbine engines. On a gunnery range in the Mojave Desert, where they actually strafed and were blowing up things, shooting rockets, I got some good material: explosions and swooshes and sounds that were used for some of the laser effects. I also had a friend who was a gun collector, from old black-powder guns up to M16s. We checked out about twenty weapons. We shot up the hillsides, got a lot of ricochets. I tried recording them in an unusual way by putting a mike near the gun and by putting a mike next to the target as well, so in stereo you'd hear the bang and the hit."

ROBOT ARMOR

In England, Lucas and Mollo were busy creating the last costumes, with the latter being the next department head to be impressed by the former's spartan directives. "George made pronouncements of a general nature," Mollo says. "First of all, he wanted the Imperial people to look efficient, totalitarian, fascist; and the rebels, the goodies, to look like something out of a Western or the US Marines. He said, 'You've got a very difficult job here, because I don't want anyone to notice the costumes. They've got to look familiar, but *not* familiar at the same time.' That was it! It then came down to asking George, 'Well, is this color right, is this material right?' and going from there.

"We didn't look at any films specifically, but had a lot of books—all the

books there were on science fiction and science-fiction films, books on World War II, on Vietnam, and on Japanese armor," he adds. "I started going around the area in London where all the electronics firms are and buying £20 worth of things. I would say, 'You know, I'm going to be sticking this on a robot.' "

The one outfit for the film's robot-like villain, Darth Vader, had a budget of £500 pounds ($1,173). "Vader was fixed in the McQuarrie painting," Mollo says. "To realize that costume, Vader became a combined operation between the costumiers and us. The costumiers made the basic costume out of leather, while we in the studio made the masque, the armor, the belt, and the funny chest box with lights on it. To me it looks like a Nazi helmet and pieces of trench armor that they wore in World War I. So it wouldn't be too hot and uncomfortable for the actor, we made it in pieces, so that you could take bits off quickly on the set."

While Vader was to appear in only a few scenes, Anthony Daniels as C-3PO was going to be in nearly the whole picture. He also had only a single outfit, but it was budgeted at the much more grandiose sum of £7,750 ($18,189). The road to a finalized C-3PO design had begun with Lucas; gone through McQuarrie's mind, then the shops of John Stears and John Barry, where Liz Moore took over; and finally returned to the hands of Lucas on February 11, 1976. "George had this concept of what the thing should look like, but I did a lot of very simple line drawings of little expressions," Barry says. "Then George wanted to go for a slightly more humorous, silly look, so Liz Moore modeled nine faces. We stood them up at head height all the way around the stage, so that George could look at them, but they were kept well apart so that they didn't interfere visually with one

John Barry's sketch (top right), based on the designs of McQuarrie and Johnston, helped his crew draw up blueprints for the sandcrawler base and tracks, dated December 9, 1975 (far right). Ingenious production design enabled the wheel assemblies to be broken down and packed into trucks for transportation to Tunisia (bottom right).

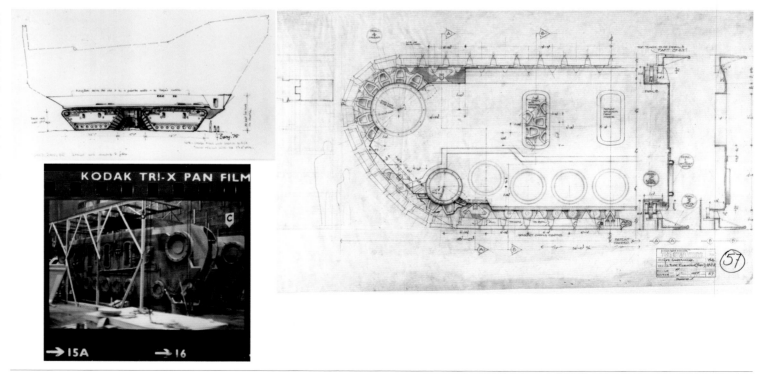

another. Then George, in fact, found two coins for the eyes, and we poked into the clay to make the mouth. He didn't quite like the made-up mouth."

Following the costume show for Lucas, the art department concentrated on personalizing the robot exterior to fit its sole inhabitant. "They told me they had to cover me in plaster," Daniels says. "The glamour of films really hit the dirt when I was standing there cold and shivering, with practically nothing on, and these two laborers came up with buckets of plaster and Vaseline. It was one of the most disgusting experiences in my life. They were very worried about doing my head because they said a lot of people faint. So they stuck a couple of straws up my nose. They said if you feel at all funny about it, wave your arms and we'll yank you off straightaway."

After creating the plaster molds from Daniels's body, from which the metal pieces would be cast, the process hit a snag. "Unfortunately, a few days later they called me up and asked if I had a twisted spine," he explains. "I didn't think I had a twisted spine, but I went into the studio and there was this poor little warped me. The weight of the plaster had pulled me over. So I had to go through the whole body-cast process again. Fortunately Liz Moore was a love and made sure I was as comfortable as possible. She was very beautiful, and there I was wearing ladies' tights wrapped up in sandwich foil, and she was slapping great jars of Nivea all over me. George kept coming in and fiddling around with my elbow or my knee or my shoulder, trying to work out how to make this garb work for a robot."

A cover letter to Bunny Alsup (below right), assistant to the producer, came with a copy of a press release (below left) sent out by Roadrunner Productions Ltd. in which they described, with breathless excitement, the departure of the first road trains—shown here waiting embarkation at Dover on their way to Tunisia—on February 16, 1976 (left): "This is believed to be the first operation of its kind undertaken by a British haulier. Despite lack of time, the most meticulous planning has been necessary, particularly with regard to customs documentation... Within a matter of days, the first convoy of three drawbar pantechnicons and one specially constructed scenery van, with a combined capacity of 24,000 cu ft, was en route to Calais..."

DEBONAIR DIALOGUE

Throughout the first quarter of 1976, Lucas somehow managed to find time, as usual before dawn, to revise his fourth draft into what would be the shooting script. Most of his changes occur in the first two-thirds. However, no matter how much Lucas worked on the spoken parts, they failed to impress him. He decided to hire his screenwriting friends Gloria and Willard Huyck for their verbal expertise. "Just before I started to shoot I asked them to help me rework some of the dialogue," Lucas says. "At the very last minute, when I'd finally finished the screenplay, I looked at it and wasn't happy with the dialogue I had written. Some of it was all right, but I felt it could be improved, so I had Bill and Gloria help me come up with some snappy one-liners."

"I met George at USC, when we were both in film school," Willard Huyck remembers. "A friend of mine and I had made a short film and it got stuck in the lab because we didn't have the $80 to get it out. George was working at a commercial house on weekends, and I didn't know him that well—but out of nowhere, he said, 'You know, I've got the $80 and I heard that you couldn't get your film out of the lab.' So I thought this was such a wonderful thing to do, and we became friends after that."

Lucas and the Huycks had already collaborated on *American Graffiti* and the development of *Radioland Murders*, so they had a solid working relationship that was actually built upon, at least in Willard's case, a similar upbringing. "Willard and I come from exactly the same background," Lucas says. "He came from San Fernando Valley, and his father is almost like my father. Same small-business owner. Small town. Middle-class WASPs. We are of the same social, economic, religious group, and we therefore relate on a lot of levels; there are a lot of similar things we understand and are amused by."

Already familiar with the film, having read several of the previous drafts, the Huycks tightened and lightened the dialogue, while Lucas remained fundamentally frustrated by the whole experience of authoring *The Star Wars*. "It's very hard to write about nothing," he says. "*Graffiti*, I wrote in three weeks. This one took me three years. *Graffiti* was just my life, and I wrote it down. But this, I didn't know anything about. I had a lot of vague concepts, but I didn't really know where to go with it, and I've never fully resolved it. It's very hard stumbling across the desert, picking up rocks, not knowing what I'm looking for, and knowing the rock that I've got is not the rock I'm looking for. I kept simplifying it, and I kept having people read it, and I kept trying to get a more cohesive story—but I'm still not very happy with the script. I never have been."

HIGH NOON

Two weeks before shooting was to begin, the last of the road trains left for Tunisia—without the landspeeder and robots, however, because they were still not ready. The first road train had departed the end of January, and the second in February. Each journey took five days, by ferry to France, by road to Italy, by ferry from Genoa to Tunis, then by road from Tunis to Djerba in trucks—twelve trucks total. The first construction crew was already in Tunisia for six weeks of prep.

The production crew brought with them four Land Rovers, a mobile kitchen, tons of equipment, and, of course, the sets. "I designed the sets that

(Continued on page 135)

The Adventures of Luke Starkiller, as Taken from the "Journal of the Whills" (Saga I) Star Wars, Revised Fourth Draft, Shooting Script, March 15, 1976

The roll-up is the same as in the third draft. Most of the developments in the revised draft are subtle or inherent in the dialogue polish. Biggs and Luke's conversation is less confrontational. The homestead is now placed on a salt flat, in a hole, from where Beru calls Luke before the robot sale, reminding him to get a translator that speaks Bocce. In a now extended version of that scene, it is C-3PO who suggests they consider his astromech friend after the first robot blows his top (it was more arbitrary in the last draft, a result of haggling between Uncle Owen and the Jawas).

In the homestead garage, the conversation between the robot and Luke has been sharpened:

FOURTH DRAFT	REVISED FOURTH DRAFT
LUKE	LUKE
Not unless you can change the unchangeable or alter time.	Not unless you can alter time...speed up the harvest...or teleport me off this rock.
THREEPIO	THREEPIO
I'm sorry sir, I'm only a "droid" and not very knowledgeable of such things... not on this planet anyway. As a matter of fact I'm not even sure which planet we're on.	Uh—I don't think so, sir. I'm only a droid and not very knowledgeable about such things...not on this planet anyway. As a matter of fact, sir, I'm not even sure which planet I'm on.
LUKE	LUKE
That's all right. There is nothing anyone can do about it. You can call me Luke.	If there's a bright center to this universe, you're on the planet that's the farthest from it.
THREEPIO	THREEPIO
Thank you, sir. I'm Threepio, Human Cyborg Relations and this is my counterpart, Artoo Detoo.	I see, sir.
	LUKE
	You can call me Luke.
	THREEPIO
	Yes, Sir Luke.

And now Leia's message is addressed to "Obi-wan Kenobi ... help me!" That is, Ben now has a full name "Obi-wan" (the "wan" resurfacing from the very first list of names Lucas had written). Other small but notable changes are: R2-D2, through C-3PO, suggests that Luke remove his restraining bolt; Owen tells Luke to have R2-D2's memory "flushed"; and when Beru says Luke is too much like his father, Owen mutters, "That's what I'm afraid of."

With the alteration of Ben's name, Luke and Kenobi's dialogue is different when they first meet; the fact that Luke now doesn't understand

A blueprint for
the cantina interior
dated January 23,
1976.

that "Old Ben" and "Obi-wan" are the same person makes the scene play differently:

> BEN
> Obi-wan Kenobi...Obi-wan. Now that's a name I haven't heard in a long time...a long time. Most curious...
>
> LUKE
> I think my Uncle knew him. He said he was dead...
>
> BEN
> Oh, he's not dead, not yet...not yet.
>
> LUKE
> You know him?
>
> BEN
> Of course, of course I know him, he's me: I haven't gone by the name Obi-wan since before you were born.

Within Obi-wan's cave dwelling, C-3PO now shuts down while they talk, and Ben introduces the "lightsaber" for the first time with new dialogue:

"This is the weapon of a Jedi Knight . . . not as clumsy or random as a blaster. An elegant weapon . . . for a more civilized time." And the connection he makes between the death of Luke's father and Vader has become more personal: "he was betrayed and murdered . . . by a young Jedi, Darth Vader." Obi-wan then asks Luke to come with him and learn the ways of the Force, which, because he can't commit to that, makes plain the farm boy's indecisiveness and fear.

In Mos Eisley, Obi-wan does the Jedi mind trick on Imperial troopers, who let them pass without checking their identification papers. After the fracas in the cantina, we cut outside to the robots, who see stormtroopers approaching; in the previous draft, their activity was indeterminate. Back inside, the negotiations between Ben and Han are longer, and the pirate ship has a name: the *Millennium Falcon*.

> HAN
> It's the ship that made the kessel run in less than 12 par-secs! I've outrun Imperial starships, not the local hulk-cruisers mind you. These are the Corellian ships I'm talking about. I think she's fast enough for you, old man.

Mollo's costume concepts for the cantina patrons.

(The "par-sec" is a navigational calculation, not a measurement of time; that is, the ship is fast because it's smart.) Instead of cutting away from the cantina after Ben and Luke leave, Han is caught inside by an alien sent by one Jabba the Hutt.

                    ALIEN
    That's the idea, Solo. You will come outside with me or
    must I finish it here?

                    HAN
    I don't think they'd like another killing in here.

                    ALIEN
    They'd hardly notice...get up. I've been looking for-
    ward to this for a long time...

                    HAN
    I bet you have...

    Suddenly the slimy alien disappears in a blinding flash
    of light. Han pulls his smoking gun from beneath the
    table as the other patrons look on in bemused amazement.

                    HAN
    ...but it will take a lot more than the likes of you to
    finish me off.

    Han gets up and starts out of the cantina, flipping the
    bartender some coins as he leaves.

                    HAN
    Sorry for the mess...

A scene aboard the Death Star has been cut, as Vader no longer senses Obi-wan's entry into the story. Now after Luke and Ben sell the speeder, we cut to Jabba the Hutt, who banters with Han about the money he owes Jabba—for dumping his illicit spice shipment, not for the building of his ship ("aura spice" was first mentioned in the treatment as a valuable commodity)—with the result that Han is given more time to pay. We then cut back to the Death Star, where Vader simply decides to send more men to the planet's surface. The banter in the pirate ship as they try to escape Mos Eisley is different:

FOURTH DRAFT	REVISED FOURTH DRAFT
HAN	HAN
Traveling through hyper-space is no mean trick. Without very accurate calculations we could pass through a star or near a supernova. And that would end our trip real quick.	Traveling through hyper-space isn't like dusting crops, boy. Without calcula-tions we could pass right through a star or bounce too near a supernova. And that would end our trip real quick.

In the revised draft, when Tarkin threatens to blow up Alderaan, he actually does so in the same scene—and for the first time we *see* Alderaan blown to pieces, with the script cutting straight to Obi-wan, who senses it. The gunport scene has been moved from before their arrival at the Death Star to during their escape from it. Instead of Han, it's Luke who says, "I have a very bad feeling about this," when they approach the space fortress for the first time.

New dialogue indicates that Leia has lied about rebel bases on Dantooine, while the Death Star scenes are less numerous and the action tighter. Now when Luke enters the princess's cell, she remarks, "Aren't you a little short for a stormtrooper?" Luke explains that he's here with Obi-wan— which triggers the scene where Vader senses Ben's presence, which used to come after Luke and Leia escaped from the prison cell. In the prison corridor shootout it's Leia, not Luke, who blasts open a way out—straight into the garbage masher, which used to come much later in the story; moreover, the Dia Noga and garbage masher scenes of the second, third, and fourth drafts have been combined into one, more compact, scene.

In addition to being more active, Leia's character is consistently strengthened with sassier dialogue. Upon seeing the *Falcon,* she says, "You came in that thing? You are braver than I thought"; and she gives Luke a kiss "just for luck" before they swing across the chasm.

When they arrive on Yavin, a new character, Willard—named for Willard Huyck—greets them. When Han leaves, it's to pay off his debt to Jabba, not just because he doesn't feel like fighting. During the attack on the Death Star, Leia is also given more prominence with a couple of lines and more written reactions to the fighting.

STAR WARS PROGRESSION

- Homestead is in hole
- C-3PO suggests to Luke that Owen purchase R2-D2 after first astromech droid blows its top
- Ben Kenobi now "Obi-wan Kenobi"
- Luke removes R2-D2's restraining bolt
- Now Kenobi asks Luke to accompany him and learn the ways of the Force, and Luke hesitates
- Kenobi does mind trick on stormtrooper in Mos Eisley
- Pirate ship named *Millennium Falcon*
- Han shoots an alien in the cantina
- Han is in debt to Jabba the Hutt for dropping an illegal spice shipment
- Han Solo blasts off in ship after shootout with stormtroopers
- Alderaan is blown to smithereens on-screen
- Escape from detention area leads straight to garbage masher scene, which now has the Dia Noga in it
- Gunport battle follows escape from the Death Star

went out on location so that they nested one inside the other, so that we would get a lot on the trucks," Barry says. "I made the track units of the sandcrawler in three sections so that we could get them one folded up inside the other— because if it won't go on the truck and it won't go over the hill, then it won't be in the film. It's those sorts of considerations that really pin you down."

Three weeks before shooting began, all of this carefully if frenetically planned work almost became a lost cause. Because back in the United States, negotiations between the Star Wars Corporation and Fox were dragging on and on, up to the beginning of March—at which point Lucas had to call their bluff. A number of elements, which Kurtz characterized as "deal breakers," were fueling the fire: 1) a dispute over who should pay $45,000 in legal fees; 2) still unsigned agreements that affected the chain of title to the picture; and of course 3) all of the details inherent in the production-distribution contract.

"About three weeks before we were going to shoot, I gave Fox an ultimatum," Lucas says. "I said, 'I'm not going to start shooting this picture until all these outstanding points are agreed upon.' Because once I'd started the picture, they would've had me. Once you start shooting, you don't have any more leverage."

In late February 1976, Kurtz flew to LA and met with Alan Ladd. Following the meeting Kurtz called Andy Rigrod, telling him he wanted Tom Pollock and Jeff Berg to talk with Ladd and Dennis Stanfill, chairman of the board of directors, and obtain their verbal commitment that Fox would pay the $45,000. Rigrod's notes reveal that, if these issues were not resolved, Kurtz and Lucas were ready to "fly back"—i.e., abandon the picture. Now that Fox had invested heavily in the film, this was a serious threat—which was made doubly so given the last and most critical piece to the legal puzzle: the American Security Interest and the British "Charge"—two pieces of insurance essential to Fox's ownership of the film, both of which were in peril because the studio had no signed agreements.

For two weeks, negotiations must have hit high gear—because seven days before Lucas was either going to shut down production or board a plane for Tunisia, Fox blinked. Compromises were reached, and though they didn't have the exact language for the final production-distribution contract, the studio gave in to Lucas's main demands. Pollock signed key papers on behalf of the Star Wars Corporation to help Fox, which agreed to pay the legal fees, and Lucas signed agreements formalizing his directing and writing services, which gave Fox its desperately needed "chain of title."

"It wasn't until a week before we started shooting," Lucas says. "Gary went over and got the agreement, brought it back, and I signed it."

In this Mollo costume sketch, Solo's costume directions are: "T-shirt, long sleeves, black jeans, yellow stripe into boot."

MINDSTORMS IN THE SAND

MARCH 1976 TO APRIL 1976

CHAPTER SEVEN

As last-minute preparations were made during the final few days in London, Alan Ladd, newly appointed as Fox's senior vice-president in charge of worldwide production, arrived from Los Angeles to go over some "final points" with Lucas and Kurtz. One dilemma was that ILM was behind. "They hadn't done any special effects," Lucas says. "ILM was supposed to have all the plates for the front projection with the spaceships done by the time we started. It was a key part of the production schedule—but they only had about three of them."

Into this high-tension situation came the first of the leads. "The whole thing was such a parallel of the film," says Mark Hamill, former short-order cook at McDonald's, ice cream scooper at Baskin-Robbins, and copyboy at Associated Press. "Here I am, off on this great adventure to make this movie. I had never been to England, never been to Africa. I was on the plane, and we came down through the clouds, and I saw all of those quaint houses. After landing, I was anxious to hear people talk with their English dialects. Someone picked me up and we went to the hotel. I put my bags down, took a shower, and went straight out to have a costume fitting. The next day they took me over to EMI where I met George and Gary. I was scared of them.

"George took me around and showed me all of the sets," he continues. "They weren't painted or anything; the *Millennium Falcon* was just wood. You can't imagine how it's going to look. And he's explaining all of these things—'We're going to shoot the exterior here and when you walk into the house, this is where you'll be'—and jet lag is setting in while I'm meeting all of the crew. Then George says, 'Do you want to go and see some test footage of the robots?' I said sure and we went to the screening room, and they were all waiting for George. And George says, 'Oh, this is Luke Starkiller.' Everybody just went 'Oh' and went back to their job, and I fell into a chair. It was really exciting, but no one cared. They were all

blasé. I was really interested in what was going on, but I just couldn't keep my eyes open.

"Afterward, I left to go back to my hotel—and got lost. I thought I'd walk around and see things. Well, nothing's on a grid in England. Three hours later, I'm still trying to find my hotel. It got so bad that I tried to get help in another hotel. I'm looking through my wallet for something, a matchbook, and they're starting to get very worried—with the Tube bombings and the IRA—so they want my passport number. But I couldn't think of it, so they called the police. And I'm sitting there with the police in a paddy wagon, and they're asking, 'Was it the Dorchester? The Grosvenor Square?' Finally, magically, we hit upon it."

LAST PLANE TO TUNISIA

As Ladd and Kurtz finalized cost estimates, the wardrobe budget came out to about £90,000 ($220,000). "In fact it was really quite a comfortable budget," Mollo says. "The materials that were used were so cheap, you see." One item that stood out, however, was the cost associated with the stormtroopers, who ran up a tab of £40,000 ($93,000)—and whose final outfits were still not ready a week before location shooting was to begin. "Stormtroopers were the nightmare costume," Mollo explains. "We got a model in of suitable size, did a plaster body cast, and Liz Moore modeled the armor onto this figure. Then everybody used to go in and say, 'Arm off here, arm off there,' and George changed all the kneecaps. This went on for several weeks. Finally that was all taken away and produced in vacuum-form plastic—but the next question was: How does it all go together? And I think we had something like *four days before shooting,* but we just played around until we managed to string it all together in such a way that you could get it on or off the bloke in about five minutes.

While last-minute preparations were completed in England, last-minute construction of the sandcrawler and other sets were under way in Tunisia, with the arrival of the road trains from England (left)—though even mules were necessary for additional transportation (below).

"On top of all this, George announced that he was going to take some stormtroopers on location, and he wanted them to be in 'combat order.' I said, 'Oh yes, George, what's combat order for stormtroopers?' and he said, 'Lots of stuff on the back.' So I went into this Boy Scout shop in London and bought one of these metal backpack racks; then we took plastic seed boxes, stuck two of those together, and put four of those on the rack. Then we put a plastic drainpipe on the top, with a laboratory pipe on the side, and everything was sprayed black. [laughs] This was the most amazing kind of film! George asked, 'Can we have something that shows their rank?' So we took a motorcyclist chest protector and put one of them on their shoulders. George said, 'That's great!' We painted one orange and one black, and that was it!" Mollo concludes, happily.

Last-minute solutions were also found for the C-3PO costume. "They finally did hit on specially engineered wheels and rings that fit in beautifully with each other," Daniels says. "But all this took so long that I only put on the complete costume once, just before we flew to Tunisia."

One of the major cost overruns occurred because these sort of final adjustments were being made so late, due to the studio moratorium. Certain sets and equipment didn't make the last road train, which would've cost around $5,000. Instead production had to charter a Lockheed Hercules C-130 aircraft at a cost of $22,000, round trip, for the last shipment just two days before shooting began.

To celebrate their impending adventure, Lucas and Kurtz threw a cocktail party for the cast and crew at the Hotel Africa in the Maghreb room on March 17 at 6:30 PM. "I guess I came in on Tuesday," Hamill says. "Thursday I had off. Friday, I had lunch with George and Gary in a Chinese place. Then the big day arrived. It was Saturday, March 20: We were down at Heathrow Airport and were ready to zip out to Tunisia. That was the first time I saw any of the crew that were going to be shooting. That was fun. That was like field-trip day. You got your bags with STAR WARS stickers on them. I thought to myself, 'I'm going to Africa!' And off we went."

THE FIRST NIGHT

Lucas, Hamill, Daniels, and company flew from London to Djerba on a chartered British Airways flight. That night was a layover before they continued by car and truck to Nefta. The week before, Anthony Daniels had been playing in *Rosencrantz and Guildenstern Are Dead* at the Criterion Theatre in Piccadilly Circus. "It's a very taxing play," he says. "But I still didn't sleep the first night in Tunisia, because there were a lot of German tourists trying to find their rooms at four in the morning, and we had to get up at six."

"We landed in Djerba, and there was a huge hotel complex," Hamill says. "Four hotels all next to each other—you could get lost on the way to your room. It was insane. It was all one story, just spread out. Golf courses, restaurants, discothèques—I thought, *Is this what Africa is going to be like?* But the next day we started out real early and drove forever in the rain to the salt flats."

At Nefta, the biggest nearby town was Tozeur, "which was tiny," Robert Watts says. No stranger to location shooting, Watts had handled productions all over the world, including Japan, Finland, Spain, Germany, Colombia, and the Kalahari Desert. "A lot of nomadic people used to come out of the Sahara, these black-dressed Berber women who still cover their faces. You can only see one eye like that. And they were a terrible hassle at night driving through the town because you couldn't see them."

After running smack into the bargain-tour crowd in Djerba, the newly arrived crew had to deal with the Franco Zeffirelli television production of *Jesus of Nazareth* (1977), which was also lodged in Tozeur. "It was a twelve-hour miniseries," Kurtz says. "And they had used up all the local technicians, all of the plaster and rental cars—and all of the hotel space. The big hotel was closed due to remodeling, so people had to double and triple up, and stay in fourth-rate hotels. That was okay for two weeks. We could survive that. But if it had been two or three months, we would have had a riot on our hands."

The Star Wars location crew numbered about a hundred people from England and twenty-five Tunisians. The two groups communicated in French, primarily through the assistant directors and the Arabs from Tunis, as Tunisia used to be a French colony. The night of Sunday, March 21, those who could got some sleep in their cramped quarters, preparing for a production that had already been almost three years in the works, but still wasn't ready for prime time.

REPORT NO. 1: MONDAY, MARCH 22, 1976
CALL: 06.30; SALT FLATS AT NEFTA; SETS: EXT. LARS' HOMESTEAD; SCENE NUMBERS: 26 PART [PURCHASE OF C-3PO AND R2-D2]; 29 PART [LUKE AND GIANT TWIN SUNS]; B29 [LUKE AND C-3PO RUSH OUT OF HOMESTEAD TO LOOK FOR R2-D2]
Note: Not every scene shot is listed; some scenes were shot over several days, which is signified by "Part" or "PT."

Cast and crew arrived on the salt flats at Nefta, where the sandcrawler partial set was ready for them. Lucas needed only the bottom portion for his location shoot, including scene 26, in which Owen Lars purchases the robots. (Above) Lucas talks to Phil Brown (Owen) and Mark Hamill (Luke).

The first day's scenes featured Hamill, Daniels, Kenny Baker in the R2-D2 shell, and Phil Brown as Uncle Owen. Lucas's notes reveal that Brown was cast because he was a "good Owen-type, a scruffy American"—something that Brown could relate to. "Uncle Owen was a straightforward curmudgeon—which I am anyway," Brown says.

The day's most complicated scene was the purchase of the robots. Extras included twelve local children as Jawas. Struggling to join them was a tired Daniels. "I couldn't sleep in Nefta, either," he says. "The first morning of filming I was so tired, I didn't care at all about anything. The final costume took two hours to put on. It fit tightly. Two bolts went into the neck, and it was bolted just above the waist, so there was no way on earth that I could get out of that thing. It was precision-engineered, and if I got in the way, I got very badly cut up. By the time I walked ten paces out of the tent on the Tunisian salt flat, it hurt so much that I couldn't make it to the set about three hundred yards away. I kind of hobbled and lurched over to the set and we began filming—but I just felt I wasn't going to make it through the film."

Hamill, on the other hand, was enjoying the first day. "It was really great," he says. "All of that stuff was supposedly happening on my planet, Tatooine, so there was a modicum of continuity. That was the beginning of the movie and I really got to know Threepio, the actor playing him, as well as the character. It was real easy; it was like it was happening in the film."

As the sun rose, Daniels, encased in his armor, learned a valuable lesson. "On the first day's shooting, the script had a lot of technical vocabulary. I had to say 'binary loadlifters,' which I still can't say. And we must have done quite a few takes before it occurred to me that it didn't matter what I said, because my lips weren't moving."

While Daniels resolved one problem, however, others waiting in the wings came to the fore. "Things started to go wrong," Kurtz says. "The Artoo unit was not working right, the batteries would run down too early,

Anthony Daniels (below): "I saw a chair one day and it said ANTHONY DANIELS on the back of it, and I was very excited about that. But I never got to sit in the chair because I could never sit down. I had this terrible leaning board, a kind of medieval thing with arms that allowed me to recline at about seventy degrees, which was very little use at all, because the weight still went down to your ankles. I wore ordinary nylon leotards and tights and some very nasty little sailing shoes from Libby White's in London—I wore one pair throughout the film, and they got very battered. I had gold shoes under the gold legs, which went up onto a pair of trousers made of fairly thick plastic bolted together at the hip. It had a rather large crotch, which I think George liked to define as 'space eroticism.' And then I had a kind of corset, which was made of very thick rubber and sewed by hand. It had lots of spare wires and junk, which during the course of the film changes incredibly. Fitting above that is a front and back piece. The front piece contains the left armhole and the back piece contains the right. The arms were slid up and hooked on the shoulder. The hands were special gloves made by a sculptor who decided that they should be sheet steel. The first time I put them on, I could hold my hand up for about twenty seconds before it would clunk on the table. They were so heavy, I said they had to make me something else. That was an example of production gone haywire."

and they were hard to replace. The kick-down leg didn't work, and the head didn't turn right. The very first day we had that sequence where Uncle Owen picks the red robot and Luke walks away and says, 'Come on, Red!'—and the red one is supposed to roll out there and its head is supposed to blow up. Well, the radio-controlled robot had all the controls *in* the head, so we couldn't put the exploding head on it.

"So we all stood around for a few minutes looking at each other and saying, 'Wait a second. The script says the robot is rolling along and the head blows off. Now, you guys are supposed to know better than this. You're the ones who designed this stuff.' But we knew that nobody had had enough time to get ready," he adds, "so we accepted all the problems on location. We had rushed and rushed to get ready for Tunisia, and I even considered postponing for two weeks, but we would've gotten into hotter weather, and that would have been a real disaster. So we went ahead with it.

"We ended up taking the fiberglass backup robot, putting it on a piano wire, and putting the exploding head on that. Les Dilley ran off and repainted it to match the red one."

"There were all kinds of robots careening over the desert," says Kenny

Baker, who was inside R2. "They were all charging around on the flat desert. Jack Purvis was yelling, 'Look out! There's a robot coming!' and it just crashed into me, tipped me over."

Though this was surely not the best way to start the shoot, Lucas's demeanor had an effect on at least some of the crew. "He's always calm. Even if he has a storm going on inside of him, he's very calm and soothing," Hamill says. "Amazing things would go wrong technically. He'd be working with four robots in one shot and one's radio-controlled, one's hydraulic air-powered, one has a midget inside, and another's on strings like a big marionette. If two of them hit the mark, it's a print. I was amazed, because George moved really fast. I never felt he was really slighting the film, though. I'm sure there was a certain amount of compromise, but we moved really fast."

"George is very good at compromising," Barry agrees. "When Artoo falls off the ramp or something, he doesn't mind because he knows he's going to not use the shot at that point; he'll cut away to something else. He's prepared to ride the punches, as it were."

By the time the unit wrapped on the first day, though the first of 355 scenes had been shot, they had failed to capture Luke and the "twin suns" because the Tunisian weather hadn't cooperated. As for Daniels, who had started out relaxed, he was suffering terribly. "At the end of the first day, I was covered in scars and scratches," he says. "I was very, very tired and very cross. That was the last time I ever wore the costume all day."

UNIT DISMISSED: 19.20; SCS COMPLETED TODAY: 1;
SCREEN TIME TAKEN TODAY: 2M 43S.

With "Red" on a piano wire, the robot was made to explode on cue after some frantic scrambling (left).

Scene B29, in which Luke looks for the little robot who has fled, was shot at the end of Day One (below right).

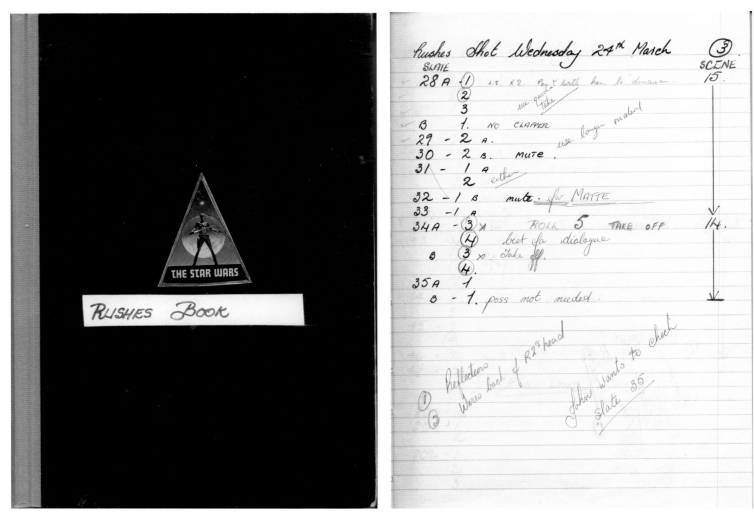

REPORT NOS. 2–4: TUESDAY, MARCH 23–THURSDAY, MARCH 25, 1976
CALL: 06.30; SALT FLATS AND SAND DUNES AT NEFTA; SETS: EXT. LARS' HOME-
STEAD; EXT. EDGE OF DUNE SEA; EXT. DESERT WASTELAND; EXT. SANDCRAWLER;
SCS: 26; 15 [C-3PO AND BLEACHED BONES]; 14 [C-3PO AND R2-D2 ARGUE ABOUT
WHICH WAY TO GO]; B32 [STORMTROOPERS FIND EVIDENCE OF DROIDS]; C42 [LUKE
DISCOVERS DEAD UNCLE OWEN AND AUNT BERU]; 3 PART [LUKE IN WASTELAND WITH
DROID THAT MALFUNCTIONS]

At the end of the second day they again failed to get the sunset shot, as clouds unloaded "torrents" of rain on the desert, and the trucks carrying equipment got stuck in the mud. On the morning of the third day location auditor Ralph Leo left with the first day's rushes, so John Jympson could start editing back in England, and Daniels's difficult life in his metal prison continued during scene 15.

"If you look carefully when I'm walking past the big bones in the desert, you'll see that I can barely move," he says. "In fact, just as I got 'round the corner, I fell over. I was found with my arm sticking in the sand at ninety degrees, because, once I fell down, I couldn't retrieve myself. And if nobody stood in my immediate range of vision, I was totally alone on that sand dune. My hearing wasn't good, either, so I would spend many hours in my own little world unable to join in and chat with people. In the evenings I would seek out the biggest group of people making the most noise to relocate myself as a human being."

That afternoon, Sir Alec and Lady Guinness arrived in Tozeur, but weather conditions continued to worsen, forcing Lucas to halt shooting at 5:57 PM due to "bad light."

By the fourth day, despite the several setbacks, cast and crew were becoming familiar with their surroundings and one another. The location caterers, working in the mobile kitchen, managed to produce steak-and-

Daniels had to be pulled out of the sand after he'd waved on camera (below) and then walked off camera behind a sand dune and fallen over. The bleached bones were first assembled and approved in England (middle strip) before being shipped to Tunisia.

(145)

kidney pie, while Mark Hamill and Gary Kurtz had discovered a mutual love of Carl Barks's Donald Duck comics.

"We worked like stink, twenty hours every day," Robert Watts says. "It was a very good shakedown period for a crew. To really get together out on location, and do it up front before you get to the studio, is good—to eat out of each other's pockets, particularly in a small town like Tozeur."

Because the production stayed in that one town for a few days, word went around that they were sometimes hiring, and Watts ended up employing a local youngster. "When I'd leave in the morning and every night when I'd come back, this kid is standing outside the hotel. So I'm not going to give him a job, because the minute I do, all his buddies will ask me for jobs. In the end, though, I decided I needed an office boy. He worked out very well because he worked very hard."

But in order to make up for the time they were losing, production had to split into two units. The second unit covered "Jawa activity shots with robots in front of sandcrawler," while the first unit shot scene B32 with stormtroopers, played by "six local men" who were paid 8,500 dinars for the day ($6.50). The delays necessitating two units were partly due to unusually bad weather, but also to the earlier, unnatural holdups caused by the studio.

"It was purely a case of Fox not putting up the money until it was too late," Lucas says. "Every day we would lose an hour or so due to those robots, and we wouldn't have lost that time if we'd had another six weeks to finish them and test them and have them working before we started. Whereas before there were only about five or six people involved in the special effects, once we were on location with 150 people involved, we were paying much more in salaries—so that six-week delay cost an enormous amount of money. Ultimately, we had to scrap whole days out there in Tunisia and say, 'Okay, we'll try to pick that up when we get back to the United States.'"

Another robot crisis occurred when the truck carrying several of them caught fire, and two robots slated for the homestead set were damaged.

SCS COMP: 5; TIME TAKEN: 6M 46S; DAILY STATUS: 3/4 DAY OVER

"We had a black all-in-one leotard for the stormtrooper costume," Mollo says, "over which the front and back of the body went together; the shoulders fit onto the body, the arms were slid on—the top arm and the bottom arm were attached with black elastic—a belt around the waist had suspender things that the legs were attached to. They wore ordinary domestic rubber gloves, with a bit of latex shoved on the front; the boots were ordinary spring-sided black boots painted white with shoe dye. Strange to say, it all worked."

Problems with the landspeeder also played a part in the decision to do pickups in the United States. The scene with the banthas, however, which were to be portrayed by elephants, had always been scheduled for later. "By the time we would have dragged out two circus elephants and fought with them and waited around endlessly with the crew, entailing all those associated costs, it was clear that it was not a practical idea," Barry says.

Despite slow going, the one scene completed on Day Five—in which Luke finds an errant R2-D2—helped Hamill better understand his character. "George is Luke," Hamill says. "He is. I always felt that way. We were in the desert one time—it was the scene where I had just found Artoo after he ran away—so I ran up and said, 'Hey, where do you think you're going?!' And to Threepio, 'Do you think I should replace the restraining bolt?!?' But George came up to me and said, 'It's not a big deal.' He acted it out, just walking up and saying, 'Noo, I don't think he's going to try anything.' At that point, I was thinking, *Well, he's doing it so small, so I'll do it just like him—and he'll see how wrong he is.* So I did it like that—and he said, 'Cut. Print it. Perfect.' So I thought, *Oh . . . I see.*

After Sir Alec and Lady Guinness were greeted upon their arrival by Lucas (above left), they chatted with Mark Hamill (left) while the director conferred with his DP, Gil Taylor (below). Later they shot Luke looking into the skies while tending to a moisture vaporator (above right). "Luke's poncho was just a straight blanket with some edging to it," Mollo says. "There were all sorts of funny sombreros and hats, but eventually we abandoned the hat for Luke." In total, five outfits were made for Luke at a budget of £2,020 ($4,700). "The moisture collectors were made out of airplane junk," John Barry says, "but somehow they look believable."

When Luke (jumping out of his land-speeder perched on its carousel arm, left) finds his dead aunt and uncle, Hamill thought it would be appropriate for his character to fall on his knees sobbing, but Lucas preferred a more neutral performance, so that audiences would be able to project their feelings onto him. Lucas knew that later on he would edit the sequence in keeping with the art of montage as explained by early Russian filmmakers such as Sergei Eisenstein and Lev Kuleshov, in which the juxtaposition of shots would arouse emotion, rather than just the actor's performance.

Mules once again were used to help carry equipment to remote areas, such as the spot where they filmed the arrival of Ben Kenobi (right); while Lucas conferred with his crew, however, delays with the little robot persisted (below).

Opposite: Lucas, Guinness, and Hamill watch and wait before filming Obi-Wan's first scene.

THE MAKING OF STAR WARS

"After that, I often felt like I was playing George; I even went so far as to do his little beard gestures," Hamill adds. "George even gave me his nickname, *The Kid*; they used to call George The Kid until he grew his beard."

Daniels was also getting into character. "See-Threepio is a kind of English butler, a cross between Laurel and Hardy with his friend," he says. "He loves being around Luke because that's his purpose—to look after people—he wants to make them happy. I think that's one reason why the part works. This unlikely shape has all the human attributes and possibly more, though it seems outlandish, because he isn't human. The odd thing was I kept acting the whole thing out, facially, if I were emotionally upset in a scene or angry, even though no one could see me."

Friday's shooting again wrapped early due to heavy rains—and on Saturday the bad weather reached its peak, developing into a terrific storm. "We get up in the morning, and though we are supposed to be in the sun-drenched southern part of Tozeur, it is pissing rain and there's a wind like you wouldn't believe," Watts says. "So I call a rest day, and I go down to Les Dilley and take him out to the salt flats. We drove out in the Land Rover all right—but when we got out of the car, it was so slippery we couldn't even stand up. Luckily the local security guards had these Wellington boots, with the heavy treads on the bottom. We had one each supporting us, so we could get out to see the damage to the sets. The top had gone off the homestead and that was already halfway to Algeria somewhere."

"It had blown away," Barry says. "It blew three miles in the night, it just rolled and rolled and rolled."

"The sandcrawler had been completely blown apart!" Lucas recalls. "Stuff had gotten stuck in the mud. Then the army trucks that came to pull the stuff out of the mud got stuck in the mud—and stayed there until the weather changed."

The crew regrouped and rebuilt, however, and on Sunday, Guinness appeared for the first time in costume as Ben Kenobi. "What I remember about Sir Alec Guinness was that, before going on camera, he lay down in the sand in his brand-new clean costume and dirtified himself," Bunny Alsup says. "I thought this was unique and wonderful. Only later did I realize that George probably asked everybody to do this because one of his goals on the film was for everything to be used and dirty."

Having arrived several days earlier, Guinness was playing the scene in which he finds Luke in the canyon after the Tusken Raiders have attacked. "We worked about a week without him, but we'd see him," Hamill says. "I think Tony Daniels and I had dinner with him and his wife, Lady Guinness, twice."

As they quickly filmed the canyon setups, Hamill adjusted to working with the vastly experienced older actor. "At first, I felt very much like you do when you go before the principal, but then I thought I should be more myself, because that's what he's like. So we loosened up to the point where I could just sit next to him and not say anything for an hour while they were setting up. I know he really liked that. He felt that we were taking each other into our confidences. Two or three times, he would say, 'May I suggest something?' And, gosh, I wish he would do that all the time, because he was always right. He would say, 'Stop and think of what you're saying. Are you *talking* about going or are you *going* there?' Because it's

Alec Guinness as Ben Kenobi chases off the Tusken Raiders and revives Luke, who lies next to his landspeeder (its supporting post is concealed by a rock, below).

not the fact that I'm going but *where* I'm going. Little things like that. You'd think about it, and, usually after you'd shot it and were on your way home in the car, you'd understand what he meant."

"We did work in Tunisia on these extraordinary salt flats," says Guinness, who was enjoying himself. "There's a great feeling of strange space that stretches on for hundreds of miles; it's genuine, real and gritty—it's not some made-up world."

SCS COMP: 7; TIME TAKEN: 11M OS.

REPORT NOS. 8–10: MONDAY, MARCH 29–WEDNESDAY, MARCH 31, 1976
TOZEUR; ROCK CANYON; SCS: 38 [TUSKEN ATTACKS LUKE]; 47 [VIEW OF MOS EIS-
LEY, "SCUM AND VILLAINY"]; 35 [TUSKEN RAIDERS ESPY LUKE IN LANDSPEEDER];
17 [JAWAS NEUTRALIZE R2-D2]; 18 [JAWAS CARRY R2-D2 TO SANDCRAWLER]; B42
[LUKE AND BEN DISCOVER DEAD JAWAS]; E42 [JAWA BONFIRE]

By Monday, on a logistically complex day, with first and second units working on the salt flats and in the canyon near Tozeur, several scenes were completed: Obi-Wan's arrival; Luke watching the battle in space; and stunt supervisor Peter Diamond playing the Tusken Raider who attacks Luke. The veteran stuntman and actor rehearsed without costumes—but when the cameras rolled and Diamond donned the Tusken headgear, he realized he couldn't see. As Hamill dodged the blind stuntman's violent blows, his look of fear was real.

The rest of that day was spent climbing up to the cliff from where they'd command a breathtaking view of the canyon below, which would later be replaced by a matte painting of Mos Eisley. The crew gathered their equipment for the trek—including an indispensable (for the English) tea urn—and packed up the mules and porters. When they got to the top, Daniels was put into his metal outfit just in time for tea and, to his annoyance, had to wait inside his prison for the duration of the break.

At the end of that day, the shot that bad weather had foiled three or four times before—scene 29: Luke and the twin suns—was attempted once more. With the clouds dissipated, they set up the VistaVision camera, waited, and got it.

By Tuesday, Day Nine, production was concentrated in the rock canyon during what was another day of fairly intense filming for the Jawas. Playing those diminutive creatures were Kenny Baker's cabaret partner, Jack Purvis; Gary Kurtz's two children; the son of an English truck driver; Mahjoub, a little Tunisian who usually worked for the hotel in Tunis; and local children aged eight to ten. "The Jawas had to be designed from scratch," John Mollo says. "They were supposed to look like little rats, sort of grimy and filthy. George produced a prototype, which he subsequently felt was too theatrical, so we pulled it back to just a black stocking mask and these eye-bulbs, which were wired on, a little brown cloak with a Russian Cossack hood, and a scarf. Then we'd put other bits and pieces on them the day of shooting just to make them look a bit more formidable."

For the shot in which Daniels had to drop a Jawa cadaver into a bonfire, the body was placed onto his already outstretched arms; fighting his limited visibility, he then tried to coordinate his movement with Luke's, as his landspeeder was swung around by the carousel. Hidden beneath his armor, Daniels was also able to quietly analyze his relationships with fellow actors: "Without being unloyal to Kenny Baker," Daniels says, "he

Peter Diamond, without mask (below left), rehearses with Hamill and crew the scene in which a Sand Person attacks Luke with a formidable weapon—which Hamill inspects with some trepidation (below right), because Diamond would be literally blind when the cameras rolled and he was aiming blows at the actor (left, mattresses were placed to cushion their falls—and Daniels wears shoes because his feet are not on camera).

didn't read the script from beginning to end, so I was totally on my own. In fact, it was very difficult because I would say something to him and there would be absolute silence. Often it was very lonely doing scenes with him, for he wasn't there. As for Mark, I used to kid him that even when I wasn't speaking in our scenes together, nobody was going to look at him because I was gleaming and shining in all the lights, nodding and upstaging him generally—but one of the things that is a delight is the way Luke talks to See-Threepio. The same with Alec Guinness, though he must have had a very difficult time in his career to suddenly start acting with robot scrap heaps."

"I found him to not be an easy guy to get close to," Baker says of Daniels. "We didn't argue or anything, but we were not close friends."

Daniels also overheard a brief difference of opinion between Taylor and Kurtz, as they hurried to catch the fading light for a shot of the Jawas loading R2 into the sandcrawler. "I didn't grasp them all but, 'Who's

meant . . . be lighting this . . . movie, . . . or me, because . . . you're . . . it,
I'll . . . off!" Daniels says.

By the second week of location shooting, the radio-controlled robot
problems had formed a frustrating pattern: "In the morning we had
perfect reception," John Stears says. "But by two o'clock we had all sorts
of problems with interference." They would pick up other radio stations,
which Stears hypothesized may have been due to mica buildups under the
sand. Some problems were resolved by playing around with the aerials, but
as the days wore on new difficulties arose.

"We got some weird signals from Arabic radio stations," Hamill says.
"It was really frustrating. We'd get things almost all ready—and the

robots would go bananas, bumping into each other, falling down, breaking. It took hours to get them set up again."

Also by this time, several questions that had been developing in relation to the script had been posed—and a solution found. The problems
were essentially two: Ben Kenobi didn't really have anything to do in
the film following his escape from the Death Star; and the Death Star,
theoretically a very dangerous place, was too easy to escape from. In short,
the film needed more drama. The answer to both structural problems
was to kill off the Jedi Knight. At one point C-3PO and Chewbacca were
also candidates for death, but Ben was the most logical choice—as it also
enabled Lucas to make an important point about death and its relation to

THE MAKING OF STAR WARS

On Monday, March 29, Mark Hamill prepares and then plays the scene in which his character reflects on his dreams. The second sun would be added in post-production.

the Force. Kenobi wouldn't just die, he would disappear, joining the Force with his consciousness intact.

"I started writing the revised fourth draft while we were in London doing preproduction," Lucas says. "I continued it when I was in Tunisia and I didn't finish it till we were back in England. I had been toying with the idea of killing Obi-wan but I made the decision while we were in the desert. I was struggling with the problem that I had this climactic scene that had no climax about two-thirds of the way through the film. I had another problem in the fact that there was no real threat in the Death Star. The villains were like tenpins; they just got knocked over. As I originally wrote it, Ben Kenobi and Vader have a swordfight, and Ben

hits a switch and the door slams closed and they all run away, and Vader is left standing there with egg on his face. They run into the Death Star, take over everything, and run back. It totally diminished any impact the Death Star had."

As a late entry into the story, Kenobi hadn't always fit in. Even the first appearance of the old man in the synopsis, where he is essentially a vehicle for the film's spirituality, had obliged Lucas to search for plot points that would involve him. Rewrites are common during shooting, however, so Bunny Alsup was already armed and ready for script changes. "I had shipped my IBM typewriter with all of the other equipment," she says. "But the typewriter fell off the plane while they were unloading

In Tunisia, Hamill, who had realized that Luke and Lucas were one and the same (as two photos happen to say, visually, above), climbed with Guinness and company to the top of a mountain for the scene in which they see Mos Eisley for the first time. Below them was the large sandcrawler set, which cost £54,850 ($128,000), and which caused some strange reactions—or not so strange, when you recall that its tread systems were based on NASA-designed vehicles. Because it was placed on the Tunisia-Libya border, and because Tunisian military trucks were being used by production, the Libyan government registered official concern about what they perceived as a massive military mobilization on their border. "It's true about the border," Lucas says. "They had to come and inspect the sandcrawler to verify that it was not a secret weapon." The sandcrawler had been transported in pieces from its salt flats location (opposite, below) to its rock canyon location (opposite, above)—a move complicated by the fact that it had been blown apart earlier by the storm.

in Tunisia and was broken. That was pretty tough. But we had production secretaries there, and one was French and she had a French manual typewriter, not even electric. Using that was exceedingly difficult because some of the letters are in different places. Then I got sick on some fish and had dysentery. I was so sick, sick as a dog, but I couldn't afford to be sick because I had to type the pages—and I managed to get that done with a French [laughs] typewriter."

"I took Alec aside and told him I was going to kill him off halfway through the picture," Lucas recalls. "It is quite a shock to an actor when you say, 'I know you have a big part and you are going to the end and be a hero and everything and, all of a sudden, I have decided to kill you.' Alec

Lucas explains a shot to Gil Taylor (inset, above). Hamill as Luke is then filmed looking into the pit/set where the crew would also lunch (right). In one of the Hotel Sidi Driss alcoves, Phil Brown and Shelagh Fraser (Aunt Beru) were filmed with Hamill. The Lars homestead courtyard set was budgeted at £6,200 ($14,500).

was a very, very brilliant man but he was also an actor and very emotional, very human. 'You mean I get killed but I don't have a death scene?' he said. But he kept it under control."

Under control, for the meantime.

SCS COMP: 15; SCREEN TIME: 15M 48S.

REPORT NOS. 11–14: THURSDAY, APRIL 1–SUNDAY, APRIL 4, 1976
HOTEL SIDI DRISS, MATMATA (GABES LOC.); SCS: 26 [PURCHASE OF C-3PO AND R2-D2]; A28A (EXTRA); 32 [OWEN LOOKING FOR LUKE AT HOMESTEAD]; A28 [LARS' HOMESTEAD—DINING ROOM]
AJIM, DJERBA; SCS: 48 [BEN: "THESE ARE NOT THE DROIDS YOU'RE LOOKING FOR"]; 59 [MOS EISLEY: STORMTROOPERS WATCH *MILLENNIUM FALCON* FLY OFF]; ZA50 (EXTRA) [C-3PO IN FRONT OF CANTINA]; A50 [BEN TELLS LUKE HE'LL HAVE TO SELL HIS SPEEDER]; 49 [IN LUKE'S SPEEDER, THEY APPROACH CANTINA]
MOSQUE, DJERBA; SCS: 8 [LUKE IN LANDSPEEDER ALMOST RUNS DOWN A WOMAN]; 10 [BIGGS AND LUKE WATCH BATTLE IN SPACE ON TATOOINE]; 16 [BIGGS TELLS LUKE HE'S GOING TO JOIN THE REBELLION]

The morning of April 1, production moved several hours by car to the homestead location in Matmata, located within the Sidi Driss Hotel. There, Shelagh Fraser (Aunt Beru) joined the crew for the first time. Again, Lucas's notes contain his thoughts on casting: "a little British, but okay."

The sunken hotel courtyard had been transformed into the homestead hole by Barry and his crew, with ingenious dressing that included two storage tanks, toys, kitchen units from an aircraft galley, drainpipes, and yards of specially made material. Cast and crew stayed here only one day, however, before moving on to Djerba.

Shoot Day Twelve was the first in the "Old West" town of Mos Eisley. To populate the one-horse outback, production again used twelve children as Jawas; four men playing Tusken Raiders; six men as stormtroopers; four as starpilots; three as robots; and sixteen men and women as farmers. The town of Djerba had been modified by Barry, who had spotted it during one of his location-scouting trips.

"It looked very interesting with those strange low domes, which I saw just as I was going by on the way to the ferry one day," he says. "You can

just see them from the road. So we added to those domes; we created premade domes, and I put one on top of each box-like building. Then, because all the electrical supplies are aboveground on poles, we decided to mask them. I invented a strange aerial, which you can see sticking up all over the place, which we fixed to all the electrical supplies just to make them look like something else. Then there was one tree around which we built a big crashed spaceship. We had made a great big machine, a sort of roller, to make tracks across the desert for the sandcrawler—so we used that as dressing in the street. We never wasted a thing!"

Needless to say, the local population was "a bit amazed" by all these doings, and a guard was kept on location at all times. "They stood around and watched us shoot," Kurtz says. " 'Those crazy Americans!' "

By Day Thirteen the C-3PO suit was literally starting to come undone. "There is one scene where you see me walking away from camera into the cantina behind Luke, and my trousers have completely given up," Daniels says. "In fact, bits of me would fall apart. They would ask if I could play the scene with my arm bent. I would open my arm, and a greebly would fall off. Basically I was classed as a prop, so through the whole film I had an amazing prop man to look after me, Maxie, who had worked in Tunisia before. He would stand there shouting strange words in Arabic mixed with French to the Tunisian helpers, and they really liked him."

The cantina exterior that Daniels stumbled toward was surrounded by many of the landspeeder prototypes, keeping to Barry's maxim of zero wastage. Having finished the scenes in Mos Eisley, production packed up and moved to the mosque location.

For the last day of the Tunisian shoot, on April 4, Garrick Hagon (Biggs), Anthony Forrest (Fixer), and Koo Stark (Camie) arrived for their scenes with Hamill in Anchorhead. Scene 8 was a shot of a woman, played by a local, shaking her fist at Luke, who drives by too fast for her liking. In one of the odder happenings, Stark recalls that the Lucasfilm production did end up meeting the Zeffirelli production: "Operated by remote control, R2-D2 had to trundle off camera and disappear behind a sand dune," she says. "But the remote control failed to stop the robot and he wandered onto the set of *Jesus of Nazareth*!"

Despite the quantity of work scheduled for the last day, they sped through it—much to the relief of all involved. Following crew wrap, Daniels and Hamill had dinner together. "We talked," Daniels says. "We had enjoyed working together in this peculiar world."

Having decided to be an actor at a very early age, Hamill noted that it had been amazing. To celebrate, they both then attended a cast-and-crew party paid for by Lucas and Kurtz—a brief respite from the twenty-hour days on location before months of work in London. Only cameraman Jeff Glover and his assistant, Mike Shackleton, would stay behind to shoot a couple of aerial plates for the landspeeder and a few pickup shots of R2-D2.

"We made it," Robert Watts says. "We got out of Tunisia on schedule, which was important—because this picture has masses of problems. Electronic devices, radio-controlled robots, people wearing weird suits, strange sets—I mean, it's stuff that hasn't been done before. We were underscheduled in preparation time, and with the best luck in the world, you can't predict everything that's going to go wrong."

While Watts remained upbeat, Lucas didn't appear that evening, going to bed early, exhausted and disturbed. "By the end of the location shoot, I'd only got about two-thirds of what I'd set out to get," he says. "It kept getting cut down because of all the drama and I didn't think it'd turned out very well; I wasn't happy with what I had managed to get. I was very depressed about the whole thing. I was so depressed I couldn't even go to the wrap party. I just wanted to go to sleep. I was seriously, seriously depressed at that point. Because nothing had gone right. If things continued in that way, I was never going to get the movie finished. Everything was screwed up. I was compromising right and left just to get semi-things done. I was desperately unhappy."

SCS COMP: 28; SCREEN TIME: 24M 39S.

Mollo's sketch of the Jawa costume (right) and the finished costume on the day they filmed three Jawas in Djerba (middle); Jack Purvis played lead Jawa as well as several robots (far right). Djerba was first tagged as a possible location by Barry, who took several photographs during his recces (above). Peter Diamond plays a farmer (opposite, above left) in Barry's transformed Djerba, where Hamill, Daniels, and Guinness posed in front of the dressed cantina exterior (opposite, below).

Lucas survived Tunisia, but was unhappy with what had transpired there.

Alec Guinness in Djerba.

(162)

On April 4, 1976, the last day of the Tunisia shoot Koo Stark (Camie, far left) and Garrick Hagon (Biggs, left) arrived for their scenes.

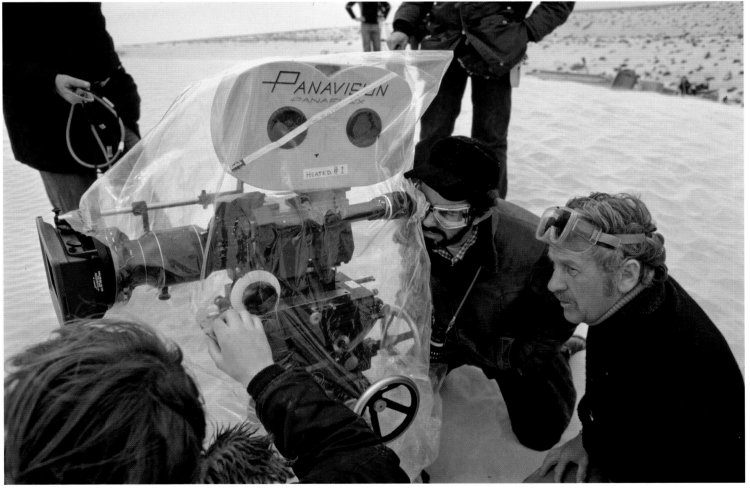

Lucas checks a shot, with the camera protected from the desert sand by a plastic sheet.

FASTER THAN A
SPEEDING FREIGHT TRAIN

APRIL 1976 TO MAY 1976

CHAPTER EIGHT

REPORT NOS. 15–17: WEDNESDAY, APRIL 7–FRIDAY, APRIL 9, 1976
CALL: 08.30; EMI STUDIOS, BOREHAMWOOD
STAGE 7: INT. LARS' KITCHEN; INT. ANCHORHEAD POWER STATION; 28 [BERU FILLS
PITCHER WITH BLUE MILK]; A32 [OWEN LOOKING FOR LUKE, TALKS WITH BERU];
9 [ANCHORHEAD: BIGGS/LUKE REUNION]
STAGE 1: INT. LARS' HOMESTEAD (GARAGE); 27 [C-3PO TAKES OIL BATH AND LUKE
DISCOVERS LEIA'S MESSAGE]; A29 [LUKE FINDS C-3PO HIDING IN GARAGE]
STAGE 3: INT. DOCKING BAY 94; AA53 PART [JABBA AND HAN SOLO]

Harrison Ford arrived in England on April 1, a few days before the location group returned. "The first contact I had with the company over there was for a fitting, at a big costume company in London," Ford says. "George had made suggestions to the costume designer, who had prepared a costume for me to try on. It included the shirt I wore, but instead of the small collar, it had a huge Peter Pan shawl-type collar. I said, 'No, no, no. That's wrong. Can't wear that.' So they took it off. Later on the set, George never missed the collar. He had a concept of the costume, but it was loose."

While Lucas and Ford had an easy rapport, apparently Kurtz retained some leftover apprehension from his interactions with the actor more than four years before. "I heard that Gary had prepped certain members of the English production group with information that I might be very difficult to deal with," Ford says. "That was based on his experience with me on *American Graffiti*, where most of Paul LeMat's antics were pinned on me."

Moving back to London and EMI/Elstree gave some members of production a chance to regroup. "As soon as we got back to the studio, I told John Stears we had to fix the Artoo unit so that we didn't have so much trouble with it," Kurtz says.

"To move forward you have to be stubborn and persistent," Lucas says. "I went back to England and got a lot of sleep, because we returned on a weekend. I got up the next morning and started all over again. I was hoping things would go better. But they didn't."

While life on the set could be much more controlled than it was in the Tunisian deserts, it was also strictly regulated by unions and long tradition. The workday began at 8:30 with a tea break around 10; a copious lunch was served from 1:15 to 2:15, with tea at 4 PM. During the tea breaks, work would continue, however, as only the assistants would stop and grab things for the people running the set. After wrap, crew members would often go out for a drink nearby. "That helped us a lot because we could run down to the pub, see if anyone was there, and ask a question or get them to come back," Kurtz says, as often Lucas and others would be working out the next day's shoot long into the night.

The crew would not work overtime unless it had been accepted by a vote earlier that morning. Even if they were in the middle of a scene, the workday would stop dead at 5:30 PM—which immediately caused problems. Scenes that could have been finished in the evening were completed the next day, which meant that a two-hour stage move that normally would be accomplished at night would take place during the day—translating into huge amounts of lost time, and wearing quickly on the independent-film-schooled Lucas.

On Friday, Day Seventeen, production moved to one of the largest sets: Docking Bay 94, in which the *Millennium Falcon* was housed. Built in what must have been close to record time, the exterior of the pirate ship had been painstakingly re-created by the construction crew and art department, duplicating exactly the miniature sent over from ILM (even down to the mistakes—like an edge of styrene coming out that was too thick to be the ship's aluminum skin—much to the amusement of Joe Johnston). "That sort of preconceived idea is very dangerous," Barry says, "because you find yourself building things that don't fit in any stage." True enough, only half the *Falcon* wound up fitting on Stage 3, and it was so large that moving it was out of the question; instead different sets would be built around it.

Friday was also the first day on set for Peter Mayhew, who had been cast as Chewbacca the Wookiee and who had signed his contract on February 27, 1976. Mayhew's route to *Star Wars* had begun when "some reporter wanted to do a story on people with big feet," Mayhew says. "A producer saw the article and cast me to play Minoton in *Sinbad and the Eye of the Tiger* [1977]. One of the makeup men on *Sinbad* was also creating the Wookiee costume, and he suggested me to the producers of *Star Wars*. So four or five months after playing a Minoton, I was playing a Wookiee. I was the new boy, new costume, and everything was strange."

"He's just the most gentle—that's how smart George is," Hamill says of Mayhew's casting. "I mean, he found this big, gangling sweet guy. He was so shy at first." Through both acting stints, Mayhew kept working his day job as deputy head porter in a London hospital, though apparently his employer didn't take kindly to Mayhew's suddenly varying schedule.

Scene 27, the protocol robot's oil bath, was also completed that day—though Daniels's costume predicament was not improved by the return to London. "I stood on a special effects platform and, as the oil bath scene began, the platform was lowered by three men into a big tank containing a mixture of oil and colored water," he says. "I'd had the foresight to have them heat the mixture first—for this was still winter in England—but it was a fairly disgusting experience, feeling this warm oil seeping up

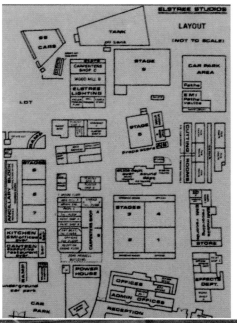

The layout of EMI Studios (aka Elstree Studios) in Borehamwood, England.

Philip Strick from *Sight and Sound* magazine visited the studio at about this time and wrote: "All nine [sic] stages were festooned with amazing architecture, including a labyrinth of curling corridors, ramps, and airlocks, a vista of one-dimensional rocket tubes, and a spectacular pirate spaceship, brooding like a huge concrete manta-ray over the meteor holes that had been burned into it."

between the costume and me. By the end of the day, we'd done it so many times the sticky tape came off and my leg began to float away. I also had a little ear microphone to hear Mark speaking, and what is so wonderful about those instruments is that you can hear anyone near the microphone, so you listen in on some very outrageous gossip."

The biggest problem—a potentially film-destroying event—had to be counteracted by Lucas during a strategic lunch on one of their first few days back. In the intervening time between Tunisia and his arrival at the studio in London, Guinness had mulled over the death of Obi-Wan, and was not at all happy about it.

"We went to a restaurant and sat down," Lucas says. "He was terribly upset. He was ready to walk off the picture—he said, 'I'm not doing this.' He didn't like the idea of being a ghost. That's the part he really didn't like, the idea of giving yourself up willingly to join the Force. So I had to convince him to come back on the picture. That was a very long lunch, during which I had to explain why I was doing it and what I was doing and how. I explained that in the last half of the movie he didn't have anything to do, it wasn't dramatic to have him standing around, and I wanted his character to have an impact. Once I explained it was much better for the movie, he looked at it and said, 'You're right. This is much better.' He started to think about what he was going to have to be doing and how it would've been embarrassing to simply be standing around without much purpose.

"The idea of having Ben go on afterward as part of the Force was a thematic idea that was in the earliest scripts," Lucas adds. "It was really a Castaneda *Tales of Power* thing."

Afterward Guinness spoke to Hamill, who says, "Alec thought it would be far more effective if he sacrificed himself."

SCS COMP: 33; SCREEN TIME: 30M 13S.

In the garage set Luke points to a hologram of Princess Leia that would be added in postproduction, while C-3PO takes a refreshing oil bath—that was anything but for Anthony Daniels.

Declan Mulholland (Jabba the Hutt) on Stage 3 with Harrison Ford (Han Solo) and Peter Mayhew (Chewbacca) (top); Paul Blake (the "Alien") is fitted with a mask while another extra holds his alien hands (above).

REPORT NOS. 18–24: MONDAY, APRIL 12–THURSDAY, APRIL 22, 1976
STAGE 3: INT. DOCKING BAY 94, SCS: AA53 [JABBA AND SOLO]; 58 [LUKE AND COMPANY ARRIVE]; B58 [HAN FIRES AT STORMTROOPERS]
STAGE 6: INT. CANTINA, SCS: 50 [OBI-WAN AND LIGHTSABER]; ZB50 [LUKE AND BEN MEET HAN]; AA50 [HAN AND ALIEN]
STAGE 8: EXT. MOS EISLEY ALLEYWAYS, SCS: 53 [LUKE HAS SOLD HIS LANDSPEEDER]; 56 [SPY TRANSMITS *FALCON*'S COORDINATES]; A58 [SPY TALKS TO STORMTROOPERS]; C50 [DROIDS HIDING]

Monday saw everyone back on Stage 3's Docking Bay 94. Declan Mulholland returned for his second day as Jabba the Hutt, along with Bill Bailey, Paul Blake, and Peter Diamond, who played his gangster henchmen. Filming and retakes continued for several days of first- and second-unit

work, as progress reports recorded various difficulties, including a defective 40mm lens and an accident with stuntman Reg Harding, who, as a stormtrooper, had a bolt inside his helmet dig into him during a fall.

"The sets were terrific and there were all these different sorts of people wandering about," Mulholland recalls. "Harrison Ford was pleasant and got on with the job. He was just one of the lads, really. We had a few chats in between takes."

On Tuesday the camera crew set up to film the interior cantina scenes—the set piece that had been in Lucas's mind since 1973. The entrance of Luke and Ben into the bar—and the reveal of all the strange creatures—was meant to come as a surprise to audiences. "George didn't really want to go way-out on the people, other than the creatures," Stuart Freeborn says. "Because that was supposed to be a kind of 'shock' scene. Everything's pretty normal up to that point in the film. Indeed, we weren't to introduce odd things like Mr. Spock *before* that scene."

To prepare the exotic cantina clientele, Freeborn worked with his wife and son, and employed another six assistants. Together they made life casts with rubber and foam pieces: fake noses, twisted lips, false teeth, cheek enhancements. "For the so-called ugly humans, I had photographs taken of all the artists," he says. "I did some sketches on the photographs, which I got okayed by George Lucas, and built them up from there."

"What happened with the cantina costumes is that George and I sat down and created a complete chart," Mollo says. "I drew a little figure for each type of person, and he decided he wanted so many peasants, so many Martians, so many space pilots, so many pirates—and that was all tied in with the heads which Stuart had designed or could produce. Then it was just a question of getting together with Stuart and making sure the heads and the costumes fit together.

"As usually happens with a crowd is that you do it on the day," he adds. "You truss them all up on the day, and change them around if you see something you don't like."

After Mollo had seen to the last costume details of the forty-two extras, they were escorted onto the cantina set. "I wanted a round bar," Lucas says. "I drew out a rough plan, with a lot of little alcoves around the side, and I wanted a big shaft of light coming down the center."

"George wanted a main part for where the action was," Barry says, "and then those cubicles off to the side—a secret part where you could have a secret discussion."

That secret discussion, filmed on April 20, was Harrison Ford's first dialogue scene with Alec Guinness. "I've always been impressed by Guinness, man. It just scared the shit out of me that I was going to have to do scenes with him," Ford says. "Before I even went over there, I would think about it—he could have been any one of a thousand monsters. But he turned out to be an honest, simple, direct kind of guy, which made working with him much easier. And he was like all good actors: prepared and ready."

"Alec Guinness had a very mischievous sense of humor," Lucas says. "He would give me a hard time every once in a while, making me explain things that didn't have to be explained. He wanted me to go through the drill. He loved to do that to me. I knew he was playing, but he would be smiling to himself almost saying, *I'm not going to let you get away with it that easy.*"

"His eye is a very pure eye," Guinness says of Lucas. "I trust that. And little things I've heard him hesitate about . . . He's kind of like a litmus paper; you can judge off him very well as to what's going on. He has a *total passion* for what he's doing; I don't think I've ever come across anyone so immersed in film. I have an idea that he goes to bed in it—wrapped up, you know, in the actual material."

The same alcove was also used for a scene with Ford and Paul Blake, a friend of Anthony Daniels. Although later in the script Jabba refers to him as "Greedo," during the cantina scene he is simply called an "Alien." A newcomer, Blake was appropriately impressed. "My first day on the set, the cantina was filled with incredible aliens. The booth sections were extremely restricted, so my movements were quite stiff."

However, because Freeborn was ill at the time and not able to finish his work, Blake's mask was not very expressive, nor his hands very maneuverable, so he had difficulty grasping his blaster and pointing it at Han. Indeed all the faces were somewhat disappointing. "Stuart was rushed to try to create the cantina creatures while we were in Tunisia," Lucas says, "because we had moved the cantina sequence up a week in the shooting schedule and I kept adding monsters all the time. But a few weeks before we were going to shoot that sequence, Stuart got sick and had to go to the hospital, so we didn't get all the monsters finished that we wanted. The ones we did have were the background monsters, which weren't meant to be key monsters."

Two other day players in the cantina, Angela Staines and Christine Hewett, played Han's female companions (or "space girls"), while Rusty Goff, Gilda Cohen, Marcus Powell, and Geoff Moon were listed as "contract artistes," adding to the total crowd. Ted Burnett played the bartender who tells Luke he can't bring in the droids. "The parallels between the film and real life were amazing," Hamill remarks. "When we got back to England, Harrison came into the picture and had so many ideas and just new perspectives on a lot of things. There were new characters coming in, so Threepio and I were split up a lot and he felt a little left out."

Mayhew, on the other hand, was quickly adjusting to his role and creating a relationship with his on-screen companion, Harrison Ford. "You first see Chewbacca in the cantina background talking to Obi-Wan . . . Bang, bang, bang, the whole scene worked," he says.

ENTER THE PRINCESS

April 20 was Carrie Fisher's first costume fitting, at Berman's, the actress having arrived the previous day. Before leaving the United States, she had been worried about her hair and her wardrobe. "One of the costume sketches had me wearing a little Peter Pan leotard," Fisher says. "But it was rejected. I was also scared about what they were going to do to my hair, because I had so much hair put on me, two different sessions of that—I had at least thirty hairdos tried on me. And they didn't like it when I got to London. When I arrived, they were shooting the Mos Eisley thing. The hairdresser woman Pat [McDermott] put on me what she had as an idea for the hair—and that was it. I went into the cantina and showed George the hair, and he said, 'That's okay.' Then they put me in a nice white dress and put dirt all over it. And from the first day on, they put a gun in my hand with charges in it, took me to a sound stage, and had me practice shooting it."

"For Leia's costume, what we did was to slit it up the side a bit so she could move around," Mollo says. "We had special boots made for her, too. Jean Harlow was the type, so we looked through a few *Vogue*s and came up with that slightly different belt."

The same day that Fisher arrived, new script pages dated April 19 were circulated among the actors, and a copy was sent to Fox back in the States. "George went off to shoot, but of course a lot of blue pages were coming in," Alan Ladd says. "That's when they decided about the death of Obi-Wan."

Another alteration, smaller in scope but with lasting impact, was the last of the name changes. Luke Starkiller became Luke Skywalker. "That I did because I felt a lot of people were confusing him with someone like Charles Manson," Lucas says. "It had very unpleasant connotations."

Skywalker was of course the original name for the general in the treatment, but for a long while Lucas didn't think it was strong enough. No scenes had to be reshot, however, as Luke's last name wouldn't be spoken until he finds Leia in her prison cell: "I'm Luke Skywalker . . . I've come to rescue you!"

SCS COMP: 42; SCREEN TIME: 39M 32S.

Costume sketches of Leia's dress by McQuarrie (top) and Mollo (below), and Fisher wearing the final product. Mollo's sketch asks the question whether Leia would be wearing jewelry on her wrist and whether she will be wearing sandals, shoes, or boots; it also indicates where the slit in her dress should be made.

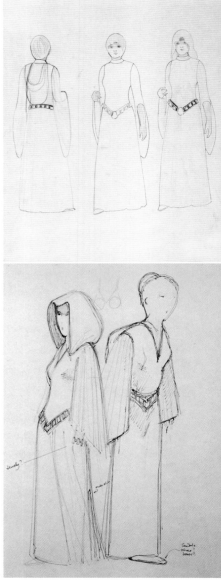

Opposite: Although ostensibly an exterior, the Mos Eisley street was built on Stage 8. Extras were suited up in alien costumes and masks, and a strange encounter between a small person and a larger one on stilts, Peter Barbour, was filmed.

Musical Names

"George kind of swapped names around," Ralph McQuarrie says. "He told me, 'I just don't want to think up new ones.'" The notes for the many drafts contain dozens of lists of names, but here's what Lucas says about his final choices:

Han Solo: "It could have been from some Solo [paper] cups."

Obi-Wan "Ben" Kenobi: "I picked *Ben* because it was a very easy name; *Kenobi* was a combination of a lot of words that I put together. The name came out of thin air."

Leia Organa: "I just picked that name. But there was a planet Organa Major in the film for a long time. And she ended up with the name of the planet because she was originally from there, though afterward her planet's name was changed to Alderaan."

Darth Vader: "That's just another one of those things that came out of thin air. It sort of appeared in my head one day. I had lots of Darth this and Darth that, and Dark Lord of the Sith. The early name was actually *Dark Water*. Then I added lots of last names, Vaders and Wilsons and Smiths, and I just came up with the combination of *Darth* and *Vader*."

Chewbacca: "I came up with a whole bunch of Wookiee words, just changing words around, and I liked *Chewbacca* the best." (The word *Wookiee* came from *THX 1138,* when actor Terry McGovern was doing wild track voice-overs and said, "I think I just ran over a Wookiee.")

R2-D2: "We were working late one night on *THX 1138,* and we were looking for 'Reel 2, Dialogue 2,' and so somebody yelled out get 'R2D2'—and Walter Murch, who was mixing the film, and I both loved that name so much that we decided that it was a good name for something. We just kept playing with it, so I put it down in my notebook and that's where it came from."

C-3PO: "Once I had *R2-D2,* I had to do something sort of like it, so I just made up another one."

Moff Tarkin: "That was just a name that was made up out of nowhere."

Jawa and Tusken Raider: "I looked around until I found a name that fit them. I knew I wanted the Jawas to be very small and very shrouded, and I knew I wanted them to have little eyes that bugged out, like in the forest when you have all those little eyes."

The long scene in Ben's home took one day of first unit and another day of second unit to complete, with pickups done a few days later because of a lens problem. "We were asking ourselves, 'Ben Kenobi—what does

In Ben's home on Stage 7 with the lightsaber (which glowed when viewed through the camera).

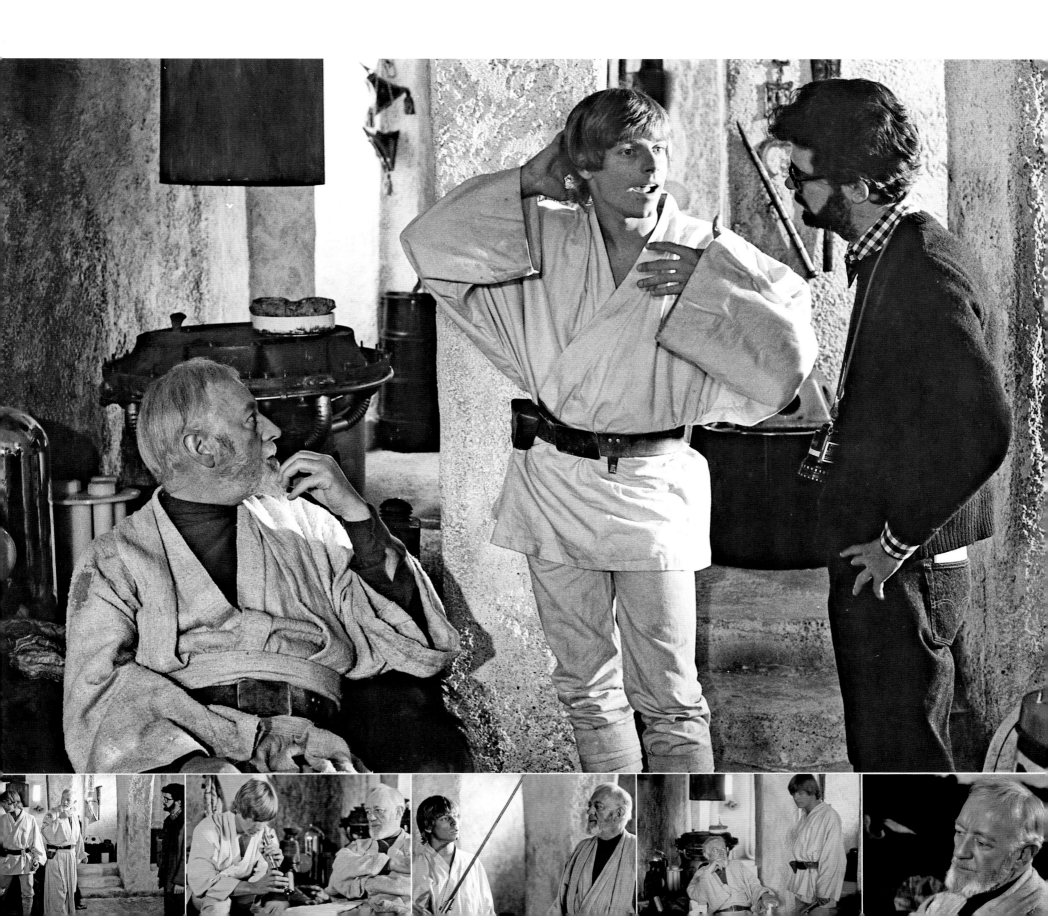

he do in his spare time?'" Barry muses. "You have to decide that before you can do his apartment. We had steps and seats, which we put furs and things on top of." The pared-down dwelling was ultimately given a rug, a trunk for the lightsaber, and what look like mementos. But the décor had to play second fiddle to the dialogue between Ben and Luke, which formed one of the two or three main expository scenes of the film. In it, the Force is explained, their mission revealed, and the lightsaber unveiled.

The middle child of seven brothers and sisters in a family that moved often, including two and a half years in Japan, Hamill adapted easily and enthusiastically to life on the set, and could relate to his character's family problems. "I think Ben Kenobi is like the father I always wanted, because I can't really relate to my uncle," Hamill says. "My uncle is an isolationist and wants to just have a farm. But when I find out that Guinness knew my father and was involved in the same sort of things, I think there's a great connection there—and it was easy for me because I couldn't help but be in awe of the actor who was playing it."

"I tried to make him uncomplicated," Guinness would tell *The Sunday Times* on May 2, a few days later. "I'm cunning enough now to know that to be simple carries a lot of weight. The laser sword seems to be a marvelous weapon. It's rather like a Japanese sword with a row of laser buttons. But I must confess I'm pretty much lost as to what is required of me . . . What I'm supposed to be doing, I can't really say. I simply trust the director."

It would also seem that Guinness was relaxed enough to improvise, for while the script had his line as "You must do what you feel" when Luke hesitates about becoming a Jedi Knight, what Guinness said was, "You must do what you feel is right, of course."

John Stears and company had worked out the problem of the lightsaber just in time for their scene. When Hamill "ignites" it, what he's really holding is a spinning wooden sword, partly coated with a reflective material that, when photographed by Gil Taylor through a half-silvered mirror, looked like it was illuminated from within.

While Hamill and Guinness did repeated takes, Daniels sat quietly in the background, worrying. "My feet crossed beneath me in a yoga position, I moved up only with the help of Alec and Mark," he says. "But I had to warn Alec that I was really a lethal instrument, because I could very happily chop off fingers without knowing. If they put their fingers where the arm went in or where the knees joined, I would just crack their fingers without being at all aware."

At 5:30 PM Lucas and company were still filming the cave scene. The director had already been obliged to stop scenes several times in midstride and wasn't about to do so again. "When we were on location we could shoot a twelve-hour day," he says. "But when we got back to the studio suddenly they were chopping me off at 5:30. I said 'Wait a minute!' Because what happens is you get a scene completed, except one or two shots that would've taken about forty-five minutes to finish—but they'd say no. If instead you finish the scene at the end of the day, then you move to the next stage that night; you don't take up shooting time for it—because they won't *shoot* after 5:30, but they *can* move their equipment. I would have picked up an hour or two every day, but they wouldn't let me do that."

"It's a holdover from the labor situation in England," Kurtz explains. "It would've been helpful had they decided to work past five thirty, but they never did, which annoyed George quite a bit some days, particularly when he only had one or two shots left to complete a scene—forcing him to make a time-consuming set move in the middle of the next morning."

"But there was a provision in the contract that said if I was in the middle of a shot, I could take what they called a 'quarter'—fifteen minutes," Lucas adds. "I was allowed to take up to four 'quarters' to finish a shot. So I set up a very elaborate, long dolly shot in the Obi-Wan scene, and I took the four quarters—but the crew was very angry with me. I was a bearded kid, around thirty years old. I was just this crazy American who was doing this really dopey movie."

That Friday evening, after the first unit wrapped Ben's cave, Lucas and Barry did a walk-through of a Monday set, the first on the Death Star: a simple corridor in which Darth Vader catches a glimpse of Obi-Wan and follows him. The following Monday the panels Lucas requested during the walk-through to close off the corridor had been added—and Darth Vader, played by David Prowse, quickly completed his scene.

"George told me he was making a space fantasy and asked me to consider playing either Chewbacca or Darth Vader," says Prowse, who had played many a large person in films such as *A Clockwork Orange*, and who owned a chain of weight-lifting gyms that made him independently wealthy. "I turned down Chewbacca at once. I know that people remember villains longer than heroes. At the time I didn't know I'd be wearing a mask. And throughout production I thought Vader's voice would be mine."

Another looming problem was taking shape in the form of John Jympson. While Lucas had been in Tunisia, rushes had been delivered to the English editor, who had started cutting the scenes together. However, Lucas hadn't been able to see the dailies himself until now, and when he started viewing Jympson's assemblies, he wasn't happy: Jympson's selection of takes was questionable, and he seemed to be having trouble doing match-cuts. Yet, just as Lucas had been patient with the robot problems, he was hesitant to criticize the editor for similar reasons: Everyone in the production was operating without enough prep time and, in this case, with less guidance than perhaps needed. "Jympson is in an impossible position, cutting material that I haven't even talked to him about," Lucas said to one of the crew at the time. "It's totally unfair for me to judge him now."

Strangely, it was the editor who became very impatient with Lucas, complaining loudly about how things were being done. "I think the editor was very unsympathetic to George," Barry would say a couple of weeks later. The situation was all the more uncomfortable for Lucas, who was now coming to grips with the more negative aspects of doing a large-scale production. "His films were always very private before," Barry says. "Because of the low budgets, no one would see them. So George is now fairly touchy about people seeing rushes, and I can understand his point of view. He knows what he's going to do with it, but someone else might ask, 'Well, why does it look like that?' He doesn't want people to start losing confidence, in him or the picture."

SCS COMP: 45; SCREEN TIME: 44M 29S.

The highly reflective floors had to be kept clean for the scenes of Darth Vader (David Prowse) and Obi-wan Kenobi (Alec Guinness) walking through the hallway built on Stage 2.

REPORT NOS. 27–32: TUESDAY, APRIL 27–TUESDAY, MAY 4, 1976
STAGE 2: INT. DEATH STAR, SCS: BA53 [VADER SPEAKS WITH A COMMANDER]; 113
PART [HAN AND CHEWIE JUMP THROUGH BLAST DOORS]; 107 PART [HEROES VIEW
FALCON THROUGH BAY WINDOW]; A110 [LUKE FIRES AT STORMTROOPERS]; B110 PART
[LUKE AND LEIA ARRIVE AT CUTOFF BRIDGE AND SWING ACROSS]
STAGE 4: INT. DEATH STAR CONTROL ROOM, SCS: A124 [VADER: "THIS WILL BE A
DAY LONG REMEMBERED..."]; D42 [VADER AND TARKIN DISCUSS LEIA'S RESISTANCE
TO MIND PROBE]; SS225 [TARKIN: "EVACUATE?! IN OUR MOMENT OF TRIUMPH?"];
66 PART [LEIA: "THE MORE YOU TIGHTEN YOUR GRIP..."]
STAGE 1: INT. DEATH STAR CONFERENCE ROOM, SCS: 22 [VADER: "I FIND YOUR LACK
OF FAITH DISTURBING"]; 76 [REPORT PER DANTOOINE]; 89A [VADER REPORTS
OBI-WAN'S PRESENCE TO TARKIN]

While Tuesday's filming was uneventful, Wednesday, April 28, featured Luke and Leia's swing across the chasm. Though the stage floor was only about a dozen feet below—a matte painting would be added much later to simulate the bottomless pit—harness expert Eric Dunning had been called in on April 21 for an evening meeting with department heads to discuss logistics and safety.

"First they practiced with two puppets on one string dangling from the roof just to see if the rope was strong enough," Fisher says. "Then they put all these cardboard boxes down on the ground, but I couldn't see how the boxes were going to prevent me from breaking any bones. After kissing Mark, George wanted me to say, 'For luck,' which sounded obscene because the words blended into one another. Then I was supposed to shoot the gun and swing. On the swing across, I was going to hold the gun, which is real heavy, and that scared me because I thought I'd drop it. I was also afraid my hair was going to fall off. But it was funny that day—everyone was laughing—and we only had to do it once."

The swing was just one of Fisher's physical performances, which dominated her first days on the film. "I'd be running down a hallway and my hairdo would start falling apart," she says. "I didn't like having my breasts taped in. In space, they don't bounce. Princesses don't do that, so they taped me."

Fisher's first appreciable dialogue occurred with Peter Cushing in the Death Star control room the following Thursday. It was here that she started to understand how Lucas worked with his actors. "Up until the scene with Peter Cushing, I was just running down corridors, and George didn't talk that much to me," Fisher says. "But in my scene with Peter, I was doing too sarcastic and George wanted real anger. But I liked Peter Cushing so much that, in my mind, I had to substitute somebody else in order to get the hatred for him. I had to say, 'I recognized your foul stench . . .' But the man smelled like linen and lavender."

"You see, I always lavishly slosh lavender water all over myself whenever I'm filming," Cushing says. "I also use a tube of Colgate Dental Cream, because I'm very conscious of bad breath. In fact, if I'm watching a boring love scene in a movie, I can't help thinking: *I do hope they've both brushed their teeth.*"

While Carrie struggled to muster her anger, Cushing, like his compatriot Alec Guinness, was trying to make sense of his lines. "There was a great deal of the script I didn't understand," he says. "Especially the technical jargon. And I wasn't alone. Many of the stagehands came up to me and asked, 'What is all this about? I can't understand a word of it.' I told them, 'Neither can I. I'm just saying the lines, and trying to sound intelligent.'"

By the end of the day, though Fisher had done her best to sound authentic, she thought she had failed. "George didn't say anything, which I took to mean, *He's mad,*" she says. "The next day, George came up to me with his hand on his beard and said, 'You were great yesterday.' And from then on I knew that when he didn't talk, that it was okay— that less was more with him. Sometimes George would just say, 'Anything goes. If you want to change the dialogue, you can,' or he'd say, 'Faster' or 'More intense'—and I didn't know what that meant, either, at the beginning. I just thought it meant that I was not very good. But then I found out that it was okay. I think Harrison told me."

Lucas shows Fisher how to hold and shoot the gun—and then she and Hamill swing across (this page and opposite).

THE MAKING OF STAR WARS

"Basically I show up and George points me to where he wants me to stand and tells me in his own way what he wants me to do," Ford says. "When I'm done doing it, we either have a discussion about it, or he says, 'Do it again, faster and better.' That's one of the nice things about George, which gives me real confidence in him. That whatever the problem is, we will be able to work it out when we get there. It's no big thing. I think that's the way he likes to work, too."

"Carrie had just started when she did her scenes with Cushing," Hamill says. "I came in about eleven and left when they finished. I watched a lot of what Carrie did, but I didn't want her to know I was on the set because it would have been a distraction. The next day, between takes, I did go and get his autograph. Cushing is the ultimate English gentleman. So distinguished. He was surprised I knew that he was in that Laurel and Hardy film *Chump at Oxford*, and he told me about working with them. Pictures were taken for publicity, and though I never worked with him, there was no way I would have missed meeting him."

Hamill had also learned that the fairly recent death of Cushing's wife had tremendously affected the actor, who wrote about it in great length in his autobiography. "He used to cycle to her grave every morning," Hamill says. "He was very fragile, but a wonderful guy, really sweet."

SCS COMP: 53; SCREEN TIME: 54M 17S.

(Continued on page 182)

INVITATION

Sir Alec Guinness has kindly invited all members of the "STAR WARS" Cast and Crew to drinks on completion of shooting on Friday, April 30th in the Executive Restaurant at EMI Studios (which is to the right of the Studio Bar and upstairs on the 1st Floor of the Studio Admin. Building).

On April 30 cast and crew members received an invitation for cocktails from Sir Alec Guinness.

Death Star Control Room

"There was a lot of ingenious work done to make one set look like a lot," Lucas says. "But most of the Death Star really is just one set."

"Because of the amount of work there was to do here, we had the Death Star panels made by an outside company in plastic," Barry says. "In fact, we have used these panels on a lot of other sets as well, because they're so quick to put up. They've been quite a big help, although they were quite expensive."

In addition to his scenes with Fisher (right), Cushing had scenes with Prowse as Darth Vader in the control room and the conference room (opposite). For the former scene, Larry Cuba had actually created a computer graphic for the big screen, with architectural representations of hallways, as Tarkin and Vader were originally going to monitor the whereabouts of the heroes as they fled through the Death Star (above and top right). The room itself, like the corridor, was also changed just before filming.

"Originally George wanted to have the feeling that you got in *Things to Come* [1936], just a huge, silent, sophisticated interior, so it was going to be just the screen," Barry says.

"All I wanted at first was a big room with a giant screen and with some control towers," Lucas says. "The rest of it was John's design. He came up with those little podiums and everything."

"When George decided he wanted another wall on the right," Barry adds, "we just cast all the panels over from the other stage and put them up quite quickly. I knew, with those panels, that I could afford to sail close to the wind."

"I was very pleased with the way that Death Star door worked [right]. I think you do get the feeling it's coming down diagonally, though it's really just sliding down horizontally," John Barry says. "The whole concept of the Death Star set was what George called the 'Tinkertoy.' The basic set was probably six units, which could be assembled in endless ways. The big panels were about six by three feet, the smaller ones, three by one foot, and so on, because we had to build those big sets fairly quickly, and then rebuild them around what George was shooting. Sometimes we'd change the 'continual corridor' while they stood and waited. I had a very good crew. Very friendly—much more friendly than I am, thank God—who would do it on the spot."

Death Star Conference Room

"That was another one of those scenes where I didn't have a very strong idea," Lucas says. "I knew I wanted a big conference room, so I said, 'Design a round room around a round table.' And John showed me the drawings and I said, 'That's great.' Sometimes I had very specific ideas about what I wanted and sometimes I had very vague ideas."

"I designed the chairs so they were all basically the same, with a slit in the back," Barry says. "Except the two taller ones, whose backs were extended, to accent the man sitting in it (above). Those chairs just weren't quite like anything we could have bought, particularly in the number we needed, so we made them."

"He decided he wanted to keep the round motif, so he made more

round rooms in the Death Star," Lucas adds. "Intellectually, it's all wrong, because of the fact that they're the enemy; the interiors should really be very angular. But it works."

In his scenes Cushing was often shot from the waist up. "The problem was, I have very big feet," he says. "I wear an English size 12 shoe, which is perilously close to the Frankenstein monster category. Unfortunately, the boots they gave me were far too small. I was in absolute agony wearing them. But there wasn't enough time to get me a pair which fit properly, so I said to George, 'I don't want you to think I'm asking for more close-ups. But whenever possible, could you please shoot me from the waist up? These boots are *killing me.*' He very kindly agreed."

REPORT NOS. 33–36: WEDNESDAY, MAY 5–MONDAY, MAY 10, 1976
STAGE 2: INT. DEATH STAR, SCS: 83 (CHEWBACCA GROWLS AT MOUSE DROID); 84
[WAITING FOR ELEVATOR TO PRISON LEVEL]; 109 [HAN CHASES STORMTROOPERS];
110 [CHEWBACCA SEES HAN RUNNING AROUND CORNER]
STAGE 9: INT. PIRATE STARSHIP HALLWAY, SCS: 80 [EMERGING FROM SMUGGLING
COMPARTMENTS]; 67 PART [LUKE TRAINING WITH SEEKER; HOLOGRAM GAME]; 63
[C-3PO: "I FORGOT HOW MUCH I HATE SPACE TRAVEL"]; AA118 [LUKE: "I CAN'T
BELIEVE HE'S GONE"]; A119 [SOLO: "WE AREN'T OUT OF THIS YET"]

Back in the United States, ILM continued to work on the plates for front projection with an increasing sense of doom. They were spending around $30,000 per week now on operating costs, but were hopelessly behind schedule. "As a result of the six-week delay and a couple of other things, we were behind just about the period of time that the hiatus encompassed," Dykstra says. "So my head was in a shit because it looked like we weren't going to have the plates out on time and people were getting really depressed. They were working really long hours, but they weren't happy about what they were doing because they knew it was second-rate. But we felt we had to do it because it was going to cost $10,000 a day to have a crew sitting around if we didn't have the plates out on time."

Their forward progress hadn't been helped by the departure of ILM production supervisor Bob Shepherd just as principal photography had begun. But he had previously committed to Spielberg's *Close Encounters of the Third Kind.* "Had someone been here who had the power to do things George would accept, it wouldn't have taken so much time," Shepherd says. "John Dykstra said to me, 'If you're going to leave then you've got to find someone else to do what you did.' But I didn't know anybody else."

Shepherd was eventually replaced by Lon Tinney, but John Dykstra's job hadn't been made any easier. One bright spot at Van Nuys was an April 1976 hire, Dennis Muren, who was chosen to work with Richard Edlund in the camera department in order to help move things along. "I was very much aware of the project for about a year and a half before I got on to

it," Muren says. "I'd heard that John had gotten the job, so I called him up and I showed him some of my footage, but I didn't hear back for about ten months, so I thought the show had folded. Then all of a sudden I got a call to come on in and meet Richard Edlund and see the place. They had already been set up there for months; they were almost hiding out, and it was just a neat place. I didn't know quite what the quality of work was going to be and I'd never seen that sort of electronic equipment before, so it seemed like an opportunity to try and figure the stuff out, plus meet a lot of people that I didn't know. I was hired on to shoot backgrounds of stars moving by and planets for the foreground spaceships that Richard was going to be shooting."

In Chicago, Larry Cuba was also struggling with his deadlines, in his case for the computer animation. "I thought we'd start work in December," Cuba says, "but the actual contract was not decided on until February, and they said the actual deadline was June 1. So based on the data, I thought we could still make it—but in the middle of April they said, 'We made a mistake. The shooting schedule just arrived from England, and we noticed that the scene we need your stuff for is May 6. So we actually need it in April for them to prepare over there.' So I called George and he said, 'Well, we can change our shooting schedule.' So they rearranged it for the last day the set was available: May 17—which meant we had to send it on May 6.

"So we went at it. All the shooting was done in the last week in April. But then the hardware just kept breaking down during the crucial weekend. I had even decided on Saturday night that I would call them on Monday and say, 'I tried but you are going to have to do bluescreen.' I decided to go to sleep. Usually the computer rooms are air-conditioned to keep the hardware cool, but I figured I'm going to be comfortable, so I turned the air conditioner off. I went to sleep at midnight; at three I woke up and I thought, 'Well, it's gotten warmer in here—I'll try it.' And the computer ran continuously all day Sunday from then on; it crashed maybe two or three times during the whole day. We were lucky and we got it out on time."

On Stage 2, Lucas watches and advises as Hamill, Ford, and Mayhew await and then board the Death Star elevator (below and opposite).

ATTACK OF THE GIANT SETS

Back in England the frenetic pace of the shoot, which was now four days behind schedule, was taking its toll on cast and crew. The scope and complexity of the sets were particularly challenging. Production supervisor Robert Watts happened to be interviewed by Charles Lippincott on May 10, 1976, so his words relate exactly what the crew was experiencing: "The biggest problem on this picture is that we have a large number of sets that we shoot on for a comparatively short period of time. So it has been a case of trying to keep up with the set construction. Though we're employing a large number of laborers, we're literally only one day ahead on the set construction. People have been working on weekends; people have been working overtime in the evenings to get this thing done. But it's been necessary, because we couldn't have kept up without it."

In the middle of all this was Lucas, whose experience on sets up to this point had been dramatically different, because he'd either been on location or on a tiny set on a small sound stage. *THX 1138* and *American Graffiti* had had a total of about 40 people on the payroll, whereas *The Star Wars* had 950 paid employees, simultaneously working on fairly massive sets within two large studios.

"We'd really be on a set for only about one day," Lucas says. "We'd finish shooting and then we'd move on to another set; and we'd have to tear down the previous one and build another one right away, because we didn't have that many sound stages. At EMI there were eight sound stages, but that's a little better than a week if you're shooting a set a day. Sometimes we'd put two or three sets on a stage, which would give us that advantage, but no matter how you did it there was a tremendous amount of pressure to get sets finished and redressed. It was really like riding a freight train at about 120 miles per hour and having the guys trying to build the track in front of you as you go.

"One of the results was to make it hard to have complete control over things," Lucas adds. "I would tell somebody to do something and that somebody would tell somebody else and by the time the guy who was actually nailing the fixture to the wall got the message, it was usually the wrong message. That was not only frustrating for me, it was also frustrating for John Barry. He would bang his head against the wall and say, 'Why can't they just do it the way I tell them?' And that's what I would say, and we were both in the same fix."

"George will sometimes tell some carpenter on the floor to change something without going through the chain of command," Watts says. "But if one thing is changed and it doesn't go over the production office desk, the ramifications of that one change may affect four different departments. So it should always come through here, which is now happening. But that's, you know, a minor consideration."

"You cannot control it, unfortunately," says Barry, who was interviewed just a week later, on May 17. "You can dictate the letter, but it's going to come out in somebody else's handwriting. It's driving me potty, doing the sets, because it's so absolutely time-consuming—and even though you work seven days a week, you can't do everything, but you can't delegate, either. That's the director and designer's problem:

On Stage 9 Guinness, Hamill, Ford, and Daniels quickly ran through several scenes in the *Falcon*'s main hold (opposite). For Ford, the line, "Kid, I've flown from one side of this galaxy to the other...," perfectly explained his character (above). Hamill, on the other hand, complained to Lucas about his line "Gee, it's lucky you had these compartments" while they were shooting their exit from the smuggling vaults (left, hair stylist Patricia McDermott). "But George said, 'Just get in the compartments and do it,'" Hamill says. "And he was right."

Basically, you are dependent on somebody else, because of the time scale. Ironically, the more you do get involved, the more it ends up like a Stanley Kubrick film, taking fourteen months instead of eight weeks. And the sets all are terrific, but nobody notices that the actors are very dull.

"Fortunately, George knows that a lot of things can be changed and altered, and is always ready to discuss it, to come and look at the sets after the rushes," Barry adds. "We're always walking around the sets at eight o'clock at night, so nothing's a horrid surprise when George gets on there in the morning."

Most of the film's numerous and rapidly built sets continued to the very outermost edge of the stages, and Lucas would photograph them with two, three, or four cameras. "I shoot fairly rapidly but I pick out shots as I go," he says. "I like to stand on the set and see the scene take place and decide how I'm going to shoot it. I'll watch the scene through the camera, move the camera around, watch the scene various ways, and get rough ideas about things. That's why I use a couple of cameras."

The combination of the size, number, and resulting costs of the sets, mixed with Lucas's unorthodox shooting style, turned out to be very confusing for Fox executives and the crew. Both were expecting lots of wide establishing shots of the elaborate sets, whereas Lucas would often start in close, or dispense with more ordinary coverage. "George says he wants to make it look like it was shot on location," Barry says. "So

if you're shooting on an ordinary suburban street, you don't do a great big shot of a suburban house, because everybody already knows what it looks like. He wants to give the feeling that everybody knows about Mos Eisley or whatever; he wants a newsreel sort of feeling."

"There was a lot of negative reaction coming back from England to the US," Alan Ladd says. "People were saying, 'We spent all this money on these big, elaborate sets and he's only shooting a piece of it!' George wasn't doing the 360-degree camera angle, exposing the entire set."

"They wondered when they were going to see more sets," Lucas says, "but they didn't really make a big issue out of it. I think Laddie kept things under control, and obviously that's the office that can come down on you and really cause trouble."

"Sometimes people get upset because of the way George shoots," Watts adds. "Maybe he'll not do a master first or something like that. But it's his prerogative—because every member of the crew, from the top to the lady who sweeps the offices out, is only here for one reason: and that's to help George tell a story. That's my belief. Sometimes you can work with a director and really think you're getting a lousy picture, and that's depressing. But that's not the case here at all. I think that if we can make as good a picture as *American Graffiti*, then I think we're in. I wish I had a piece of the action . . ."

SCS COMP: 65; SCREEN TIME: 60M 01S.

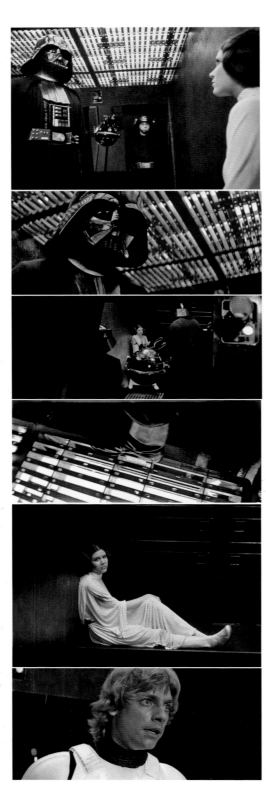

"The prison floor is made up of plastic pallets for fork-lift trucks, which we bought off the shelf," John Barry notes of the set built on Stage 4 (fourth from top).

Hamill's scene in the prison cell has him, for the first time in the film, speak the name of his character—"I'm Luke Skywalker..."— which had been Starkiller until just a few weeks before.

Production continued to speed from stage to stage, moving on to the prison cell set, with the help of assistant director Anthony Waye—one of those chosen by Watts and Lucas for his toughness—while the second unit filmed inserts and R2-D2 putting out a fire in the pirate ship hallway.

On Wednesday, May 12, in her prison cell scene with Vader and the torture robot, Fisher again had to work up fear for someone whom she found not very threatening. "I was in a little box of a room, so I used the idea of claustrophobia to make it scary," she says. "But it was hard to be afraid of Darth Vader. They called him 'Darth Farmer,' because David Prowse had this thick Welsh accent, and he couldn't remember his lines— I guess I could've been afraid of that."

The morning of the second day on that set, Fisher prepared as she usually did: "Coca-Cola first thing in the morning. I used to sit in the bathtub the night before and go over my lines, like the one in the prison hallway when I would say, "This is some rescue. When you came in here, didn't you have any plan for getting us out?' I planned a reading for it. But when I went in the next day to do the scene the entire hallway was blowing up—so there was no other way to do it but, 'THIS IS SOME RESCUE! WHEN YOU CAME IN HERE . . .' After that, I would memorize my lines and wait to see if we were being blown up or not."

"Carrie is the funniest girl I ever met," Hamill says. "She makes me laugh, almost always, and she has a great sense of humor about herself. She doesn't take herself seriously, which would probably be very easy for her to do. I actually didn't know how the Princess was going to be. I did the whole hologram scene before I even met her. So Carrie comes in and she's like Carole Lombard: beautiful to look at, but with a sense of humor."

As a child Fisher used to "read" books before she could actually read the words, making up stories to go along with the cover or illustrations. After progressing through an "*Archie* and *Love* comic-books phase," she became an avid reader of Hemingway, Shakespeare, and Fitzgerald. She would also fake being sick so she could stay at home and watch *Andy Griffith, I Love Lucy, The Real McCoys,* and old movies on TV.

As their scenes together multiplied, Fisher and Hamill were finding a rapport, as were Hamill and Ford. Played as written, they were supposed to simply exit the elevator into the prison area. The day of shooting, however, they ad-libbed, facing the wrong direction when the door opened, to add a comic touch. A few days before, they'd improvised with Peter Mayhew: As they marched down a Death Star corridor, Chewbacca growled at a mouse droid, which, radio-controlled, did an abrupt about-face and scurried in the opposite direction. In short, the actors were creating the all-important chemistry that Lucas had hoped they would. One point that seems to have drawn them all together was Ford's cabalistic handling of his dialogue.

"I had already been shooting for four weeks, going on five, when Harrison came in," Hamill says. "He visited the set once and then I went over to his hotel room. We were going to go out and have dinner, and I'm flipping through his copy of the script—and I see lines of his just crossed

Ford, Hamill, and Fisher on the set (above), and with Mayhew in a publicity shot (below).

out completely. He'd written things in the margins, saying the same thing basically, but his way. He had an amazing way of keeping the meaning but doing it in a really unique way for his character. Well, I was . . . you know, the script was the bible for me. There were lines I just couldn't say, but I learned to say them. It might have even helped my character, in a way, that sort of stilted dialogue. But I also kind of kicked myself and wished that I had been loose enough to do what Harrison was doing."

"I used to go over lines with Harrison and Mark," Fisher says. "Harrison would always change his lines. I was very impressed that he could do that. I didn't know what to do with them. They seemed fine like they were. I was also being agreeable because I kept thinking they were going to realize their mistake soon about hiring me."

"Mark makes this big point about my changing dialogue," Ford says, "but I don't remember really changing that much. I would change the phrasing slightly or put a line or a group of five lines in a different place. But I would usually discuss those with the script girl, rather than George."

Nevertheless, Hamill seized upon the prison-level scene as an opportunity for some of his own line changes. "When we were bringing in the Wookiee, the guard [Malcolm Tierney] asks, 'Where are you going with this thing?'" Hamill says. "And the line was something like, 'It's a prisoner transfer from cell block . . .' And then lots of letters and numbers. But

Alan Ladd Jr. and George Lucas at Elstree Studios in late April/early May 1976 (left). Ladd with an unidentified crew member (right).

I love in-jokes, so I said, 'This is a prisoner transfer from 1138.' But George came over and said, 'Don't do that.' But we did four more takes and by the end I was doing it again. I think I did it on the one he printed."

He did. "Working with actors is like working with any professional," Lucas says. "All you have to do is explain what you want and help them try to get it. It's communication more than anything else. There are a lot of theories, but ultimately, at the practical level, it's just a matter of getting across what you want the character to do. If the part is cast properly and you have a really good actor, he can do it. In terms of changing their lines, well, that's a matter of letting them have their way. Lots of times actors have very good instincts. They're thinking about the character a lot more than you are. You're looking at the whole thing—they're looking at only that particular person. If they're uncomfortable or something doesn't work, it's usually because there is something wrong with it.

"If I have a disagreement about something with an actor, I'll do it both ways," he adds. "I'll spend the time and money on the set to let him have what he wants, but that's just a matter of give and take. There are some crazy actors in the world, obviously, but the best thing to do is to avoid them. I only want people who are good, talented, and easy to work with, because life is too short for crazy actors."

The Rebel briefing and war room sets occupied the same stage at Shepperton. Alex McCrindle is General Dodonna, next to Fisher as Leia (middle right). On display are the computer graphics hurriedly created by Larry Cuba for a grand total of $10,200 (below right).

"You like George so much as a person, and feel so at ease with him as a friend, that you want to please him," Hamill says. "He would never embarrass you or make you feel foolish for trying some things—and I tried really amazing things that were really wrong, thinking back on them. I did have a couple of disagreements with him, not big ones, where he'd say, 'Well, I don't think he should do it that way.' And if George thinks you are wrong, there is no way you can convince him that you are right. He might be open to a hundred thousand ways of doing something, but if you pick the one that he thinks is wrong, there is no way you can show him you're right."

CONFLICT

While the on-set camaraderie between the actors and their director increased, the department heads were having a more difficult time of it.

"John Barry and Gil Taylor didn't get along very well," Kurtz says. "They really didn't talk much, unless I forced them to by having a meeting. There were some problems John created for Gil by not allowing enough room for lighting the sets, and Gil created a lot of problems for John."

One particular problem was the color of the Death Star walls. "I always wanted to use a navy-blue steel color," Barry says. "We went through various tests with that, but it does seem to have been too dark, as events have turned out. It didn't seem to be able to light up enough in the Death Star conference room. But I have changed it now to a lighter gray. I also gave Gil a bad time because it's really tough to light a set that's that dark with characters in it who are wearing either black or white. The light panels were metal, and they started to distort because Gil had to use, and very wisely I might add, thousands of photo floods. But I learned long ago that if you give the lighting cameraman an extremely bad time, it makes the lighting very interesting."

"When you get a person like John Barry," John Stears explains, "who is really so interested in the artistic merits of the film, it's very, very difficult—because he builds sets that don't work for us. We've had problems

two or three times now where things don't work for the lighting cameraman. Gil's had awful problems; I've had several problems, too. But it's one of those things you have to get around."

Unfortunately, Taylor became the locus of more bad feelings, a result of the fallout after Alan Ladd came over to see the dailies in late April and early May. "Up until that point I had been getting very negative feedback from London about the picture," Ladd says. "And the picture was escalating in cost, so I thought I'd go see for myself."

Ladd's trip was primarily to placate certain executives at Fox who were in an uproar. "I remember people saying, 'How can this be?! *Star Wars* is going to cost us over $10 million—how are we ever going to get our money back?!'" Warren Hellman says. Ladd was also interested in shoring up his own base, as rumors were circulating that he would soon be fired due to the horrendous fiasco of a film he had championed called *The Blue Bird*, released on April 6, which would eventually be referred to as "without a doubt the turkey of the decade."

As Lucas was busy filming, Ladd and other visiting Fox executives were shown film footage without the director's presence. "I was warned up

On Shepperton's H
Stage, crew make ready
the floor of the
throne room (above)
for the scene in which
Mayhew, Hamill, and
Ford walk down the
aisle to the dais
(opposite, with extras
in the background
clothed in Mollo's
last-minute find at
Berman's: olive green
US Marine outfits—with
buttons).

front that it was a very rough assembly, and that they were quite unhappy with the editor," Ladd continues. "The picture started, and all I could say was, 'That's interesting; it looks good,' and so forth. But, and I never said this to George, my real reaction was: *utter and complete panic*.

"I didn't sleep that night. But the next day I spoke to George, and when I heard specifically what his concerns were, and how things should be changed, I must say I lost the anxiety about it. Had George said, *Didn't you love it?* I would have been very scared and very nervous. But he said, 'This is *not* what I want and this is *not* what it's going to look like.' He explained that he hadn't even seen a lot of the footage himself yet."

Lucas also allayed the studio's anxiety about the end battle. The last two drafts of the script described each shot in so much detail that it had covered a lot of pages—and pages meant screen time, which meant money. "There was a lot of concern about the page count, people saying the picture would run three hours," Ladd adds. "But George told me in London that the battle sequence was timed out completely, and that the whole movie would not go over something like two-ten."

After Ladd returned to the States to give his report, another Fox executive carried out an end run in London—again influenced by the company's experience with *Lucky Lady*. "It was after Laddie and those guys came over

and looked at the first few weeks of dailies," Lucas says. "They said it all looked fuzzy. I think part of it was an overreaction on their part to *Lucky Lady*, which had not done well. It had that gauzy look, and they were afraid that that was why it wasn't a hit. So I think Peter Beale told Gil, without telling me, to stop using the gauze, which was unfortunate. Because a day later I noticed a difference in dailies, so I asked Gil, 'Did you have gauze on that?' And he said, 'No, no, I think on the Death Star we shouldn't have gauze 'cause I think it's too black,' and he gave me all these excuses. Then I found out a few minutes later that the studio had told him not to do it."

Already unhappy because Taylor hadn't been giving him the documentary style of lighting he'd requested, Lucas, who had been working more with the camera operator on the framing of shots and movement, felt understandably betrayed by both his DP and the studio. The production was five days over, R2-D2 still wasn't working properly, costs were escalating, and the pace was not about to let up.

SCS COMP: 69; SCREEN TIME: 62M 43S.

The award ceremony scene (right), with Daniels, Lucas, Hamill, and Fisher sharing a light behind-the-scenes moment (opposite).

REPORT NOS. 39–47: THURSDAY, MAY 13–TUESDAY, MAY 18, 1976
SHEPPERTON STUDIOS, H STAGE: INT. MASSASSI OUTPOST, THRONE ROOM, SC: 252 [CELEBRATION]; INT. MASSASSI WAR ROOM; SCS: 135 [DEATH STAR ATTACK BRIEFING]; 137 [DEATH STAR ARRIVES]; 190, ETC. [LISTENING/REACTING TO BATTLE]

Production traveled across London to film on Shepperton Studio's H Stage from May 13 to 18. Although it was an enormous cavern, Lucas was going to have to carefully film angles that would make maximum use of his extras. Additional Rebel personnel and the missing parts of the set would be created later with a matte painting. The extras he did have needed to be briefed as to the story, which Hamill, who by this time was thoroughly invested in the movie, took upon himself. Clothing them was John Mollo's job.

"That scene wasn't in our budget," Mollo says. "Someone came in and said, 'Of course, you realize there are 250 extras in it.' So we asked George and he said it was more like four hundred, so we really had to make do. Nothing was made at all; it was all stock items. We took our gray Rebel combat jackets and our pilot outfits, and we added funny caps. At Berman's, in boxes, we found something like two hundred US Marine olive-green stand-ups, which we left well at the back because they had buttons on

them. We also found two hundred French Foreign Legion costumes, khaki jobs with collars, so we added hats, scarves, and things. For the Rebel generals, George came in with a still from *Once Upon a Time in the West*, where they were all striding through the dust in Rangoon coats. Gary came in with a khaki jacket with leather patches and a bit of metal hanging on it. One of the art directors wanted an American cavalry shirt . . .

"I think we asked George, 'Is Luke wearing his flying suit in his last scene, or does he go back to his own clothes?'" Mollo continues. "And George said, 'No, I think he ought to look a bit more like Han.' It was a very last-minute thing, but we concocted an outfit like Han's in different colors."

Carrie Fisher wore the same white dress, but her hair was changed to what was referred to as the "hot plate special"—an arrangement dreamed up by Lucas and Pat McDermott. Although suffering from a cold, Anthony Daniels took the stage in spruced-up attire. "All through the film I was covered in grime," he says, "but for this shot, I am absolutely gleaming, which of course gave all the camera people problems."

Because the robots couldn't climb the stairs with the three heroes, they were placed with the Princess at the top—which was still a perilous place. "I could come down stairs purely by force of gravity," Daniels says,

"and nearly had a couple of nasty accidents where I miscounted the steps; once I set off there was no stopping me until I reached the bottom. When Luke comes up to get his prize, I played the whole thing a bit like a Jewish mama seeing her son at his bar mitzvah."

The scheduling of the award ceremony couldn't have been better. The actors had really gotten to know one another by this time, and their camaraderie spilled over and into the scene, with Fisher's infectious humor and smile mirrored by Ford and Hamill—and caught forever on film.

SCS COMP: 78; SCREEN TIME: 69M 41S.

VANISHING POINT

MAY 1976 TO JULY 1976

CHAPTER NINE

REPORT NOS. 43–51: WEDNESDAY, MAY 19–TUESDAY, JUNE 1, 1976
EMI STUDIOS, STAGE 4: INT. DEATH STAR PRISON CORRIDOR, SCS: 88 PART; 91
[SOLO: "MAYBE YOU'D PREFER IT BACK IN YOUR CELL?"]; 96 [LEIA BLOWS OPEN
GARBAGE CHUTE]; 88A (EXTRA SC: LUKE IN CORRIDOR)
STAGE 8: INT. PIRATE STARSHIP COCKPIT, SCS: 60 PT. & 62 [SOLO: "WATCH YOUR
MOUTH, KID, OR YOU'LL FIND YOURSELF FLOATING HOME"]; A67 [COMING OUT OF
HYPERSPACE]; 73 [FALCON SPOTS TIE FIGHTER]; A74 [LUKE: "HE'S HEADING FOR
THAT SMALL MOON"]; C74 [OBI-WAN: "THAT'S NO MOON . . ."]
STAGE 3: INT. DEATH STAR, MAIN FORWARD BAY; SCS: 77 [OFFICER REPORTS
FALCON IS EMPTY]; 81 [STORMTROOPER CARRIES SCANNER EQUIPMENT ONTO
FALCON]; A101, A102–04 PART [R2-D2 PLUGS IN, C-3PO TALKS WITH LUKE]; 117
PART [VADER AND OBI-WAN FIGHT; OBI-WAN IS CUT DOWN; HEROES ESCAPE]; 116
PART [VADER: "WE MEET AGAIN AT LAST"]

For logistical reasons, the fight between Obi-Wan and Vader was filmed first, for three days beginning on May 27, before their actual meeting was shot on June 1. Stunt coordinator Peter Diamond had started thinking about this duel the day he had met the director. "George said, 'I've got these laser swords—I don't want broadswords and I don't want fencing. I want it somewhere in between,'" Diamond says. "So I had to create a style that was unique."

He trained Prowse and Guinness in that special style, but the day of the shoot things went a bit slowly. "It's a natural tendency when you are cutting at someone's head to bring it down as hard as you can," Diamond says. "The fight took slightly longer to shoot than anticipated because of that problem . . . and David Prowse is such a heavy-handed man, every time they touched swords, the blades kept breaking."

A few days before the duel, on May 17, Lippincott had interviewed John Barry. One lingering aspect of the shoot that hadn't yet been tackled was bothering the production designer. "Front projection gives

us enormous problems," he says. "We can't build front projection to full size, because that'll push us too far away from the screen—and you've got to keep the screen fairly tight up behind the cockpit, otherwise we get this terrible fringing problem. It really is a perfect case of the cart before the horse. It's really going to cause quite a bit of problems, for George, ultimately."

Barry wasn't alone in his apprehension, so, on May 27, the second unit started front projection tests on Stage 8 using an extra in the pirate ship cockpit after the principals had been filmed. "I was worried about the approach to the Death Star sequence," Kurtz says. "We desperately needed the plates, but we weren't getting them. And the shots that ILM *did* send were not right. I said we needed long shots of the approach, and they were giving us short pieces for front projection. They kept saying that we'd have to cut away. Instead, we spliced them all together to make them long enough."

Back at ILM, there was disagreement as to the quality and quantity of what was being delivered. "We delivered sixty plates; we thought they would work," says Robbie Blalack.

"When they reached the point in live-action shooting in England when they needed the process plates, we didn't have 'em," Dykstra says.

Once everyone saw the second-unit experimental footage, however, the verdict was clear. "We saw the tests as they came back and there were a lot of problems," Blalack admits. "Problems of focus in the process rig in England, some problems of contrast coming from the way we were lighting the ships on our end, the way we were compositing them. In total, it simply wasn't working."

"I don't know who the technician was and I don't know what kind of problems he ran up against while he was doing it, but it didn't appear to be usable," says Dykstra, who, in retrospect, saw it as a flawed concept—

On May 19 cast and crew returned to film more of the prison shootout (below right, the slate for that day, Take 1).

"When we were wearing the stormtrooper uniforms, you couldn't sit down," Mark Hamill says. "They built us some sawhorses to sit on and that's the most we could rest all day. It was terrible. You get panicky inside those helmets. You can see the inside of the helmet and it's all sickly green, plus you've got wax in your ears, because of the explosions, and you just feel eerie. I only once freaked out and said, 'Get me outta here!' It really was uncomfortable."

trying to time an actor's performance to perhaps only a few seconds of pre-filmed footage—and he felt somewhat responsible. "That's real hard, right: You cue the actor and he looks up and he can't *see* anything but gray and he's only got 60 frames to get his line out with feeling. It's pure luck for him to hit that timing. You can burn film for weeks like that, so that was ridiculous, and it didn't work. I didn't foresee that problem. There was no talent in that because I didn't have any consideration of what they were

really trying to do, so I got busted for that one. It was our fault that they didn't use the front projection. It was another moment for which I felt very bad about things."

It was also another setback for Lucas and his crew members, who, according to the progress reports, were increasingly ill and having physical mishaps, from principals to stagehands. They were nine days over, and an essential part of the plan had simply disintegrated. Things also came to

a head with editor John Jympson, whom Lucas dismissed about halfway through production.

"Unfortunately, it didn't work out," Lucas says. "It's very hard when you are hiring people to know if they are going to mesh with you and if you are going to get what you want. In the end, I don't think he fully understood the movie and what I was trying to do. I shoot in a very peculiar way, in a documentary style, and it takes a lot of hard editing to make it work.

"I got rid of some people here and there, but it is a very frustrating and unhappy experience doing that," he adds. "I realized why directors are such horrible people, in a way, because you want things to be right, and people will just not listen to you and there is no time to be nice to people, no time to be delicate."

SCS COMP: 98; SCREEN TIME: 79M 18S.

REPORT NOS. 52–62: WEDNESDAY, JUNE 2–WEDNESDAY, JUNE 16, 1976

STAGE 2: DEATH STAR COMMAND OFFICE; 82 PT [LUKE CONVINCES HAN TO HELP RESCUE LEIA]; 94 [C-3PO TALKS WITH LUKE DURING PRISON BATTLE]; 99 PART [DROIDS PRETEND THEY'D BEEN TAKEN PRISONER]
STAGE 2: INT. POWER TRENCH; A105 PART [OBI-WAN SHUTS OFF THE TRACTOR BEAM]
STAGE 8: INT. SANDCRAWLER; 20 [C-3PO AND R2-D2 ARE REUNITED]
SHEPPERTON STUDIOS
H STAGE: INT. MASSASSI MAIN HANGAR DECK; 136 PART [LUKE REPROACHES HAN]; A132 [HEROES WELCOMED IN CRUMBLING TEMPLE]; 251 [LUKE RETURNS WITH R2]
EMI: STAGE 8—INT. PIRATE STARSHIP; 62 PT RETAKE, A67–E74 RETAKE

"I did say some rubbish to Alec once in the control room because I couldn't think of the right words," Anthony Daniels says of their scene in the Death Star. "Rather than screw up the tape, I mumbled. He never batted an eyelid and just carried on. Of course, that takes his kind of skill."

After Guinness as Obi-Wan left to disengage the tractor beam, on June 2, Hamill, Ford, Daniels, Mayhew, and Kenny Baker completed the scene in which they plot out their ad hoc strategy to rescue the Princess. "Occasionally, I would stop like a real actor and deliver a line absolutely still, like 'the Princess is going to be terminated,' " Daniels says. "You can't fool about with that line because it is really quite serious. What George instantly spotted was that I only existed when I moved. If I didn't move, the voice could be coming from anywhere. So I very carefully had to think out how to move as I spoke, to speak the lines with my head, physically."

The physical side of the robot costume was not improving for the walled-up thespian: Numerous progress reports attest to his continuing discomfort, chafing, and skin irritation. "There was a very strange system of filming, which did very much get on my nerves," Daniels says. "It took a half hour for me to get dressed up in this thing for the master shot. Then, generally, we'd do everybody else's ones and twos and close-ups, and then we'd get to me. But toward the end of the film, I couldn't bear the costume any longer. I'd take it off as soon as I finished a shot, which meant wasting a lot of their time because I'd have to get dressed again. And they never got on to the fact that if I'd been allowed to do all my scenes at once, it wouldn't have taken nearly as long."

Daniels's partial solution was to dress only as much as was needed for

Although quite far apart in the script continuity, nearly all the scenes in the *Falcon* cockpit were filmed one after the other on Stage 8 late in May and mid-June.

the shot. "I would, whenever possible, look through the viewfinder in the camera and discover how much of me was visible," he explains. "Believe me, if you see just my arm or just my head and shoulders, that's all I'm wearing in that scene. There is a magical shot in the control room where you see just my hand come into frame and pick up a comlink. But it still took about twenty attempts to do that; they had to put a sticky pad in the palm of my hand. Then I had to watch very carefully out of camera, watch this sticky pad come somewhere near, and then close up, because my hands were hit and miss. Every day was a new experience."

Lucas's experiences with the robots, however, had become maddeningly similar. "See-Threepio hasn't been fixed, and neither has Artoo-Detoo," he says. "Artoo cost us at least a week just because his head wouldn't work. It just wasn't well designed and it was not that well executed in the end. I said I want those heads to work, to turn, and we gave them a lot of time and put on more people during production toward the end when we were really using them—and they never worked."

"There was a problem with Chewbacca's eyes," Stuart Freeborn says, listing another headache. They would separate from the hair on the inside

and look as if they were separate from the mask. "It's quite a problem, and really we haven't got a 100 percent answer to it, and we never will."

While all of these irritations persisted, the solution to the front

On Stage 3 in mid-May several scenes were shot with the half-*Falcon*: the arrival of the stormtroopers via the elevator (top right) and the shootout (below right—with sandbags in the elevator shaft). Stunt coordinator Peter Diamond, Guinness, and Lucas (opposite) discuss Obi-Wan's duel with Vader in the forward bay on the same stage. Following two pages: Lucas demonstrates to Guinness how to surrender himself to the Force, and the scene is shot with a special effects rig standing in for the departed Jedi Knight.

projection shots was to opt for bluescreen instead. New plans and budget estimates were made, and Dykstra, Edlund, and Blalack were scheduled for a trip to Elstree. "Everyone was very clear that if photography in England of the actors against the bluescreen, which was to be shot in VistaVision, wasn't correctly lit, then we were going to have to do a salvage job on top of our normal workload," Blalack says.

SHOOTING ON A CRANE STRING

From June 9 to 14 production moved back to Shepperton Studios, where the throne room had been converted to the giant Rebel hangar. "We changed that in maybe three or four days," John Barry says. "They were both enormous sets, but they'd been built on huge wheeled units, forty feet tall. We had trucks lug them into place, and then George came back again."

As the earlier conversation between Taylor and Lucas had suggested, H Stage was too small for the hangar, which was supposed to be hundreds of square feet—as big as a real one. Attempts had been made to rent a genuine hangar, but permission to film there proved unattainable. Instead they had to use light and magic. "The sound stage at Shepperton, although it's 250 feet long, is a little bit small for the Massassi hangar," Barry says. "So the back half of that set is all in perspective, where the lights go away on the back of the runway. Although they are good old-fashioned tricks that they've used all the way through things like *Gone with the Wind*, it does limit the director. And people don't like that, which is why those tricks are unpopular."

Another trick of the trade included using painted cutouts for the starfighters in the background, as well as filming the two real ships that they'd built in such a manner that they could be multiplied in postproduction. But even the real ships created difficulties. "We got the guy into the X-fighter and the hydraulics brought down the canopy," Barry explains. "That was great. It closed. But then we couldn't get it open again. We were all struggling with it—but we had to drill a hole, finally, in order to get him a screwdriver so that he could let himself out. That's moviemaking, of course.

(Continued on page 202)

In the Death Star command office, Ben leaves on his mission (with Larry Cuba's computer graphics in the background), and Luke then convinces Han to go on a more spontaneous adventure to rescue the Princess. When the robots are discovered (opposite), Daniels had to shoot an insert of his robot hand picking up the comm unit—a shot that proved quite difficult to accomplish (opposite, bottom right).

Sir Alec Guinness (right)

"When the X-fighter takes off and it goes up in the air, there was a lot of fuss about it," he adds. "People were saying, 'We can't get a crane in here and we can't do this and that.' So I said, 'I'll tell you what: Get one of those gigantic cranes.' So we had a huge crane outside the biggest stage in Europe, way over the top, and we hacked a little hole in the roof, and the wire came right down through the roof and just lifted the ship up."

A FAREWELL TO GUINNESS

Back at EMI on Guinness's last day, June 16, the first unit filmed a retake in the pirate ship hallway. It was during this sequence that the actor felt his skill at one moment sagged. When the planet Alderaan blows up, Obi-Wan reels backward and clutches his forehead—"an unpardonable cliché" in Guinness's opinion. "I still go hot and cold when I think of that scene," he says.

His own criticisms notwithstanding, Guinness's performance still stands today as part of the essential charisma that was found during filming—something the other actors were well aware of at the time. "He was the strongest, most solid thing," Hamill says. "From the very first day he worked, he just had something there. You could see it. A lot of times you couldn't see it on the set, but when the film was developed, you'd say, 'I didn't know that was going on.' There was just an aura. I think he was playing a wizard, but he had magic all of the time."

One evening after the day's filming, Guinness, Fisher, Hamill, and some others went out and got to know each other a little better. "He was funny the night he took us out to that Greek restaurant for dancing, Carrie and all those people," Hamill remembers. "The owner came out with his daughters and taught us Greek dancing, and we rolled up our pants. Alec has a really whimsical sense of humor. It doesn't come out all of the time, but in spending a long time with him, I found out that he's real funny. He was real funny that night. He talked about experiences, and so forth, but if you ask him about what he thought about winning an Oscar, he's more thrilled at getting nominated for his screenplay *The Horse's Mouth* [1958]. That was much more important to him."

"I gather he displayed his real personality to much greater effect than I ever saw," Ford says. "Got real drunk and started dancing around with his pants rolled up. But I never saw him that loose. He revealed his personality to me by doing things like trying to find me a place to live on one day's acquaintanceship."

"Good actors really bring you something, and that is especially true with Alec Guinness," Lucas says, "who I thought was a good actor like everyone else. But after working with him I was staggered that he was such a creative and disciplined person."

SCS COMP: 112; SCREEN TIME: 92M 30S.

John Barry came up with the idea of putting a giant crane outside the studio, whose hook could descend through a hole cut in the sound-stage roof in order to lift up the X-wing so it would look like it was flying (right).

REPORT NOS. 63–70: THURSDAY, JUNE 17–MONDAY, JUNE 28, 1976
STAGE 8: INT. PIRATE SHIP HALLWAY AND COCKPIT, SCS: A125 PT [HAN: "NOT A
BAD BIT OF RESCUING"]; C120 PT & C121 PT [FALCON/TIES FIGHT]; 118 PT [SOLO:
"I HOPE THAT OLD MAN MANAGED TO KNOCK OUT THAT TRACTOR BEAM . . ."]; 239 PT
[SOLO: "YOU'RE ALL CLEAR, KID"]; 245 PT [SOLO: "GOOD SHOT, KID. THAT WAS
ONE IN A MILLION"]; A122 [LEIA AND CHEWIE HUG]; AA58 [CHEWIE IN COCKPIT];
A-Z120 [DOGFIGHT SCENES]; INT. X-WING AND Y-WING COCKPIT (WITH BLUE
BACKING), SCS: 140, 143, 152, ETC. [CHATTER DURING DEATH STAR ATTACK]
STAGE 2: INT. SANDCRAWLER, SC 25 [C-3PO SENSES SANDCRAWLER STOPPED];
INT. DISUSED HALLWAY, B105 [LEIA AND HAN ARGUE AFTER ESCAPE FROM GARBAGE
MASHER]; INT. DEATH STAR HALLWAY, SC: G163 [VADER: "WE'LL HAVE TO DESTROY
THEM SHIP TO SHIP"]
STAGE 4: INT. GARBAGE ROOM, SCS: A97 PART [SOLO: "WHAT AN INCREDIBLE
SMELL YOU'VE DISCOVERED"]; A100 [WALLS CONTRACT]; A102 & A104 COMP [LUKE'S
SIDE OF DIALOGUE WITH C-3PO]

As first and second units scrambled to complete the film, which had fallen
more than fourteen days behind, the situation wasn't helped by a nagging
sense that special effects work had stalled in the United States. "That part
was the biggest problem that we encountered. Our biggest frustration,"
Kurtz says. "Because we were shooting and shooting and getting closer and
closer to the end—but we knew that nothing was being accomplished in
Los Angeles."

But at ILM, the feeling was mutual. "George is in England, you know,
and I don't care how articulate he is at describing what he wants, or how
articulate I am at understanding what he wants, the truth of the matter
is without him being here to see the film, it's really tough to get that cohesive spirit of working together," Dykstra says.

The reality was that during the entire length of principal photography,

Back at Shepper-
ton Studios, Hamill
suited up in Rebel
pilot gear, as did
others in the dress-
ing room (opposite).
Lucas and com-
pany next to the
full-sized X-wing
(above).

On Stage 2 Daniels worked with children as Jawas inside the sandcrawler interior.

ILM completed only two shots, in which the escape pod disengages from the Rebel ship and sails toward Tatooine with the robots inside. "George had gone to England and John was busy, so Richard Edlund designed this whole shot, and Jamie Shourt and I stuck it all together," Grant McCune says of the first shot. "We took the escape pod and tied the entire box that held the tube and took it up to the roof of the building. Then we took a great big volleyball net, with four guys holding it. I had a trigger to push the electronic pulse through the whole system. Richard took the high-speed camera that was mounted on top of the box, and we said, 'We'll try it and hope that the pod doesn't break when it hits the net.' We dropped it twice that day. When we got the film back the next day, the first shot was perfect—just exactly what they wanted. For three or four months that was the only shot that the shop was able to put out, so everybody was real happy about it."

The second was shot by Dennis Muren about a month later during the latter part of principal photography (with Doug Smith and Edlund, who took a look before his departure to London). "Richard was gone to England for four days, with John and Robbie," Muren says, "so when they needed to do this shot of the pod dropping, they already had the background painting, so I composed the shot and gave some motion to the background through the stars and shot the pod using the big camera. I think it was Grant that came up with the idea, or maybe John, to have the pod mounted off-axis, so it would look like it was tumbling. When it goes down a distance, I had it sweeping in toward the planet all of a sudden, like the planet's gravity is taking over. We didn't want it to go in front of the planet, though, because we hadn't worked out all of the bluescreen problems. I lit the shadows of the pod with orange light, as if it were being reflected off Tatooine. That was about it; it was very smooth. I shot it in one afternoon."

Meanwhile, Ben Burtt, when not working at ILM, was diligently collecting sounds. "Seventy percent of the time I was recording," he says. "About every two weeks I'd send a tape representative of what I'd recorded to England. I probably sent about twenty tapes during their shooting. I'd have my voice on the tape, saying, 'Here's ten examples of explosions;

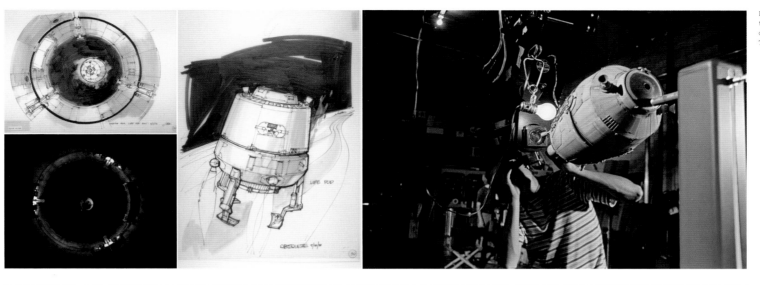

Dennis Muren shot the pod as it descends toward Tatooine.

Joe Johnston did concept sketches of the escape pod being jettisoned, dated May 11, 1976, along with those of it landing (top left and middle). While it was decided later that the pod didn't need to be filmed actually landing, Grant McCune describes how they shot the pod being jettisoned: "We took electric solenoids and put three of them inside the tube that held the pod. The pod had a ring around it where these claws would hold on to it, which were connected to the solenoid, so that when you tripped the button, all three claws would pull out and drop. Down lower in the tube we put three-inch aluminum tubing in it with a number 44 flashbulb that lasts for 1.7 seconds; at the end of the tubes were the flashbulbs. Closer to where the pod was, we'd cut little square tables out and laid fish scales and mica dust on it, and we'd put air jets in with an air solenoid—so the final effect when it fired was the pod dropped through the tube, the explosive bolts would go off and then all the junk that was sitting around it that got exploded would float around in space right behind it [bottom left]."

here's some examples of jet planes; here's a whole bunch of bear sounds.' I even tried to make them do some phrases. I said, 'Here's a Wookiee getting angry, here's a Wookiee being lovable.' I never got any response, but they told me they did hear it. I honestly think they were so busy they probably never had a chance to listen to the tapes. I think Bunny Alsup heard them, you know, but I don't think George had time. But that was the only way they knew I was doing anything. The other 30 percent of the time I was doing odds and ends at ILM."

BLUESCREEN SLINGERS FROM THE FAR WEST

Burtt was right about Lucas, who by this time was suffering not only mentally but physically from the strains of making his movie. When John Dykstra, Richard Edlund, and Robbie Blalack arrived in England, via TWA Flight 760 on June 23, to oversee the switch to bluescreen, Lucas was hoarse and ill. "George is flying by the seat of his pants at all times— I mean, it is an enormous project," Barry says. Stories of Lucas's plight spread through his circle of friends, making their way to Spielberg on the set of *Close Encounters* where Bob Shepherd remarked, "George was getting wasted badly; I'm surprised he's still alive."

Despite his worsening condition, Lucas met with the ILM trio, and together they strategized as to how to best utilize the bluescreen technique. "The biggest change during filming was from front projection to bluescreen," Lucas says. "We had shot the approach to the Death Star, but once we got the results, we realized it wasn't going to work."

"So we decided we were going to do a bluescreen," Dykstra says, "and then we really got rolling again. We went over to England to check it out. At that point I think George felt like I knew as much as Tommy Howard [special photographic effects supervisor on *2001* and many other films], that there was some validity as to what I was saying—not that I was always right, but that I knew enough so maybe I could help."

"We were faced now with remaking all of those shots at a later period of time," Blalack says, "so the energy level went sky-high and we flew over there, helped them, worked with them to set up the shooting. We converted the VistaVision camera to take Nikon lenses, so it was compatible with what we were shooting; we did testing; and I went over to Kodak to see that we got the correct and best perforations on all the stock that they gave us. We did all of this coordination, running around, and spent about a week there, got over jet lag about three days into it, and flew back.

"But it was very exciting, actually seeing the full-sized pirate ship, seeing all of these people walking around and the stormtrooper extras resting in the sun, with half of their stormtrooper suit on," Blalack adds. "We had fun in the midst of it, but we also realized what we were faced with. All the plates that we had sent to England, except one or two of the TIE ships going toward the Death Star, we never used again; that was all shelved, and we started over."

"John Dykstra came to London when we started the bluescreen," Kurtz says. "We wanted to make sure that we weren't going to go back to the US and hear, *None of this stuff is any good and you didn't do it right.*

Lucas directs May-
hew, and then the
cameras roll in
the garbage room
(right). The next
scene was filmed in
the "disused hall-
way" (below right).

So he and Richard and Robbie all came to London, and we stood on the stage with Stan Taylor from Technicolor and went over everything very carefully. Then we sat down with John and went over the optical effects. We said, 'We have 360 shots, that makes one shot a day projected out—are we going to finish on time or not?' And John sat there and said, 'If things go right, yeah, we can do that.' We gave them the last chance at that time."

News of the technical change didn't go over well at Fox, where Ray Gosnell was monitoring costs back in the States. "Fox is very thorough," Robert Watts says. "Particularly Ray Gosnell, the head of production—he knows his business. And it's good for us because if we feel we're being looked at carefully, it keeps us on our mettle."

"The bluescreen cost another $100,000," Lucas says, "but there wasn't anything we could do about it, so there wasn't any issue about it. We had to stay on schedule and we had to get the stuff shot. But lighting the bluescreen really slowed us down—it would take forever, hours and hours."

MONSTER TENTACLE

While bluescreen tactics were decided upon, Lucas steered the first unit into the garbage masher set on Stage 4, where the actors got to slog around in increasingly nasty water on June 21 and 22. In addition to the walls that were rigged to contract, the special effects and makeup department had combined to create the Dia Noga. For everyone, however, the creature was less than it could have been. For Lucas, who had already tried a trash compactor escape scene in *THX 1138*, it was a case of another compromise, for what had started out in his drafts as a semi-transparent, fairly enormous monster with almost magical powers had been repeatedly scaled down by necessity and unworkable concepts.

"It's a cross between a jellyfish and an octopus, a transparent muck-monster," Lucas says, "which can take any shape. It presses itself against the floor or in the nooks and crannies of the trash masher, or even in the trash itself, to survive. I had that same scene in *THX* and it failed miserably, so I had to cut it out."

"The Dia Noga is a bit of a sad story," Stears says. "I made the mock-up of the monster for George to see. He thought about it and came back, and we redesigned it. There was an awful lot of work that went into that monster, and it really is superb. Unfortunately, we can't use it in its entirety. You'll never see the body, just the tentacles." During early preproduction, in fact, the plan had been to use diodes to inflate the monster, so it would seem to emerge from the water—but that idea went by the wayside when budget cuts forced Lucas to combine scenes. "We needed a smaller tank because we combined the two sets: the garbage room and the Dia Noga cave," Stears explains. "Now it's not physically possible on the set we have."

"They started constructing the Dia Noga out of this very heavy plastic, and it started to get very cumbersome and big," Lucas says. "It had to be run by ram jets, which I didn't like, so I rejected that idea and I kept rejecting things to the point where all we had left was a tentacle."

To protect themselves from the slimy water in which the tentacle lay, the actors had the option of wearing a wet suit under their clothes. Fisher, however, thought it was mandatory and soldiered through the two days. "I liked jumping through the garbage chute, but I didn't like wearing the wet suit," she says. "It was under my white gown, for protection—or I was going to look like Walter Brennan [a leathery and wizened actor] from the waist down from being in the water so long."

Later on the same set, the ad-libbing of Ford and Hamill became comically contentious. "Then, of course, there is that famous fight between me and Harrison," Hamill says. "In the scene where we're trying to get out of the garbage masher, I was supposed to say, 'Threepio, open the . . . ,' and give this long serial number. So I had planned all along to say, '2——,' so my [own] number would be forever preserved on film. But the way the scene was blocked the day of, I wasn't near the door—so Harrison got to say the line and he started doing *his* number and that really burned me up. I said to him, 'Come on, say mine, I thought of it!' But he kept doing his own and I got madder. Finally, Harrison read my number and said, 'Happy now, you big baby?' And I laughed because I felt busted 'cause I'd been acting like a two-year-old."

Filmed in continuity, the next scene was shot in what they called the "disused hallway" (which would explain why it wasn't crawling with stormtroopers who would've noticed four wet Rebels emerging from a garbage masher). "It was 105 degrees outside," Fisher says, "so I wasn't standing up straight and I was acting crazy. I was walking too fast because I wanted out of that hallway. But George said, 'Now, act more like a princess. Stand up straight.' Very black-and-white direction. Not anything weird and bizarre like other directors would say. It was very specific. 'Faster' you can do. 'More intense' you can do. And he did that in the disused hallway when it was so hot and he was the only one who seemed to know what was going on. He'd also refer to other scenes: 'Remember how you were in the scene with Peter Cushing? Now just do the same in this scene.' So it was never scary. I totally trusted him."

Thursday, June 24, was Harrison Ford's last day. "I get a concept of the character," Ford says, "but I don't get a concept of the way the character will behave until I see how the other people are going to act in a scene and until I get to see what the set is like and the situation. If you can develop a kind of confidence in the people you're working with . . ." In the interview,

Lucas has a rare smile as he looks at a collection of photographs taken during principal photography and assembled by Lippincott and Stanley Bielecki of SB (International) Photographic. "There was one point during filming when George and I figured we were making about $1.10 an hour, with all the time and work we were putting into it," Kurtz says.

Peter Mayhew, upon completing his role as Chewbacca, returned to his day job as a hospital "porter" or orderly.

On Stage 8 more cockpit scenes were quickly shot, with Lucas taking a look at Vader in his TIE fighter (right). The Panaflex camera used for filming Biggs (opposite, Garrick Hagon) had a list on it of the other films in which it'd seen action.

On Stage 4 Hamill and Ford finish their gunport scenes (below middle).

he trails off, but the conclusion is fairly clear: Han Solo was a result not just of Ford's own interpretation of the character and Lucas's direction—Solo was also the right response to the performances of his fellow actors.

On Monday, June 28, Ford flew to Los Angeles, along with Fisher, who was taking a break. And it was another last day, this time for Peter Mayhew. The Princess and the Wookiee had enjoyed some good times together. "We'd go to lunch at the Chinese restaurant, and I'd have my 'hairy earphones' on, and Pete Mayhew is seven foot two," Fisher says, "but they'd serve us like we were regular people. That was my favorite part. I'd go out to get cigarettes and magazines in my entire outfit, and . . . nothing. They would just give them to me."

That Monday also saw Dykstra, Edlund, and Blalack return to ILM.

Indeed, for the first time the progress reports mention "blue backing," in shots of X-wing cockpits, as production entered a new phase.

SCS COMP: 173; SCREEN TIME: 103M 08S.

REPORT NOS. 71–84: FRIDAY, JUNE 29–JULY 16, 1976

STAGE 8: INT. COCKPITS, SCS: 170 [BIGGS IN TROUBLE]; I220, 148 [WEDGE: "LOOK AT THE SIZE OF THAT THING"]; N220, ETC. [ATTACK ON DEATH STAR]; 240 [BEN TALKS TO LUKE, WHO SWITCHES OFF HIS TARGETING COMPUTER]; LUKE'S SPEEDER ON EXT. DESERT WASTELAND (FP), SC: 34 [LUKE SPOTS FUGITIVE R2-D2] STAGE 2: GUN EMPLACEMENTS, SCS: 158, Q163, ETC. STAGE 4: INT. GUNPORT, SCS: 232, A120–A123 (CLOSE-UPS OF MARK HAMILL)

PANAFLEX 21

1974	THE WIND AND THE LION
1974	FRENCH CONNECTION II
1975	THE MAN WHO WOULD BE KING
1975	YOU ARE MY DESTINY
1975	THE NEW SPARTANS
1975	THE SECRET LIFE OF PLANTS
1976	THE STAR WARS

One last attempt was made to do front projection with Hamill and Daniels in the landspeeder, also on Stage 8.

STAGE 9: INT. REBEL STARFIGHTER, SCS: 11 [LEIA: "LORD VADER . . . ONLY YOU COULD BE SO BOLD"]; 6 [THE DARK LORD BREAKS THE REBEL'S NECK]; A6 PT [C-3PO: "DON'T CALL ME A MINDLESS PHILOSOPHER . . ."]; 4 PT [C-3PO: "WE'LL BE SENT TO THE SPICE MINES OF KESSEL . . ."]; C6 [STORMTROOPERS STUN LEIA]; 2 PT [C-3PO: "DID YOU HEAR THAT? THEY'VE SHUT DOWN THE MAIN REACTOR"]; A3 ["THE AWESOME, SEVEN-FOOT-TALL DARK LORD OF THE SITH MAKES HIS WAY INTO THE BLINDING LIGHT OF THE MAIN PASSAGEWAY"]

With cast and crew fifteen days behind schedule, Fox insisted that the *Star Wars* production split up into several units and shoot as many things as possible at the same time. The progress reports from the last two weeks are thus filled with statistics relating to multiple crews working on different stages and sets as they shot inserts, pickups, close-ups, and miscellaneous coverage as rapidly as possible, while Lucas continued with the first unit. The director tried to explain to Fox that it would cost much less to simply extend the schedule, but executives were adamant that the film had to finish no later than mid-July.

"Alan Ladd just couldn't go to the board and say the film wasn't finished on a given day," Lucas says. "It had to be finished."

One by-product of the intense need to wrap things up was that even though front projection had manifestly failed, a last attempt was made

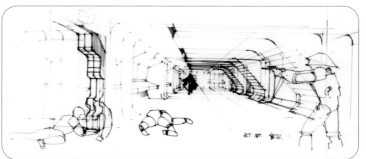

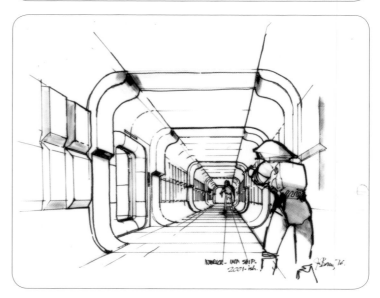

for a few shots of the landspeeder traversing the desert. With Hamill and Daniels in the physical vehicle, they were filmed against front-projected plates in an effort to save time that would have to be otherwise tacked on to the US pickups. Meanwhile, the second unit traveled with the actors for a shot outside the Cardington Air Establishments in Bedfordshire, a stand-in for the exterior of the secret Rebel hangar on Yavin.

Work was complicated by the fact that during his performance in the grips of the Dia Noga tentacle, Hamill had burst a blood vessel in his eye, making it impossible for him to shoot his X-wing cockpit close-ups until the very last days, and forcing scenes to be rescheduled. Other mishaps were recorded, including an increasingly ill Gil Taylor, and a larger and larger number of electricians who had to be called in for the intricate bluescreen lighting. The conflict between DP and producer came to a head when the former discovered the latter rearranging the lights. In some stills taken from this period, Ronnie Taylor is the acting director of photography.

Carrie Fisher returned to this melee on Sunday, July 4, bearing a gift for the beleaguered Lucas. "Carrie brought him a Buck Rogers helium pistol," Hamill says. "And George wouldn't put the thing down. We saw him in the hallways up at EMI, just kinda twirling it around. Couldn't pry it out of him."

Fortunately Lucas was able to compartmentalize, reserving space for amusement while also driving his troops on—but still only to 5:30 PM. It didn't help that Lucas would speak to his friends Steven Spielberg and Marty Scorsese, who were making their respective films with 120-day shoots of twelve- to fourteen-hour days—more than twice the time that Lucas had.

"Magazines were calling and asking, 'Is George unhappy?', and I said, 'Well yes, George is unhappy,' " Barry recalls. "And they asked why was that, and I answered, 'Because making movies is very difficult. Movies are not done in a jolly atmosphere of self-congratulatory lunches at the Polo Lounge.'

"The potential problem on a picture like this is it can become a committee movie," Barry adds. "There are so many people involved and so many forces working on you, working on George, that the amount of choice you've got is limited all the time by these outside pressures."

THE WHITE CORRIDOR

Lucas nevertheless had the wherewithal to make a last crucial decision. Walking through the sets one night with John Barry, they toured the Rebel ship, which was really the redecorated main hold of the *Millennium Falcon*—and Lucas found it wanting. "Sometimes we tried to re-dress a set and use it again," he says. "But I looked at it about a week or so before shooting, and I said, 'I can't possibly shoot the sequence on this set.' The original set was the little alleyway with the Princess and the robots. That was all we had. And I just realized I couldn't shoot a battle, five pages of

dialogue, and all these people running around, and have it all take place in one little hallway.

"So I said, 'John, you have to build another big hallway next to this little hallway'—and that created a whole big ruckus with Fox and everybody, because it cost a lot more money. I got a lot of flak—everybody came down on me. There was a lot of screaming and yelling. But ultimately, as the director, if you decide that it is vital to the film, it is vital to the film. We had to have it; I couldn't make the movie with half a set. I had really tried to cut corners wherever I could, but once in a while we'd reach a point where we needed to spend the extra money. So John built a new white set. I was very concerned that the opening, the first interior of the film, be spectacular and look opulent, and not just be a set re-dress. We had a lot of problems with that but eventually John, who is a genius, did it."

"One set we changed quite a bit was the interior of the opening spaceship," Barry says. "We added a great white hallway to it, because it had been a revamp of the interior of the *Millennium Falcon*. Also, I think George wanted the set to look, at first sight, like you are in your conventional all-white interior *2001*-type spaceship—and then the door blows down and in comes Darth Vader—*black* against a white hallway!"

The explosives ignited during that opening shootout caused at least one stuntman to go to the hospital. "John Stears got a little ambitious and blew the walls off the set a couple of times," Kurtz says. "But any powder man does that occasionally. Misjudges a little bit. But he did a really good job on the gunfights in the white hallway. He was much faster than any other powder man that I've ever worked with."

"When the laser blasts hit a wall, I didn't want it to be just a little squib like you normally have on a gunshot," Lucas says. "I wanted it to be a big, huge flash every time it hit. So we tested out large squibs so we could make big explosions."

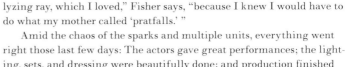

"I remember that I had to shoot a gun and that I got felled by a paralyzing ray, which I loved," Fisher says, "because I knew I would have to do what my mother called 'pratfalls.'"

Amid the chaos of the sparks and multiple units, everything went right those last few days: The actors gave great performances; the lighting, sets, and dressing were beautifully done; and production finished on time. The progress report for July 16 reads, "Completion of principal photography in U.K. today. Mark Hamill and Carrie Fisher completed their roles today and will travel to Los Angeles tomorrow, Saturday, July 17, 1976. George Lucas will travel to USA on July 17. Anthony Daniels and Kenny Baker also completed their roles today. The editing equipment and film will arrive in the U.S. on July 27. Scenes remaining to be shot (in USA) are now as follows . . ."

A list of those incomplete scenes follows, mostly with R2-D2, the banthas, the landspeeder, and the sandcrawler—pretty much all shots that had been handicapped for technical reasons. There would also be one more day of shooting in the United Kingdom. The first official day of postproduction was the following Friday, when an insert shot of Luke's gloved hand turning off the targeting computer and of C-3PO in the Rebel ship corridor were needed, so stand-ins were used. Derek Ball, the sound man, also traveled to the home of Shelagh Fraser (Aunt Beru) to record "wild track"—lines that can be inserted anywhere when the actor is off camera. On July 23, second-unit cameraman Brian West used his Arriflex to capture: R2-D2 for scene 2; various hands on various controls, in assorted cockpit shots; and, once again, the landspeeder with a Luke double against bluescreen.

"I kept checking and asking, 'Do you realize I'm working on that day,'" Daniels says. "And they said, 'Yes, you'll be finished.' And of course I wasn't so they asked my stand-in to do it. She was a beautiful blond debutante, a girl small enough to get into my costume. She was really quite good."

By the end of the 84-day shoot, which finished twenty days over schedule, production had exposed 322,704 feet of film, with 226,717 feet printed, and recorded 219 magnetic rolls for sound. They had shot an average of one minute and thirty seconds of script a day. Hamill led the field of actors, with 70 days worked, next to Daniels's 54, Ford's 42, and Fisher's 37—all performed on about 100 sets. "But what we did was group the sets all together into composites, so there were only about 40," John Barry says.

Principal photography cost more than planned, but not wildly so. "Gil Taylor's lighting budget was the source of the biggest overage, along

with transportation," Kurtz says. "He'd looked at the sets, all the plans, and worked out with his gaffer that the average was supposed to be 10 electricians a day." But they ended up with 20, some days 40 electricians on the big sets, most of whom were called in for the shift to bluescreen. "That automatically kicked it up, because we had to dig out about 50 extra arc lights," Kurtz explains. "The days that we were going blue backing, we had 60 electricians working on the set. Every 20 minutes those guys had to change the carbons on about 70 white-flamed carbon arcs. So that was a huge overage right there. That wasn't Taylor's fault." Nor were the Death Star hallways and hangar, which John Barry had to repaint about seven shades of gray lighter, so they wouldn't require so much illumination.

Gil Taylor would eventually express regret about the way things turned out. "I only wish I could have my time over again to have a slightly different relationship with George," he says.

"Most of the rest were just nickel-and-dime overages," Kurtz adds. "Set construction overages, rescheduling . . . The rest was more or less okay." Circumstances aided the bottom line, when the British pound was devalued that year, creating a windfall of about $450,000, which decreased the total overage in the UK to approximately $600,000.

The final appreciation of the experience in England was mixed, but edged toward the positive. "Some of the people were enthusiastic about the picture and some of the people were indifferent," the producer says. "I think 60 to 70 percent worked out well. We were working with people we had never worked with before, so I don't consider that a particularly bad record."

Lucas agreed: Some worked out, some didn't. "Part of the problem is that you're asking the impossible of people," the director says. "And they can either do it or they can't. But you can't blame or fault somebody for not being able to do the impossible—by definition, it's impossible."

SCS COMP: 344; SCREEN TIME: 124M 02S.

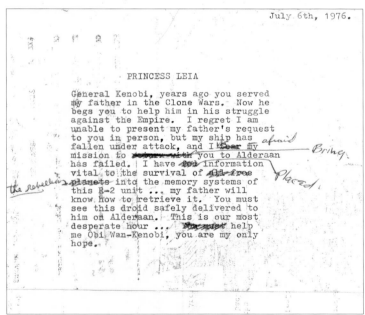

One scrap of paper dated July 6, 1976, contains Lucas's changes to Princess Leia's hologram monologue (above), which was shot around that time, while another indicates the last day of second-unit shooting on July 23, 1976 (left).

ACE-PEOPLE AND THE WIZARDS

JULY 1976 TO DECEMBER 1976

CHAPTER TEN

A shattered Lucas made a couple of stops before returning to California: Mobile, Alabama, to visit Spielberg on his set; and New York City to say hello to Brian De Palma. Lucas had assembled booklets of black-and-white production stills, on-set photography of *Star Wars*, which he gave to his friends, including film critic Jay Cocks.

"When he wrapped at Elstree he came straight to my set in Mobile, where I was shooting *Close Encounters*, and he was so depressed," Spielberg says. "He brought a whole bunch of stills—the sandcrawler and the Jawas—and I was just amazed, but George was so depressed. He didn't like the lighting; he didn't like what his cameraman, Gil Taylor, had done for him. He was really upset."

Back in Los Angeles, Lucas attended a screening of *Carrie* with its editor Paul Hirsch and director De Palma. Lucas then returned to ILM on August 1, 1976, to face a situation even more dire than the one he'd left

in England. The pressures awaiting him were such that, even decades later, they haunted him. At the 30th anniversary of ILM in 2005, during his short speech at their new San Francisco Presidio headquarters in the Letterman Digital Arts Center, Lucas recalled his experience: "When I got back, they'd spent half their budget, and had only one shot in the can. There were 45 people and about 360 shots left—and they thought they'd be able to finish the film easily in only eight months.

"On my way back from ILM," Lucas says, "I started getting severe chest pains, since my life was collapsing around me. I had to recut the movie from scratch and ILM hadn't created a single shot that was viable. I was really hurting, so when the plane touched down I went straight from the airport to the hospital." They kept Lucas overnight. By morning, the doctors determined that he had not been having a heart attack, and Lucas was allowed to leave.

During most of May and June, Ralph McQuarrie had worked on other projects, but from July 19 through July 22, 1976, he worked on the "roughs for S.W. book cover." On August 11, 1976, he finished the illustration (right and opposite) and started work on "I.L.M. *Star Wars* T-shirt art." By this point, Lucas had dropped *The* from the title, at which point it became *Star Wars*.

Even if the ILMers were right, *Star Wars* would just barely make its release date in the spring of 1977. As Lucas mulled over the situation at Industrial Light & Magic, he came to certain conclusions. The first was that it was being run as a research facility rather than a film production unit. The equipment, though fabulous, had taken longer than predicted to build, tests were still being carried out, and the experimental explosions hadn't looked good. Procedurally, they were completing a shot and then waiting until the next day to make sure the rushes were okay before moving on, despite the Dykstraflex. "George ended that as soon as we got back," Kurtz says. "No holding any shots. You finish the shot, you break the set up. If you have to do it over, you reset. We can't worry about the rushes. That was a part of the delay. They were experimenting and they were working under a different set of rules."

"We didn't even know how to do a bluescreen shot at the beginning of *Star Wars*," Richard Edlund notes. "So I brought in Bill Reinhold, an old-timer who had done *It's a Mad Mad Mad Mad World* [1963], to teach Robbie Blalack how to do bluescreen."

While Lucas and Kurtz came to grips with one problem, an equally important task was beginning up north in San Anselmo, within Park Way's converted carriage house: the editing of the film. ILM's initial goal—the one that had been abandoned during principal photography—was to finish the escape from the Death Star scenes. But now that ILM was going to be adding special effects to the bluescreen elements already shot in England—the reverse of what had originally been planned—a work print of that sequence had to be created before they could start. The first and primary task of postproduction was thus to cut together that sequence so ILM would know how long each shot was, where the camera would be, and so on. Fortunately, this was the moment Lucas had been working toward for more than three years—to have the raw material that he could meld into a cinematic experience.

"I really enjoy editing the most," he says. "It's the part I have the most control over, it's the part I can deal with easiest. I can sit in my editing room and figure it out. I can solve problems that can't get solved any other way. It always comes down to that in the end. It's the part I rely on the most to save things, for better or worse. Everybody has their ace in the hole—mine's editing."

Harrison Ford, who had already experienced the before and after of *American Graffiti*, was well aware of what Lucas would do in editorial. "That's one of George's great virtues: putting a movie together to create an experience for the audience," he says. "That's where a touch here of this character and a touch there of that one will seal up your impression of what he is going for. It's not fully resolved until it's done by him."

"I think of it in terms of cinematic style, which is why there is a lot of cross-cutting in my movies," Lucas says. "Cinematically, it's the way I like to tell a story. But no one had been editing on the movie for several months, so the first thing we had to do when we got back to San Anselmo was to reconstitute everything that had been cut in England, put it back in dailies form, and start from scratch. It turned out to be even more of a horrendous job than we thought it was going to be. We were running against a terrible time problem, so we hired an editor, Richard Chew. He and my wife, Marcia, who was also an editor, raced to get a first rough cut of the movie ready by Thanksgiving."

CUTTING GUNS

Chew and Lucas had originally met through their mutual acquaintance, John Korty, and Chew of course had been Lucas's first choice as editor the previous year. "I had gotten other offers because of the success of *Cuckoo's Nest*," Chew says, "but nothing had come along that I felt I wanted to live with for six months or a year—when the chance came again to work on this. I had already heard that George was coming back from England and that they were very unhappy with what the English editor had done with the film. George wanted the whole thing redone. He asked Marcia to work on the final battle sequence, so ILM could start, and he needed someone else to start at the beginning. And since I'm neighbors with him and he was familiar with my work . . ."

The overarching concern was to cut things as tightly as possible, with no unnecessary special effects footage, so neither money nor time would be wasted. But before anyone could begin, they had to create coding systems and standards that would enable the editors and ILM to work together. Coordinating that effort was Mary Lind, who ran the Film Control Office down in Van Nuys. She had actually started back in August 1975, recruited by Jim Nelson, who was an old friend of hers, after they'd met accidentally in a Schwab's drugstore. She and her team were responsible for the whereabouts of every frame of film—a monumental task, particularly as postproduction wore on. Eventually, she wound up with 23 cross-referenced notebooks tracking each frame as it traversed often a dozen departments (top right). "I remember we had about 60,000 feet of live-action VistaVision out of England," Lind says. "It was sent here and reduced from 8-perf to 4-perf so that Marcia and Richard could cut it."

This initial mechanical work took about four weeks; another two weeks was spent coding the reduction prints to the VistaVision prints. "If you were going to pick up a code number to find negative and it was code number 400, it was actually code number 800 in VistaVision," Lind says. "Oh God, it got crazy!" Another complication occurred when Film Control discovered that "the film put together in England was damaged," Chew reports. "As though people hadn't cared what they were doing—to the point of slamming it all together and saying, 'Screw this job!' So they were a bit upset at ILM because they had to go through the whole thing."

While they were waiting up north for the processes to be completed down south, Chew started at the beginning, on the Rebel ship and the droids. "One great thing about working with the robots was there weren't any lip-sync problems for an editor to worry about," he says. "We just chose whatever looked good and then we could cheat in anything else. For See-Threepio we had at least the production guide track, where Anthony Daniels is speaking underneath the mask, but for Artoo, whenever we came to him, either George or I would say, 'Phoove-orvr-ovrrrrrr!' We'd do something that would sound appropriate as a reply. It was a good way for me to ease into the style of this film."

As soon as the properly coded and reduced 35mm special effects footage was delivered from Film Control, while Marcia concentrated on the end battle, Chew turned to the escape from the Death Star. "I started working on the picture the beginning of August 1976," Chew says. "George said he had to lock that sequence by September 15 for ILM to do all the optical work and the miniatures, but he was so busy, the only thing

In the Film Control Office, film librarians Connie McCrum and Cindy Isman work with film control coordinator Mary Lind (top right). Peeking out of the drawer is an ILM shot tracker. In the same room was ILM editorial (middle and below right, with Lind).

Every department was fairly cramped, including editorial, optical, the machine shop (above, with Dick Alexander, Doug Barnett, and Bill Shourt), and the back room, which was filled with models used for kit bashing (left). In fact, ILM spent about $1,700 on art supplies and $2,900 on model kits.

he could say to help me was, 'Here's the scene—don't look at the English cut, because it could influence you and I want you to start from scratch.' So I was stepping into the project cold. I had all this material, with blue-screen, and I had no idea what we were going to see out there. The only guide that George could give me was this black-and-white dupe of World War II dogfight news footage. So during the first three days, while keeping in mind what George wanted, I was already indicating with grease pencil the paths that the TIE fighters would take, where the explosion would come from, and when laser beams would fire out of the guns.

"We wanted to establish the spatial relationships," Chew continues. "There were some very nice angles that George had shot; and when Han or Luke pivoted in their chairs, they cast these nice shadows on the wall behind them. We would choose stuff like that, not taking into account where the TIE fighters were. There were some lines like, 'Here they come,' or 'Do you hear me, baby, hold together,' but those were the 'wild cards' that we were able to shift around to bracket whatever action was occurring."

After Chew was able to piece together a rough cut of the sequence, as it was a precedent-setting moment in postproduction, Lucas took over. "George is enough of a film craftsman, besides being the 'general' of this huge army, that he really wanted to get his hands dirty," Chew says, "to cut frames off and manipulate things, because I think he is happiest when doing that. So he had me put together the gunport sequence so that he would have something to play with. Then he went upstairs to his editing room and Steenbeck editing table and looked through all the trims, while I continued working from the beginning of the film and Marcia was working on the end. He worked on it weekends up until the time that he locked it on schedule."

"I cut one sequence myself," Lucas says. "It was too hard to explain what I wanted, so I just cut the whole thing. It had to be cut right away because of the special effects. We had to know how to do it, so I sat down and cut it."

"After the live-action editors had their time to work with the material in San Francisco, it hit our room—when it all had to be done at *once*," Mary Lind recalls. "And of course they couldn't give us little sections at a time, so when those escape from the Death Star rolls arrived, it was 18 hours a day just figuring out numbers. There were people sleeping here."

Once the film had been logged, ILM began its first true sequence— with a year of investment in equipment and experimentation on the line.

CONTRACT FOR VICTORY

"Kissinger always said that the essence of negotiating is having an ass that doesn't get tired," Tom Pollock says. "The one that sits there the longest, and says the same thing over and over and over again, is the one that survives."

Perhaps spurred on by the return of Lucas, Twentieth Century-Fox finally agreed to the official wording of every single item, the result of years of hard deliberations between, representing their client, Andy Rigrod and Tom Pollock, and, representing the studio, Mort Smithlise, Donald Loze, Lyman S. Gronemeyer, William Immerman, and often two or three people from production.

"Studios are very traditional and precedent-oriented," Rigrod says. "If you ask for something that they normally don't give, no matter how small it is, they get very defensive about it. So I remember the negotiations as endless. We were in this huge paneled room at the studio—it looked like a meeting of the board of directors. There were sometimes as many as eight people sitting around this huge table. We would sit there for days and negotiate and argue. Every line of the agreement was read and changed. It went through four or five revisions. It was the most lengthy, complicated, and difficult contract negotiation I've ever seen.

"The thrust of it was that Lucas was very concerned that all versions of the picture would be controlled by him," Rigrod adds, "with as little interference by the studio as possible. We were actually having a race to see whether the contract or principal photography would be done first." The movie won by more than a month.

The seventy-four-page "long-form" contract was signed on August 27, 1976. The most important part of said document is Exhibit D, which begins with the phrase, "[The Star Wars Corporation] owns all Sequel Motion Picture rights in and to the picture." The intricate legalese, which necessitated its own in-contract glossary, also stated that Lucas would maintain control over the licensing of his movie and the sequels, with profits from merchandise—which historically had meant T-shirts and movie posters—being split fifty-fifty for *Star Wars*.

BATTLE STATIONS

The lone wolf of production, Ben Burtt also had to be taken care of when Lucas returned. "By the time they came back, I was pretty nervous as to what was going to happen," Burtt says. "I'd had very little feedback and I was still under the impression that Walter Murch was going to step in and take over. I thought that maybe I was through with being employed. Gary would say things like, 'Now a real sound effects editor is going to run the picture . . .' I had no previous track record in this area, and they were not about to give the responsibility for a film of this magnitude to some completely inexperienced sound editor, which is what I was. Of course I was offended by that, because I'd spent a lot of time on the film. This was my first big job, and I wanted it to turn out good.

"Finally in August, they said they wanted me to go to San Anselmo for a week or two just to make up some effects for the temporary version of the picture," he adds. "Basically I was going to transfer the sound

library up there. I had it really well organized and cataloged so that anybody could go through it, so I kept thinking I was going to turn it over to somebody, and maybe that's what they intended. I don't know. But I went to San Anselmo and stayed for seven months instead of three weeks."

In September, as the effects house was about to begin on the escape from the Death Star sequence, changes had to be made at ILM. With Bob Shepherd gone since March, Jim Nelson had been the production supervisor, working with John Dykstra—a combination that, according to the producer, didn't work out well. Dykstra, as the leader of his troops, was perceived by different people in different ways. For Shepherd, Dykstra had been the totally committed leader, but Kurtz felt differently. "John wanted to be buddies with everybody," he says. "He didn't like yelling at people. From a technical point of view, he had the broadest range and knowledge of the various areas, from opticals to mechanics and electronics, but he didn't like to push people. He was the kind of person that likes to tinker with his cars, go scuba diving, and do motorcycle racing out in the desert. He pals around with those guys a lot; they were a big family. All of ILM had that college fraternity feel."

"I'd say about 125 people passed through here," Dykstra says. "We didn't fire many people on the show; we did lay a lot of people off, but we didn't have too many personality conflicts. But it was pretty scary, bringing it all together, because I'd never had anything like that before. You get these creative people together and one guy says, 'I'm going to bite your head off.' And the other guy says, 'I'm going to kick . . .' Someone would come downstairs and say, 'Up in roto—they're killing each other.' So I'd wait until the ceiling would start pounding, and then I'd call up and say, 'Get down here!' "

To remedy the situation, Lucas decided to look for an experienced production supervisor—something that would also partially appease the execs at Fox, who were putting a lot of pressure on the production. On June 25, 1976, the studio had released *The Omen;* it was doing well at the box office, which took some of the pressure off *Star Wars*, but nowhere near all of it. "Fox's production department was continuously harassing us," Kurtz says. "Because they were as uneasy as we were. They didn't see any paperwork to

Richard Chew uses Lucas's Steenbeck editing table at Park Way (far right). In an office on the ground floor of ILM, Lucas goes over storyboards with his new production supervisor, George Mather (right). Lucas's hire, Mather put into place key reforms at the struggling facility.

tell them what we were doing. On a normal production schedule, you know exactly where you are. At ILM, we had nothing. We had no schedule. The only way we could placate Fox was to invent paperwork."

It was decided that ILM's "average" would be five shots a day. Shots were numbered and divided into categories—complicated, medium, simple—and a percentage system was worked out. By September 18 ILM was at a somewhat fictional 10-percent-complete mark. "It was the only way that Fox felt a little more at ease with what was going on," Kurtz says. "We were having a terrible time."

In late September, Lucas hired George Mather as the new production supervisor at ILM. "Then we really pushed very hard and whipped the place into shape, from a production point of view," Kurtz continues. "From a technical point of view it was fine. They had worked out the bugs in the camera, the bluescreen process had begun well, both optical printers worked like gangbusters—they were raring to go. It's just that they should have been in that spot *three months* earlier."

"Mather was brought in by Twentieth or whatever combination of powers," Dykstra says. "But it was an unnecessary hindrance to my work and my communication with George."

BLOWING THINGS UP AT NINE-TEN

Additional specialists were hired to placate the studio, but also because ILM's explosion tests hadn't worked well. Having sat in the audience so many years ago and heard Lucas announce his intention to make *The Star Wars*,

it must have been a thrill for Joe Viskocil to join the production. He and Bruce Logan had formed Nine-Ten, an ad hoc special effects house, and they were employed in mid-September 1976 to destroy miniature ships in a convincing and spectacular fashion. They also were tasked with trying out alternative-method effects shots. Logan was yet another from the class of *2001*, having worked on that film as animation cameraman, animation artist, model builder, and shot designer for more than two years.

"Nine-Ten was formed when things were going pretty laboriously at ILM, in terms of what was being turned out, and there was pressure from Fox to produce more footage," Logan says. "I think George wanted to try a lot of ideas that were different from what was happening. It was a very experimental setup, an attempt to do some things in a simpler form to expedite the huge number of shots that were needed. They were looking for eleven-frame cuts, or nine frames of this or that. Just flashes through the frame to see how it would integrate with what ILM was doing with the repeatable camera—plus explosions, which was not the main function at the beginning. But it did turn out to be the main contribution of Nine-Ten."

Logan, Viskocil, and their small crew started on Borendo's stage, which was quickly deemed too small for the noxious chemicals they were using. The group therefore moved to the Producers' Studio, where additional space enabled them to set off bigger bombs at 100 frames per second instead of 300, using a VistaVision camera. The size of the detonated models also went from around three feet in diameter to about six feet.

"John Dykstra showed me the data of what they'd done at ILM," Viskocil says. "They'd used a lot of acetylene bombs, so it was mainly sparks and the disintegration of the model. It looked very cartoonish, which wasn't what George wanted. But through Greg Hauer at ILM, I was able to do the explosions legally because he had a powder card.

"George wanted the outline of the ship to be on fire, the entire outline of the ship sparking away, and then it would blow," Viskocil continues. "Figuring out how to do that took some time. Finally, I used just a paste—a special blend that I made up and applied right to the model—and that would be set off first. You would then have the outline for quite a few feet of film, a few frames, and next you would blow it up. George wanted to see the fireball effect, the World War II type of footage where the ship just disintegrates and you see this big ball of gasoline flame. One thing that I appreciate George for is the fact that he just gave me full rein to do what I wanted. He gave me a concept as to what he'd like to see, and I just elaborated from that."

Nine-Ten decided to use mainly silt, magnesium, and gasoline-based explosives, electronically detonated with squibs. "We had only one day to shoot something like eight or nine X-wings and Y-wings exploding at the Producers' Studio—and it was really something!" Viskocil says. "I remember we all came in Saturday: Terry Bowen, David Lester, Brent Bryden, Jerry Deets, Mike Myer. It took a lot of time to actually put all the explosives in the ships and prebreak them and wire them up. We didn't test out anything. We went for the shot—and we were lucky."

At one point pieces went through the ceiling, and at another Viskocil burned his hand. "I did have a little flaming debris on my arm at one point," Logan says, "but I was able to put it out with the fire extinguisher."

Nine-Ten did seventeen days of work—seven at Borendo and ten at the Producers' Studio—with a crew of eight people. The results were successful, but they did run over budget, costing over $65,000 instead of the projected $35,000. Logan and Viskocil would later work at ILM, however, using their experience to help create additional explosions.

Other outside houses, such as DePatie-Freleng Enterprises and Ray Mercer & Company, were also used from this point on to complete certain shots for which ILM was not equipped. Located on West Cahuenga Boulevard in Hollywood, Van Der Veer Photo Effects worked on the animation for the laser bolts and lightsaber effects (about thirty shots, according to Blalack), while Modern Film Effects composited 35mm anamorphic footage taken in England with VistaVision elements created at ILM.

STATE OF THE PRODUCTION

On September 14, 1976, Lucas sat down with Charles Lippincott for his first extended interview since before principal photography. The answers to the questions (here organized by subject) are spoken by a man who is

clearly exhausted and somewhat disappointed about much that had passed and much that was still going on. But it's possible that, like the earlier interview that took place after the green light, this one was related to the signing of the long-awaited contract.

The studio: "Fox still doesn't know what the film is. They're not a model of confidence. They're still worried that they've got a big and expensive 'something' on their hands, which they can't describe or understand."

ILM: "Given another five years and another $8 million, we could get some pretty spectacular effects out of there. But we don't have the time or the money. I don't know what else to say. That's the biggest problem."

Principal photography: "After trying to improve the script and trying to find the right story, the movie became itself, it took over. It was very hard. It found itself and became the movie that we were making. It wasn't particularly the movie I started out to make."

Concept: "When I came up with the idea for *Graffiti*, it was astounding to me that nobody had ever done it. I just could not believe that nobody had ever done a movie about cruising, one of the top national pastimes. Same thing here: It's inconceivable that they aren't making hundreds of these adventure movies. It's part of American culture."

Visuals: "The thing I like about this film is the fact that it was written and designed as a movie. The elements that are interesting in it are cinematic elements, not literary elements. It was designed as an emotional, visual exercise, not as an intellectual exercise. I'm sure we are going to get a lot of backlash because of that, but I'm not afraid of it being called a comic-book movie."

Predictions: "*Star Wars* could be a type of Davy Crockett phenomenon. I don't know whether I've done it. I don't know . . . But I know I've got a better one in me, one that is more refined. Gene Roddenberry wrote about his *Star Trek* series, and pointed out that it wasn't really until about the tenth or fifteenth episode that they finally got things pulled together. You have to walk around the world you've created a little bit before you can begin to know what to do in it.

"Someday I'll do another movie like this, maybe, which will be much closer to my original plan. I didn't get the illusion that I'd seen in my mind. I got something else, which is all right, but wasn't what I started out with. Whenever you make a movie, a force takes over and directs the movie, and there's nothing you can do about it. It takes on its own shape. It's chemistry, the chemical reaction between people; the wind and the weather, and everything. All that has its own influence; it all has a life of its own.

"The film's only hope is that it is *Jaws* and not Godzilla versus the Gila Monster."

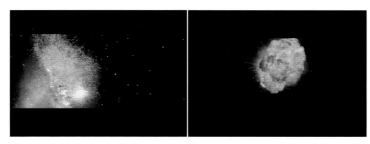

The long shot during the escape from the Death Star of the TIE fighter blowing up (far right): "That consisted of two separate explosions shot off at the same time, so it looked like one was coming through the other," says Joe Viskocil. "Alderaan blowing up was a gas explosion that consisted of wood fibers," he adds. "The pieces of wood would silhouette to give the feeling of the core of the planet (right)."

Richard Chew was the second editor hired (below), while Paul Hirsch was the third (left). With director Brian De Palma, he attended a dinner (far left, standing: Hirsch, De Palma, and Hirsch's wife, Jane; sitting: Verna Cocks, Lucas, Jay Cocks, and De Palma's future wife, Nancy Allen) and a discussion with Steven Spielberg (below, in cap, with Hal Barwood on the railing, De Palma, Kurtz, and Lucas).

A BLACK MOOD

Lucas's feelings about his film made themselves felt as he began the constant shuttling back and forth between his Park Way offices in Northern California and his special effects crew in Southern California.

"I recall one comment he made when he was having a hard time with one of the scenes that I was cutting," Richard Chew says. "I could tell that he was really unhappy, but I couldn't tell if he was unhappy with what I was doing or with the film. But George admitted to me that all he could see were his mistakes every time he looked at the scene, that it was like free association for him. He remembered all the traumas he endured while working in England: the day so-and-so had a cold, or someone had a sore throat and this guy was late, and that lens broke or he had to use the lens that he didn't want to.

"Plus, he had dozens of people down at ILM, where he was spending three days a week, and then he'd come back up north and he would look at something and say, 'Oh, this doesn't work—did I mess up in directing this?' It was just another straw on his back."

Hal Barwood and Matthew Robbins, whose offices at Park Way were a stone's throw away from the editors, were witnesses to the process. "Matthew and I would go to lunch with George frequently," Barwood says. "We'd go down to the carriage house at about lunchtime and George would be sitting there with the Moviolas, cutting away, and every now and then he'd say, 'Hey, take a look at this.' One day we saw Princess Leia with this sort of cardboard gun, peeking out, and then a coupla guys in these plastic suits that looked silly said, 'Set for stun.' Matthew and I walked outta there and had a wonderful lunch with George, and when we went back to our office, we joked around for about an hour saying, 'Set for stun. Set for stun! Oh my God, it's a disaster!' "

Despite his feelings of despair, Lucas forged ahead and was often able to aid Chew by recalling the best line readings of a given scene. "At the end of the week, he would spend all his time just looking at what we'd done while he was at ILM," Chew says, "and then looking with us at what we were going to do the following week. Usually we'd approach a scene by looking at the dailies. He would tell me what he liked, and then I would make something out of that. He has a very good memory, so we almost never had to go through the outs [discarded dailies]. George would spend anywhere from a half hour to a couple of hours appraising each scene."

But even with two editors, work was not proceeding fast enough. According to the postproduction calendar in the long-form contract, they were more than a month behind. Brian De Palma had heard they were in need of help, so he recommended his New York editor, Paul Hirsch, whom Lucas had recently met in Los Angeles, but who was now back home.

"Marcia Lucas called me," Hirsch recalls. "And she said, 'Things are going a lot slower than we had hoped; our editor in England didn't work out and we're having to recut everything. We've got Richard Chew working on the picture—but we're just not getting enough done! Are you available to come out?' And I said, 'My wife is expecting a baby, but let me ask her.' The timing was crazy, but I went home to Jane and said, 'I'll understand, whatever you say: I have an offer to go out and work on *Star Wars*.' And she said, 'Go do it.' "

A former architecture student at Columbia University, Hirsch had opted instead for film, so he dropped out and found work at a "trailer house" that had the MGM and United Artists accounts. His first mini success was when he cut down a ten-minute featurette on *The Thomas Crown Affair* (1968) to three and a half minutes. Before leaving for the West Coast, Hirsch had to spend a week finishing up on De Palma's *Carrie*, arriving in San Anselmo on October 16. "I was a little intimidated," he says. "Because both Marcia and Richard had been nominated for Academy Awards before, and I was just this kid from New York, but they were great.

"At first I was working on the Moviola. But I had forgotten how many years it had been since I had worked on one, so I was all thumbs, breaking the film, dropping it, and wasting a lot of time just trying to get the film to go through the machine. So Marcia said, 'I don't care. I'll work on the Moviola.' After that, I was working upstairs in George's room on the Steenbeck."

Hirsch's first encounter with Lucas in the small carriage house was instructive. The editor was given a scene that Jympson had assembled that seemed to already conform to what the director said he wanted. "I was overcome with a great feeling of dismay," Hirsch says. "It seemed to be exactly what George was after. But he said, 'This is your test.' So I started to get into it, looking at alternate takes and really examining the possibilities of the scene. The original scene had been cut to about four minutes; when I finished the scene, it was down to three minutes—but there was more in it."

Once Ben Burtt understood the lay of the land, he, too, grabbed a room at Park Way, in the main house basement. "I got to know George better since I was near him," Burtt says. "He told me, 'We're going to start editing the picture. What I want you to do is just start cutting in sound effects that go with the picture so I can see whether I like them or not.'

"I was alone in a room with the sound equipment and the library. So the first day I walked over to the editors and I asked if could see the reels they'd cut, so they ran reels one and two. It was the first time I'd seen anything in the picture, and I was overwhelmed. When they were finished with those reels, I just took them back and the first thing I started working on was the big fight in the beginning. There was no spaceship shot, no titles, so I started working on different laser gun sounds. I worked with the basic laser gun sounds for about a month. At the same time, I started working on Artoo-Detoo, since he spoke right off the bat."

FINALLY MAGIC

Lucas would fly down to Los Angeles every Monday and work at ILM until Wednesday evening. Slowly, over a period of months, he was able to put things together and become better acquainted with the personnel down south, though stress levels remained consistently high. According to the fictitious but—judging by ILM's internal reports from the time—strangely accurate estimate put together by Kurtz and Mather, 18.1 percent of the effects work had been completed by October 16.

"When George came back from England, we'd been operating autonomously for some time building the equipment and learning how to use it," says Edlund, whose first job had been working at CBS News, out of Seattle, Washington, as a television cameraman—this after graduating from UCLA with a philosophy degree and dropping out of Harvard Law

Darth Vader's TIE fighter: "This was another quickie design, based on a two-by-two-inch sketch," Joe Johnston says. "George wanted to use the basic TIE ship cockpit, so he said, 'Make it look like a faster, newer TIE model. It's the general's ship, the command car.' I did a dozen sketches and he picked one [top]. Steve Gawley took it and pinned it to his model-making workbench" (below).

Starfields: Before any shot of spaceships flying around could be completed, ILM had to solve the problem of a key element that would be common to them all: the starfield. "I created the stars," Joe Johnston says. "The starfield was two four-by-eight-feet sheets of Plexiglas, lit from behind, and placed in a semi-circular box."

The four-by-sixteen-foot starfield was painted silver and then black so that it would be opaque. It was curved into two arcs, and lamps were placed between the arcs to create a light-box effect (below, with Doug Smith). Then Johnston went in and created the star patterns by poking holes in the black paint—a long process, because at first he ended up with a polka-dot look. The stars had to be painstakingly re-formed into nebulae, constellations, and so on.

School a few years later. "But George wasn't satisfied with the look of the shots we'd done, so he spent some time with me on the stage. I would program a shot, so that he could see all of the parameters, and he'd say something like, 'It looks like it pans a little bit too much, can you fix that?' I'd correct the pan, then shoot it in black-and-white, develop it here in fifteen or twenty minutes, and put it on the Moviola. George could see exactly what we'd done, and he'd say, 'That looks better, but let's do this.' On two or three shots, we went over it ten times—but it was great, because after that point, if I had a problem, I could call him if he happened to be in San Anselmo, and he knew what I was talking about. The telephone became a successful communication device."

"We finally got up to sixteen people in the optical department, working on two shifts, eleven hours a day, six days a week," Robbie Blalack says. "After about six months of testing and playing around, we got the process of printing from the bluescreen shots and all of the other elements down to where it was fairly good."

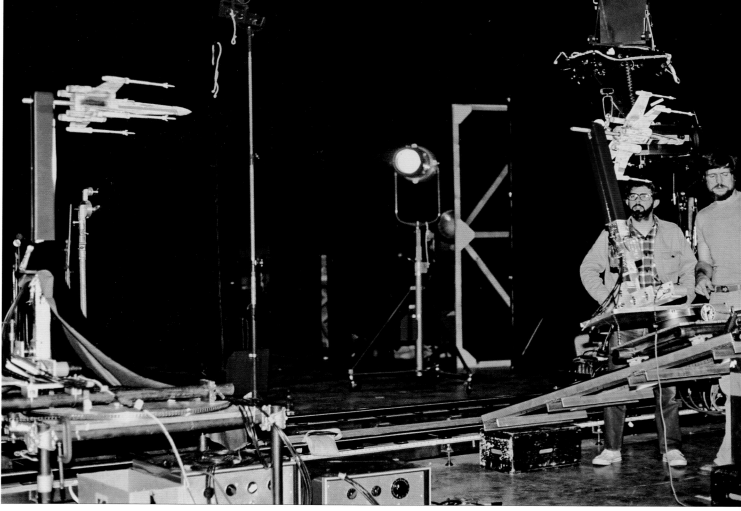

On one of the stages at ILM, Edlund and Lucas talk (right, and below with X-wings supported by blue pylons—one of Dykstra's innovations that greatly facilitated the bluescreen process). Standing around a Moviola (opposite, left), Lucas powwows with Joe Johnston, who designed the T-shirt being worn by Edlund (inset). One shooting stage had the Dykstraflex on a 40-foot track with its boom (opposite, right, with Lucas, Paul Huston on stool, and Kurtz kneeling). The second stage had a 14-foot track with a Technorama camera. Both stages were equipped with turntables, motorized trolleys, and bluescreens.

THE MAKING OF STAR WARS

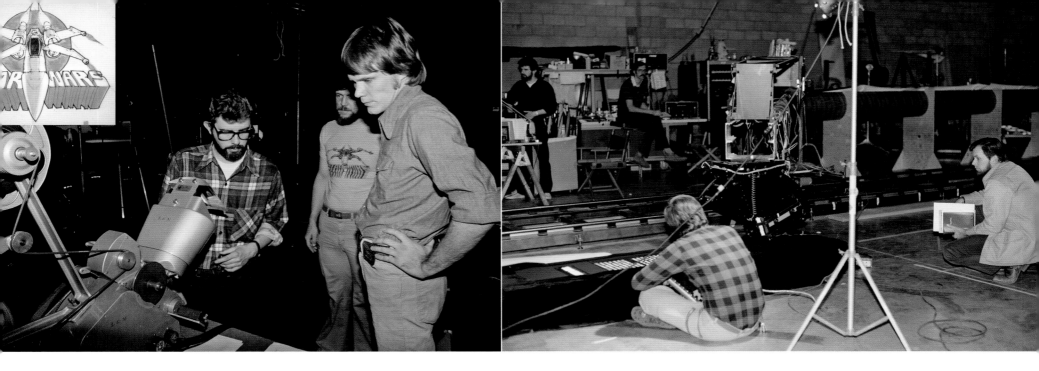

To do the "lineups," Blalack hired Dave McCue, John Moles, Bruce Nicholson, Donna Tracy, and Eldon Rickman, who had been recommended by Disney—all young people ready to work very long hours. Jim Vantress, who used to run the insert department at MGM, was brought in as an "operator," as was David Berry, who was imported from the stage area. Much of everyone's concern was keeping the printing room ultra-clean so no dirt would contaminate what had to be an always pristine negative; eventually a vacuum suction machine was purchased that could suck up dirt from people's shoes.

ILM's change of course continued as Bob Shourt managed to remedy R2-D2's mechanical problems in two weeks, much to Lucas's relief—something John Stears's special effects department hadn't been able to accomplish in six months. George Mather also had a small but crucial first victory when, according to Lorne Peterson, he was able through his Hollywood connections to speed up the time in which ILM's VistaVision film was being developed; up until his intervention, the processing houses were apparently ignoring the low-level production.

"They needed to get the film done in time," Dennis Muren says. "I tried shooting some spaceship shots on our older secondary camera, but eventually the decision was made for me to work nights and Richard Edlund to work days on the main camera, starting in August or September, for about five months."

"George was our general," Muren's assistant Ken Ralston says. "We were his soldiers and we were all fighting this single battle to get the film out."

As shot production increased, and more shots were approved by Lucas, the sixteen months of preparation began to pay off. "There wasn't a lot of enthusiasm until the people around this organization started seeing some product," Dykstra says. "And then they would go, 'Hey, look at that, that's pretty neat.'"

The comments, offhand in August and September, became more deeply felt by October, and the place began to really gel. It had begun with an odd combination of people with specific talents, many of whom had never been involved in filmmaking before. Finding themselves in a situation where they could apply their distinctive creative abilities to a unique purpose, they now realized they were learning quite a bit, which, in turn, inspired them to put even more into their work—to the point where they actually started to compete for extra duties.

"We hired renaissance people who understood enough about film and drawing, about mechanics and carpentry, and who could interrelate," Dykstra says. "But all of a sudden we had people going, 'That's my responsibility, you're taking my responsibility!' And it gets to be a knotty problem keeping everybody happy. It's the first time you ever found people arguing about taking more work, right? These guys were crazy, but it was a nice switch."

ILM was often dealing in contradictions. Outsiders saw the effects house as disorganized because it was unorthodox, but internally everyone knew they were under duress and on a timetable. The paradox worked fairly well, led by the department heads who, by this time, were working together harmoniously. "Those people—McCune, Blalack, Edlund—came in all at once so that they could develop their own spaces and a method of communication. There were no memos, not one single memo pad," Dykstra explains. "There were memos to the outside world, but the information that was done around here was done by word of mouth. The people upstairs knew what was happening on the stage and the people on the stage knew what was happening upstairs. There were problems, but overall it worked really smoothly. It could've been a lot worse. Not one person killed anybody else, although it came close a couple of times."

The noncorporate way of working added to ILM's mystique and people began to call it the "Country Club." Because the facility had no air-conditioning and the temperature on the two stages often rose above 100 degrees beneath the hot lights, a makeshift cold tub was constructed outside. Filled with overheated longhaired employees, it was eyed with horror by visiting studio executives. Another way to cool down was provided by Joe Johnston, who purchased an airplane escape chute from a manufacturer across the street and transformed it into a water slide. For relaxation, the model shop was used for dances, and film nights were scheduled with pizza (and the occasional porno film snuck in). A Friday-evening tradition became known as "launching ship night," because ILMers would take model rockets and blast broomsticks, old X-wings,

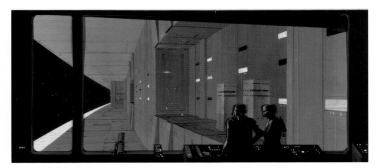

plastic models—and once an old car—as far into the sky as their rocket fuel would carry them.

The atmosphere during working hours was deceptively calm, however, as much of the photography was done late in the afternoon or at night. The facility literally didn't have enough electricity during the day at times, because of industrial plants down the street that tended to hog the neighborhood's resources. Once the factories closed at five, shots lined up during the day could be completed. A lot of people therefore slept on the premises, with their sleeping bags on cots, in a state of enthusiasm mixed with high anxiety.

"People don't understand this and I doubt that they ever will," Dykstra says. "If you do special effects, you work in a black room all day long and you get totally paranoid about your film. Everything happens slowly and you can't tell if there's a glitch in the shot until you get the process back the next day. People are on edge a lot and under pressure all the time."

By October 30 ILM was up to the mirage-like statistic of 25.8 percent complete. But they were making progress, and Lucas's feelings had gone from almost entirely despondent to somewhat hopeful. "I remember George visiting my house in Los Angeles," Martin Scorsese says, "and complaining about the special effects and how he never wanted to direct again. He said he'd really had it. But he was thrilled with certain shots, like a spacecraft crossing the frame and the camera panning with it."

SPLICING THROUGH SPACE

"George was the only one who had seen the whole picture," Paul Hirsch says. "I had no idea what the stuff looked like and wouldn't know until I finished the reel and got into the next reel. I was trying to do about a reel a week because of the time pressure. I'd finish a reel and go to George, and he would discuss what I had done and we'd make changes and get it right. Then I'd go on to the next reel—and it was just a whole world. I remember looking at reel nine with George—which has Ben going into the power trench, then the Tarzan scene, with Luke and Leia swinging across the chasm, and the swordfight and the shootout when they escape—and I looked at that reel and I thought, *My God, this is going to be a lot of work*."

"I was working with three editors at once," Lucas says. "I was spending half of my time in Los Angeles working on the special effects, so I could only work with them for three or four days a week. I would tell them what I want, say this is the shot that I want, and this is the way I think the scene should work. Then I would come back the next day, look at what

they'd cut, and we would discuss the changes and problems. I was going from editor to editor to editor, all day long."

As the editors went as fast as they could toward a first cut, with Hirsch working upstairs and Marcia and Chew downstairs near the assistant editors and the coding machine, both Chew and Hirsch were able to assess Lucas's editorial style. "George likes to keep things simple and gets his energy from the cutting," Hirsch says.

"He was pretty spare," Chew observes. "Coming off *Cuckoo's Nest*, it especially struck me. Milos Forman would have four or five printed takes of a master; then he would have the singles and the two-shots, and four or five takes of those. George, either for aesthetic or budgetary reasons, was much more controlled about that."

Although there were certain scenes that each editor "owned," they began to trade off just before completing the initial cut. "We put it all together and then spent about three or four days as a tag team," Hirsch says. "George, Richard, Marcia, and I would sit at the machine each for a couple of hours, taking turns and making suggestions. The last day, we did this for about twelve hours."

PRIVATE PREMIERE

From the aggregate interviews, it's not clear exactly when the first cut was finished, though it was probably late October or early November. The scene chronology of the first assembly corresponded almost exactly with the shooting script, with Biggs, Luke's friends, Jabba the Hutt, two trench runs, and so on. Those who saw this cut, either together or at intervals, were Lucas, his three editors, Kurtz, and Burtt, who had done a "scratch mix." Temporary sound effects thus accompanied the whole picture, but it had only scattered special effects shots, primarily from the Death Star escape sequence.

"At that time very few optical shots were completed from the end battle," Burtt says. "But they had a work print based on old World War II movies. So I cut the spaceship sounds and lasers to that. We had Spitfires going by that sounded like spaceships; we had lasers being fired from Messerschmitts. It was relatively insane."

"I'd always seen the film in bits and pieces, only the parts that I was working on, or looking over someone's shoulder," Chew says. "So the most lasting impression I have of the film was after watching the first cut the first time—and when I saw it, I was really astounded by the *entirety of*

On October 11, 1976, Ken Ralston (top right) helped photograph elements for a complex shot of the *Millennium Falcon* being pulled into the Death Star. McQuarrie's production illustrations were the guide (opposite) as Lucas directed second unit (left and above). "When the *Falcon* is drawn into the Death Star, that's a matte shot with a number of elements," Richard Edlund says. "That was actually Joe Johnston down there in the foreground—in fact, it's Joe Johnston *and* Joe Johnston. We only had one Imperial suit at that point, because the other had been stolen, so we shot it split screen. We also needed two cannons, but we only had one."

George's vision. I don't think I was able to get up from my chair afterward for about ten minutes in the screening room. I realized the look of the film, the thrust of the film, the characters of the film were so uniquely George—if you know George in any way, you had to realize that all of this came as a result of this *one man.* And it just knocked me out. It was coming from the recesses of George's mind, this basic seed that he had grown into a thousand trees."

Chew was evidently impressed, and the others could also see the film's potential. But it was very far from finished, and the screening led to several changes and two substantial cuts. First Lucas decided to begin the movie the way he'd written it in his second draft, before intercutting the scenes of Luke and his friends on Tatooine with those of the robots, Darth Vader, and Leia in space.

"In the first five minutes, we were hitting everybody with more

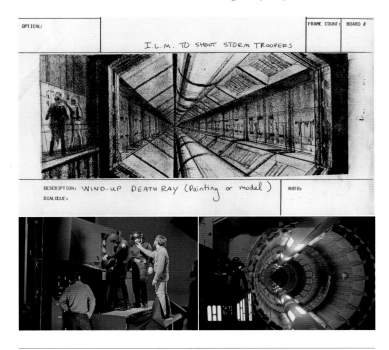

At ILM, Lucas shot inserts of Death Star technicians preparing to fire the laser including Joe Johnston and Jon Erland as those occupying the laser tunnel (above left, with Edlund holding a light meter as Lucas looks on). "That energy tunnel was fairly difficult, because it was not that easy to do circles in perspective," animation supervisor Adam Beckett says. "The shots that did have interesting requirements received, possibly, excessive attention because of their rarity, but that energy tunnel has everything in it but the cat's meow. It's got light effects, a live-action element, two guys, with light effects on them. That platform is hand-drawn by Pete Kuran, who also created the light effects on the wall of the tunnel with Jonathan Seay. I'd do the key drawings and Diana Wilson would do a lot of the in-betweens. There were probably 160 pieces of artwork in 42 frames; the only reason there are so few is because most of the animation is in cycles that can be repeated over and over again. Those concentric rings going down the energy tunnel are just repeats. The miniature of the infinite tunnel was done by cutting a hole in a front-surface mirror and photographing it through that hole with another mirror behind it—just like at the funhouse."

information than they could handle," Hirsch says. "There were too many story lines to keep straight: the robots and the Princess, Vader, Luke. So we simplified it by taking out Luke and Biggs, instead just presenting the Princess and Vader, which is clearer. The Princess has the plans—the thing that everyone in the film is very much concerned about—and she gives the plans to the robots, and the robots go to the planet and they meet Luke. So that's now relatively simple.

"But it also made the picture a lot weirder," he adds, "because the main characters became the robots, which is a wonderful idea. It's very George. And the reason it works is that George invested the characters with a human sense of humor. It also made the planet they land on work as an alien place. Before, by showing Luke on the planet, there was no mystery: You knew the planet was inhabited by people. But now when you go to the planet with the robots, you don't know what you're going to find—the first characters you see are Jawas—which gives it a whole air of exotic mystery."

George also felt that there was no reason to see Luke until he became an active participant in the story. But it was not an easy decision to make to just delete those sequences; Marcia fought to keep them in, and the four scenes with Luke and his friends were tried in different places. But more arguments for cutting came from the fact that George didn't like the performances, and that the later relationships Luke creates are stronger.

"One of the big topics that came up was how do we speed up getting to the cantina scene?" Chew says. "The answer was to stay with the story of the robots, also because it's so much more unconventional. That's when George told Paul and me for the first time that that was initially how he had written the story. To us, who were new to the picture, that just seemed the way to go."

The second major sequence to be cut was the scene in which Jabba the Hutt spars with Han Solo. Lucas realized that ILM would not be able to complete the complicated stop-motion Jabba he'd wanted in time to finish the movie. Again, though she knew the scene had problems and would be hard for ILM, Marcia lobbied to keep it. In this she was joined by Harrison Ford. The problem once again, however, was pacing and performance. "George also thought there were too many phony-looking green Martians that looked like Greedo in the background," Hirsch says.

Once again, different methods for salvaging the scene were mulled over. "George considered putting subtitles under Jabba, and I think that idea got transferred over to Greedo," Chew says.

"There were certain expositional elements in the Jabba scene—the fact that Han was a smuggler, that he was wanted, that he needed the money—so we incorporated those into Greedo's sequence and that solved that problem," Hirsch adds.

The first cut ran about 117 minutes. And even though they were dropping some scenes, the editors knew the film would stay about the same length because it was missing "personality" shots of the Death Star, establishing shots, the roll-up, and the credits. Indeed, so much was still in the works that Ladd, sitting in his office at Fox, was pessimistic about the film being released on schedule. The film had already been pushed back from its initial April 1977 date, and he was concerned it might slip again.

"In September, George, Gary, and I had met with Laddie, Jay Kanter, and the future head of marketing and distribution, Ashley Boone," Lippincott says. "We told them it would be ready at the end of May. They spent a few days talking it over and called back—they agreed."

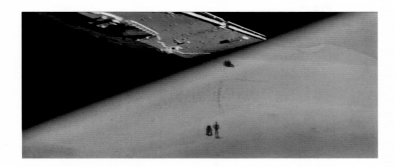

Chew-ing Editorial

Working on the first cut under the supervision of Lucas, each editor tackled certain scenes. Though there was occasional overlap, Richard Chew recalls the following anecdotes about some of the sequences that he cut together:

Rebel ship shootout: "What was interesting was how George staged that twice, and shot it with three cameras each time: first from behind the Rebel soldiers, and then from behind the stormtroopers. Because of the time and expense of having explosions and guys falling all over, I'm sure that George had judiciously placed his cameras. So we just doubled up on stuff and were able to take about twenty seconds of time on the set and turn it into two minutes. George asked me to indicate with grease pencil, in every instance where a laser gun was firing, the path of the lasers. In most of these instances the laser bolt was never more than three frames long, but I would indicate with a circle whatever laser gun was firing. It would take me a couple of hours to mark up a whole gun battle with grease-pencil marks. When we'd play back the film, all you'd see were a bunch of circles with some asterisks for explosions and streaks with arrows indicating directions and angles of incoming laser bolts—but George, with one look, would be able to spot problems, 'Okay, you need two more laser bolts up here.' He would be able to instantaneously pick out all the gaps in the flow."

Luke in garage with robots: "One thing that had concerned George on this scene was that he didn't have enough coverage on Artoo. Because of things that happened on the day he was shooting, he ran out of time and didn't shoot close-ups for Artoo, so we were missing angles for when Luke leans into Artoo, starts scraping him, and the robot plays the hologram—there was nothing else that could be used for Artoo at the beginning and the end of the scene. But I was able to find a couple of feet here and a couple of feet there, before the slate and after 'cut,' of Artoo making certain moves, which I was able to edit into the right overlap of dialogue either from Threepio or Luke. I remember that was the first time George got excited about something, because it worked perfectly well as a reaction on the part of Artoo, especially as we were also cheating new dialogue for Artoo, which George had yet to make up."

Dinner with Luke, Uncle Owen, and Aunt Beru: "Normally, George would cover a scene like this from, say, three angles: a single on each and

then one two-shot. He wouldn't shoot a lot of takes, seldom going beyond take three—whereas that dinner scene, as I recall, he went to take seven, nine, and even eleven. He knew that he was in trouble with the actor playing the uncle, so he had to get as much coverage as he could."

Rebel hangar: "There are very few scenes that I can recall that had complicated staging moves. They were usually very direct. It was A to B: Darth Vader comes in the room, and goes to Tarkin, who is sitting. He didn't do the kind of baroque movements that Francis would have, where the editor could probably use the entire master shot because it was constantly changing frame size and who was included in the frame. I think probably the most interesting camera moves George did were in the hangar, in scenes that got dropped from the film; that is, Luke getting ready to go to battle, stopping to talk to Han, going over to Leia, and then coming to see Biggs."

Richard Chew also worked on the cantina scenes, while Paul Hirsch edited the droid sale, Ben's cave, and all the scenes from the moment they blast out of Mos Eisley up until the escape from the Death Star—which Chew and Lucas cut. Marcia Lucas worked primarily on the scenes that were deleted of Luke and his friends on Tatooine—and on all the scenes from the moment the X-wing pilots close their canopies up until the end of the film.

In keeping with the tradition of the old serials and swashbucklers, Lucas decided to revive the use of editorial wipes, a transitional device for going from scene to scene (above left). On the ground floor of the converted carriage house at Park Way (below), a Moviola was used for editing the film, along with other equipment and the obligatory trim basket.

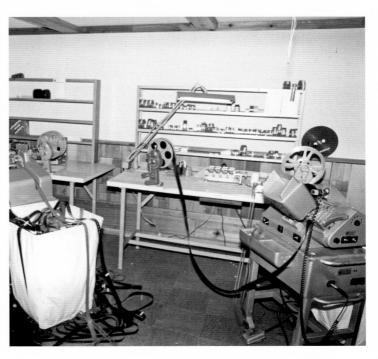

INDUSTRIAL LIGHT & MAGIC INC.
6842 VALJEAN VAN NUYS CALIFORNIA 91406   PHONE 9895757

```
MEMO FOR GEORGE LUCAS - SAN FRANCISCO - 11/30/76


1)  GL:  GET OUTTAKES FROM SAN FRANCISCO OF X WING
         COCKPIT SHOT AND Y WING COCKPIT SHOT.  These
         outakes will be tested as comps with trench shots
         with and without lazers.

2)  NOTE TO TOD:  OPTICAL HOUSE REQUESTS THAT GUN
    BARRELS BE SCRIBED DIFFERENTLY THAN YOU HAVE
    BEEN SCRIBING THEM.  THE CURRENT WAY OBLITERATES
    GUN BARREL.
```

NO   YES

An ILM memo dated November 30 (above) illustrates the correct and incorrect way to animate blasterfire. Upstairs in the ILM dailies room (below) are: (front row, from left) Jon Berg, Rick Baker, Ken Ralston, Dennis Muren, and Lorne Peterson (in armchair); (second row) Grant McCune, Jibralta Merrill, production assistant Mikki Herman, Penny McCarthy, Gary Jouvenat, and Jim Nelson; (in the back) Dave Jones, Jerry Greenwood, Gary Kurtz, Rose Duignan, and George Lucas.

"We met at the time to discuss it, because there had been much contemplation of not opening the film in the summer of 1977," Ladd says. "That they were going to get October instead, because there were hardly any effects, and they were so far behind that the feeling was they would not be ready. But George said, 'I will be ready.' And he explained how he was doubling up on some things which would allow him to make the date."

Around this time, Lucas also asked Ladd for funds to reshoot parts of the cantina sequence for Greedo's new dialogue, and to enhance the scene with more aliens, but no immediate decision was forthcoming.

ELECTRONIC BABY TALK

The scratch track on the first cut did not include finished robot sounds, because each one was a special case, and none more particular than that of R2-D2. "Discussing Artoo, George said, 'I want an organic sound, like it was a five-year-old kid, but he's got to sound electronic,'" Burtt says. "The first I did were too electronic, pure synthesizer, too impersonal and cold. George wanted to add an emotional side to it. We had Artoo talking to Ben Kenobi, so we had to be up on a level with Alec Guinness, to come up with a character who was going to make him look good, not silly. We had to achieve a performance through sound, which is not easy, and that is what I struggled with the most.

"George pushed me a great deal on it," he continues, "and many times I think I stopped too early. I was satisfied with it, and he wasn't. He would say, 'No, no, no.' I'd work for a long time on something I thought was just perfect, and I'd play it for George when he'd come back on Friday—and he'd say, 'It's not any good.' And I'd be upset and resentful, because I had a feeling I was failing. But I was inexperienced. I had never worked with anyone like this before. He'd never be harsh, by any means, he'd just say, 'No, it's not what I want.' As he was in every area, he was meticulous. He wouldn't let anything slip by without his approval.

"But it worked out great," Burtt says. "The final approach we took was this: I'd look at a reel, and I'd write down what I thought Artoo would be saying in English, like 'I'm hungry,' or 'Look out, the stormtroopers are coming,' or 'Gee, look at that explosion.' Then I'd show George, and he'd say, 'Yeah, that's about right. Try to come up with some phrases for that feeling.' So I would make up a phrase. We went one phrase at a time in the picture. It started out very slow. It took forever to finish reel one—six weeks, I think. After that, it began to go a little bit faster. Originally, I tried actually making sounds that had the same intonations and inflections as the line in English, but that didn't work. In the end it became a matter of establishing basic emotional levels: excitement, cute squawks, inquisitive whistles. I'd play his 'words' on the synthesizer while I made sounds into the microphone at the same time, and the two would be blended. I'd whistle and coo—a bunch of coos, that's the sound that George does very well, it's one of his ideas—I'd sigh and groan, and move the oscillators of the synthesizer. So it was almost always a blend of a human sound with an electronic sound. We got the organic and the electronic combined. Once we had the technique down, I would audition my performance for George."

"The first effect that Ben Burtt laid in was the exclamation of Artoo when he got hit by that Jawa shot and fell over," Richard Chew remembers, "and it just broke me up. The film really came to life."

DOGS AND MONSTERS

The adventures of ILM continued in November 1976. Joe Viskocil and Bruce Logan were now helping Richard Edlund do explosions, eventually blowing up seven models in the Van Nuys facility. "We had one really glorious explosion of one of the TIE fighters," Viskocil says, "and Richard almost lost his ear."

In the ILM editorial department there was another close call. "I used to take pieces of film I was working on and put them over my neck," Dykstra says. "Every once in a while, I'd screw up and put one of the pieces of the film that was around my neck into the Moviola—and almost cut my head off!"

Upstairs, in a room with some fairly dilapidated couches, dailies of special effects shots began to be a regular occurrence. The attendees would offer their critiques, but would also begin to scratch themselves after a while (some ILMers were bringing in their flea-ridden dogs, who would sleep on the couches). The critique most often heard was, "Bluespill! Bluespill!" Because the blue of the bluescreen—the part of the shot that was supposed to disappear—could be seen invading, spilling into the miniature or even principal photography.

"I have a feeling that it's impossible to totally avoid bluespill in this situation," says Adam Beckett, who ran the rotoscope department. "I've heard some grumbling that 'they weren't as careful as they could be' in England, but that would derive from our initial failure to supply the plates. So various excuses on both sides were made."

"It was a real difficult thing having to learn how to use this new camera equipment, having to start and stop motors, and vary the speeds of motors during the shots to make it look as though ships are actually making believable aerodynamic rolls and banks," Dennis Muren says. "Some of those shots were absolute killers. I had to come up with a lot of ways to *not* use the motors, so I could use what I'd learned on space films to give realistic-looking motions."

"I think John Barry and I conversed a couple of times, but he was so far away," Dykstra says. "And given how much there was to do, it was simply impossible that problems would not happen on the set that would make the special effects more difficult to do down the line. In the compressed span of time he had to complete all of those sets, he could not be there to make certain there wasn't a bluespill problem or that there were no yellow lights or whatever."

Apart from noting the technical shortcomings of what was shot at EMI, the ILM crew was seeing the story of the movie for the first time. "None of us realized exactly what it was about until we saw some footage from England," says Richard Alexander. "Suddenly, the day we saw the dailies, we came out of there saying, 'Hey, this might be pretty neat.'"

While the make-believe percentages disappeared in November, a new system of tracking took its place, with each shot followed until it was deemed "OKAY G. L."—approved by Lucas. Though the escape pod shots were completed first, the very first shot "accepted" was the Death Star firing a laser cannon, photographed by Muren. The schedule indicates that two other shots were approved by Lucas on October 16, 1976, but only a few more had met with Lucas's okay by November. "This whole thing has been pretty strange for me, because I came from a traditional way of doing special effects," Muren says. "To come in and work with electronics and everything—it's just something that I'm still getting used to."

A November 15 memo in the ILM archives indicates that a November 22 meeting was scheduled with the "monster people" so they could review the cantina sequence and prepare for the reshoot, whose funding was still in question. Meeting notes explain how elephants were to be made into banthas: "New tail will be dragged. Should be made of light, furry and durable material. Head piece depends on what elephants will tolerate." Attendees also discussed whether it would be a good idea, for the safety of everyone, if the elephant trainer might be disguised as a Tusken Raider, so he could remain close to his pachyderm player.

One story that comes to a close around this time concerns ILM and the union. About three-quarters of the way through production a number of "established" industry people developed a renewed interest in what ILM was doing. Word was circulating about some of their more unique approaches to special effects. "It finally came down to a meeting," Tom Pollock says. "Jerry Smith and Joe Berna came down to the facility, and ILM put on a rather brilliant performance."

"When the union boys came in to look us over, I had a program in the camera," Richard Edlund says. "I pushed a button, and the camera went through its gyrations, down the track with no one touching anything, with the lights flashing and the counters buzzing—and stopped right in front of them. They were kinda taken aback because they had never seen anything like this. They knew that we had brought home the bacon. So they said, 'Okay we'll take you guys in.'"

MOTION OUT OF MODELS

Two key individuals in the race to complete the film were Edlund and Muren, who were alternately using the main camera, each with his crew, literally night and day. "We split the shots up pretty much however we felt like it, and that worked out pretty well," Edlund says. "We got along quite well, and there weren't a lot of egos involved. Everybody knew what the project was and were giving their input because everybody had this common cause."

"The Rebel blockade runner was almost the last ship finished," says Joe Johnston (above). "On the first pirate ship, there wasn't really enough detail on it; it didn't look like it was done by real movie model builders, and the paint job was amateurish. The second version was real nicely done. We'd had the chance to do all those other models in between and then go back to the blockade runner. It really showed what everyone had learned about model building. It was supposed to look like a ship that had been assembled from other ships. George said he wanted something that looked like a fish head, after we'd taken the original cockpit and put it on the *Millennium Falcon*. I think he finally did me a little sketch of this hammerhead thing, and that's what it ended up like." The ship sits on a table in the model shop with Dave Beasley, David Jones, and Paul Huston working on another ship (above).

The two special effects photographers divided up the work along the following lines (though sometimes a shot would have several parts that would be subdivided):

> **Richard Edlund:** "The opening shot, most of the pirate ship shots, most of the bigger ships I did; and I did the trench itself." "Richard liked the dogfights," Muren says, "where there's one ship pursuing another and two ships racing along the trench. He also shot the training remote."
>
> **Dennis Muren:** "The multiple ship shots, like the Y-wings diving down together and going into battle, that's the stuff that I did. I did most of the shots with the ships flying through the trench, the ship elements, although Richard shot the trench element; and I did all the shots of the ships flying toward and away from the Death Star." "Dennis did a lot of the X-wing stuff," Edlund says. "He did the armada scene and the approach to the Death Star, and the peel-off shot."

As Edlund and Muren appraised certain shots and sequences, they had to always maintain an equilibrium between technology versus artistry versus necessity. They thus made "maps of the galaxy" to show where the sun would be at any time, "but it really worked out best when the shot dictated how it was lit," Edlund says. While Lucas hadn't been enthralled by the lighting in earlier shots, the later ones were much improved by his increased communication with Edlund. Muren had his own learning curve. "I was very skeptical of the Dykstraflex at first," he explains. "It was used for a lot of shots—dogfights and ships moving quickly—that it didn't need to be used for. I think those elements could've been shot at high speed with wires or poles against blue. But everything was set up for this system."

The more Muren worked within that system, however, the more he came to realize its advantages. In fact, the experimental attempts made at Nine-Ten, using more low-tech approaches to fly ships, ultimately were not compatible with the high level of work that began to come out of ILM. "You're working in a very slow-motion situation," Muren says. "And a lot of ideas come just as you are doing the work; you have an idea on how to make something better just as you see it happening. If you were trying to do something with ships on wires and you got an idea to change a motion, it would be a big deal: You'd have ten people who would have to do the work, and they would start grumbling because they don't want to do it, and the producer would be pacing back and forth. But out here nobody has to know about that but me. I can just reprogram a shot. It takes me only two minutes to change the entire direction of the ship by just running a motor [in the Dykstraflex] to the left instead of to the right. That's one of the neatest things about it. You can get very spectacular-looking shots done by an individual instead of a group. It's the neatest tool that's probably been made to do aerial footage."

But even with the innovative equipment, the poetry of the flying ships had to be implemented by humans. "What is more interesting is getting into the pantomiming of the ships, the motions of the ships," Muren says, "which are completely created by Richard and me. That was really difficult! To make these ships look like they're flying, like they've got weight, because you're creating motion out of nothing."

```
150          INT. LUKE'S STARSHIP - COCKPIT - TRAVELING          150
(86A)                                                            (86A)
             CU. Luke.  Grim determination sweeps across Luke's face as
             he flips several switches above his head and adjusts his
             computerized target readouts.

161          INT. LUKE'S STARSHIP - COCKPIT - TRAVELING          161
(97)                                                             (97)
             CU. Luke.  He nosedives radically starting his attack on the
             monstrous fortress.  The Death Star surface streaks past the
             cockpit window.

                              LUKE
             This is Blue Five, I'm going in.

                              BIGGS
             I'm right behind you, Blue Five.

163          INT. LUKE'S STARSHIP - TRAVELING                    163
(99)                                                             (99)
             CU. Luke.  Terror crosses his face as he realizes he won't
             be able to pull out in time to avoid the fireball.

                              BIGGS
             Pull out.  Luke, pull out!

C163         INT. LUKE'S STARSHIP - COCKPIT - TRAVELING          C163
(102)                                                            (102)
             CU. Luke.  He adjusts his controls and breathes a sigh of
             relief.  Flak bursts outside the cockpit window.

                              BIGGS
             Are you all right, Luke?

                              LUKE
             I got a little cooked, but, I'm OK.

                           BLUE LEADER
             Blue Five, give yourself more lead time,
             or you're going to blast yourself out
             of the sky.
```

Lucas's ongoing corrections to the final script make plain the decision to change the "Blue" Rebel pilots to "Red," though in the final film at least one pilot still wears a helmet with a blue insignia.

"No matter how sophisticated your equipment is, no matter how neat it all is," Edlund adds, "whenever you get into production, you invariably wind up making do with what's at hand. You've got a little bit of light flare coming from sunlight, so you tear off a piece of cardboard and tape it on—and it looks quite amazing and that's real professionalism."

EDITING, THE SPIRIT OF '76

Following the first cut, there was a new temp cut every couple of weeks, which only the same small group would review. After the first major structural changes, other adjustments were made to the successive cuts: for example, to the opening shootout. "There were two shots of actual humans getting hit, with big explosions on their chests," Lucas says. "But I cut those out after I saw it; it was a little too extreme. I did have big blasts on the stormtroopers, but I avoided them on humans."

The scene in Obi-Wan's house was rethought, too. As originally scripted and shot, Luke and Ben watched the hologram, discussed the Force, and then decided to save the Princess—which, upon viewing, seemed a bit heartless because of the lag between her plea for help and their decision to fly to her rescue. The scene was re-edited to start as if they'd already begun talking about the Force—then, as soon as they see the hologram, Ben decides to travel to Alderaan. To smooth over the edit, a brief shot of R2-D2 beeping impatiently to play them the hologram was inserted, culled from other footage of the robot.

In the hangar, lines were shortened and dialogue about Luke's father being a great pilot was cut. But it was the end battle, by far the most complicated part of the story, that required the most editing work. One of the first changes was to clarify the number and characters of the supporting pilots, some of whom were cut. "That decision was really made in terms of what would be easily identifiable," Lucas says. "We had a Blue crew but we couldn't use blue because of the bluescreen [parts of their ships would've disappeared]. So we were left with Gold Leader and Red Leader."

The end battle was also running too long, so Luke's two trench runs were combined into one. This created tighter storytelling, but also several editorial challenges. Within one trench run, the following would now have to be conveyed either visually or verbally: Luke's initial intention to use the computer, Ben's dialogue, Vader's actions, R2-D2's drama, Han's arrival, the fate of the other pilots, Leia's feelings—all within the believable length of physical space along the trench. To draw out the suspense, Lucas had decided to shoot second-unit footage at ILM of the Death Star preparing to fire, some of which would be added to this sequence, along with coverage taken of Peter Cushing, stolen from an earlier scene that had been shortened. "It was all editorially manufactured," says Marcia Lucas, who, just after Thanksgiving, left the picture to help Martin Scorsese on *New York, New York*.

SOUND EDITING

Just before Christmas, another cut was ready. "For the second screening we hadn't tried to keep Ben's tracks in sync," Hirsch explains, "so we looked at the picture with just the work track. There were no sound effects, and everyone thought it was a disastrous screening except me. I believe it's good to look at something with no sound effects and no music, because they can mask your understanding of what's happening editorially."

From that point on, however, Burtt's sound effects work more consistently dovetailed with what was being done in editorial. As soon as they finished a reel, he would mix in the sound and give it back to them so they could hear as well as see how it played—an unorthodox but effective methodology. Usually, sound work would have come as the last step before the film's release, with someone given a final cut of the film and asked to simply fill in the sound holes.

"The editor would cut a reel and a week later he'd see the mixed version of it," Burtt explains. "I would add all the sounds—lasers, spaceships, Jawas, Sand People. The editors would eventually work with nothing but mixed tracks. In fact, they began to depend more on the fact that Artoo could talk and they would cut to him much more often—because they knew he could talk. They would say, 'Why don't we bounce to Artoo and get a reaction?' That would not have happened had they not known they could get the sound in. So it was a really unique experience in that respect."

"As Ben evolved the Jawa language, it integrated so well," Chew says. "Each cut that we saw not only showed us the effects of structural and dramatic changes, but we also heard the evolution of what new things Ben and George had come up with."

To create the Jawa language Burtt had studied several African dialects; next he recorded other employees at Park Way speaking and yelling the words, which were then sped up or altered before being mixed into the film. "They cut the Jawa sequence originally with just the cute guys running in and picking Artoo up," Burtt says. "And then I took that reel and added the Jawa voices. When we showed it, one of the editors was just rolling on the floor laughing. The Jawas talking made so much difference, because it created a feeling that there were little beings in those costumes."

Some time before Marcia left, the editors also started building a temporary music track. "Dvorak's *The Planets* was used at the beginning," Chew says. "And Liszt preludes over the breaking into the jail sequence. George was having a lot of fun. He would bring in a record whenever he got back from LA. He would have a new idea for the temp track, which was the best way for him to convey to Johnny Williams what he wanted. But I didn't know which way he wanted to go with the music at first. The first time we talked about it was when I was editing that cantina sequence, so I said to him, 'Hey, George, have you ever heard Tibetan music, because I think the chanting and the animal-bone instruments might really be appropriate.' And he said, 'No, I'm going to use Benny Goodman.' And I went, 'What?!' And he said, 'Yeah, they're gonna play swing, man!'"

BLAZING TRAILERS

In addition to overseeing the film's special effects, editing, and sound effects, Lucas was also very much involved in its marketing. Charles Lippincott had been trying to energize the burgeoning science-fiction and comic-book convention circuit, and word of mouth was beginning. The novelization had just been published, and a Marvel comic-book adaptation was well under way—but one of the biggest draws to any "coming soon" film is its trailer. Plans for the preview had begun in the fall of 1976 and crystallized in November. But the reality, given the few special effects completed, was that the best production could hope for was a short, powerful burst that would alert audiences to the upcoming movie.

Presumably because the pressure was so great to tightly control costs, assistant optical editor Bruce Green kept a day-by-day itinerary of his time and travel while he acted as go-between on last-minute adjustments to the trailer, uniting its disparate elements and troubleshooting. The following is his (abridged) saga:

Ben Burtt in his basement editing suite at Park Way; playing bocce ball with Walter Murch; and petting Indiana, Lucas's dog and inspiration for Chewbacca.

"TIE fighters flying by was an elephant howling slowed down and stretched out electronically . . . I went back east for a short vacation and recorded the subways in Philadelphia, while riding to both ends and getting various air doors and mechanical noises. Those were used for all the doors in the spaceships. A lot of the clatter of the trains was used for the sandcrawler and its basic motor sound . . . I went on a hike in the Poconos of northern Pennsylvania, which has a huge radio tower on the top of the mountain. The wind is very strong there, which makes for a very eerie singing in the wires, almost a minor key sustained note. It was hard to record but ultimately it was used for the sound of the Y-wings and the howling sound they had . . . When I came back to Los Angeles, I went to all the different radio towers in the area, up on Mount Wilson, and struck the wires with a hammer. They're all different pitches and tones, so I collected a whole orchestra of that particular material. It's a very high-pitched twang, but very explosive. I mixed that in with a bazooka sound, and that became the basis for the lasers . . .

"I have a lot of favorite sounds effects from old movies. Some of these I sought out and used. One is the Fox thunderclap; it's probably a combination of actual thunder and someone striking a sheet of metal, but that explosion was used several times in *Star Wars*—it's part of the explosion of the main hatch blowing up on the blockade runner; I also used it at the end in the battle over the Death Star anytime there were full-frame flashes. In the shot when the spaceships dive into the trench, there's a number of full-frame explosions and at that point, you hear a sweetened-up version of the Fox thunderclap . . . Another very esoteric sound effect is what I call a 'Wilhelm.' This is a man screaming on a recording that has been used exclusively by Warner Bros. for about twenty-five years. It's been used in many Westerns and horror films. I call it a Wilhelm because one of the first films it was used in was a Western called *Charge at Feather River* [1953], where a cavalry private named Wilhelm gets an arrow in the leg and screams—this particular scream was dubbed in for his voice although he didn't really make the sound. I had an idea that perhaps the first time the scream was used was

Not only did Peter Diamond play the main Tusken Raider and the stormtrooper who is shot off the ledge, he appeared, by his count, more than fifteen times in the film. In fact, Diamond and his two stuntmen, Reg Harding and Colin Skeaping, did so many falls that they became known as the "The Three *Star Wars* Stooges."

in a film called *Distant Drums,* in 1951, with Gary Cooper, for a guy being eaten by an alligator. So I asked the Warner library if they would send me a sound of a man being eaten by an alligator—they actually had a card in their library with that designation on it—and lo and behold, it turned out to be the scream that I was looking for! So that's in the film. It's the sound of the stormtrooper who gets shot by Luke and falls into the power trench. It's a great scream . . . I had the satisfaction of making use of some of the legacy left over from the great days of sound in Hollywood."

November 26: I drove to the editor's cutting room in Hollywood and met with him, Gary Kurtz, Charlie Lippincott, Adam Beckett, and three people from the ad agency. We discussed the storyboard, the animation and opticals, the time factor, and other related materials. (3 hrs.)

November 29: We saw the rough cut [same place and people, minus Beckett] of the trailer and discussed what shot could not be used because of problems with the effects. We talked about the music. (3 hrs., 18 min.)

November 30: Phone calls to editor and optical to coordinate effects for trailer. (2 hrs.)

December 1: Editors meeting; prepared fx budget. (3 hrs., 18 min.)

December 2: I drove to Tech 20 to pick up negative; talked with negative cutter about problems he was having finding certain scenes and his stolen dog, and how to find that, too. (1 hr., 13 min.) Bring neg to MFE [Modern Film Effects] and explain to lineup person the order to assemble the IPs and the time element. (2 hrs., 7 min)

December 6: Drove to ILM to view trailer work for any possible last-minute changes. (37 min.)

December 7: Drove to MFE to discover a matte for the exploding title had not been made. Had animator reshoot matte and had this developed at MFE and cut in. Made last check at optical house of all elements and went over all effects with the printer operator before actual printing began. (6 hrs.)

December 9: Viewed first answer print at 8 AM at Deluxe and made timing changes. Cut in reshot scene. At 1 PM viewed second answer print—authorized striking of 10 prints from original negative and making one CRI; drove back to ILM to be told agency wanted to adjust explosion at end of trailer. Went to MFE, recut last scene and authorized reshoot of this scene. (8 hrs.)

December 10: Viewed reshot scene at MFE and cut into trailer at Deluxe. (6 hrs., 4 min.)

The budget for the trailer, compiled on December 2, for 107 seconds (160 feet of film) was $3,915.10, of which $1,268 was spent on MFE's opticals. The special effect of the exploding *Star Wars* logo was created by Joe Viskocil and Bruce Logan. Ironically, the shot in the trailer of Leia and Chewbacca in the pirate ship cockpit was a front projection one; the other special effects consisted of a few finished shots from the gunport battle.

"The trailer was more about the spirit of the film; it introduced a lot of different characters," Ken Ralston says. "One thing they did have was a couple of the very early lightsabers."

After Lucas approved the final trailer, problems arose with Fox—whose collective anxiety concerning the film was not being mollified by its progress.

"There was a lot of the tension building up at the time," Ladd says. "People were saying, 'Change the title' and that we couldn't go with this trailer. I told them to show the research to everyone and to discuss the title change, but that I couldn't think of a better one. It was a case where all the research strikes were against the film. The board of directors did see the trailer themselves at their meeting in December, and, although they didn't like it, they didn't make a big issue of it. But one of the board of directors disliked the title very much."

Apparently the title conjured up, for some, images of Hollywood starlets at war. "My way of handling it was to say, 'If you want to change the title, come up with more titles and we'll see if we like them,'" Lucas says. "We essentially put the problem in their half of the court. I realized they probably wouldn't be able to do it, and they didn't, so we let it go at that."

Nevertheless, the issue of title and trailer persisted even after the

trailer was released in time for Christmas. Saddled with what sounds like part of Antonio Vivaldi's "Winter" from his *Four Seasons*, the slow, ominous classical music was at cross purposes with the trailer's upbeat visuals, making it play like a schizophrenic excerpt from *2001* and helping to create a divided reception. "It was obviously drawing certain people in through curiosity," Ladd says. "I saw it play here at the Avco where it wasn't very well received, and I saw it in Tucson where it was badly received. There was also all kinds of new market research saying that the picture will absolutely not work if we call it *Star Wars* and if we keep the trailer on—and that the picture really had *no chance*. But we kept saying, 'We've got to have something.' I mean it had to have a chance just to at least get its money back!"

The teaser poster, along with frames from the trailer for *Star Wars*—including one of the two or three front projection shots in the film (left), "very early" lightsabers, and the exploding logo.

CELLULOID TRANSFIGURATION

DECEMBER 1976 TO APRIL 1977

CHAPTER ELEVEN

The work ethic at Park Way gave way to the occasional break. Howard Hammerman, who started in June 1976 as the general repairman, remembers: "Everybody in the whole company could come and sit at one table and have Christmas dinner. All the people that worked there and their families and kids, we all came to the Park Way house and sat and talked about movies and harassed George and teased him about why is there sound in outer space. I questioned him about that at the first Christmas dinner, and he looked at me and said, 'I'll tell you what. We're going to put a little platform out there floating in space [laughs] with an orchestra on it so that it'll make sense.'"

In January 1977, with editorial well in hand, the director decided that only Paul Hirsch needed to stay on. "I went up to San Anselmo and was originally supposed to stay until the end of the year," Hirsch says. "But George asked me to stay until the end of the picture, which I wanted to do because I loved the picture and I loved working for George."

Farther south, while Ladd pondered a bleak future for the overbudget and late film, ILM kept making steady progress. They had begun working on the escape from the Death Star sequence on September 29, 1976, after Joe Johnston had painstakingly reboarded the sequence; by late January 1977 Lucas had approved most of the shots. While things were not always well between the director and the head of the special effects crew, on the whole Lucas's estimation of ILM was continuing to grow—and their situation had vastly improved when Luke's two trench runs had been combined into one.

"I had heard that all of a sudden things were much easier, because we didn't have this entire run to do," Dennis Muren says. "I was still working independently at night with my crew, with Ken Ralston, who was my assistant; and Richard was working with Doug Smith in the

Van Der Veer Photo Effects was given written instructions on how to do the laser gun battle animations (top right), which included the number of cuts, bolt directions, and so on. The effects house worked on the lightsabers as well (opposite, top right), while ILM's animation department took care of the Death Star blast (opposite, top left) and vetted all outside work (below right, animator Pete Kuran, production staffer Rose Duignan, Lucas, and animation supervisor Adam Beckett study laser sword possibilities).

Battle #	Sequence	Begin/End	# cuts
1	Opening battle on blockade runner	Stormtroopers come thru door/ 3PO & R-2 cross corridor to explosion	24
2	Corridor chase on blockade runner	Stormtroopers firing on run/ Rebel troopers run away	21
3	Princess captured	Princess fires / Princess falls	5
4	Escape from Mos Eisley	Stormtroopers fire/ Han Solo run up gangway to his ship	12
5	Control station assault	Han fires/ Imperial officer falls	2

LASER GUN BATTLES

daytime. And as it went on, George would give me a rough storyboard representing one frame of what he wanted and would say, 'I'd like it to go from here to there, and make it run about 86 frames.' We'd discuss if he wanted to use a telephoto or wide-angle lens, but after a while he came to trust us pretty much."

"We figured that once all the personnel were trained and everything was moving," Robbie Blalack calculates, "that we could do a medium-difficulty shot in about two and one-half weeks."

Upstairs in Film Control, Mary Lind and her group were reaching peak activity. "There were five editorial benches," she says, of the increasingly crowded work space. "When I first put the shelves up, everyone was saying, 'You'll never fill them.' I filled them and emptied them three times. When George, Gary, and John would all come up to the room and have a discussion, you literally had to raise your arms in the air to walk

by, so we finally knocked out the wall between us and Joe Johnston's art department, because you couldn't even breathe anymore."

OVERTURES

Before showing a cut of the film to John Williams, Lucas and Hirsch added to the temp track. The director had designed his film as a "silent movie," told primarily through its visuals and music, so great care was taken to obtain the right moods. "We used some Stravinsky, the flip side of *The Rite of Spring,*" Hirsch remembers. "George said nobody ever uses that side of the record, so we used it for Threepio walking around in the desert. The Jawa music was from the same Stravinsky piece. We used music from *Ivanhoe* by Rózsa for the main title. George was talking about having a majority of the film set to music."

(Continued on page 246)

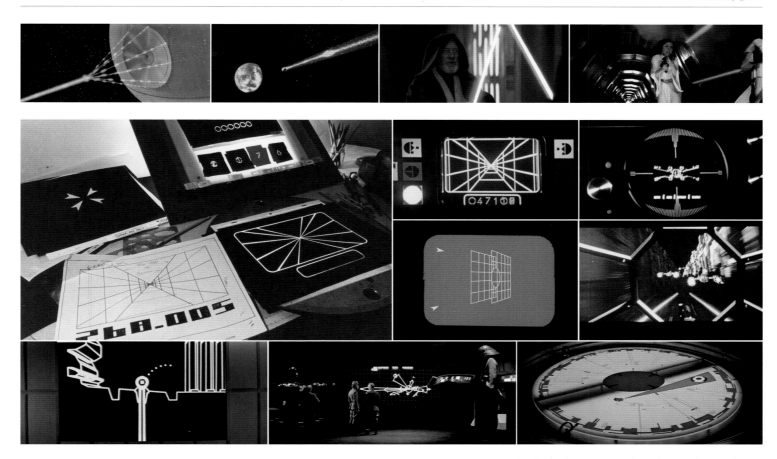

On December 14, 1976, animation supervisor Dan O'Bannon delivered a status report to Gary Kurtz listing his shots. On the "gunport targeting device," work was finished (middle, by Jay Teitzell); the "bomb down shaft" in the Massassi briefing room was also completed (bottom left, by John Wash); the "schematic wall screen (tractor beam)" had finalized artwork and would be on camera "this week"; the "rebel targeter" [middle right] also had finished artwork and awaited camerawork. The only unfinished artwork was the "Death Star wall screen (approach to Yavin 4)"—"considered by all to be the most important of the series," O'Bannon writes. "I have withheld this shot until computer animators Wash & Teitzell had finished their individual responsibilities and could work on it together. Imperial technology should appear more advanced." This graphic would eventually involve Teitzell, Wash, O'Bannon, and Image West (bottom middle); the graphic showing the approach of the Death Star was "produced" by John Wash (bottom right).

"I remember George brought in this sequence and played it for us," Robbie Blalack says. "It represented about 15 percent of the optical department's total output, and that was the first time we had seen our work tied in with the live action—and I think the energy level went up significantly. It was nice to see the entire thing finished with the sound. It was exciting."

127-P (*P* signifies "processed"): The docking bay miniature, based on the set blueprints from England, came apart into four different pieces (below right). The ceiling was used for other background miniatures later on. "Up on the ceiling on one of the gantries in the Death Star docking bay is the most exact miniature of the Dykstraflex," says Grant McCune. "It's upside down hanging from the roof."

129-P: "George and I had gone through and boarded all this stuff," Joe Johnston says, "and we were talking about it—when he suddenly goes, 'Now I've done it! We drove them right in there, and now they're escaping, but it's hard for them to escape—if they're *backing* out!' So we talked about solutions, like making the docking bay go all the way through the Death Star; but it's supposed to be the size of a planet, so that wouldn't have worked."

In fact, that had been the original idea in the third draft, when the ship was supposed to land on the cloud city prison. "Alderaan was the mushroom city where they were going to go out the other side, and we used to laugh about how they were going to take off and shoot their way

through this city going clear out the other side," Johnston remembers. But in the craziness of last-minute budget cuts and script changes, no one had anticipated this singular visual problem. "Ultimately, the ship had to back out of the Death Star, spin around, and take off. That was done with a very tricky model mount that allowed the model to rotate on its central axis in a horizontal plane and also rotate on its vertical axis in a rolling sense."

"That was a very complicated program," Richard Edlund agrees. "It probably took most of the day just to get the program right, whereas, generally, we could generate a program in about twenty or thirty minutes once we had the model up [below and opposite]."

132: This shot made use of McQuarrie's Death Star matte painting, which was about three feet in diameter (opposite, middle left). They photographed it with blue where the stars would be placed, then the starfield was photographed with a matching move (pan from right to left); then the model of the *Millennium Falcon* was filmed with the same move. The three elements were combined in the optical printer.

133-P: Luke's stars were left to right, and Han's right to left. ILM added yaw and subtle variations to differentiate them. They also generated multi-directional roaming stars that could be used repeatedly, by using "icons" off the original negative, in front or behind. The original negative was never used as a printing element (opposite, middle).

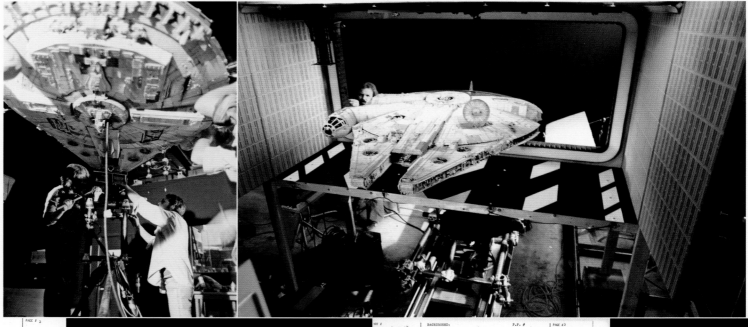

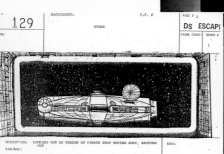

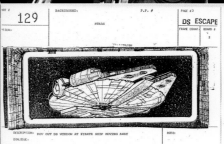

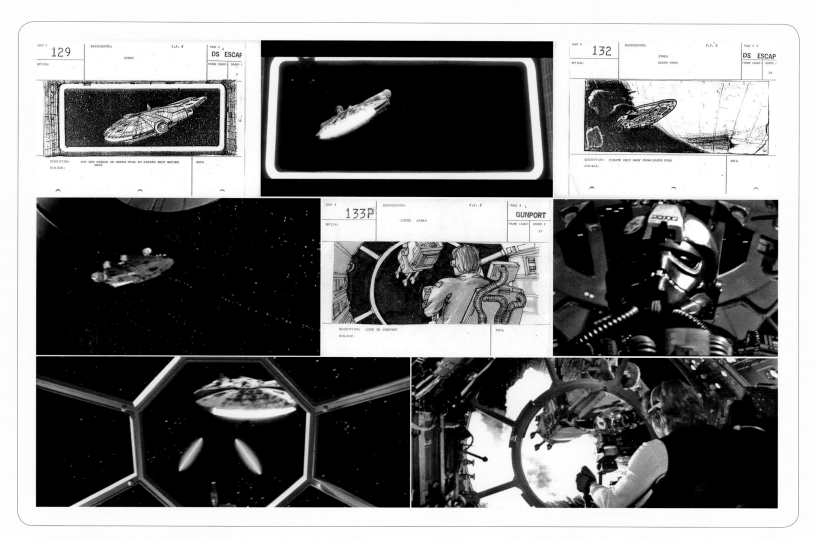

137-P: This shot created some confusion and remained problematic: "This is an example of the less-than-perfect communications that existed at ILM," Adam Beckett says. "George would say one thing, and a week later I'd get the information from Robbie Blalack, interpreted by Robbie, that 'George doesn't like light effects.' The fact is that George neither likes nor dislikes light effects; he dislikes light effects that look like matte lines. He likes light effects that look like light being cast by laser beams. Robbie made a general judgment on light effects rather than a discriminating one."

The cockpit with the TIE pilot, with bluescreen placed behind the back windows, was shot in England; ILM laid in the stars with the appropriate motion. Once they had finished the other effects, however, the black-costumed pilot had become greenish black, which didn't please Lucas, because the man looked as if he'd been rotoscoped in and wasn't part of the original set (middle right).

138-P: Once Lucas had established where the lasers would have to hit, ILM would supervise their animation. "Lasers are a terrible pain in the ass,"

Dykstra says. "You have to come up with some cockamamie perspective that makes it look like the lasers are going away or coming at you." Despite many tests and experiments, Lucas was never happy with the effect (bottom left).

153-P: "This was the first explosion that was shot at ILM that the roto-scope department got to try enhancing," Beckett says. "We did a ton of artwork for a couple of elements, because all we had to start with was this ship that kinda flew apart and had some sparks coming out. It all was sent to England and was apparently approved because we went on and prepared another shot after that. We found out later that it wasn't approved at all—in fact, it didn't have anything to do with what was needed. So the explosion was redone using gas and powder and metal flakes [bottom right]."

"We had a lot of trouble with the wings of the TIE ships warping in the heat of the stage lights," Joe Johnston says. "Sometimes they had to hang for quite a while while they were lit and rigged for explosions—and if there was any kind of delay, it would warp all over the place because we used thin beams around the perimeter of the wings to hold the paper in."

"George had listened to a lot of records and done a lot of research, and people had given him records," Burtt says. "He had picked out some material from Dvořák's *New World Symphony* for the end sequence of the great hall and the awards. He had chosen some of Bruckner's Ninth Symphony for Luke's theme. We slowly built up temporary music tracks and mixed them in with the film, so we had a temporary version of the film with an essentially complete sound effects track and a patchwork music track that highlighted various moments in the picture. At this point Johnny Williams was brought in."

"I started with George just after New Year's," Williams says. "I went up to Park Way and he showed me the film."

Lucas, Williams, music supervisor Lionel Newman, music editor Ken Wannberg, and Hirsch gathered together and rapidly spotted the cues; that is, they decided where the music should go and what kind of music it should be, using the temp track or "source music" as a guide.

"We sat and went over the film reel by reel, over the course of two days," Hirsch says. "The way it developed, there was a lot of music in the first three-quarters of the film. The idea, though it was never explicitly stated, was to open up some space so the music that came in at the very

end would have an even greater impact. So after the gunport sequence, there was no music for a long time, which was contrary to the pace of music that we'd established in the first part of the film. You have to go slow in order to go fast."

"What the source music did was convince me that George was right about the idiom of the music in the picture," John Williams says. "He didn't want, for example, electronic music, he didn't want futuristic cliché, outer space noises. He felt that since the picture was so highly different in all of its physical orientations—with the different creatures, places unseen, sights unseen, and noises unheard—that the music should be on fairly familiar emotional ground. I think what George's temp track did was to prove that the disparity of styles was the right thing for this picture.

"So I came back to my little room and started working on themes," he adds. "I spent the months of January and February writing the score."

Even before the new year, veteran sound editor Sam Shaw had also started on the film, with the greater part of his crew joining him mid-January 1977. Shaw had worked on *American Graffiti, Cabaret,* and *The Candidate,* among many others. "Ben Burtt worked on the film creating sounds for a couple of years," Lucas says, "and then when we got down to the final crunch, we brought in a regular sound effects editor from Hollywood to cut the sound effects and do all the other sound effects that had to be done. Ben did mainly the special intricate things that had to be created."

The large-scale and miniature landspeeders were needed for additional shots (right, with Bill Shourt at the wheel; far right, David Jones spray-paints the miniature).

With understandable trepidation, Burtt handed over his sound library so that Shaw could build the final tracks. "I was uneasy about that," he says. "I didn't like the idea of someone else making a lot of creative choices as to where you put it and how you put it in, and so on. I was worried. I asked George if we could do it ourselves. But he and Gary said, 'No, we don't have time; we've got to have these sound effects editors do it.'"

Shaw's first task was to create the sounds for the motors in C-3PO and R2-D2. "That was a huge job," Burtt says. "I had never gotten to that on my list; we hadn't established that as a priority."

"Everything was a problem on *Star Wars*," Sam Shaw says. "The biggest problem was the time, together with the fact that it was very demanding. There is more sound in that one picture than there is in ten average pictures put together. There were over a hundred effect units for each sound reel, so over twelve hundred reels. Everything was just very special; everything you did was something that you hadn't done before. You never got bored!"

THE FOX PREVIEW

Toward the end of January, Lucas felt ready to screen a cut for Alan Ladd. "It was the first time I showed it to an outside group," Lucas says. "We did a mix for Johnny Williams with the temp track, and right after that we showed it to Laddie, his wife, Gareth Wigan, and Jay Kanter. A very small group."

Wigan and Kanter constituted with Ladd a power triumvirate at Fox that had been shepherding their films through the studio labyrinth. After they and Fox executive Leonard Kroll, who also attended, settled into the seats of the screening room constructed behind Park Way, and as the film neared its finale, Lucas noticed that one of the execs was becoming emotional. "I was sitting right next to Gareth, and he turned to me and he had tears in his eyes," Lucas says. "I couldn't believe it. I couldn't believe Gareth Wigan was crying—I thought he was crying because he was thinking, *Oh my God—our whole careers are destroyed. Our lives are destroyed!* But he said, 'This is the greatest film I've ever seen.' And I thought, *No way!* I'd never had a studio executive say that at the end of a screening. I thought, *This is really weird.*"

It must have been all the more surreal when Lucas remembered the previous reactions of Warner Bros. and Universal to his first two features. Wigan was so moved that upon returning home, "I sat my family 'round the kitchen table and I said, 'The most extraordinary day of my life has just taken place. I want you to remember this day because I never thought I would have a day's experience like the day I've had today in seeing this film.'"

The others had varying opinions. "Laddie didn't know what to think," Lucas says. "His wife loved the movie. She was going on, but Laddie was quiet and said, 'Gee, George, you did a really good job.' After they all left, Paul and I looked at each other, shrugged our shoulders, and said, 'What was *that* all about? It could've been worse!'"

Around this time, Hal Barwood's estimation of the film also changed. "I got invited up to a screening that George was having," he says, "in a little screening room, with William Morris fabrics on the wall and these big easy chairs you could sit in. I brought my two kids, who were about

Color Relations

As the picture took on its final shape, certain aspects of Lucas's visual plans became clear. "You are sitting in a nice light room for the first half of the film," he says, "but in a darker room for the second half. So for the first half you feel happy and sunny, and during the second half you might feel more oppressed and moody. It's subtle, but I think it will have an effect on people."

The characters' costumes and design also play a part in the director's larger look. "Leia is dressed in white and is part of the technological world—black, white, and gray," Lucas says. "She has a spaceship, but she would've been a stranger if she'd gone to Tatooine, the natural world: tan, brown, and green. She would be like Artoo. I really liked the idea that when Luke, Ben, the Wookiee, Threepio, and Artoo are all together, everyone except Artoo blends into the real world, Tatooine; it works very well. But when you go to the Death Star, it works just the opposite. Artoo fits in with everything because everything is black and white, and he is primarily white. We made the stormtroopers white, too (also to mix things up, so not all the bad guys were dressed in dark colors). Even Threepio is out of place in the Death Star, more than Artoo. That was a creative decision to make Threepio part of the people, earth side, which was an esoteric idea, but I liked it."

"The only thing that we varied a little bit was the Han Solo costume: He's dressed in browns, and has a spaceship, because he is an eclectic. He takes a little from everything."

The sandcrawler model's proportions (left) were worked out retroactively to fit the bottom third that production had built in England. ILM used as a point of reference a shot of the sandcrawler on a hill where its "headlights" could be seen, matching that to the miniature's. Its mechanics were designed by Jamie Shourt, who installed an electrical system that supplied voltage to the treads based solely on how much was needed, so there would be no spinning wheels (below left).

ten, and we sat down and we watched this thing. It was just all sorts of slugs and leader with Magic Marker marks—but I was just knocked silly by the movie. I was just thrilled to the core by this fantastic film. I couldn't believe it. Of course, I'd been set up to be stunned because of my doubts previously."

Although the reactions of Barwood and Wigan were similar to Richard Chew's, the businesspeople who would have a large impact on

the success of the film—the theater owners—had no idea what the film was like, and they were proving hard to educate. Their lack of financial enthusiasm was causing anxiety throughout the studio, because *Star Wars* was backed solely by Fox, whereas its two most recent big-budget films—*Lucky Lady* and *Hello, Dolly*—had been co-financed with another studio, and hence less risky.

"*Lucky Lady* had star names and theater guarantees," Ladd explains, "so even though it didn't do what everybody had hoped, the cash loss on the picture wasn't going to be worrisome. With *Star Wars* nobody was able to get the guarantees. It was a very negative response. One of the key things with a film is getting the appropriate 'house' [movie theater in which to open]. So we had to go out early to get the proper houses, and we got absolutely no response at all. Exhibitors were going heavily into *A Bridge Too Far, Exorcist II, Sorcerer,* and *The Deep.* So we had great problems getting guarantees for *Star Wars.*"

Fox had actually started the process back in October, without a print of the film to show, by sending out bid forms to every theater owner throughout the United States. Almost schizophrenically, the form listed the conditions for the rental—an exclusive 12-week run and a 90/10 profit split—which were strangely exorbitant given the studio's precarious confidence in *Star Wars,* and which had the effect of scaring off most exhibitors.

During that first month of the year, with the film close to being locked, Lippincott interviewed the three principals, who were also in the dark as to its future. On January 4 Carrie Fisher said, "The great thing about *Star Wars* is that when I see it, I'm going to be as surprised as anyone, because I've not seen any of the effects. Are they going to have my planet blown up? I'm very curious to see what my planet looks like blowing up, what I look like flying through space."

On January 5 Mark Hamill said, "I would do anything for George. I'd go paint his house. Seriously. But I may never get to work with him again . . . He told me once that he didn't want to make features anymore, that he wanted to go back and make student movies. I'll do those, too."

"I don't know what it is going to look like, not at all. No idea," Harrison Ford said on January 20. "When I was filming, I had no idea how they were going to do some of the things that were in there. It was a mystery. And still is to this day."

NO END IN SIGHT

From mid-January to early February 1977 second and third units were scheduled to do pickups and reshoots. Nearly all the shots were going to be on location, with the only set a reconstitution of the cantina alcove.

"The other big argument with Fox was over the cantina set and the Death Valley pickups," Kurtz says. "In a production meeting at the studio someone said the cantina set was going to cost us $100,000, so the studio said no. They wouldn't authorize the expenditure. We were talking about fifteen or twenty creatures—the elephant suit would cost $25,000—so I really had to go to Laddie, go down to the studio, and tell them that we estimated that it was going to cost from $30,000 to $40,000, certainly under $50,000, and that it was extremely important for that sequence to be right.

"This was also at the time where they were arguing over paying the Huycks," he adds. "They wanted $15,000 for their dialogue polish. Fox wasn't going to pay it. They insisted that George pay for it out of his writing fees. That's why we were so pissed at the studio. They made no effort to help in any of these areas at all; it would've been a goodwill gesture, more than anything else."

The funds for the cantina reshoot were necessary in part to pay Rick Baker and his small crew, who had been engaged to make the cantina creatures. "A good animator friend of mine was friends with Dennis Muren," Baker says. "He heard that they were looking for people to do these aliens, so he gave them my name." Baker had started doing puppets and makeup for low-budget films like *The Thing with Two Heads* (1972) but had recently graduated to big-budget films with the remake of *King Kong* (1976).

"George explained that there was a scene in the film where there is a bar and there are a whole bunch of aliens in it," Baker adds, "and he just wanted some more aliens. George and I talked for a great deal of time and we were both very excited about what we were talking about, I think, and maybe that's why he went with me." Baker's bid was accepted, with the caveat that only Stuart Freeborn would get a credit on the film, as he was the primary artist. Baker agreed and started his team, which consisted of Jon Berg, Phil Tippett, Laine Liska, and Doug Beswick.

While they began sketching out alien concepts, Kurtz's negotiations with Fox netted them $20,000 for the sequence. Though less than what they'd wanted, getting anything may have been a result of Ladd's positive reaction to the preview. "We just cut down the number of weeks that we had to work," Baker says. "I think at that point George wanted like seven monsters. Well, we were all fans of science-fiction films. All of us wanted the opportunity to show what we could really do, so we did a lot more work than we got paid for. We ended up with about six weeks to do as many aliens as we could."

THE UNITED STATES DESERTS

A few ILMers began construction of the alcove set on a small sound stage in Hollywood, while Grant McCune, Lorne Peterson, Joe Johnston, and others began photography of the miniatures on location. "I think there were six trips made to the desert," Johnston says. "Four were made just to shoot the sandcrawler; on two others they took the landspeeder along for canyon shots. The sandcrawler was constantly breaking down: the tracks would jam, the tread would come off. The sandcrawler probably ended up costing more per second than anything else in the film, because it involved taking that model, a camera, and a crew of six guys out to the desert, where they usually had to spend the night. We left the model once in a van, and it got cold that night. We were in a motor home twenty yards away, but we could hear the pieces of styrene popping and cracking on the model."

On the first trip one of the sandcrawler's inner lightbulbs broke and they didn't have a replacement; the second time it was too windy and cloudy; on the third trip the lighting exposure was done incorrectly; only the fourth shoot was perfect.

Lucas was leading the second unit, and had called in Mark Hamill for their pickups. Hamill was driving himself out to the location in mid-January, the Friday night before the rest of the crew left, when he had a bad car accident. According to Kurtz, Hamill was taken to County General and then, because of the severity of his wounds, to Mount Sinai Hospital. "They operated from about nine o'clock in the morning until about four in the afternoon," Kurtz says. "I saw him at four thirty, and Mark said, 'Oh. I'm sorry I got delayed. As soon as I get out of here this morning, we can go.' He evidently had no idea what he looked like."

With Hamill out, Lucas and his crew set up their gear to capture foot-age of banthas, Tusken Raiders, and whatever they could. "There were a lot of things I wanted to shoot with Mark that we had to do without—bits and pieces, at least ten close-ups—but that was just fate," Lucas says. "We ended up using a double for the landspeeder shot."

"I was real concerned about the elephant wearing the bantha head-gear," Rick Baker says. "It weighed something like three hundred pounds."

"We all fell in love with Mardji," Lucas adds. "It was the first time she'd ever been out in the real world. They led her down to a creek in Death Valley and she just loved to play around in that creek."

Fortunately, the elephant was good-natured and her shots were recorded without incident. Next up was the full-scale landspeeder, whose hovering effect had so far eluded production.

"We tried several ideas during filming, and none of them seemed to work," Lucas says. "We finally tried using a mirror, and that came close, but it didn't work, either. So when we went out to Death Valley, we redid the mirror and made it sturdier and made it longer, raised the car a little bit higher, and found a lake bed that had topography that was easier to work with. Then we shot it again, but that didn't work because not enough care was taken to make the mirror and to get the speeder going fast enough. Finally, Bob Dalva came back with a crew and made it work. But he only got one shot, and we needed three. So then we sent *another* cameraman to get the final two shots using the same method."

A student at USC with Lucas, Dalva had gone on to be one of the founding members of American Zoetrope. Another old friend of Lucas's was Carroll Ballard, whom he'd gotten to know while making *The Rain People* (and who would direct *The Black Stallion* in 1979, with Coppola producing), and he became Lucas's second-unit DP. "George did get some money to do some retakes," Ballard recalls. "So I went out and shot out in the desert for about two weeks. Then we went back to Hollywood on a tiny stage right across from Kodak and shot the bar scene."

John Dykstra, Richard Edlund, and Grant McCune in the desert of Randsburg shooting the sandcrawler miniature (top). Doubles of C-3PO, Obi-Wan, and Luke in the land-speeder with its mirrored skirt for more pickups (middle), which also necessitated transportation of R2-D2 (left) and other material in a truck (above).

In Death Valley, Kurtz, DP Carroll Ballard, and Lucas (below right) shot pickups of the bantha (below left, completely dressed). The "bantha" was named Mardji, a 22-year-old, 8,500-pound female Asian elephant, who was normally a resident of Marine World Africa U.S.A. (above, partially dressed, with Doug Beswick in the Tusken Raider outfit). "It took six men to build up [her costume] and they worked for a month," says Ron Whitfield, director of general theater at the amusement park. The base was a "howdah," or elephant saddle. The curving horns were made from flexible home ventilation tubing. Mardji's shaggy coat was created from palm fronds, while the head mask was molded from chicken wire and then sprayed with foam to give it shape; the beard was made from horse hair. Although she was able to water-ski for spectators at the park, the bantha tail, made of wood and covered with thick bristles, gave Mardji problems—but her handler gave her apples, which compensated for the costume.

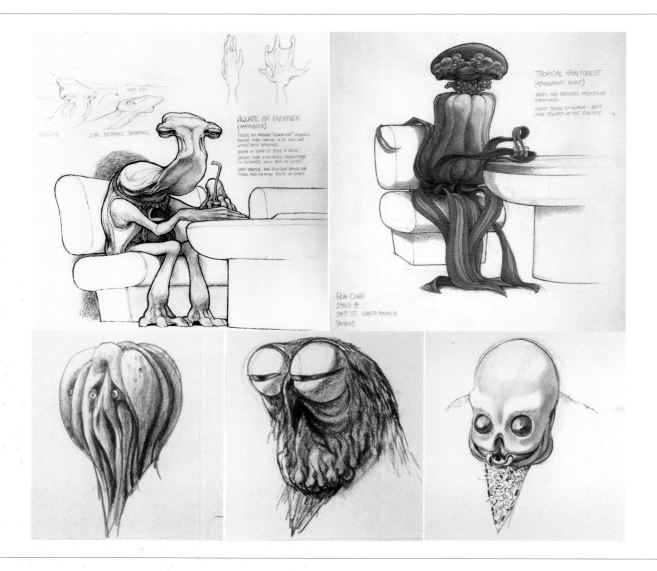

A TALE OF GOO

The inserts needed for the cantina scene took two days to shoot, at Dovington's small studio on La Brea Avenue, on January 24 and 25, 1977. The new dialogue was typed up for reference on February 5, 1977:

```
Han and Chewbacca slide out of the booth, a slimy
green-faced alien with a trunk snout pokes a gun in
Han's face. He speaks with an electronic intonation.

                    GREEDO
OOOH TAHTOO TAHT SOLO?

                    HAN
Yes, Greedo. As a matter of fact I was just going to
see your boss. Tell Jabba I've got his money.
```

```
                    GREEDO
SOM BEJA LAY. SARA TRAMPEECA MOCK KEY CHEEZKA. JABBA
WANINCHEKC BA WOO SHANEE TY WANYA ROOZKA...HEH, HEH,
HEH, HEH. CHASK IN YAWEE, CHOOZO.

                    HAN
Yeah, but this time I've got the money!

                    GREEDO
EL JAYA KOOLKA IN DE KOOLY KUU SOO AHH.

                    HAN
I don't have it with me...Tell Jabba—
```

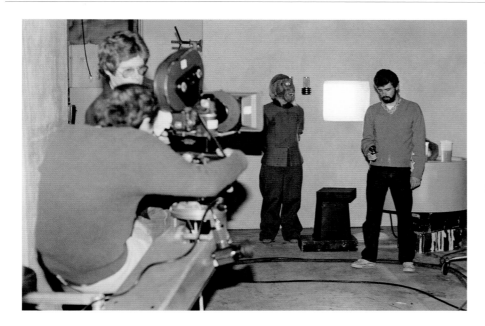

Back on September 30, 1976, McQuarrie had already started making sketches of aliens for the planned reshoot of the cantina scene (opposite, below). Ron Cobb also contributed a number of illustrations (opposite, above). With Ballard on camera, Lucas shows how to handle a blaster during the cantina pickups in late January 1977 (left). The notorious "drooling arm" monster (above) was a hand puppet that could generate goo on command.

GREEDO
JABBA HI TISH KEE!!! SO GUU RUUYA PUU YA YA OOR WAH SEE PATKEEKA KUU SHOO KUU PON WAH SCHREEPIO!

HAN
Even I get boarded sometimes. You think I had a choice?

GREEDO
DLAP JABBA, POOM PAH KOOM POTNEY AH TAH POM PAH!

HAN
Over my dead body...

GREEDO
OOHKLAY YUMA, CHEEZT OE KUU TOO TAH PREEZTAH KRENKO... YAH POZKA!

HAN
Yes, I'll bet you have...

Harrison Ford would loop his lines later, as only the alien, now referred to as "Greedo," would be on camera. "George showed me the Greedo mask, which I think is one of the ones he liked the best of Stuart's," Baker says. "He said, 'You know, we've got this mask, but with the person wearing the mask, it didn't work. He was moving his head and it didn't look like he was talking.' Fortunately, it was made out of foam rubber, so Doug Beswick added a little mechanism that works the mouth. The only other thing we did was put in a mechanism to work the antennae. The funny thing is that the mouth mechanism broke just before they shot. It was real delicate. But somebody got the idea to stick a clothespin in the girl's mouth. So she just had a clothespin between her teeth, which went to the end of the mouth on Greedo, and she just moved that around."

The "girl" was Maria de Aragon, whom George Mather had recruited for the Greedo reshoot. "It was hot under the mask, and I almost lost my life because I was out of breath," she recalls. "I started to make gestures that were out of the ordinary, and George Lucas noticed and made sure I got help. I had a very bad three or four minutes there."

Another monster that caused gagging was the one known as "drooling arm." As Phil Tippett explains: "I had some ideas for a really weird, gross thing, something that wouldn't look like a man in a suit. You could just put your arm in this thing, like a hand puppet. The jowls would breathe in and out, and it had a line through its mouth that dripped red oozy liquid. They were preparing to do that shot, so I was trying to get it ready real fast, sticking the tubes in and getting all the gook ready, when Kurtz walked up and did a double take, and then said, 'George, come here!' And Lucas walked up and looked at it, too. He said, 'That's really a gross-looking thing! What kind of a rating do we have on this, Gary?' 'Well, I think it's a PG.' So then they said, 'Yeah, let's go ahead and shoot it!'

"Laine Liska was working on that setup with me at the time," Tippett continues. "First George shot it a couple of times without the goo, because it dripped all over the tail and was messy. And then he said, 'Well okay, let's do the goo in this next take.' On 'Action,' I put my arm in this creature and reacted to the 'Wolfman' and Lucas said, 'Okay . . . *Goo!* . . . C'mon, let's have goo.' And I said, 'Laine, quick, the goo!' And Laine had this plunger filled with all this red goo, so he forced it really quick and it let out this really big, kind of farting sound—and all this goo went *phoosh!* Just everywhere! It was so disgusting! George said, 'Cut, cut, forget it, that's it.' You know, just everyone got grossed out! So that's the story of how the goo didn't get shot."

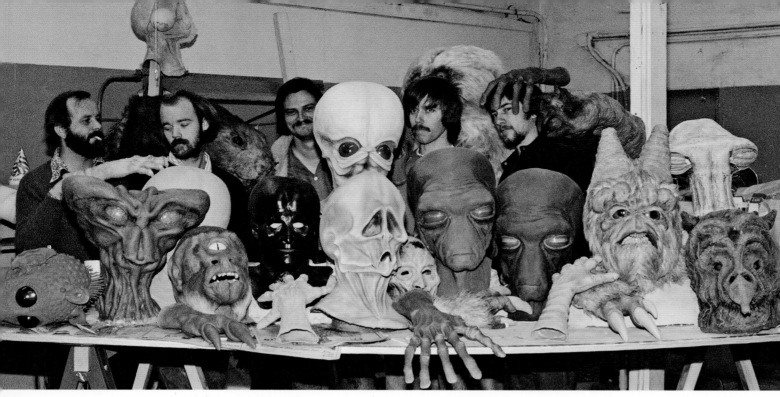

The People

Rick Baker: "George came in and said, 'You know I'd like to do a scene here where we've got a band of aliens playing some music.' He wanted a whole bunch, but I said I didn't know how we were going to get that done in time. Then he noticed one mask and said, 'Something like this would be good.' So I said we could mass-cast them; they could all be basically identical, and George said, 'Fine!'"

Jon Berg: "We had a great deal of freedom. We worked primarily from some key drawings by Ron Cobb."

Phil Tippett: "There were four or five of us, Jon, Laine Liska, Doug Beswick, Rick Baker, and an assistant of Rick's, Rob Botine, did some work on it. I think at the end we had something like fifteen or sixteen different makeups, and then Rick donated a number of things that he'd already made, so we had about twenty-five monsters. Originally, the contract was for like seven. The characters that Rick donated were things that he had done on his own; they weren't from any other project, so they'd never been filmed before."

Jon Berg: "George showed us a cut of the cantina sequence as it stood at that point, and we saw what was going on at ILM—and it was just really exciting. This was the movie we'd all wanted to see, and here it was happening right in front of us! So we got a tremendous amount of energy, and that's why everybody just said, 'Well, we got to seven—come on! Let's keep grinding away at it!' George's enthusiasm was depicted on the screen, and all that wonderful imagination got us going."

The Monsters

As described by Jon Berg and Phil Tippett:

Spider-guy: "The silver furry creature with the little nose and the four eyes, who scratches its head in the scene—that had the most extensive body of any of the characters [behind Doug Beswick, above]."

Hammerhead: "You know you don't see it in the film, but he had a torso and two arms constructed for it. I was operating one part of it, but the arm couldn't quite pull the thing toward it, and just spilled the canister on the table. Apparently everyone was cracking up, because it looked like a lush who was trying to get his drink and couldn't quite make it [top right]."

Brain-guy: "A blind old man who had his brain exposed [above, fourth from left]."

Skull-head: "A four-armed hooker; half insect, half octopus, with butterfly wings on it and tennis shoes."

The band: "Doug Beswick sculpted that from one of Rick's designs and made a whole bunch of them. Phil was in one, and I think they had some of the girls from ILM out there in those costumes getting ready to pass out—we were nearly killed by our own creations. There was one tiny hole that the mouthpiece of the instrument was supposed to stick into—and that was just not enough space to get air through! Particularly when it's plugged by the mouthpiece of the instrument! We had to dance to the beat of an old Benny Goodman tape that George brought in, and the instruments had been designed at ILM. The thing Jon had weighed a ton. I think it was made from a buoy or a sea anchor. Awful! But it looked neat. Some of the girls from ILM came for the shoot kind of nicely made up, but by the end of the day we all looked just like drowned rats; their makeup was running, the lipstick was smeared …"

GONZO ILM

In February 1977 complex work was being completed at ILM at a good pace, but still under less-than-ideal circumstances. Aside from technical problems, personality issues had to be worked through during this particularly intense make-or-break period. Fox production head Ray Gosnell had intensified the studio's crack down on the effects house, which had a significant impact on everyone as they tried to meet impending deadlines. It was still no sure thing that the film would be released on time in May, only three months away.

"I got into arguments with George over this and that and the other thing," Dykstra says. "But it was predicated on what I consider a paradoxical situation. He was working incredibly hard and had the rest of the show to do, but at the same time he couldn't understand why I couldn't do things the way he wanted them done. We had a lot of discussions about how things should be done, but he was sick and he does drive himself pretty hard. It was a nightmare for both of us.

"I was another obstruction, because I had a lot of the film in my hands," he adds. "And I was paranoid as hell. I figured that things were going on behind my back because Mather had been brought in. I asked, 'Do I get to fire Mather, if I don't like him?' It was really unfortunate, because I truly really like George."

"John has a tendency to talk everything to death," Kurtz says. "You sit down to discuss a problem and he will explain to you for an hour why it won't work. Well I don't need that. I already know what the problem is. What I need is someone to say how we intend to solve it. So both George and I were rather frustrated about that. John assembled

a lot of talent, but it was never run properly. It was like organized anarchy."

"'You're not being cooperative,' they would say," Dykstra says. "You end up in the position of being the bad guy. But I'm not the bad guy! I'm not the bad guy! That's what was crazy about that. That's why I want to get out of doing this and do something else . . ."

Dykstra also had run-ins with Robbie Blalack in the optical department. "They fought a lot," Kurtz says. "Blalack was able to composite that material with a minimum amount of dirt, with the very minimum of matte lines, but he and John didn't always get along too well. Everybody has their problems and you never know for sure until you work with them. The trouble is, on a movie, you only have one shot at it."

As for the ongoing technical puzzles, internal ILM memos attest to dozens of reshoots; misunderstood verbal and written instructions; the wrong negatives being used; starfields moving the wrong way; bad matte lines; and on and on. Nevertheless, throughout this whole period, only two people were fired, and no one ever quit.

NOTORIOUS PREVIEW

Because he had shared his successive drafts with his close friends, Lucas screened his rough cut for many of the same sometime in mid-February 1977. Among the attendees were Brian De Palma, Matthew Robbins, Hal Barwood, the Huycks, Steven Spielberg, Jay Cocks, and a few people from ILM. "I usually show the rough cut to several friends and let them tear it apart and find out if there is anything I can do to improve it," Lucas says. "So a week or two after I ran it for Johnny Williams, I showed it to them. Some were confused by it and some weren't sure if it was going to work. Only Brian, as is his nature, said anything really negative about it."

"I think we went a little overboard at that point," Hirsch says. "We got so excited with the fresh material, the new monsters, and everything from the pickups that we overdid it a bit. And the opening prologue was still the one from the third draft, about what happens in the hundred years before the film, but Brian and Jay felt that it should be explaining what happened right before the film starts. Plus, Brian didn't pick up the

(Top left) A surprise birthday party for Grant McCune with women in a cake and homemade costumes featuring Paul Huston as Chewbacca and Joe Johnston as Darth Vader; (far left) an exhausted Connie McCrum, film librarian; (left) long hours led to Mary Lind and Paul Huston sleeping on the ILM premises; (above right) the "cold-tub" crowded with (from high noon) Grant McCune; the daughter of ILM landlord Jim Hanna; Doug Barnett, Lorne Peterson, Paul Huston, bookkeeper Kim Falkinburg, Joe Johnston, and Mary Lind (in sunglasses). (Top left and left, photos from the private collection of Lorne Peterson.)

idea that Kenobi was turning off the tractor beam; Matt Robbins had the same problem. We solved that by just substituting some of the robot's dialogue and by shooting one insert."

"The film was really not ready to be screened for anybody yet," Spielberg says. "It only had a couple dozen final effects shots; most of them were World War II footage. So it was very hard to understand what the film was about to become. I loved it because I loved the story and the characters. But the reaction was not a good one; I was probably the only one who liked it and I told George how much I loved it."

"Steven said, 'This is the greatest movie ever made and it's going to make a hundred million dollars!'" Lucas says. "The Huycks were dubious;

they were worried about it and about me—but Brian was saying, 'What's all this Force shit?! Where's all the blood when they shoot people?' If you know Brian, that's the way he is. He does that to everybody; he's very caustic."

"George has always invited honesty," Spielberg explains. "He's never said, *Come see my movies to heap praise on me.* He invites you to give your honest opinion, but Brian kind of went over the top in terms of his honesty. That night he and George had kind of a verbal duel in a Chinese restaurant, which was pretty amazing to have witnessed. But out of that conflict came a wonderful contribution. De Palma inspired the new crawl, which gave the audience some kind of story geography."

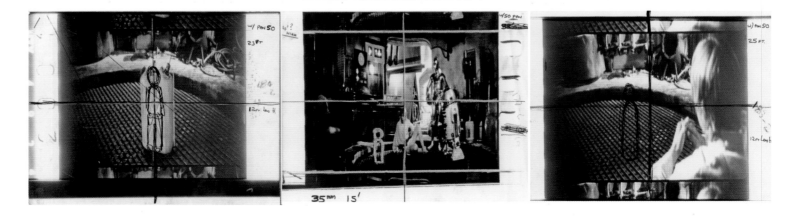

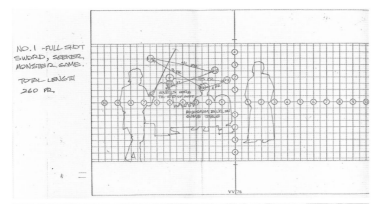

NO. 1 - FULL SHOT SWORD, SEEKER, MONSTER GAME.

TOTAL LENGTH 260 FR.

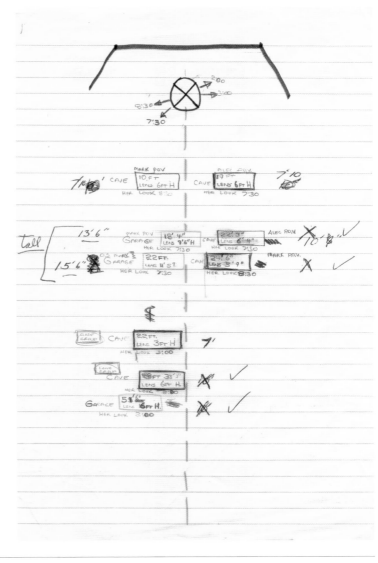

The seeker ball was made in the ILM model shop in two hours, and shot against bluescreen. But because all anamorphic shots had been filmed with the 35mm production camera and not the VistaVision, the "Jedi Lesson scene" had to be sent to an outside effects house to be completed. Precise instructions per Lucas (far left middle, dated February 19, 1977, with red tracking numbers in the margin) were written on how the shot should work. Additional instructions were sent by means of a "Field Chart" that was unique to ILM (far left top). Using 22 fields across, this diagram could be placed on a Moviola, then traced onto the appropriate frames, so the movement of the added elements could be calibrated exactly (final frame, far left).

STAR WARS   2/19/77

JEDI LESSON SCENE: OPTICAL EFFECTS REQUIRED FOR SEEKER ELEMENT.

JL1: (FIRST SHOT IN SEQUENCE REQUIRING SEEKER ELEMENT) SEEKER ELEMENT TO BE REDUCED IN SIZE BY 25%, BUT: IN EACH FRAME OF THE SHOT, THE REDUCED SEEKER BALL MUST BE IN THE SAME FRAME LOCATION AS IT WAS FOUND ON THE ORIGINAL SEEKER NEGATIVE. FTG: 8' 13 FRAMES

JL4: NO SPECIAL OPTICAL FX REQUIRED.

JL25: SOME REPEAT PRINTING IS REQUIRED WHICH IS DESCRIBED IN DETAIL ON WORKPRINT ITSELF.

Carrie Fisher had performed her hologram dialogue while standing on a turntable. She was thus rotated and filmed from different angles that could then be composited into footage from the scenes in the garage and Ben's house. Based on the various points of view, measurements were worked out (top right). To help complete the shot, rough drawings were made on the 35mm squeezed anamorphic film (opposite bottom; final frames, above).

"Brian was the one who actually sat down and helped me fix the roll-up, he and Jay Cocks," Lucas says. "The next day we rewrote the roll-up; Brian dictated it to Jay. He typed it up and it got rewritten a couple of times after that."

An important coda to the story is that Ladd, who was still quite anxious about the film, called Spielberg after the screening for his opinion. "He was very nervous and asked, 'What do you think?'" Spielberg remembers. "And I said, 'I think it's going to make a fortune.'"

Martin Scorsese also viewed the film around this time, though not all the way through. "I saw pieces of it on the KEM, battle scenes with bluescreen," he says. "My first reaction was that it was going to be tapping into this extraordinary revolution in technology, particularly in video games." (In 1972 Atari had released Pong, which had become a sensation.)

Editorially, the collective feedback led to the cantina sequence being shortened. A subsequent screening for Francis Ford Coppola resulted in the only structural changes. "Francis thought that there was too much explanation in the beginning, I think," Hirsch says. "So we moved the first scene inside the Death Star to much later in the film." Originally the conversation between Darth Vader, Tarkin, and other Imperial officers took place in the second reel, right after C-3PO was reunited with R2-D2 in the sandcrawler; after Coppola's reaction, the Death Star debate was placed after the scene in Ben's cave, in the fourth reel.

"What that accomplished was really terrific," Hirsch adds. "Before, you had no idea of the relative importance of who these guys were; you didn't see the scene in its proper perspective. But once you'd followed Luke and picked up Ben, you knew how *bad* the bad guys were. And once we moved that one scene down, it set off a whole chain reaction of other things that had to be shifted. We dropped some scenes that didn't serve much purpose, like the scene with Vader and one of his aides walking through the Death Star halls, where he was saying something about searching for the robots—we knew all that stuff anyway."

"It was a little hard to judge," Coppola says. "It was so filled with grease-pencil lines, and missing shots, and Japanese fighter planes diving . . . I didn't know how to quite take it. I thought it was maybe a tad repetitive."

"Francis saw it later on and his projector kept breaking down, so he saw it out of order," Lucas says. "Carroll Ballard was living in Francis's pool house at the time, and he saw it then, too."

"George always has been unbelievably tight, in terms of how closely he plays his cards," Ballard says. "He doesn't reveal anything. Finally, he had a screening—and I felt so unbelievably sorry for George, because there were no special effects, just the performances, hardly any music . . . After the screening, I remember going up to George and trying to console him, saying, 'You can probably fix it. Maybe we can do some retakes.' It was just appalling. Had I been in the studios at that time, I would have pulled the plug."

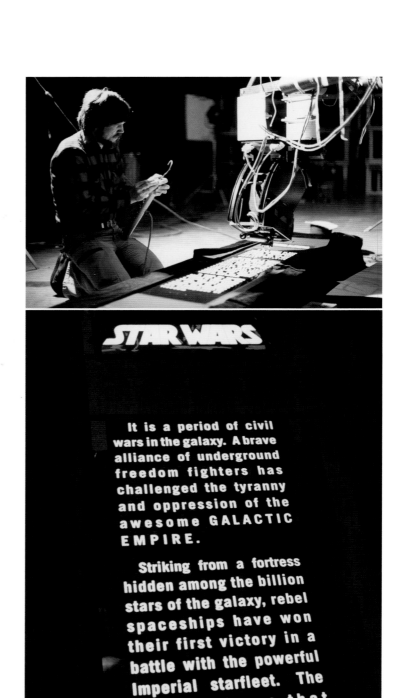

STAR WARS

It is a period of civil wars in the galaxy. A brave alliance of underground freedom fighters has challenged the tyranny and oppression of the awesome GALACTIC EMPIRE.

Striking from a fortress hidden among the billion stars of the galaxy, rebel spaceships have won their first victory in a battle with the powerful Imperial starfleet. The EMPIRE fears that another defeat could bring a thousand more solar systems into the rebellion, and Imperial control over the galaxy

Back in the spring of 1976, McQuarrie had done several matte paintings of planets, including Tatooine. These were composited in creative ways with shots of miniatures so that, for example, a single painting detail (top left) could be used in several shots: with the escape pod, one or two Star Destroyers, and the *Millennium Falcon*.

MATTE MAGIC

From February 20 to 25, 1977, Ralph McQuarrie worked on the *"Star Wars* one-sheet roughs"—that is, the poster. While he'd been busy working on matte paintings of the planets and the occasional rough sketch for effects such as the one in Luke's binocular shot, his duties were winding down—while the skills of a more experienced matte painter became needed. In fact, Harrison Ellenshaw, the son of celebrated matte painter Peter Ellenshaw, had been contacted nearly a year earlier.

"Jim Nelson said, 'Hey, we're doing a film called *Star Wars*. George Lucas from *American Graffiti* is directing—would you be interested?'" Ellenshaw says. "I said, 'Yes, sure.' This must've been January or February of '76. Then about a week later Gary Kurtz came by with Ralph McQuarrie's production paintings. I thought those were terrific. That looked exciting, and Gary said, 'This is the look we want to get.' When George got back from England, I met him and he completed the deal, because he was so full of his normal enthusiasm that I got wrapped up in it. I thought, 'Yeah, we're going to make some matte shots you're not going to believe!'"

Many years before, Ellenshaw had at first resisted following in his father's footsteps. But under the tutelage of veteran matte painter Alan Maley, he had quickly fallen in love with the art. By the time he was hired by Lucas, such was Ellenshaw's reputation that even though he was heading up the matte department at Disney Studios, a deal was arranged whereby the painter received approximately $1,050 per week as the sole freelancer in the one-man company called Master Film Effects. "I was hired on the outside but Disney didn't mind," he says. "They've been very good about that and have allowed me to do an outside film on a rare occasion." In fact, it was because Disney had allowed him to be considered for *The Man Who Fell to Earth* (1976) that word had gotten around to Lucas that its matte department would do outside work, which until then had been true only for Universal.

The big push to complete the *Star Wars* matte paintings was during the months of February and March 1977. Ellenshaw worked an average of four to six weeks on each, but many were done simultaneously. To photograph the completed works, he used a stop-motion Bell & Howell camera box, originally made in 1912 for Disney, with torque motors and "funny added things," he says. "It's very simple, very reliable; it has a one-second turnover, which is what we used to film the painted matte shots combined with the live action. That's what goes onto the negative, so that's what goes into the film.

"The first three I did very roughly to see how they went," Ellenshaw continues. "George loved them and that just boosted my ego. He said, 'Wow, those are terrific!' I was sucked in. From then on, it just continued. Normally, you like to sell the first version of the painting and hope there's not going to be changes. But because of his personality, I really didn't mind redoing them if he had changes, in order to make them as good as we possibly could."

One of his successes was the great hall, which had been causing problems at ILM. "We turned it over to Harrison Ellenshaw," Robbie Blalack says, "who used the actor elements, painting in the rest, and he did a really magnificent job."

(Continued on page 264)

Storyboards were given to Ellenshaw as guides (some are marked DISNEY, as he was freelancing from that studio, while others are marked PETER— he officially changed his name to Harrison from Peter, so he wouldn't be confused with his father, also named Peter, sometime after the release of *Star Wars*).

The great hall: "George had wanted a shaft of light to illuminate Luke, Chewbacca, and Han as they walked down the middle of the hall, with everyone else almost in black, in nothingness. But the production footage hadn't achieved that look, so he wasn't pleased with the result; he felt that the people standing at attention on the sides were overlit. In fact, we couldn't make our matte shot as dramatic as we might have because it wouldn't have intercut. Instead, we compromised and made them dark, but not all that dark. The great hall, I repainted completely three times. Now it seems a relatively simple shot, which is what I thought, too, at the beginning—but it just wasn't working. The columns were too thin, the blacks would go funny. So I added people on the side, then I reduced the plate again and added men in black; then I added another plate partway down the hall and added the shafts of the windows with burning light coming down the middle."

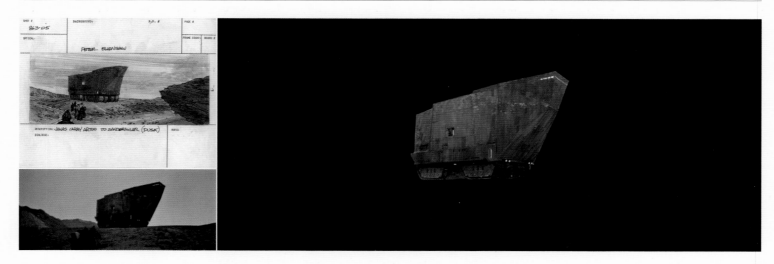

Sandcrawler at dusk: "The sandcrawler was done on the plate that they took in Death Valley, where the Jawas are carrying Artoo-Detoo. We took the Jawas right up to where their heads almost go behind the painting, but not quite. That was shot at a nice time of day, magic hour with a very light sky; it was supposed to be dusk and I thought it worked well, because it allowed us to glaze the sand color down and give it a real nice rusty glow."

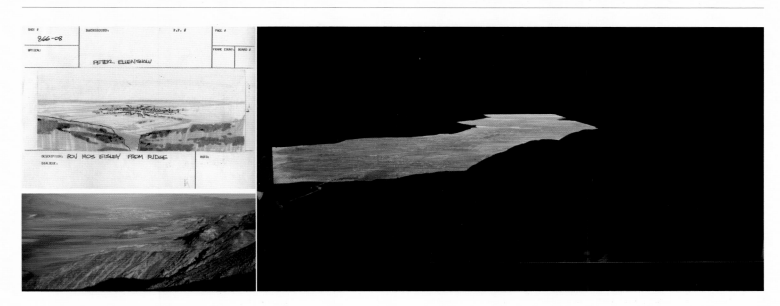

Point of view of Mos Eisley from ridge: "Originally there was a shot in Tunisia where we were looking over Alec Guinness's shoulder at the town, but we ended up not using it because there was a jiggle on it [which rules out using a matte painting]. So they went to Death Valley and shot a valley with nobody in it, a straight point-of-view shot. On this one George kept saying, 'I want the buildings bigger and taller, I want to see them more.' And I kept saying, 'You wouldn't see the buildings at that distance; they're just little specks way out there.' But he said, 'Yes, you do—go out to Mulholland Drive on a clear day, you can see tall buildings and big.' So I kept making the buildings bigger and bigger, but not as big as he wanted, so he kept saying, 'Make them bigger!' I think we came to a happy compromise."

Luke and Leia in power trench: "We created a laser blast as Leia shoots, in addition to the matte, by doing it as an added exposure ourselves rather than sending it out and having it go another generation (above left). I just blacked out a piece of glass and left three slits in, which I successively exposed one-two-three—I think we gave them three or four frames—and it matched well."

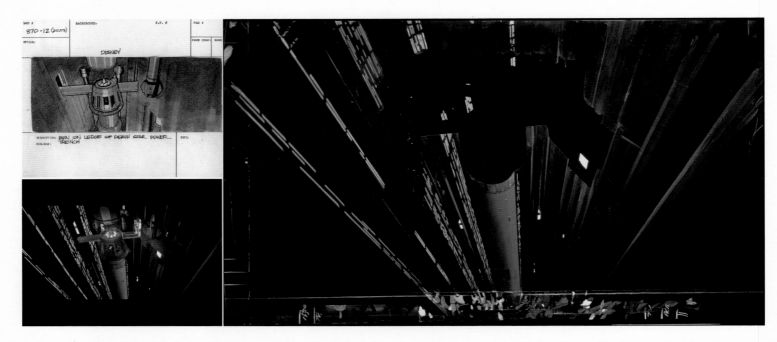

Ben on power-trench ledge: "George really wanted to create the impression that Alec Guinness was way the hell up there, above a very scary chasm. Above the tractor mechanism, he wanted a 'blue power glow' that would go on and off. So I took that plate and reduced it slightly, to help maintain quality and also to position him in a better place, where we could show more beneath him. I then painted on the sides; added a burn-in blue glow through a ripple glass up top, which went on and off,

very big exposure; and put it all together. That one went together fairly nicely."

"When Alec Guinness goes out to take care of the tractor beam, that machine has screens," Larry Cuba adds, "little versions of the Death Star that actually relate to the Death Star I used later in the briefing room scene, which in a way makes sense because they got the data from the Death Star—they stole it."

Chasm near elevators: "Ralph McQuarrie started this one [on February 7], and I finished it. He would go to my den and work on it, but this one took me about thirty hours. It was done bi-pack method. The disadvantage there

is you cannot reduce the plate, you have to live with what you have, and the quality sometimes is not as good. Ultimately, it came out slightly soft. I was disappointed in that."

Massassi hangar, interior: "They had one complete X-wing, a Y-wing, and some bits and pieces, painted ships. So I took the plate, reduced it, and then put it down in the left center; then I took the same plate, reduced it even more, and put it in the background on the right-hand side of the frame; then I painted around it, just lots of little lights in the back, a couple of shapes, a few hoses hanging down. You would be amazed at how little is on that painting, but that's not what counts—what counts is the two plates combined with the light, combined with the fact that they're composed correctly."

Massassi hangar, exterior: "I had done squares, almost Mayan-like. I put it together, showed it to George...and he sat there in dead silence, which means he doesn't like something. Then he said, 'Would it be possible to make it look more like Ralph's?' So I went back and repainted it to make it look exactly like Ralph's painting. But when we put the painting with the plate of the men walking along the bottom of the frame, it didn't quite come off as it should. So it was decided to add some foreground foliage that would move on bluescreen, and the whole thing ended up being put together on the optical printer: the VistaVision plate on the bottom, the painting, and then the foreground foliage. And that helped it."

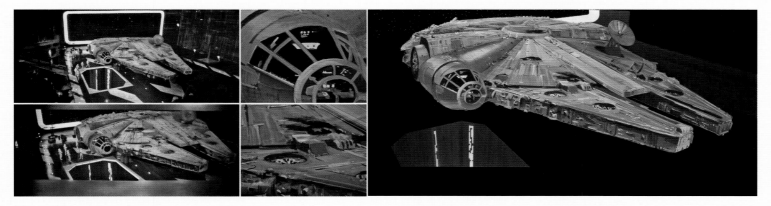

Millennium Falcon in hangar: "There is a quick shot when Leia says, 'You came in that thing?' [bottom left] And there is an establishing shot that is a little bit longer at the beginning [top left]. That quick cut was one painting, and the establishing shot was another [right, with details, middle]. There we once again reduced the plate, added onto the sides, put the top of the opening in for the shaft going down the center, all sorts of little goodies, lights and things like that. I used the original plate shot in England, the stormtroopers running up, and then I shot the miniature on regular 5247 film in a still camera, single-lens reflex. That I rear-projected and put the miniature together, matched it up size-wise, added some painting so it would match and blend, and put those two things together so it's really the stormtroopers running up to the side of the set, which is connected to the miniature. That one worked well, too."

McQuarrie's matte painting of Yavin was also used in at least two shots.

VADER'S VOICE

On March 1, 1977, a new actor took the stage at the Goldwyn Studios, albeit only for one day, and only as a voice. James Earl Jones had been chosen to do the Darth Vader dialogue, for $7,500. "George Lucas always wanted a voice in the bass register," Jones says. "I understand that George did contact Orson Welles to read for the voice of Darth Vader before he contacted me. I was out of work and he said, 'Do you want a day's work?'"

"He was the best actor that I could possibly find," Lucas says. "He has a deep, commanding voice."

With Lucas's prompting, Jones watched the pertinent scenes, studying his character's lack of emotion, and ultimately investing in him a menace that would've been difficult to imagine before. Because Vader is masked, Jones didn't have to worry about lip-syncing; he completed his work in about two and a half hours. "Vader is a man who never learned the beauties and subtleties of human expression," Jones says. "So we figured out the key to my work was to keep it on a very narrow band of expression—that was the secret."

Armed with Jones's magnificently voiced readings, the director then utilized a technique that he'd originated with Walter Murch on *American Graffiti* whereby Vader's lines were given a spatial dimension. "They did what they call 'worldizing,'" Sam Shaw explains. "It's a technique where they try to eliminate that 'looped' sound by playing the sound back through speakers in a regular room, so it has a natural presence to it, and then re-recording it."

It was next Ben Burtt's task to find the appropriate breathing sound to go with Vader's voice. "He did about eighteen different kinds," Lucas says, "through Aqua-Lungs and through tubes, trying to find the one that had the right sort of mechanical sound. And then we had to decide whether it would be totally rhythmical like an iron lung—that's the idea, which was a whole part of the plot that essentially got cut out."

Perhaps on the same day that Jones performed as Vader, Larry Ward did the voice-over for Greedo. Once again it was up to Burtt to enhance his readings to create a sound for the overly confident alien. "We had one word, which was just a person going 'Oink-oink,'" Lucas says. "If you did it fast enough with the right rhythm and electric equipment, it sounded like a very bizarre language, but that didn't work. So Ben got together with a graduate student from UC Berkeley, who is a real expert in languages, and he and Ben went through languages and languages and then they finally made up a language. Ben took it and edited it down, and we had the dialogue written out. Then we processed that electronically to give it a phasing sound and, well, it was a lot of work."

ROMANCE AND MUSIC

John Williams had worked quickly and was able to begin the soundtrack recordings on schedule in England on March 5, 1977. The decision to produce the music overseas had been presented to Williams as a fait accompli, probably due to continuing budget constraints and because the sessions coincided with the looping of the principal actors.

"We recorded at the Anvil Studios in Denham, which used to be the old J. Arthur Rank Studios," Williams says. "It's one of the most popular places to record music for film in London. It is out in the country very near Pinewood. It is a fine facility. I did *Fiddler on the Roof* [1971] there. Also did *Jane Eyre* [1971] there. So that was the logical choice. We had fourteen sessions with the orchestra, which represents about seven working days. A session is a three-hour sitting. Normally, we had a morning and an afternoon session. A couple of days we did three sessions, which was rough on everybody, because that is a lot of concentrating. With meal breaks that ends up being about a twelve-hour day."

The total forty-two hours was performed by the London Symphony Orchestra, a first even for the veteran composer. "I had never used an organized symphony orchestra before for a film," he says. "None of my assignments either coincided with the availability of an orchestra and/or the need for one. In this case we wanted a symphonic sound, and we were in London where great orchestras are available. In London you have a choice of four or five. I think they played beautifully, particularly the brass section. I think it has such nobility and such a wonderful heraldic sound. I think it really brings something to the film."

Williams wasn't the only one. Lucas had made the flight overseas to produce the sessions, and as he heard the first few cues, and saw the music's marriage with the film he'd labored on for four years, he was incredibly happy. He even phoned Spielberg so his friend could hear over a phone directed toward the musicians half an hour of the melodies and themes as they were played for the first time.

What they both heard was one of the pinnacles in movie soundtrack history, ranking with Bernard Herrmann's *Vertigo*, *Psycho*, and *North by Northwest*, and Maurice Jarre's *Lawrence of Arabia*, Max Steiner's *Casablanca*, and Erich Korngold's *The Adventures of Robin Hood*. Williams's was an emotional score with operatic leitmotifs. "I think the music relates to the characters and the human problems, even when they are Wookiees," Williams says. "This is the gut thrust of the thing in music—a very romantic theme for the Princess, a heroic march for the Jedi Knights—all of this material has to do with the fairy-tale aspect of it.

"I didn't want to hear a piece of Dvořák here, a piece of Tchaikovsky there," he continues, commenting on a discussion he'd had with Lucas. "What I wanted to hear was something to do with Ben Kenobi more developed here, something to do with his death over there. What we needed were themes of our own, which one could put through all the permutations of a dramatic situation. This was my discussion and my dialogue with George—that I felt we needed our own themes, which could be made into a solid dramaturgical glue from start to finish. To whatever extent we have succeeded, that is what I tried to do."

"I was very, very pleased with the score," Lucas says. "We wanted a very Max Steiner–type of romantic movie score. There were a lot of little discussions about if this or that would make it go too far, would it be too much? I decided just to do it all the way down the line, one end to the other, complete. Everything is on that same level, which is sort of old-fashioned and fun, but going for the most dramatic and emotional elements that I could get."

Whenever there was a break in the recording, Lucas would run to London to loop Alec Guinness, Mark Hamill, et al.—though at least a couple of actors read their lines at Anvil. Anthony Daniels arrived for voice-over work despite the fact that dozens of others had auditioned for the speaking role of C-3PO.

"It was primarily because of the fact that it was a British voice," Lucas says. "I really wanted to keep the whole thing American. Tony had the most British accent, so I said, 'No, I want to make him American because he is one of the lead characters.' I wanted Threepio's voice to be slightly more used-car-dealer-ish, a little more oily. More of a con man, which is the way it was written, and not really a fussy British robot butler. So I tried and tried, but because Tony was Threepio inside, he really got into the role. We went through thirty people that I actually tested, but none of the voices were as good as Tony's, so we kept him."

It's possible that Lucas, often loath to part with an idea that he likes, was thinking of the used-car dealer who had been cut from *American Graffiti* by Universal and wanted to get the concept into *Star Wars*.

"With dubbing you get the *beep, beep, beep—speak*," Daniels says of the audio cue. "It's quite hard sometimes to deliver, for instance, a jokey line,

Harrison Ellenshaw at work on the Massassi temple matte painting (above); McQuarrie on the elevator shaft (below).

The film editor who worked the longest on *Star Wars*, Paul Hirsch, was also at least partly responsible for the late career resurgence of legendary composer Bernard Herrmann. It began when Hirsch had laid in Herrmann's music from *Psycho* (1960) as the temp track on a film he was editing, Brian De Palma's *Sisters* (1973), and everyone responded enthusiastically. "Benny—Bernard Herrmann—had fallen out of favor with Alfred Hitchcock, and no one else would work with him," Hirsch explains. "But they sent Benny Herrmann the script for *Sisters* in London, and he agreed to look at the picture. Then he came over and did the film, and that was very exciting. When *Sisters* came out, a lot of its success was due to the reception that the score got—and in a sense it revived his American career."

Hirsch did something similar as they were creating the temp track for *Star Wars*. "The scene where they pop out of the hatch in the *Falcon*, I laid in a very famous piece of *Psycho* music there," he says. "It was a three-note motif that Scorsese had insisted that Benny use in *Taxi Driver*. It was a dark, ominous three-note motif. Curiously enough, Johnny—I don't know if he did it deliberately or what—but it's now incorporated into his cue for that moment in the film. He's got the very same notes that appear in *Psycho*, they appear in *Taxi Driver*—and now they're in *Star Wars*" (below).

all those bits about, 'No, I don't think he likes you at all; no, I don't like you, either.' But I enjoyed dubbing very much—I was very excited by what I saw on the screen in front of me. I'd often stop dubbing just to watch what was happening. I must say I think the banthas are one of the best things in it, and George of course won't tell me how they were done. I realized, watching it, that I used to see George standing up against all these physically big people—surrounded by people trying to tell him what to do—and in fact he was getting his own way very quietly. And if he couldn't get his own way, then accepting the fact. He really knew what he was doing."

Coincidentally, as Lucas left London, the looping and soundtrack completed, Ralph McQuarrie, his *Star Wars* work finished, arrived in England on March 25 to begin creating concept art for the first *Star Trek* motion picture.

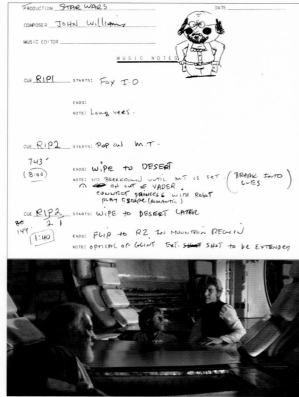

A caricature of John Williams adorns a page of "Music Notes" for the scenes of R2-D2 in the desert and mountain regions.

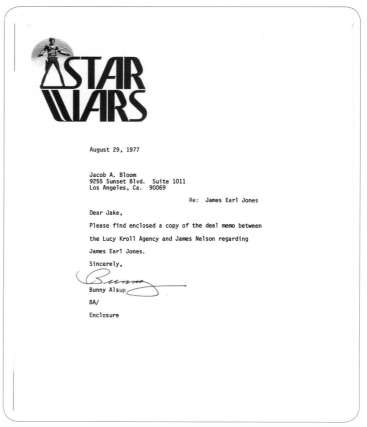

Just a few days before James Earl Jones took the stage, on February 25, 1977, a note from the Lucy Kroll Agency to James Nelson stated the agreed terms for which Jones would become the voice of Darth Vader (top). Much later Bunny Alsup sent the deal memo with her own cover letter to Jacob Bloom per the hiring of Jones for the legal files on August 29, 1977 (above).

John Williams conducting the London Symphony Orchestra to the rhythms of the film as projected above the heads of the musicians.

GARBAGE CANS AND THE TEMPLE OF TIKAL

While Lucas was in England during much of March 1977, things were relatively calm at ILM, which meant that two camera crews weren't necessary. It was thus the perfect time for Richard Edlund to lead an intrepid duo on an adventure in Guatemala. Their mission: to shoot the plates needed for the creation of Yavin, the jungle planet. Armed with twelve Joe Johnston storyboards as conceptual guides, Edlund embarked as the DP, with Richard Alexander to oversee the material and Pepi Lenzi as their translator and guide during a seat-of-your-pants journey.

"As a bonus, we got to take a little vacation, one week in Guatemala," Edlund says. "Of course, we had to take 1,200 pounds of luggage with us. Pepi is the fellow that Ray Gosnell knew. He'd been on staff at Fox for fifteen or sixteen years as a 'get-'em-there' guy. He could speak ten languages—and he was so cool, he would just roll through customs."

Hauling thirty-five cases filled with equipment (like the Technorama camera, built in 1931 as a Technicolor camera for Disney) through various airports, the trio eventually reached Guatemala, where they boarded a derelict DC-3 for the flight to Tikal. "Central America is a haven for used airplanes," Edlund says. "It was really funky; oil was just dribbling down the sides of the plane."

"We were sitting on this plane, which had about six seats that were covered with Levi's," Richard Alexander remembers. "There were big boxes and chickens, and there weren't enough seat belts. It was ridiculous! But it was one of the best flights I've ever had—we flew only a couple of hundred feet above the jungle at about eighty miles an hour. The food was

Ben Kenobi and Darth Vader: "I think of Ben's theme as also being the theme of the Jedi Knights, the Old Republic that Ben remembers. It also overlaps into the area of being the theme for the Force, the good Force that Ben represents. There is a lot of English horn in Ben's theme, which is often heard under dialogue, which is another reason for that instrumentation. Vader's theme is a lot of bassoons and muted trombones and low things, since he is the bad side of the Force."

Luke: "Luke's theme is fanfare-ish and brassy and bold and masculine and noble, and all those things. When this music is done softer, it tends to be done in some sort of brass, horns if it is more heraldic. It's the full glow of the glorious brass section of the London Symphony Orchestra [LSO]."

Leia: "The princess theme is very romantic. The first time Luke sees her, he says how beautiful she is. It really is a fairy-tale princess melody."

Sunset: "George asked for Ben's theme there once he had heard it. I had originally scored that scene with Luke's theme, but when he heard the other, he said, 'Could you put Ben's theme in there?' He liked it for some reason or other better for that scene. It is difficult to explain why. It is contemplative and reflective, and it works really very well. I think I have to say in the end he was very right."

Cantina: "George found a record that he liked. He used it for a temp track and he shot to that, which gave him a rhythmic continuity shot to shot, cut to cut. What he said to me was, 'Can you imagine these creatures in some future century having found in a time capsule or under a rock an old 1930s Benny Goodman swing-band record? Can you imagine what their distorted idea of how to play it would be?' So that's more or less what I tried to do, and I think it looks pretty cute with the monsters, you know."

Ben's death: "I used part of the princess theme in the beginning of it, for two reasons: I took dramatic license because it was the most sweeping melody in the score, but I'm also playing it because it is what's inside of her and Luke during their reaction to his death" (below).

Death Star battle: "During the last battle there is a lot of exciting battle music, which I think is beautifully played by the LSO. Very, very difficult, and they read it just brilliantly—and that battle music includes most if not all of the themes in this picture."

Throne room: "The entrance to the throne room has a big fanfare as they come in, and Ben's theme is used in a kind of parade way. In this sense it represents the triumph of the values of the Old Republic. I don't know how George thinks of it, literally, but at least musically that is how it works. That is followed by the presentation of the medals, which is a theme I am very fond of. It is a kind of 'land of hope and glory' bit. It is almost like coronation music, really, which the scene seemed to want."

beans and rice and TV dinners, and it took like twenty-one hours to get there. We landed in a jungle; the 'runway' was just a strip of mud. It had been pouring, so there were puddles everywhere."

Next stop was the Jungle Inn, so they loaded their gear on a Volkswagen bus and climbed into a jeep for the drive. "We set up most of the cameras in the hotel," Alexander continues, "which was a series of little grass huts with rooms. It was really quite romantic—big peacocks running around, snakes slithering all over the place. It rained every now and then, but it was about ninety degrees; the humidity was so heavy that Richard was blowing smoke rings that would stay in the air for about twenty minutes."

The next day eight guides led them on a scouting trip to the temples, about five or six miles through the jungle. "George had a picture in mind as to what he wanted," Edlund says. "We had storyboards, and I had already shot the pirate ship that goes in one scene, so I had that clip to match."

"Eventually we found the perfect shot to match the storyboards," Alexander says. "We found the exact place on top of temple number three, I believe. It was the first ledge, which was probably a couple of hundred feet up, and it was only about six feet wide."

"So we had to climb the highest of the old pyramids," Edlund remembers. "This particular one was a ways away from the center; it was overlooking the others. So we climbed all the way up there with all the cases, all of the equipment; when I first got to the top, a little coral snake was in the middle of ingesting a bat in this cave."

A McQuarrie sketch and painting from late 1975/early 1976 (far left, top). The latter was later extrapolated into storyboards by Johnston (far left, below). Though the small second-unit crew departed for Guatemala to capture the jungle footage, early in 1976 the planned destination was Mexico.

Richard Alexander, Pepe Lenzi, and Richard Edlund set up Lorne Peterson in the garbage can/lookout tower atop pyramid number three in Tikal, Guatemala (left, photo from the private collection of Lorne Peterson).

Phil Tippett and
Jon Berg posing the
stop-motion crea-
ture sculpts on the
black velvet (below
left), working out
shots that had been
preplanned to some
extent using the
grid/field method
(right: shots 3
and 4 are shown,
with frame counts,
but the drawings
indicate slightly
different "mon-
sters" from those
that appeared in
the film).

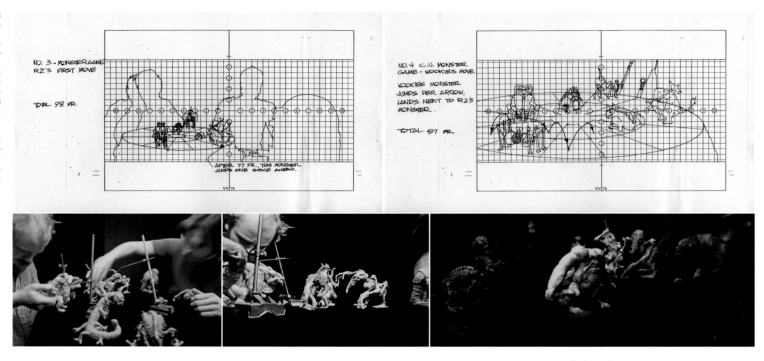

Having found their location, Edlund hired two guards with shotguns to stay overnight with the equipment. "The first day with the baggage, that was okay," Alexander says. "The second day, we got up at four o'clock in the morning. It was dark and just ridiculous."

"I decided that on the second day, we'd get up real early in the morning," Edlund says. "That way, we'd get to the top of the pyramid before the sun came up and get some shots in the early mist."

One of the key shots consisted of a Rebel in his lookout nest—which was yet another ready-made prop. "The biggest box in our luggage was a trash can," Alexander recalls. "The guard's little post was really two $28 trash cans joined together and stuck on an aluminum pole with guide wires. We'd already tested it in the middle of Sepulveda Dam, before we'd left. As soon as I'd shinnied up the pole, the police came along and stopped to look at these idiots in a trash can twenty feet up in the air."

After climbing pyramid number three once again, they took the trash can out of the crates, found chinks in the stones to keep the poles stable, and then placed the trash can on top of the poles so it had a command-ing view overlooking the jungle. "We got it up there—but then nobody wanted to climb into it," Alexander says. "So first a local did, and then I did—and I must admit, it was kind of scary looking down. The temple dropped away at an angle, but I figured that if I fell, I'd probably get stuck in a tree halfway down."

On the third day model maker Lorne Peterson joined the trio in Tikal—and was immediately coaxed into the crow's nest. Edlund also had him dress up as the Rebel who tracks the pirate ship with what's supposed to be some sort of fantastic contraption, but which was really a Minolta spot meter, with a tube and batteries taped onto it like a gun, "to make it look sci fi."

"I think we were actually shooting five days and were away eight,"

Alexander sums up. "Getting back, we had a flat tire on our truck in the middle of the San Diego Freeway, during rush hour with all the luggage—*that* was the worst part of the whole trip."

STOP-MOTION CHESS

"George had said that he wanted some really gross-looking, ugly things for the cantina sequence to punch it up," Muren recalls. "So Phil Tippett and Jon Berg made up some little sculptures that I thought might sell George on it; they were ideas for people standing on their heads and two people bunched up together in a suit. I brought them in and showed George, and he really liked them."

He liked them so much that, after returning from England in late March 1977, he hired Tippett and Berg to do the chess set scene in which the droids match wits with Chewbacca. "Originally, they had planned to use little people in costumes placed on a giant chessboard," Berg says. "But when they saw *Futureworld* [1976], which had already used the concept, it took the wind out of their sails. We had done some little clay figures for the cantina characters, and George saw those things and thought we could maybe do the sequence instead with stop-motion animation."

"Lucas just said, 'Make them about six inches tall,'" Tippett recalls. "Propulsion was one of our primary considerations, but he said, 'I don't care. They can slither and slide, or you can put wheels on them.' So we had complete freedom to do what we wanted to do."

Because both Berg and Tippett came from the less elastic world of commercials, the liberty was invigorating and they started working intently on ten small sculptures—using latex, foam rubber, and plastic foam—while Grant McCune made the chessboard itself. "When we finally got the figures and the board set up," Tippett says, "George came over that afternoon, before going over to do the sound mixing, and talked to us about what he had in mind. He blocked the sequence in, asking, 'Could this hop out, or could this guy do this?' And so we were working *with* him rather than having a preconceived set of ideas that he wanted very rigidly performed. It was a collaboration, and that was very exciting."

"I set up the shots for them," Muren says. "Jon and Phil did the stop-motion work, and the whole thing was done in a back corner at ILM. We did two shots that aren't in the film, some low-angle close-ups on the figures, but George felt they just weren't necessary. Once the audience had seen a thing in the movie, he didn't want them to see it again later on."

In order to match the backgrounds that had already been shot on 4-perforation film, Muren rented a regular 4-perf Mitchell with a squeeze lens. "Dennis was working on the night crew then," Tippett says, "and he set up all the camera stuff and lighting against black velvet. We'd roll in about three o'clock in the afternoon and get shooting by about nine o'clock at night. We had about eight figures on the chessboard, so, for the master shots, we split the board right down the middle; Jon took four and I took four, and Jon did all the primary animation for the lead characters.

"We'd start with one figure on the left-hand corner and move one of his arms, his wrist, and his leg, and then go to the next one and bend his neck, and then go to the next one and flip his antennae, and move his feet—one forward, one backward—and then take one frame of film. Then I'd go back to the very first one in the left-hand corner and duplicate the entire process, trying to remember which way we were moving one of the legs, and so on. We'd end up getting out like eight o'clock the next morning, just at dawn."

"We shot the chess game all in singles," Berg says. "It takes more time and it's harder. Boy, it gets rough when you have the number of figures we had."

Despite the continuity difficulties, Berg and Tippett finished the sequence in five days.

THEY KEPT ON TRUCKIN'

By the latter half of March 1977, the kaleidoscopes of editorial, ILM, music, and sound mixing were nearing their respective ends. Most of the effects shots had taken on their final forms, though many did not achieve what

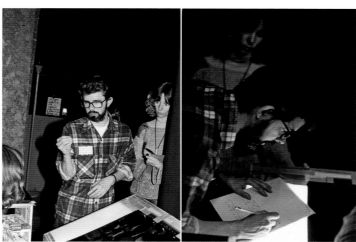

Lucas supervising work at ILM (left, with Rose Duignan; and with Kurtz, below).

PRODUCTION REPORT

BEGIN GOLD TRENCH RUN

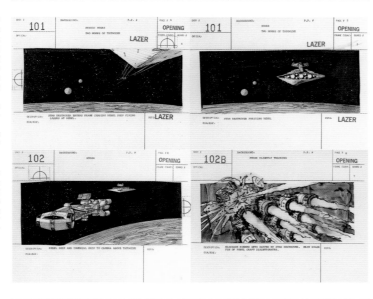

Special effects shots for the attack on the Death Star were tracked with ILM's ongoing production report (above), from September 1976 to March 1977, with columns for elements, cameras, optical, compositing—up to "Okay G. L." Storyboards (right) by Gary Meyer, Paul Huston, Steve Gawley, under the direction of Johnston, show the opening shots designated "101" and "102."

would've been nice if there had been another three months at the end of it—although we were pretty burned out."

On the editorial front Lucas and Hirsch were still tweaking the film. "We constantly made changes to the movie," Hirsch says. "It had made things difficult for Johnny Williams, because he'd been obliged to score the picture before it was locked. He'd even started writing music before we'd shot second unit. Luckily, our music editor Ken Wannberg was great in tailoring what had been designed for one thing to fit with another thing. He cut it and made it fit."

"There was always this seesawing back and forth between the music and the sound effects," Burtt says. "Music was dropped out of two places in the film. Initially there was a lot more music when Artoo-Detoo gets ambushed by the Jawas, but the scene played better without any music at all. There was also music originally over the sequence of the Dia Noga. Again it was more frightening and suspenseful without the music."

With a close to final mix in place, another screening was scheduled. Though no doubt buoyed by Spielberg's prediction, Alan Ladd had yet to get Twentieth Century-Fox's sales team on board. Given the theater owners' continuing indifference, Ladd would have an almost insurmountable task of booking *Star Wars* into movie houses without their support.

"Fox asked, 'Can we bring up all the marketing and distribution guys? Because we have to start marketing the movie,' " Lucas says. "So they came over to Park Way from the airport in a rented tour bus. The room held about twenty-five to thirty people—and that's the screening for which Laddie was holding his breath."

"I was sitting poised by the phone," recalls Ladd, who was back in Hollywood. "I had said, 'The minute you've seen the film, will you please call me?' So I was expecting a call . . . and expecting a call . . . But they didn't call, so I thought, *Oh, God, they don't want to hurt my feelings.* I broke my luncheon date because I still hadn't heard from them. And I am waiting and waiting and waiting. I finally get a call—and they were absolutely ecstatic. Everybody was crowded into a phone booth saying, 'The picture is extraordinary. I don't even believe what I've seen!' "

"After they saw the picture the end of March, their attitude changed a bit," Kurtz recalls. "They felt a lot more positive. They were much more relieved, and Ray Gosnell and the production office got off our back."

GIANT IMPERIAL STAR DESTROYERS

Intermittently from December 1976 to April 1977, Lucas, Edlund, and others at ILM were working on perhaps the most important moment of the film—the opening shot. "It's the first two or three shots in the movie, where the big ship is chasing the little ship—that was my vision of the movie," Lucas says.

Budget cuts and pared-down storytelling had reduced the number of Imperial ships from several to one. Other modifications and corrections sprinkle the ILM paperwork, which includes several references to shots 101 and 102, the two opening images:

DECEMBER 21, 1976: SHOT 102, REBEL BLOCKADE RUNNER NEEDS TO BE RESHOT. THERE IS A PROBLEM WITH THE MATTE LINE.

Lucas had originally envisioned. Often it was a case of abandoning ideas because either time or money or both were simply running out; other times it was a case of the ideal outstripping what was technically possible. "George's visits started dwindling to Mondays and Tuesdays, and then just Mondays," notes Edlund, "as we started getting closer and closer to the finish line."

"I worked a lot on Saturdays toward the end to get the thing done," Muren says. "We would shoot as many shots as we could in a row, Ken Ralston and I, without unloading the camera. That would save twenty minutes right there; if you're doing that three times a day, you've saved an hour, which means one more shot for the day. That was the philosophy I had, because I didn't see how it was ever going to be finished in time. But George compromised on his end and we compromised on our end. I don't think quality was hurt too much, though it could've been better. It

JANUARY 25, 1977: SHOT 102, PROBABLE RESHOOT OF STAR DESTROYER ELEMENT IN ADDITION TO DEFINITE RESHOOT OF REBEL SHIP. GL WANTS STAR DESTROYER ALMOST TWICE AS BIG, SO THAT IT FILLS THE SCREEN. REBEL SHIP WOULD GO OVER THE STAR DESTROYER FOR ENTIRE SHOT.

APRIL 8, 1977: SHOT 101: LAZERS ARE TO BE OPAQUED OUT OF TAIL OF MOST RECENT COMP (TEMP ON APRIL 7). ALSO, JOHN DYKSTRA IS GOING TO CHECK AND SEE IF ANY OTHER TAKES ON STARS FOR 101 ARE BETTER THAN SELECTED TAKE. JD MARKED ON PRINT WHERE LAZERS ARE TO STOP FOR FINA COMP (3 FRAMES BEFORE KEY #D6X89474).

Lucas also requested that the Rebel ship enter from the upper right-hand corner of the screen instead of directly overhead. "The opening shot, I felt, and of course George felt, was the most important shot in the show," Edlund says. "It was the shot where everybody was going to have to make the 'leap of faith.' If everybody was just boggled by the opening, they would accept the stylistic integrity, the actual look of *Star Wars*. If

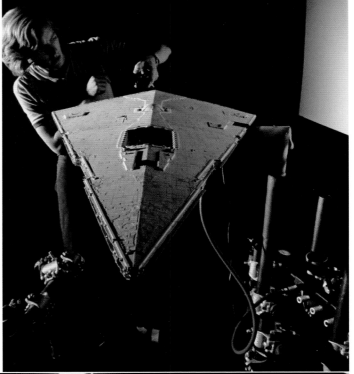

Richard Edlund and Jamie Shourt prepare the Rebel ship (below). "We built everything but the right top-side of the Star Destroyer," Grant McCune says, "which wouldn't be on camera—that became the access point for getting to the electronics and everything inside of it. The docking bay (above, with Doug Smith) was very intricate with 20 to 30 light-bulbs, and extremely fine modeling using ten-thousandths-thick materials. David Beasley and David Jones detailed it, which took them about six weeks."

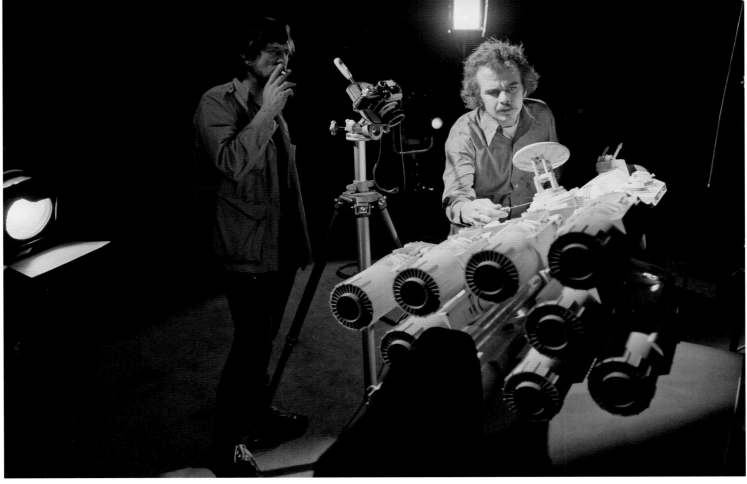

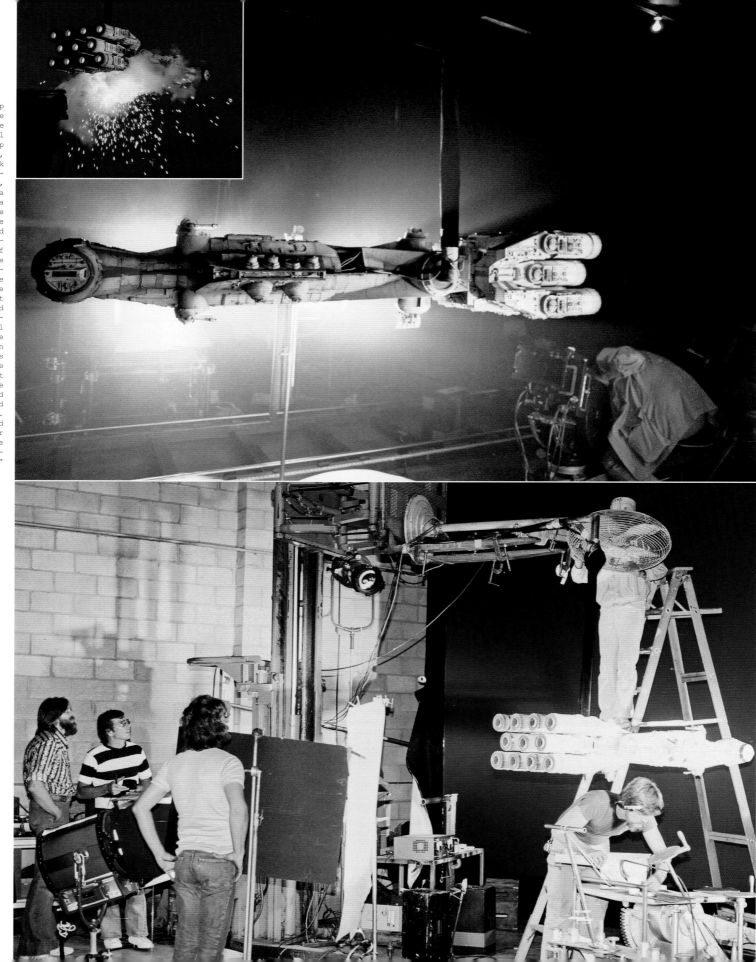

The Rebel ship was shot with the Dykstraflex on the motion-control stage, with the help of John Dykstra, Bill Shourt, Dick Alexander, and Richard Edlund (below, with an ILMer on a ladder adjusting a fan). "We hung the rebel ship upside down [above and inset, to simulate the vacuum of space], and then we set up a pyrotechnic in one of the nooks behind the radar tower," Grant McCune says. "We had time to put a pulse-motor in the central column and made the radar antenna spin around. The guns that had been made for the side of it [when it was the pirate ship] had been taken out and used on the *Falcon*. We lit it off and did about five or six takes with the high-speed VistaVision camera."

On February 4, 1977, Doug Smith held the slate for the day's work on the Death Star trench and surface (far left). Explosions were shot outside in the ILM parking lot with Joe Viskocil supervising their preparation (middle), and Edlund setting them off through cables (above left). It was also the opportunity for a group shot (below left).

I lost any sleep during the show, it was when I was worried we might blow it by making one shot that would make someone in the audience say, 'Model!'"

Much, if not all, of production's anxiety concerning shots 101 and 102 did center on the models. The Star Destroyer was only about three feet long, but in the first shot it was going to have to fill the whole of the screen for a relatively long time—about fifteen seconds—and if it looked fake, it could ruin the film. The Rebel ship, ironically, was more like six feet long—but in shot 102 it was going to have to look as if it were being swallowed by the much smaller model's underbelly docking bay, which was only five or six inches long.

"George at one point wanted to build a huge model for the Star Destroyer," Edlund says. "We were getting to the point where we had to either do it or not, and he was thinking of revamping the opening, although he had his heart set on the Rebel ship coming in, followed by the big ship with 'no cut,' so that you got the entire effect of the big ship. But he was worried that the miniature wasn't going to hold up. So I shot a test for him, by putting a tiny model on a piece of wire sticking out in front of the Destroyer, and just making a camera move on it against black."

"George knew he wanted the ship to come in and to be big," Kurtz says. "But he was worried that they could not shoot that with the small model, so we were talking about building a fifteen-foot section. Then Richard convinced him that with the right lens and angle, we could make that ship look really large. He tried it a couple of times, with a couple of

different lenses, and finally George reluctantly agreed that it might work right, but we put that on the back burner as a potential redo."

"We knew that the Star Destroyer was going to be in that opening sequence and we knew that it was going to have a real slow, close pan by it," Johnston recalls. "And at that time we had some extra people from the model shop, so we just put two guys on detailing the Star Destroyer, detailing for weeks, especially on the docking bay."

"Richard had to make the six-foot Rebel blockade runner appear to be about one-tenth the size of the three-foot Star Destroyer," Blalack says, "and that had to be handled by optics, choice of lenses, and choice of shooting distance. We wanted to improve on that one, but we never got that shot right."

"On shot 101 I used four synchronizers, two sawhorses, and a door," Lind says. "We had so many separate elements—stars, large moon, small moon, horizon, Rebel blockade runner, mother Star Destroyer, two different elements of flak, two different elements of lasers, plus all the mattes for the planets. There is no synchronizer that can take all of that at once, so what you do is you find a four or five gang-sync and hook them all together."

Following the many modifications, experiments, innovations, and ruses, Lucas signed off on the two shots in mid-April 1977, and then the audio elements were mixed in. "There were a few places in the movie where the music and the sound effects conflicted," Burtt says. "One of the first places was at the very opening of the film, when the first spaceship flies overhead. We had always wanted to have that sound effect of the spaceship come exploding through, and be a big shock on the audience's

A long time ago in a galaxy far, far away....

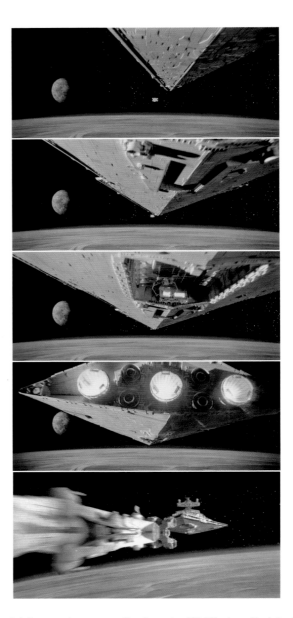

ears. However, the music composed for that point was also very loud, and was of such spectral composition that it camouflaged the explosiveness of the sound effect. We were never able to quite achieve the right blend there of music and sound effects, so we compromised, half and half of each."

IN THE TRENCHES

Lucas and his editors had started handing over pieces for the end battle sequence back in the middle of December 1976, but the complexity and quantity of the shots meant that ILM didn't finish this part of the film until the middle of April 1977. Many shots were photographed more than once, and nearly all were altered to some extent. Before each was begun, Joe Johnston would do a storyboard for it. "George would decide he'd want a board changed here and there, so we'd go through the sequence," Johnston says. "He'd pick out a shot or even pick out a frame and say, 'Move the ship forty-two degrees this way,' and that's how most of the boards were done. He was real complete about everything, every little angle of every ship. He knew exactly how he wanted it. It's really amazing."

Of course, the object of all these intricately maneuvering ships was to obliterate the Death Star. In real life, however, it was building up the

Imperial fortress that monopolized much of ILM's time. Back in 1975 Colin Cantwell had made a conceptual model; Ralph McQuarrie had also done two matte paintings. But as ILM delved into the shots themselves, it became clear that the variety of work demanded a variety of Death Stars. A shot could move in on the matte painting, straight-on, but as soon as the shot wanted to pan, then the surface perspective would have to change, and they couldn't make the matte painting appear to rotate. Moreover, the battle was to take place above and then within the Death Star trench—two entirely different locations, miniature-wise. Also, the size of the Death Star increased exponentially early on. "The Death Star became a sphere of enormous proportions," McQuarrie says, "when the guys at ILM decided

A "threshold scale"
Death Star was used
for low passes
over the surface
(right); a "sub-
miniature scale,"
another Death Star
surface, was made
from photographs
of all the little
parts reproduced
at 150-to-1 and pasted
on a big curved sur-
face (below left,
Mark Hamill inspects
this one, with Mary
Lind wearing glasses
next to him), which
was used for even
higher-altitude
shots (below right).

that it had to have a flat surface in order to run their camera above it and then we calculated the size of the sphere that would have a flat horizon when you were standing on the surface."

Initially the scale of the trench was dictated by the length needed and the length limitations. As they could move the Dykstraflex only forty feet at one go, and because the trench was supposed to be about forty miles long, the scale came down to a mile a foot. To fill those feet/miles, eight different modular units of three different-sized trench pieces were created; these could then be put together in an almost limitless number of combinations. For the surface of the Death Star a similar technique was used, with six pieces. The cost was about $5 or $6 per square foot. It was so

inexpensive because the company that mass-produced the modules wanted a film credit, so they gave ILM a discount; but in the end the manufacturer went bankrupt instead.

"There was disagreement in the beginning between Richard, John, and George about what size the trench should be and how the surfaces should be arranged within each other and how the shots could come out," McCune says. "At one time it was three feet wide and three feet deep; then it was two feet deep and three feet wide. The first time we built it, it took us a month to arrange all the parts, the second time it took us two weeks, and the third time it took us about three hours—it was just boom, boom, boom! Finally there was about sixty running feet of trench, including the end piece where the target area was.

ILM also built two trenches (top, threshold scale), though the wider
version was ultimately discarded in favor of the narrower one. With the
threshold scale trench on its side, Doug Smith helps prepare a shot of
X-wings (middle left); Richard Edlund, wearing the red helmet, is pro-
pelled down the track while shooting an explosion in another trench
against greenscreen (middle right). Another explosion is prepared by Joe
Viskocil (on ladder above TIE fighter), with Edlund behind the camera
(bottom left; bottom right, final frame).

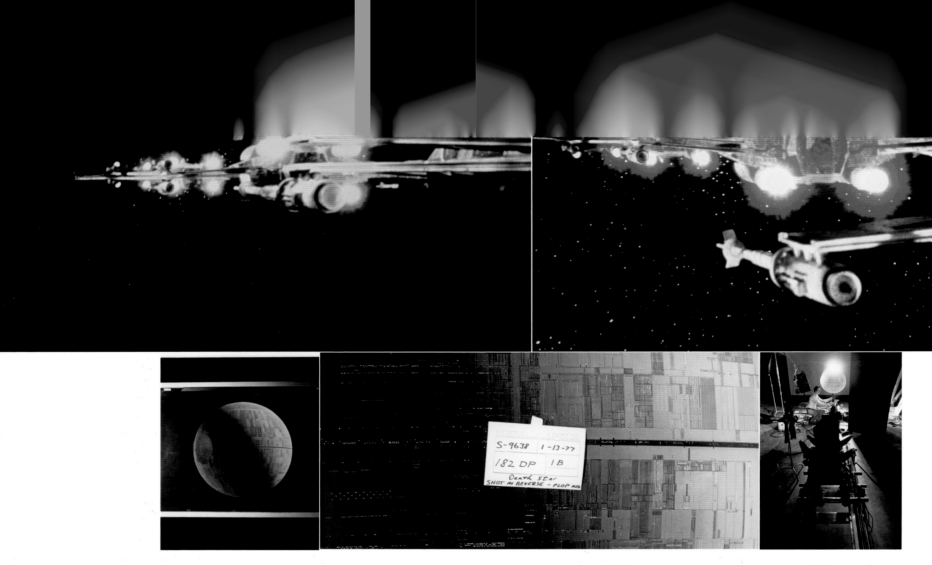

"Then we went through and put on probably ten thousand little sixteenth-inch-by-sixteenth-inch chips of retro-reflective tape, the stuff they use on freeway signs, as windows. I'd made a ring with cortelage and bulbs around the lens that would shine against the tape and reflect back, so it would look like rows and rows of windows. But George thought they were all too big [laughs], so me, Lorne Peterson, and Steve Gawley had to go through with brushes and paint out half of the sixteenth inch on ten thousand little squares."

"At one time we had about ten people working on the Death Star trench," Joe Johnston says. "It was the equivalent of being sent to the Russian front in World War II. It was like being exiled to Siberia to be sent to work on the Death Star—and it was always there, you know. It took us months to build."

Many ILMers assumed that the trench went around the equator of the sphere, but, according to Johnston, it was really one of eighteen trenches that started about halfway up from the equator and continued to the northern pole of the Death Star. For his part, Lucas had a hard time convincing others of just how fast the TIE fighters and X-wings should be going in that trench—because he wanted them to really move. Others argued that the trench was so wide that the background walls would

remain relatively static given the scale no matter how fast the starcraft were going—whereas Lucas wanted the walls to be close to a blur.

"The trench bothered George," Kurtz says. "He felt that the trench didn't go by fast enough and John's biggest argument was that if the trench is three hundred yards wide, the walls are not going to go by fast. The faster the walls go by, the smaller the scale, and that argument

A model of the Death Star was used for some shots, which McQuarrie painted between November 12 and December 13, 1976 (above right). He also did a matte painting of the Death Star (above left), and specific parts of same. A piece of paper taped to one painting (middle), completed in the spring of 1976, is dated January 13, 1977, for shot "182 DP," which featured the fortress and three X-wings. That same day, according to ILM notes, the negative for "X-wing #1" went missing. "I had my first piece of negative disappear," Mary Lind laments. "It didn't get logged or something, shot 182, #1 X-wing. I looked high and low for three days, tore everything apart, could not find it, and finally asked the guys to reshoot it."

On January 21, Muren reshot all three ships. On February 25, the Death Star color was toned down, because Lucas found it too blue. On March 18, notes reveal that one X-wing was still problematic, and Lucas considered going with only two—though ultimately all three appeared in the final shot (top).

George and John had a lot. It's how you perceive speed versus distance, in your mind."

The director eventually made his point, and the breakneck race to the exhaust port was completed. The explosion of the Death Star was shot by Richard Edlund on the Borendo stage with a special "super trick 35mm anamorphic camera from Photo-Sonics, which ran up to 300 frames per second," says Bruce Logan.

"We used a special titan blend—my own concoction at the time," says Joe Viskocil. "The first time we did a titan blend was when we had the 300-speed camera; it was a gas explosion, then silver sparks came through, and you could see a faint, gas-type aura in the air. We showed it at dailies one day at ILM—and George just flipped and said, 'There's our Death Star, no doubt about it!' The explosion just brought down the house."

TRANSFERENCE

In mid-April 1977 the end battle was sent over to Sam Shaw, who was supervising the sound mix during the day and the dubbing at night. The burden of finishing the film had now passed to him from ILM, so Lucas was often up all hours with Shaw.

"Let's take the battle just before they blow up the Death Star," Shaw says. "You have, say, two thousand feet of film. When you get it, it's completely silent. First you have to get all the sound you're going to use, which was mostly from the library that Ben Burtt had made up, but all of it had to be augmented. So that made it easier, and yet made it harder—because we had to keep the sound that George wanted, yet do it in such a way that it would technically come across. So first we added all the gunshots for the ships. Then we went through and put in all the explosions, then the ricochets, then the spaceship passbys, the interior sounds. We would start dubbing at maybe six or seven o'clock in the evening, and we would dub until eight or nine the next morning.

"And then I'd have to go wherever the mixers were working—they were working all over town—and deal with whatever problems they had, until at least three in the afternoon," Shaw adds. "Then I'd go home and try and get some sleep, but I'd be up at five to go back to work. That went on for a long time. What happens is that you don't have a life other than the film and what it needs. I can't remember eating dinner or lunch or breakfast at home; it was all take-out stuff. Every night on the stage, you'd see George sitting there with his fast-food burger. He works very hard, too. He worked as many hours as any of us did, probably more. He was the one who was really under the ultimate pressure."

"The hardest task was just getting our material there at the right time on the right day," Burtt says. "Just barely making it day after day. And then there'd be mistakes, but there'd be no time to correct them." Because the mix continued for quite a while, Lucas's presence was often needed elsewhere, so Burtt became his representative. "Since the mix was being done in Hollywood, all the mixers went to Sam Shaw with any questions," Burtt explains. "But then I started showing up at the mixes, and pretty soon there were some sparks. I would ask them to change things, which would infuriate them. In the end it's the subtleties and the nuances that really add up, but George would concur when he came, and they did do many things excellently."

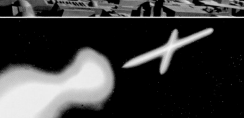

Top: Final frame with threshold Death Star surface.

"There's this shot where you're up above the Death Star diving down toward the trench and then you're in the trench flying along [left]. I shot the first half and Richard had shot the second half, flying through the trench," Dennis Muren says. "That was really tough because he shot his part first with specific motions, finishing the dive part, and then the camera is leveling off and flying through the trench. So I had to find the same motions moving in on this painting that Ralph McQuarrie had done of the Death Star for the opening part."

A group photo taken circa February 4, 1977, includes many, though not all, ILM staffers (all job titles taken from 1977 in-house contact information): (from the top, left to right) John Dykstra, special effects photography supervisor; Jon Erland, model builder; Joe Viskocil, miniature explosions; (standing, last row) Dick Alexander, camera and mechanical design; Eldon Rickman, optical printer operator; Bill Shourt, camera and mechanical design; (at far right) Gary Jouvenat, auditor Twentieth Century-Fox; (next row) Doug Smith assistant cameraman; Paul Huston, model builder; Joe Johnston, design and illustration; Adam Beckett, animation and rotoscope design; Richard Edlund, director of special effects photography; Grant McCune, chief model maker; (next row) Bruce Nicholson, optical camera assistant; Rose Duignan, production staff; Dennis Muren, second cameraman; David Jones, model builder; Mary Lind, film control coordinator; Ciñdy Isman, film librarian; Peter Kuran, animator; (next row) Jonathan Seay, animator; Jibralta Merrill, part-time librarian; Rhonda Peck, production staff, head of prop union; David Robman, assistant cameraman; Bruce Green, assistant optical editor; Steve Cullip, auditor/secretary; Don Trumbull, camera and mechanical design; (sitting, back row) Connie McCrum, film librarian; David Scott, special mechanical equipment; David Beasley, model builder; Steve Gawley, model builder; Lon Tinney, production manager; (sitting, front row) Doug Barnett, special mechanical equipment; Alvah Miller, electronics design; Jim Nelson, "chief mushroom"; John Dykstra's dog; Kim Falkinburg, bookkeeping; Penny McCarthy, assistant auditor; Paul Roth, optical photography coordinator; George Mather, special effects production supervisor; Mark Kline, production staff.

FAIRY-TALE CINEMA

APRIL 1977 TO DECEMBER 1977

CHAPTER TWELVE

As the May 25 release date drew close, and the last editorial adjustments were made, Paul Hirsch came to share Sam Shaw's estimation of Lucas's ability to keep on target. "George is the iron man," the editor sums up. "He's indefatigable. He just goes on and on, and I've got to hand it to him: The picture is an enormous accomplishment."

While Hirsch, Gareth Wigan, Richard Chew, Steven Spielberg, and a growing number of insiders were feeling bullish about *Star Wars*' chances, audience reaction was still a giant unknown. In any case Lucas and his closest collaborators were far too busy finishing the film to start prematurely congratulating themselves. One fear that actually disintegrated due to the mad dash at the end was the question of who would have final cut. Time became the ultimate arbitrator, because the final cut was simply not final until only weeks before it was due out in theaters, though, according to Lippincott, Ladd had agreed informally in early 1977 that no one at Fox would touch a single frame of the film.

"By the way, it was George's idea to open the film in May," Gareth Wigan says. "Nobody had ever opened a summer film *before* school was out. His idea was to open it on Memorial Day, that three-day weekend holiday."

"The big weekend to open movies was Christmas, ever since movies began," Lucas says. "The second time is the Fourth of July weekend. But I said I want my film to be released in May for Memorial Day weekend. And the studio said, 'But the kids aren't out of school'—and I said, 'Well, I don't want the kids out of school; I want the kids to be able to see the movie and then talk about it so we can build word of mouth.' They thought I was out of my mind."

PARTING SHOTS

As of the end of April and the beginning of May 1977, ILM finished up its last photography. One of the shots, number 114, the jump to hyperspace,

had been months in the works. Dennis Muren had begun the shot, creating the sense of great speed that Lucas had requested with a "streak thing" by keeping the shutter open and adjusting the start and end position of the camera to give a "punch" to it. Muren had left the production, however, by the time Lucas asked for the length of the shot to be changed, so Edlund completed it, adding the pirate ship to the second half of the shot.

"When the ship zips away into infinity," he says, "the only way that I could get it that small that fast was to use a Polaroid shot of the ship with a zoomback on it."

Another late effect was Luke's blast that blows up the Death Star. "The last sketch that I worked on was the exhaust port model sketch," Johnston says. "I think that was the last model built, too." In fact, that model was a re-dress of the Death Star laser tunnel model.

The title sequence was also one of the last elements to be finalized. Following the critique and De Palma's rewrite, Lucas had massaged it several times to coincide more exactly with the opening of the film:

```
It is a period of civil war. Rebel spaceships, striking
from a hidden base, have won their first victory over
the evil Galactic Empire.

During the battle, Rebel spies managed to steal secret
plans to the Empire's ultimate weapon, the DEATH STAR,
an armored space station with enough power to destroy
an entire planet.

Pursued by the Empire's sinister agents, Princess Leia
races home aboard her starship, custodian of the stolen
plans that can save her people and restore freedom to
the galaxy.
```

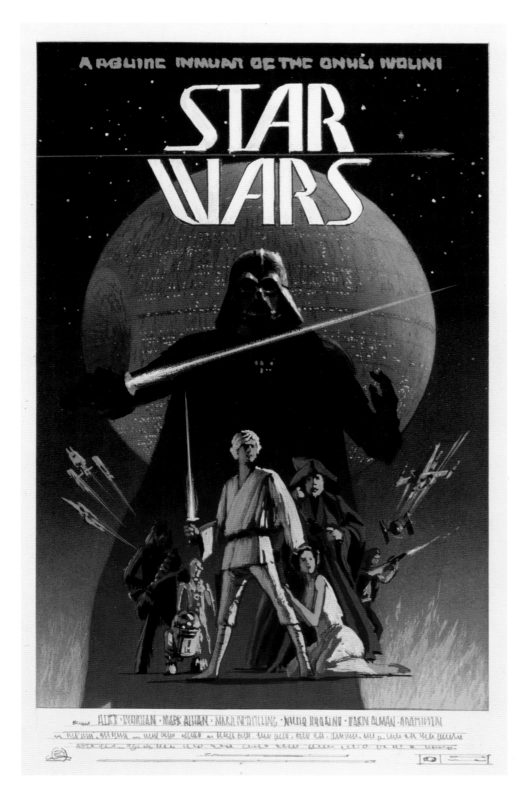

Ralph McQuarrie's sketches led to his two concept artworks for the one-sheet poster, which he completed circa March 1977. Though neither concept was ultimately chosen, matte painter Harrison Ellenshaw says, "The greatest sales tool this film ever had was Ralph McQuarrie's production paintings, in my mind."

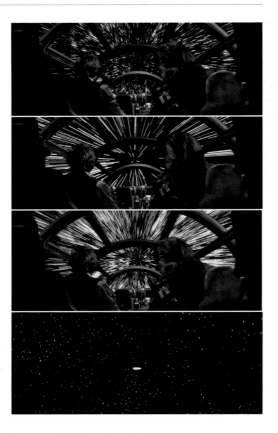

The *Millennium Falcon* makes the jump to hyperspace (right) and eventually comes back to normal time in a shot that used "Mylar junk," according to Lorne Peterson, for the eerie effect (below right). A storyboard contains a humorous sign that reads, YOU ARE NOW LEAVING HYPERSPACE. COME AGAIN! (below left).

Lucas had to insist on keeping the roll-up in the film, as Fox was pushing hard to replace it with a narrator who would read the words aloud. "I suppose there are kids that aren't going to be able to read it," Lucas says. "But they're going to have to learn to read sooner or later. Maybe *Star Wars* will give them some incentive."

"That was an interesting shot because it was one of the last ones we did, about three weeks before release," Blalack says. "We worked with Richard, who created the perspective by using a tilting lens board and a wide angle, to get the correct exposure on his photography for the recedings, as STAR WARS gets smaller and smaller. The problem is that it gets very, very small, and the image begins to break up. It's also being compressed through the anamorphic lens, so resolution problems are more severe. We shot it possibly six times to get the color, the fade-out on the logo, and all of that balanced out. It was the longest single shot that we ever dealt with."

An eleventh-hour creature add-on was the Dia Noga head. In England they had filmed only the tentacle, but Lucas decided to give more personality to the trash masher occupant. "I got a call from Jim Nelson," Phil Tippett says, "and he said, 'We need another monster—it's kind of an eyeball, with tentacles and things.' I think that was the last thing we did."

He and Jon Berg quickly sculpted, and Lucas approved, a creature whose eye could blink. They then went to the stage at ILM, where the model shop had created a miniature trash masher pond with debris floating in it, leftovers from the Death Star and exploded starfighters. "They cut a circle in the floor of the pond, which was up on sawhorses," Berg recalls. "So I had to sit under there with the stuff leaking all over me, and just jam the puppet up through the thing, turn it around, and pull it back down."

Yet another emergency was the point of view of the cantina exterior, which had yet to be completed—so the services of Ellenshaw were again required, but fast. "They never shot a good establishing point of view of

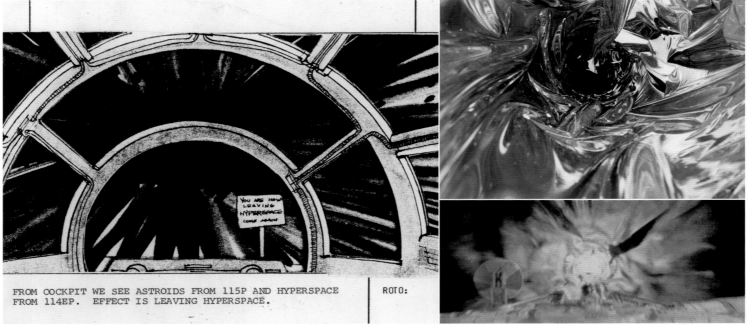

FROM COCKPIT WE SEE ASTROIDS FROM 115P AND HYPERSPACE FROM 114EP. EFFECT IS LEAVING HYPERSPACE.

ROTO:

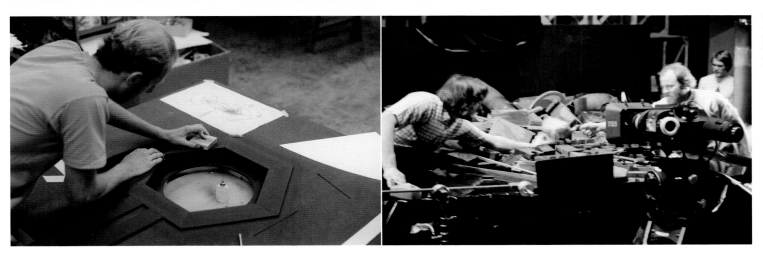

the cantina," he explains. "The only time they did, Alec Guinness and Mark Hamill were coming down the side, but of course it's impossible to have their point of view with them in the shot. So they sent it to Van Der Veer to mask those people out. But George wasn't happy with the result. So an assistant editor came rushing over one day, after I thought I'd finished with the film completely, with a piece of negative in his hand and said, 'Here, George wants to know if you can paint out the people?' This was a Tuesday, and he said, 'Can you have it by Thursday?' 'I can have it about three months from Thursday,' I said. 'Thursday's a little early.' But he said they were actually cutting negative and they needed it to finish a reel!

"So I told him we could do it by a week from Thursday—and then we ran around like chickens without heads for a week and a half. It's probably the fastest matte shot I've ever done in my life. You know, I think it was probably the last bit of film to go in the picture."

YOU CAN HISS THE VILLAIN, BUT THE FILM CAN'T HISS

Dolby Labs was founded by Ray Dolby in England in 1965, but he moved the company to the United States in 1976, right on time for its use in *Star Wars*. The Dolby system was designed to reduce unwanted background noise that, up until then, was almost unavoidably picked up during dubbing. The system also made dialogue easier to hear and enabled film-makers, at least in theory, to create more complex sound designs.

"We chose Dolby right from the start," Lucas says. "We looked at other systems like DBX, in terms of noise reduction, and realized that Dolby had the only really good stereo optical setup, and we really wanted to do the film in stereo. It was really the only option with systems that could be set up in theaters and worked right. It's just a little box that they clipped onto the Nagra."

The "only option," Dolby was far from a sure thing. It was first used on *A Clockwork Orange* in 1971, but had achieved only middling success in the intervening years.

"I did have concerns," Alan Ladd says, "only because we had already done a couple of pictures in Dolby. One was *The Rocky Horror Picture Show*,

The POV of the cantina exterior for which Ellenshaw painted out Luke and Ben (top). "George wanted a shadow under the landspeeder (bottom). We were completely inundated, but Adam Beckett said, 'I can do a shadow that will look real.' But after Adam started to do the shadow, he could see the immensity of trying to generate a shadow where none existed," Blalack says. "So I asked George to take that shot away from us; it was too much of a nightmare. It ended up going to Ellenshaw at Disney, and they struggled with it, so it ended up going to Van der Veer, and he finished it. Our prediction was that it would never work."

in 1975—it premiered in the UA Westwood Theater, and the Dolby fell apart on opening day. We also had a picture called *Mr. Billion*, which had just opened in March, which was done in Dolby. We took it down to Tucson to preview it—and it blew out the whole system. I mean, it was a mess. So there was a big concern about using Dolby. There was a lot of pressure from people saying, 'Don't use Dolby!'

"But the whole thing is that George knew how to use Dolby," Ladd adds. "The other people, I think, were just using a process, and that was the difference. They just finished the picture, and then added Dolby. George, on the other hand, designed shots that would work specifically for the sound system, which is, I think, the first time that's ever been done."

"I was very satisfied with the Dolby system," Burtt says. "We have much quieter tracks. The Dolby stereo sound consultant, Steve Katz, was a valuable influence on the mix, because of his technical knowledge."

"Dolby didn't create any problem at all," Shaw says. "When you start dubbing something down, you get a lot of hiss. When you re-record any track, you get a lot of noise. The more you dub, the more background and surface noise you pick up. The Dolby's main advantage is that it eliminates all that hiss. So for a picture like this in which there's a lot of pre-dubbing, Dolby was excellent."

The Dolby mix, however, was just the beginning of sound for *Star Wars*, as only parts of the English-speaking world were equipped for it. For crucial foreign markets and much of America, monaural and other stereo system soundtracks had to be prepared as well.

THE LEGENDARY SHOW—AND SECRET DUDS

Although the film's sound mix was not complete, Lucas decided to go ahead and preview *Star Wars* for the general public on May 1 at San Francisco's Northpoint Theatre.

The lights went down as they always do, but the movie began in a way that no movie had ever begun before. The shot that Lucas and ILM had labored on for so long—his vision from so many years ago—unfolded as the seemingly endless Star Destroyer roared onto the silver screen and the eyes of the public. Accompanied by John Williams's incredible score and Ben Burtt's fantastic sound effects, the three-foot-long model created by teams of model makers and photographed by Richard Edlund succeeded in its intention: It made the Northpoint audience instantly and enthusiastically believe in the first modern fairy tale since the Western.

"May 1 was the best, was the strangest experience I have ever had," Alan Ladd says. "I am not very prone to emotions, but when the picture opened up and all of a sudden they just started applauding, the tears started rolling out of my eyes. That has never happened to me. Then at the end of the picture, it kept going on, it wasn't stopping—and I just never had experienced that kind of a reaction to any movie *ever*. Finally, when it was over, I had to get up and walk outside because of the tears."

"They started rolling the movie," Howie Hammerman says, "and when the Star Destroyer came over the top of the frame and kept rolling

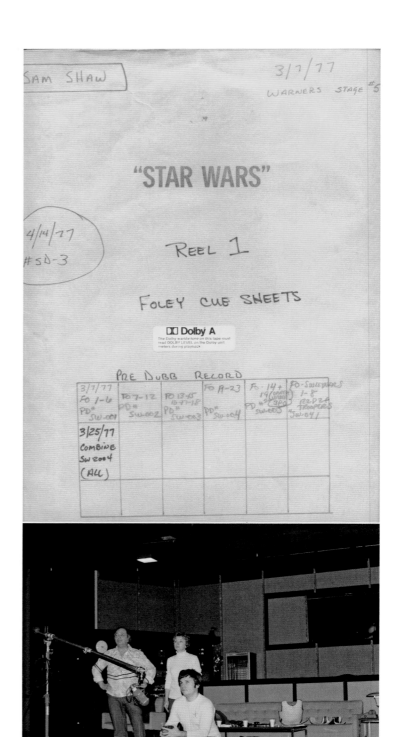

The invitation to the May 1, 1977, preview screening at San Francisco's Northpoint Theatre (left), where the regular show was the Paul Newman film *Slap Shot*, which had bowed on February 25 (far left—the "uproarious lusty entertainment and world premiere" for "Alaska" could be a wink to *Star Wars*, as no film named *Alaska* came out in 1977).

Following the Northpoint preview, Lucasfilmers gathered round the table at Park Way to tally the written appreciations of the film (below—among those around the table are Charles Lippincott, Bunny Alsup, Ben Burtt, assistant film editor Colin Kitchens, and film librarian Pamela Malouf).

on and on and on, the audience just went *nuts*. They stood screamin' and yellin'!"

Richard Chew was present that afternoon and was reeling afterward: "When I ran into George in the lobby, I expected him to really be exhilarated, and maybe he was, but certainly he didn't show it. I was going to compliment him on the film—but the first thing he said was, 'Well, as you can see things haven't changed much since you last saw the picture, and we're still trying to make it work.' And it was like, 'George! [laughs], man, you've got this wonderful movie I think a lot of people are going to want to see, and you're so humble about the whole thing!' And George's father was around pumping hands saying, 'Thank you, thank you very much for helping out George.' [laughs] But George was being just old George!"

Although the May 1 preview was a huge success, it did cause Ladd some apprehension. He sensed that the younger kids were scared by the noise, and felt that they'd been right to ask for a PG rating. "It also moved

very fast for most of them," he says. "I sat behind a little girl and it moved too fast for her."

"Fox was worried, Laddie was worried," Lippincott says, "because several people had walked into the lobby, gray in the face."

While Kurtz wasn't sure if the rating would be PG back in January, Ladd's comment reveals that the studio was favoring it. But *Star Wars* could have been rated G just as easily, for when the film was submitted to the Motion Picture Association of America's Code and Rating Administration, the vote, as reported by *Daily Variety*, "was split evenly between G and PG." In an unusual move, Twentieth Century-Fox "asked for a stricter rating."

The reasons were two: Some scenes were arguably scary for children—but the studio was also concerned that there would be a "backlash effect from teenagers if the film were to receive a G, which is sometimes considered an 'uncool' rating."

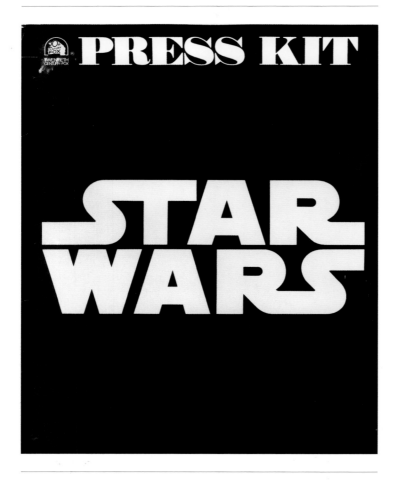

"I had a kid about five years old sitting in front of me," Lippincott says. "And when Darth Vader appears on the bridge of the Princess's ship at the beginning and grabs the guy and chokes him, the kid began crying, and just really broke down. So I said to George, 'This film is a PG.' Well, a friend of mine was on the rating board, and she was one of I think two females on the board, and she was one of the few who actually knew the film. She said the men were absolutely bored by it, a couple of them fell asleep, and they all voted it a G movie. The only one who was concerned about it was a mother, the only other woman there, who felt it was a little too intense for kids. But all the guys dismissed her, so it came out with a G rating—you know, the worst thing we could possibly get. I said, 'This is not a G-rating film.' So we went back to them for a PG. They had never had this done to them before by anybody, and they couldn't believe it. So the board reneged and gave it a PG because we wanted that."

After the general success of the Northpoint show, a second public screening was planned for the very next evening at the Metro Theatre—which added exponentially to Ladd's concerns and justified Lucas's hesitation to join the celebration. "People don't know about the next night at the Metro," Ladd explains. "I went there and there was not the same kind of reaction *at all*. I went to dinner afterward and I was so depressed; I was saying to a couple of people, 'You should have been in San Francisco, you should have been in San Francisco . . .' The next reaction I got was when we showed it at the board of directors meeting."

The members sat down in comfortable gray chairs, Warren Hellman recalls, in a screening room on the Fox lot. "I remember the evening the directors were shown the finished film," he says. "We walked outside afterward, and they handed us this little piece of paper that said, '*Star Wars* will 1) Be a breakout film, 2) Return our money, 3) Lose all of our money.' Because I'm conservative, I was going to check the center column, but my wife, Christina, said, 'Are you crazy?! This is the best movie I've ever seen! You're going to make more money on this movie than you've ever dreamed of! Erase that!' So I did and I checked the number in the first column."

"There were sixteen board members," Gareth Wigan says. "I remember clearly that three of them really loved it; three of them thought that maybe it would work, two of them fell asleep—they had just had a big dinner—and the rest of them really hated it. They really didn't get it at all and were very distressed indeed, very worried about how they were going to get their money back."

"Supposedly only two directors voted for 'breakout.' Most of them were neutral to negative," Hellman adds. "We were all standing around outside and only Chris was saying, 'This is great, this is fantastic!' "

"It played like a drama with the board of directors," Ladd says. "I must say that there were more who didn't like it than liked it. There was also a screening for radio and record people—and about ten people walked out . . .'"

THE LAST AUDIBLE GASP

By the middle of May 1977, with the release date a mere ten days away, the final mix was still incomplete. The number of different facilities that had been used over the last few months make obvious the magnitude of the sound job, while hundreds of yellow legal-pad pages, tracking the minutest of details, attest to the intricate Foley—footsteps, kisses, shirt rumpling, scuffling, et cetera—recorded at Glen Glenn, on Stage A, during the month of March. Additional dialogue recording was completed in April at the Producers' Sound Services, on North Highland Avenue in Hollywood, while much of the pre-dubbing was done at Burbank Studios. Dubbing was also done at Warner Bros., on Stage 5, and the final mixing at Goldwyn.

"The biggest problem of all was time," Sam Shaw sighs. "Everything was just very specialized. There's a thing called Foley in a picture, where you synchronize footsteps and all sorts of action. Everyone has done this dozens of times—but with *Star Wars* it was just mind-boggling! The amount that you would do for each reel was the equivalent to an entire normal feature film. It took special props, special microphones, tremendous adjustments. Professionals who had been doing things for twenty years would look at it and just be taken aback—they'd have to stop and psych themselves up. Normally you would have three mixers who would stay on the picture all the way through; we used about eight or nine mixers in the course of the show."

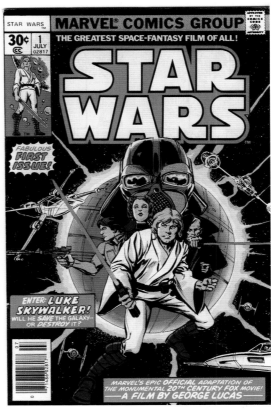

Kurtz, Lucas, and Lippincott examine publicity material (above left). The latter helped organize pre-release publicity at sci-fi and comic conventions (above middle and right), where a poster by artist Howard Chaykin was shown and sold (below left)—which Chaykin later modified for the first Marvel *Star Wars* comic-book cover (below right, which came out in March 1977, the first in a six-part series). Meanwhile, the novelization "was the fastest sellout of a first edition for a sci-fi movie novelization [Ballantine] had ever had," Lippincott says, "which surprised the hell out of me—and them. It had sold out by February [after being published in December 1976, edited by Judy Lynn]."

"It was the blending of the sounds that was the biggest source of frustration," Burtt says. "We had to depend on Sam Shaw's people—and though the mixers did a tremendous job, they weren't the filmmakers that had been on it for a couple of years and it was difficult for them to totally understand what we wanted.

"But George has a good attitude," he adds. "Not being the sound editor himself, he has the advantage of looking at the whole thing and saying, 'I want a blend between dialogue, music, and effects that gives me the story.' We thought the sound was about 30 percent successful in view of what we intended to have."

The first mix sent out with the film, at the last possible second, was the six-track Dolby stereo version, but the first mix also had the most errors. Next up was the two-track stereo, which was derived from the six-track, yet there was still no time at that stage to make any changes. "I asked Steve Katz to do something," Burtt says, "but they were all too afraid to mess with it, 'cause the deadline was so close—the whole system with the Dolby was kind of an experiment, and they didn't want me to tamper with it."

A week before opening, there was still no answer print, but, by May 24, the thousands of elements and work-hours came together just in time—as Lucas says, the film wasn't finished, it was "abandoned," for time had finally run out.

SWR 05.25.77

On Wednesday, May 25, 1977, *Star Wars* began its theatrical run, in thirty-two theaters, including the Coronet in San Francisco. On May 26 one theater was added, the Glenwood, in Kansas City, Kansas. On May 27 ten more theaters joined the ranks. In each of the less than fifty movie houses, the result was the same. Joy. At the Coronet the audience applauded as soon as the spaceships arrived—and the cheering never stopped, except at times to boo the villain, until halfway through the end credits. The landscape of cinema in the 1970s simply had no other film like it—and the world would never be the same.

Yet for Lucas, who was still working on the fourth final mix, the monaural, nothing had changed. "We'd finished the 70mm eight-track stereo mix, which Fox had resisted, and we were working on the monau-

Star Wars posters took on several forms, one of which featured artwork by Tommy Jung (left). Much of the artwork would then be modified for other media, such as the newspaper ad in *The New York Times* that ran on May 15, 1977.

ral version for the wide release, so I was mixing at night," he says. "I was approving ad campaigns, working all night and then sleeping all day in a little house that Marcia had on the flats of Hollywood. She was working on *New York, New York*. At the end of her day and at the beginning of my night we would have dinner somewhere—my breakfast, her dinner—and I think the night before we finished the monaural mix, it just so happened that we decided to eat at a Hamburger Hamlet on Hollywood Boulevard.

"We were way in the back," he continues, "but out of the front window I could see this huge crowd in front of Grauman's Chinese—limos—and I thought someone must be premiering a movie. It never occurred to me that my movie was out, because *I was still working on it*. So we got up when we were done, and I said, 'Let's go see what's going on out there.' We walked out the door and I looked up at the marquee and said, 'Oh my God, it's *Star Wars*! I forgot the film was going to be released today! Holy moly!' But it was like six o'clock, so I had to go back to the studio to finish the mix."

Lucas must have been all the more surprised because *Star Wars* was never supposed to play the Grauman. It hadn't become a prestige film overnight—it had simply benefited from the fact that William Friedkin's *Sorcerer*, which should have been playing there on May 25, wasn't finished (it bowed on June 24). Lucas's film was the starlet waiting in the wings.

When the bemused director returned to Goldwyn, Gregg Kilday, a

staff writer for the *Los Angeles Times*, joined him. Kilday was authoring a feature on Lucas and was able to observe events firsthand, including a phone call between Lucas and Alan Ladd, with the former muttering, "Wow . . . wow . . . gee . . . that's pretty amazing," as each box-office figure was read to him, interrupting Ladd only to offer instructions to the engineers.

"I called Laddie," Lucas says, "and said, 'Hey, I forgot the movie was going to be released today—how's it doing? I was over at the Grauman's Chinese and there were people around the block . . .' And Laddie started exclaiming, 'It's a giant hit everywhere, we're doing fabulous business!' And I said, 'Wait—calm down. Remember, science-fiction films do really great the first week, then they drop off to nothing. It's a good sign, but it doesn't mean anything. Let's wait a couple of weeks.' But he kept calling me all night giving me news."

The call completed, Lucas still deflected the excitement that was fast becoming tangible in the studio. "I'm still going to hold my breath for a few weeks," he vowed to Kilday. "The movie's only been released for five hours. I don't want to count my chickens before they hatch."

Later that night, Lucas learned that the limousines in front of Grauman's belonged to *Playboy* magazine founder Hugh Hefner and his entourage, all of whom ended up watching the film two times in a row. But none of this prevented him from continuing with the job on hand. "George, Paul Hirsch,

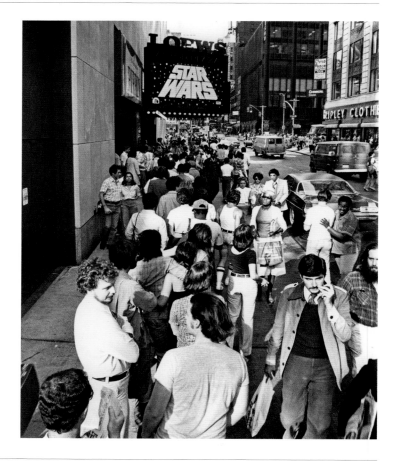

Fri., May 27, 1977 — DAILY VARIETY

'Star Wars' Heats Up N.Y. 1st-Runs With Wow 50G Opening & 4 House Records

New York, May 26 — Gotham firstrun scene was heated considerably by the opening of 20th's "Star Wars" at two Manhattan sites and three suburban situations. Opening-day take hit a wow $50,036, with house records set at four of the theatres. Leader of the pack was Manhattan's Astor Plaza, with $20,-322.

"The Greatest" mighty $510,-000 or near in opener at 73 sites.

"Annie Hall" hefty $192,596 in fifth frame at seven sites and $62,788 in first day of new break at 62 situations.

"Rocky" durable $340,000 or near in second week in latest break at 52 sites.

"Audrey Rose" okay $260,365 in first return frame at 61 sites.

"We All Loved Each Other So Much" respectable $4065 in first three days at the Beekman.

"The Car" so-so $56,000 or near in latest full round at four theatres.

"Day Of The Animals" middling $3322 opening day at State 2, Eastside Cinema and 86th St. 1.

"Smokey And The Bandit" not-so-hot $119,591 in opening round at Radio City Music Hall.

"Gums" X-rated $1186 opening day at Cinerama 1.

"Cria" nice $11,162 opening week at the Plaza.

"Black And White In Color" zippy $11,286 in first four days of third Paris frame.

"Cross Of Iron" bowed out with $28,317 in second round at Orpheum, Trans-Lux East and State 2.

"Between The Lines" roseate $10,507 in Sutton fourth.

"Cousin, Cousine" durable $9090 in second moveover round at 68th St. Playhouse.

"Cinderella 2000" disaster $1487 opening day at Rivoli, UA East and Columbia 2.

"Looking Up" dull $1593 in first four days of second Fine Arts round.

"3 Women" zippy $7456 in first four days of Coronet seventh.

Jabberwocky," commendable $13,500 or near in Cinema 1 sixth.

---

and I and everyone in the crew sat down and made a list of the things we didn't like in the stereo mix," Burtt says. "Then we tried to achieve every one of those things on the mono. And we did— different voices for some of the stormtroopers, some new loop lines for Luke, minor changes."

"We were locked in this little room, but it was important because monaural was what most people were going to hear," Lucas says. In fact, he was so intent on finishing the list of fixes that he called up Mark Hamill that very night. Coincidentally, Hamill had also been stupefied by the lines in front of Grauman's. "Imagine—the ultimate Hollywood theater," he says. "I'm overwhelmed. It's like having your career handed to you on a silver plate. But believe it or not, the night the picture opened, George called and said, 'Hey, kid, do you want to come down and loop?' I said, 'What are you talking about? It's playing. There are lines around the block!' Then he explained that the print being shown was the 70mm stereo mix, and now for the monaural mix for general release, he wanted me to add a few things. Can you believe it? The day it opened . . ."

As the sound mixing continued without Hamill, who presumably looped on another night, Lucas explained himself to Kilday. "I expect it all to fall apart next week. I guess I am a pessimist, or a realist, a

nonoptimist. I start out by expecting things to be the worst they can be, so when they're better than that I'm not disappointed."

One thing that was nagging at him was the ad campaigns. Marketing studies had been shown to Lucas claiming that women generally ignored the science-fiction genre, so he had been lobbying for, and now getting, a new promotional campaign designed to capture "female fancies," according to Kilday. To that end Lucas conferred with an illustrator who was working on a new *Gone with the Wind*–style movie poster. Lucas was then interrupted by a series of visitors, including Marcia, who showed up with two bottles of champagne; Jay Cocks, who stopped by "for a few words"— and Brian De Palma, who congratulated Lucas and joked, "Shall we call Francis and spread the gloom?"

After they'd gone, Lucas turned back to quickly finish the interview, saying that *Star Wars* was a disappointment: "I expected more than any human being could possibly deliver. A Wookiee could have delivered it, but not a human being. I needed a crew of Wookiees. With nine hundred people, I was dependent on more people than I had ever depended on before. I had a tendency to agonize a lot over things not done as well as I hoped they could be done. I felt the same about *Graffiti*—then there was no time and

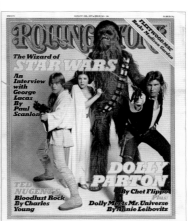

no money. It was the same thing, only more so on *Star Wars*. There were a lot more people, a larger operation, but there was also more waste and confusion, bureaucratic screw-ups going on all over the place. Obviously, from everyone's reaction, it was good enough—same as *Graffiti*. Pretty hard to believe, though, definitely beyond my capacity to understand."

Kilday then departed and Lucas went on with his sound engineers, mixing until dawn.

HAUNTING HAWAII

The lines that Lucas had observed in front of Grauman's Chinese Theatre signaled the biggest opening day in its fifty-year history, with *Star Wars* taking in $19,358, according to *Variety;* at approximately $4 a ticket, that meant around 4,800 viewers (tickets at that time sold from $2.00 to $4.50, depending on the venue). The film also broke eight records in the other thirty-one theaters, combining for a grand single-day total of $254,809— one of the figures no doubt quoted by Ladd to Lucas over the phone.

"I worked on the mix that night, the next night, and then I left for Hawaii. I was done," Lucas says. "There wasn't much publicity to do. Fox had done something for all the press two weeks before, but I hadn't been able to do it because it was at night and I was still mixing (Gary might have gone). So I took off for Hawaii with Bill and Gloria Huyck, and Marcia. But even over there we saw Walter Cronkite on television talking about *Star Wars* and we said, 'Well, this is pretty weird.' I'd told Laddie I didn't want to hear anything about it, but he couldn't help himself, and he

called me every three or four days, very excited. We got papers after about a week, just at the time Bill and Gloria left and Steven arrived."

The suddenly effusive Ladd no doubt echoed the ongoing headlines in *Variety*: The six-day box office was $2.5 million; on June 2, $3 million. But the other story, which has become legend in the movie world, took place on the beach where Spielberg and Lucas were building a sand castle and talking about future projects. Spielberg wanted to do a James Bond film, but Lucas said that he had "something better": Indiana Jones.

"George got called away to the telephone to hear about the grosses of Friday and Saturday," Spielberg says. "The 9:30 AM shows were sold out to a seat—that's good when that happens. That's a good signal."

The papers also brought articles by nearly all the major reviewers. "*Star Wars* is a magnificent film," "Murf" (Art Murphy) wrote in *Variety*. "The results equal the genius of Walt Disney, Willis O'Brien, and other justifiably famous practitioners of what Irwin Allen calls 'movie magic' . . . Like a breath of fresh air, *Star Wars* sweeps away the cynicism that has in recent years obscured the concepts of valor, dedication, and honor." Ron Pennington in *The Hollywood Reporter* predicted that *Star Wars* "will be thrilling audiences of all ages for a long time to come." Gene Siskel gave it a good review in the *Chicago Tribune,* while Charles Champlin wrote in the *Los Angeles Times,* "*Star Wars* is a celebration which, in the ultimate tribute to the past, has a robust and free-wheeling life of its own, needing no powers of recollection to be fully appreciated . . . *Star Wars* is Buck Rogers with a doctoral degree but not a trace of neuroticism or cynicism, a slam-bang, rip-roaring gallop through a distantly future world full of exotic vocabularies, creatures, and customs, existing cheek by cowl with the boy and girl next door."

Nearly all the reviewers understood that Lucas had re-imagined the serials along with the swashbuckling and monster films of his youth. The film's special effects received much notice, the actors not as much, though all were singled out for praise, especially Guinness. Several critics likened C-3PO to Edward Everett Horton, the comic sidekick in the Astaire/Rogers films of the 1930s, while R2-D2 was compared to Harpo Marx in Gary Arnold's glowing *Washington Post* appraisal. "Lucas's film is jaunty rather than portentous. One of the reasons [John] Barry's cantina seems charged with humor is that Lucas doesn't linger over it, as Kubrick lingered over the décor of the nightclub in *Clockwork Orange.* New perspectives and monsters keep turning up and moving on with astonishing and amusing rapidity. Lucas's style of sci-fi prodigality is playfully funny."

One day after the opening, Vincent Canby of *The New York Times* wrote: "*Star Wars* is both an apotheosis of Flash Gordon serials and a witty critique that makes associations with a variety of literature that is nothing if not eclectic: *Quo Vadis?, Buck Rogers, Ivanhoe,* Superman, *The Wizard of Oz,* the *Gospel According to Saint Matthew,* the legend of King Arthur

and the knights of the Round Table." *Time* magazine called it "The Year's Best Movie," and *Newsweek* was positive: "The army of credits for this serious and delightful labor implies a creative community that stands for the benign side of technology."

Dozens of other reviewers were also won over by the film, in papers throughout the county—in Santa Ana and Sacramento, California; Salt Lake City, Utah; Evansville, Indiana; Camden, New Jersey; Cincinnati, Ohio; and Louisville, Kentucky, to name a few.

Negative reviews ran in the papers of Augusta, Maine; Pascagoula, Mississippi; and Statesville, North Carolina. *The Harvard Crimson* didn't like *Star Wars,* and John Simon panned it in *New York* magazine. Another Big Apple publication, *The New Yorker,* ran a favorable review, and then a negative review a few months later. Stanley Kauffmann wrote in the June 18 edition of *New Republic,* "This picture was made for those (particularly males) who carry a portable shrine within them of their adolescence, a chalice of a Self that was Better Then before the world's affairs or—in any complex way—sex intruded."

Star Wars was also accused of racism, as its immense popularity made it a target—this because it didn't have any African American actors in it, with the exception of the "black"-robed villain Darth Vader, who, either conveniently or paradoxically, was voiced by a prominent black actor.

Another minor controversy the press got hold of was the rumor that Lucas had deliberately used Leni Riefenstahl's Nazi propaganda film *Triumph of the Will* (1935) for the throne room scene. "The truth of that particular situation is that I hadn't seen it for about fifteen years," Lucas says. "I had wanted to see it again because, early in the writing process,

I was thinking of doing a scene with the Emperor on the Empire planet, and I wanted to do that like *Triumph of the Will*. But it unfortunately got published that I was going to try to see *Triumph of the Will* and use it in *Star Wars;* evidently somebody read that somewhere and then looked at the end of the movie and thought that looked just like *Triumph of the Will*. But the end of the movie is just what happens when you put a large military group together and give out an award."

Ultimately, there was enough paranoia about a film becoming so popular so quickly that Vincent Canby seems to have felt obliged to defend his positive review of *Star Wars* (and *Annie*, the Broadway musical!) by writing a follow-up in the Sunday edition of the *Times,* in which he said, "This is not a film of the Non-Think Age."

WORD OF MOUTH

The June 22, 1977, issue of *Variety* reported that telephone operators in the Los Angeles area were being "avalanched by callers seeking the numbers of the Avco Cinema and Mann's Chinese" for show times—about 100 calls an hour, more than any number for the last ten years. "Operators have been so inundated that they don't have to look up numbers; they've got them on the tip of their tongues." On June 29 *Variety* reported that *Star Wars* had accumulated $8,780,435, but had been knocked out of the number one spot by *The Deep* and *Exorcist II—The Heretic*. However, by July 27, now in 48 theatres, *Star Wars* had recaptured the pole position after eight weeks, raking in $18,220,716.

Films had been wildly popular before—*Gone with the Wind, The Sound of Music, Rocky, Jaws*—but somehow *Star Wars* was creating even

more excitement. In fact, with very limited publicity, gigantic lines formed up in each new town, city, or suburb—fueled to a great degree by person-to-person communication.

"I enjoyed it and would recommend it to my friends," says youngster Ronnie Reed of Oskaloosa, Iowa.

"I liked the monsters the best," five-year-old Darren Pierce says. "It was worth staying up past my bedtime."

On June 23, 1977, in Chico, California, 500 people had to return home because the film's premier at the 900-seat El Rey Theatre was already sold out, thanks to a line that had started five hours before. "We've turned away people before, but never in numbers like this," assistant theater manager Richard Gorman says. In some cities, opening nights created huge traffic jams in front of the movie houses, preventing people from parking, so tenacious would-be attendees hopped into cabs to get to the show.

"My brother came to see it and said it was a real good movie," notes 11-year-old Monika Caldwell of Clarksville, Tennessee.

"I heard it was a good movie," fourteen-year-old Dennis Moore says.

"They didn't give us any money for advertising," reports Harry Stenzhorn, theater manager of Central City Mall 4 in San Bernardino, California. "They didn't have to. They've gotten tremendous public relations for this movie without even trying. People really like the good guy/bad guy thing, kind of like a Western."

Star Wars was also attracting all ages and types, from five- to 90-year-olds, from high school and college students to sci-fi fans and professionals. Whereas usually it was the moms who would take their kids to the movies,

As the *Star Wars* phenomenon grew, the film made the covers of many magazines, including *American Cinematographer* (July 1977, where a unique, composited image shows Darth Vader's ship actually being fired on by a Rebel X-wing), *People* (July 18, 1977), *Famous Monsters* (October 1977), *Newsweek* (December 26, 1977), *Cinefantastique* (1978), and *Mad* (January 1978). Shortly after the film's release, Meco Monardo's (45) disco version of the music became a Top 40 hit.

it was observed in Saint Louis, Missouri, that many more fathers were suddenly accompanying their children to the cinema.

DIRECTORS ON *STAR WARS*

Audiences were lining up, new theaters were adding it to their marquees—and fellow film directors, both present and future, were impressed.

"When I saw *Star Wars* in its finished form," Francis Ford Coppola says, "with all the effects in, and saw the complete tapestry George had done, it was very compelling and it was really a thrill for the audience. It all came together in terms of the characters and the story, the inspiration from Flash Gordon, with a little bit of *Hidden Fortress*. You know, all art, movies and otherwise, comes from something before that you are inspired by, which you borrow and make your own. That's the artistic tradition."

"I sent Stanley Kubrick a 35mm print and he ran it at his house," Kurtz says. "It wasn't in stereo or anything, but he said he liked the movie and he enjoyed it a lot. His children really enjoyed it."

"I think that certainly everyone would agree that what has been so successful about *Star Wars* is the mythic dimension," says John Korty, a Bay Area filmmaker and early inspiration for American Zoetrope. "This was somebody taking the grand myths of the past and recasting them in a form that made sense to modern-day people and especially kids."

Another Bay Area stalwart, producer Saul Zaentz (*One Flew Over the Cuckoo's Nest*), took out a page in *Variety*'s June 6 issue; on Fantasy Film stationery, he wrote an open letter to "George Lucas and all who participated in the creation of *Star Wars*: You have given birth to a perfect film and the whole world will rejoice with you."

"I came back into town just when the picture opened," Carroll Ballard says. "I couldn't believe it—there were lines around the block. I mean, it was the biggest thing that ever happened. I just couldn't fathom it. But when I finally got in to see it, a transformation had taken place."

"I had never experienced special effects that were so real," says Spielberg. "I was dazzled. It was amazing—it was amazing and depressing at the same time. I was in postproduction on *Close Encounters* and I had just come back from Hawaii where I was with George, because I'd wanted to get away from that. But when I got back to the States I saw *Star Wars* and I thought my movie just paled in comparison. I was depressed for two weeks. I didn't even want to release my movie in the same *year* as *Star Wars*. But Columbia was falling apart, and I had to cooperate, and we did great. But *Star Wars* was the star of 1977. George tapped into something very spiritual for young and old. *Star Wars* is a deeply spiritual story, yet somehow he made a war movie, too, and created a mythology of characters—he touched something that needed touching in everybody."

A twist to the story is that while together in Hawaii, Lucas and Spielberg had swapped profit points on each other's films—*Star Wars* and *Close Encounters*—because each was so sure that the other's movie would make more money. "I'm very happy to say that I won the bet," Spielberg adds with a smile.

Ridley Scott, who had just finished directing *The Duellists*, went to Grauman's to see the film, and when he came out of the theater, "I basically said to my producer, 'I don't know what we're doing—this guy's making *Star Wars*? I'm not even in the same universe as this guy—I'm not

even in the same century.'" His next two films were *Alien* (1979) and *Blade Runner* (1982).

Lucas's space fantasy also inspired a new generation of filmmakers, who were either kids or just about to start in the business. "I got really energized by *Star Wars*," says James Cameron, future director of *The Terminator* (1984) and *Titanic* (1997). "In fact, I quit my job as a truck driver and said, 'Well, if I'm gonna do this, I better get going.'"

"*Star Wars* blew my socks off. It reinforced my love of movies and my desire to make movies," says Frank Darabont (*The Shawshank Redemption*, 1994; *The Green Mile*, 1999).

"Going to *Star Wars* was one of the most exciting experiences that I ever had in my life," says Peter Jackson, who would grow up to direct the *Lord of the Rings* trilogy (2001–2003). "Not just movies—in my life—at that time. It was the first time that I saw science fiction presented in a way where everything was beaten up and oily and greasy and grimy—and you just believed in it."

"Anyone who knows me knows that my life was changed at that moment," says John Singleton, who saw the film when he was nine years old, and who later directed *Boyz N the Hood* (1991) and *Four Brothers* (2005).

For Martin Scorsese, a longtime aficionado of cinema, the verdict was simple: "I saw it when it came out. It is what it is: the classic retelling of man's mythology."

CAST AND CREW TAKES

For Peter Cushing, seeing the film with all the thousands of elements added was revelatory, if humbling. "I was absolutely knocked for six," he says. "I was riveted. There is an old saying among actors: 'Never work with children or animals.' Now we have to add to that, 'or special effects.' You swat away at your lines, trying to give a marvelous performance, and then a robot or a rocketship comes along, and the audience doesn't look at you anymore. My only real disappointment was that poor old Tarkin was blown up at the end, which meant I couldn't appear in any sequels."

Cushing's compatriot was similarly nonplussed. "I took my nine-year-old grandson to a trade screening," Alec Guinness says. "He was a little scared and wanted to know if I was going to be killed. I wouldn't tell him. The dialogue is pretty childish but the film has a lovely, fresh, innocent quality.

"My life is structured around making movies so I can do a play," he added to the *Seattle Post-Intelligencer* on September 25, 1977. "I don't imagine things will change very much even now."

The exact opposite was true for Harrison Ford, who, thanks to *Star Wars*, anticipated being able to stop doing carpentry and focus on his preferred career. "All of the characters I've played up until now have not been audience-identification type characters," he says. "They have been plot devices that set up or explain something. And the more you fill that kind of part, the more you become a function of the plot and you don't establish any kind of sympathy with the audience. It's playing the kind of charm [of Han Solo] that wins people in casting offices. It's certainly better career-wise to have done something that had an element of romance in it.

"I told George: 'You can't say that stuff. You can only type it.' But I was wrong. It worked," Ford adds.

By October 13, 1977, *Star Wars* had opened in 910 theaters in Canada and the United States, the last three in Rock Rapids, Iowa, and in Cordele and Douglas, Georgia. By that time foreign dubs had also been made for the all-important overseas markets, in French, German, Italian, and Spanish, while the film was subtitled in Chinese, Arabic, and Japanese. Because they came so late, the most complete sound effects mixes ended up being for those foreign markets, which took the monaural improvements and remixed them in stereo. All in all twenty mixes were made for overseas, some of them in funny ways.

"I didn't speak any of the foreign languages and, likewise, the people doing the mixing generally did not speak any English," Burtt says. "So I had to become somewhat of a mime, and spent a lot of time scribbling little pictures and dancing around in front of the mixing console trying to indicate what sort of things I wanted."

Star Wars made its European debut in October, where, for some reason, the Belgians found the film incredibly violent and the first day allowed only adults into the theater. Fortunately, children were permitted the second day as new prints with cuts authorized by Lucas—the severed arm, the sound of the Rebel officer's neck cracking, the two skeletons—were rushed into that country.

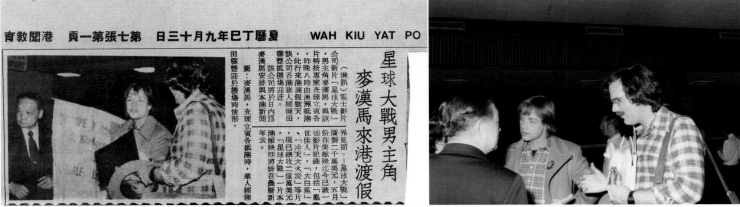

Star Wars posters from Italy (top left, with artwork by Papuzza), France (with Jung artwork), an alternate Italian poster, Israel, Hong Kong (with artwork by Tom Chantrell), and Germany. From October 23 to 26, 1977, Lippincott and Mark Hamill were in Hong Kong for the film's premiere, where a local newspaper article chronicled their arrival (bottom left; color photo taken at the same time, bottom right). In a coda to Flash Gordon's early inspiration and relation to the film, Lippincott reports that, after seeing *Star Wars*, producer Dino De Laurentiis bought the rights to the comic-strip character. He offered the movie to Federico Fellini to direct, but Fellini turned down the offer by saying that "George Lucas had already done it."

Spielberg took out
an ad in *Variety*'s
December 2, 1977,
edition to congrat-
ulate his friend
George Lucas on
the fact that *Star
Wars* had surpassed
his own film, *Jaws*,
at the box office—
becoming the number
one film of all
time (top right).
An internal memo at
Lucasfilm, written
by Debbie Fine,
lists film-rental
info accumulated by
Fox (below right).

Fri., Dec. 2, 1977 ⟶ VARIETY ⟵ 5

Dear George.
Last week "Star Wars" moved ahead of "Jaws" in domestic film rentals.
Your hyperspace performance package really did the trick.
Congratulations to the Cantina crowd and all the forces of your imagination that made "Star Wars" so worthy of the throne.
Wear it well.
Your pal,

Steven

Steven Spielberg

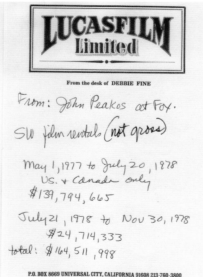

LUCASFILM Limited

From the desk of DEBBIE FINE

From: John Peakos at Fox.
SW film rentals (not gross)

May 1, 1977 to July 20, 1978
US. + Canada only
$139,794,665
July 21, 1978 to Nov 30, 1978
$24,714,333
total: $164,511,998

P.O. BOX 8669 UNIVERSAL CITY, CALIFORNIA 91608 213-760-3800

"*Star Wars* got an amazing response," Carrie Fisher says. "I used to drive by and look at the lines and think, *What?!* I haven't had a chance to absorb the madness."

"To this day [1978], people say to me, 'God, I was really dumb: I didn't realize how important this movie was . . . ,' " casting director Dianne Crittenden says of the actors who auditioned back in 1975.

"We're really surprised it's doing so well," Gary Kurtz told *The Washington Star* during a press trip to the capital in May 1977. "We knew there was a hard-core science-fiction-buff audience out there expecting it, but, frankly, we're surprised at how big it has turned out to be."

"I went to see it in a theater in a shopping center in my home town, and it was miserable," Ben Burtt says. "The audience seemed to like it, but it sounded awful compared to what it could be. Weak and dead, like an old radio broadcast. I felt very sad for the people, for all the work that we put into it, because they couldn't hear it as the film was intended to be heard."

"There is really only one sort of movie magic, and it's called *directing*," John Barry says. "It's very much like conjuring. A conjurer has his lady do something terribly interesting over here, while he gets a pigeon out of his back pocket. The jump to lightspeed is an example of conjuring, if you examine that scene very carefully. The film builds up to it—Han has to get the coordinates before they can make the jump—and it goes on quite a bit before you actually get the visual trick, which is a very short moment, but it's great. George is very good at all that."

"*Star Wars* is the first picture I really worked on that went to completion," Ralph McQuarrie says. "So I didn't really have that sense of what value the production illustrations were until I saw them on the screen."

For Alan Ladd, who was elected to Fox's board of directors in late July 1977, it was the end of many worries. The wild success of the film had proved Lucas right, to Ladd's relief. "What nobody had understood was that George's concept was to really just throw those things away, not dwell upon them, not ever give anybody the chance to say, *My God, what a wonderful set*," Ladd says. "The whole thrust of the film was movement. That's what he was going for. All of our concerns evaporated once we saw the final picture."

"It was amazing," Lucas's assistant, Lucy Wilson, remembers. "You'd go to restaurants and people were sitting around you talking about the person you work for and the movie you were working on—and it's on the cover of magazines. But we wondered, 'Well, okay, this is huge—but in two years, you know, is there a future?' "

ILM FINALS

"We calculated, at the end of the project," Robbie Blalack says, "that we had generated fourteen thousand pieces of film, given all of the separations, mattes, intermattes, garbage mattes, and lasers. All of those pieces of film had to be lined up by someone. All had to be printed by someone. The cataloging, sorting out, and the process of funneling that through was monstrous. The final count is 560 bluescreen shots compressed into 365 total shots, and it's all one generation removed, except for six shots."

On nearly all of those shots, the Dykstraflex camera was used—which amazingly had less than twenty-four hours of downtime due to mechanical

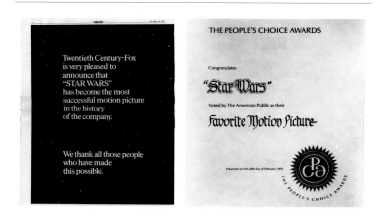

or electronic failure for the whole production. Budget-wise, ILM spent $3,619,601, $2 million over the studio-imposed ceiling, $1 million over the original estimate. The revised final budget for outside optical effects came to $273,369.

"This was my first experience with real special effects," Lucas says. "I had worked in opticals and animation before, but I hadn't really worked on the kind of problem-solving special effects that were generated by *Star Wars*. I find it fascinating. I'd like to continue to work out some of the things and try to advance them—because I don't think we took them as far as they can go."

"I think it came out fabulously, considering the limitations of time and money," Dykstra says. "It was a really unique group of people. And I really respect all of the stuff that George did to make it happen."

"George said at one point, 'I wore my favorite clothes, and never has so much money and time been spent on fun,'" Richard Edlund notes. "We certainly had a lot of fun doing the effects; it was fun to get up and go to work every morning."

"It was always difficult for me to accept George's idea of having the starfighters move at a tremendous speed and, of course seeing the film now, I agree with him completely," says Dennis Muren.

"There's a funny story," Edlund adds. "Joe Johnston went to the DMV one time when *Star Wars* had just come out, and he was standing in a line that went back to the door, and someone came in, looked at the line, and said, 'Shit, they ain't playin' *Star Wars* here, man!'"

"I remember leaving the theater and having these kids ask us for our autograph," Joe Johnston says. "We said, 'No, you don't want our autograph, we're like model builders.' But they said, 'No, no, we want you to sign this!' So we were thinking, *Wow, this must mean something—people are asking for our autographs!*"

Fan interest was mirrored to some extent by crew interest, both just before and after the film came out, as its physical props became increasingly valuable. "Once people knew it was going to be a really good film, things just started disappearing," Mary Lind recalls. "That's when everybody put locks on the doors."

As head of Film Control, Lind was also in charge of locating a secure and technologically safe resting place for the now incredibly precious neg-

ative. The optimum facility was found at the Hollywood Film Company in its vaults on Seward Street, with black-and-white optical elements stored in vaults 203 and 204, and negatives of the entire film in vault 356.

Her last duty fulfilled, Lind, who had come to work prepared to leave directly for Hawaii, jumped into a taxi and sped to the airport wearing a bathing suit and sandals.

SEVEN STORIES FOR ONE DEAL

"Fox went, in a very few years, from being a company right on the edge to being a very profitable company," Warren Hellman says.

In short, the studio's stock rose from a low of $6 a share in June 1976 to nearly $27 immediately following the release of *Star Wars*, according to Aubrey Solomon's *Twentieth Century-Fox: A Corporate and Financial History*. On June 22, 1977, *Variety* pointed out that the volume of Fox stock traded, 7,808,400 shares since May 23, exceeded 100 percent of the firm's common stock. A rumor circulated at the time saying that insider trading had taken place, given that a few individuals had bought up Fox shares right before *Star Wars* came out, while the stock was low, and then made millions when the stock soared.

"The story was that some people were sufficiently prescient to realize that there was this big hit coming and bought the stock while it was cheap," Gareth Wigan explains. "But the truth is, there were very, very few people within Fox, and certainly none of them had any stock, who believed *Star Wars* was going to be a huge hit. I think in fact the reason the stock moved up is that a lot of people thought it was going to be a *catastrophe* and the studio was going to lose all its money, and therefore the management of the studio might easily change—and therefore this was a move to acquire stock with a view to a takeover. I think they were actually trying to buy the stock with a view to getting rid of the management. But still, good luck to them; they made a lot of money."

True to character, Fox penny-pinched to the very end. Because the film's final budget was $11,293,151, $3 million over the imposed budget—though fairly close to at least one of the early projected budgets—the studio had taken a part of Lucas's directorial fee as compensation. "George was committed personally for $15,000 of his salary, as a penalty against the budget overage," Kurtz says. "That was another thing that we argued and argued and argued about with them—and they didn't reimburse him until after the movie came out."

Of course by that time, Lucas's financial situation was different from that of most filmmakers, even the most successful ones. His insistence, the help of his lawyers, and the ongoing fantastic success of the movie guaranteed him a fortune. Plus, as the film garnered what was evidently becoming a loyal fan base, its ancillary and sequel rights became more and more important. "George not only determined what products to go with, but achieved complete creative control on how the artwork looks, how the packaging looks, what ads would be used," Jake Bloom says. "Whereas I firmly believe, under the traditional Hollywood deals that were made prior to this picture, that George would not have had creative control over these deals."

One area where Lucas capitalized on this creative control was in his deal with Marvel Comics—negotiated by Lippincott—for a full-color serial

Artwork by Charles White III and Drew Struzan was featured in the summer 1978 re-release poster (right), which ran in newspapers across the country, including the July 16, 1978, edition of the *Los Angeles Times* (far right, elongated to include credits).

adaptation. The fact that it was written by Roy Thomas and penciled by Howard Chaykin, both of whom had sizable reputations and followings, gave the film a legitimacy in certain circles. "Studios minimized the comic fan," Bloom explains, "but George felt they were important in creating a base of hard-core fandom. It's a word-of-mouth business. That's something that Twentieth Century-Fox did not see three and a half years ago, but George saw it. Because of that Twentieth and George are now receiving vast benefits. I'm sure the studio will look at their contract and suddenly say, 'How could we have made that deal? How could we do that?' But they should thank God that they did it. They fell into something that they couldn't even envision."

"Yesterday [August 10, 1977], I was out at Fox, and I was talking to the business affairs people," Tom Pollock says. "And they told me that there are seven different stories circulating about why those rights were given to George—when they had never been given to anybody else before, have never been given to anybody else since, and will never be given to anyone in the future. They said there are seven stories about why they gave away the sequel rights. Because the sequel rights are enormously valuable. And they gave us half the merchandising. It was George's idea and I give it all to George."

"Recently [summer of 1977], I went to the latest comic convention in San Diego after the picture's success," Bloom adds. "*Star Wars* was probably the major thing down there; suddenly people are merchandising and trading and starting to collect *Star Wars* items. We already have avid collectors who will be there forever."

"The first screening of the completed film was at the big theater on the lot at Fox the Friday before it opened," Lippincott says. "It was a daytime screening for the *Variety* critic who blew his top because I invited 20 people from the sci-fi and comic book world who had helped me out. The critic gave us a very good review and it turned out my guests over the weekend called many of their friends around the country. The spark really took off and affirmed what many had hoped about the film."

Lucas, as well as John Williams, also struck gold when the soundtrack, which sold for about $9, went platinum with 650,000 copies selling by mid-July. The stock of General Mills, which owned Kenner, went up dramatically, too—solely based on the rumor that it would procure the toy license for the film—which it did (though toys didn't hit the market until after the holiday season of 1977). With all of his success, Lucas decided to give points or percentages of points as gifts. "Everybody has points, but the key is to make them pay off," Lucas says. "I had a chance to give away a lot of my points, which I had done with *Graffiti*. The actors, composer, and crew should share in the rewards."

Among those he gave a part of the profits to were: Gary Kurtz; Willard and Gloria Huyck; the law firm of Pollock, Rigrod, and Bloom; actors Alec Guinness, Carrie Fisher, Mark Hamill, and Harrison Ford; and Ben Burtt, Fred Roos, and John Williams.

As one might expect, news about a sequel spread rapidly—which led to a dramatic reversal of roles at Fox's negotiating table. "My understanding is that when George's agent came back for *Star Wars* two, he

Festivities included the 1978 Oscars and other parties: (top left) Grant McCune, Mark Hamill, and Richard Chew, with others; (top middle) Carrie Fisher and Anthony Daniels; (top right) Gary Kurtz, Ralph McQuarrie, and John Barry; (below left) eating dinner at the Academy Awards with their respective guests, Ben Burtt, Paul Hirsch, and Richard Chew; (below middle) Lucas chats with others at a party; (below middle) flanked by C-3PO and R2-D2, Ben Burtt receives a Special Achievement Award for Best Sound Effects; (below right, with unidentified winner on left) John Williams with his Oscar for Best Original Score. Other recipients were John Barry, Norman Reynolds, Leslie Dilley, and Roger Christian for Best Art Direction/Set Decoration; John Stears, John Dykstra, Richard Edlund, Grant McCune, and Robbie Blalack for Best Special Effects; Paul Hirsch, Marcia Lucas, and Richard Chew for Best Editing; Don MacDougall, Ray West, Bob Minkler, and Derek Ball for Best Sound. Nominations included George Lucas for Best Director and Best Screenplay; Gary Kurtz for Best Picture; and Alec Guinness for Best Supporting Actor.

said, 'Okay, one: The profit split is being reversed,' " Warren Hellman recalls. " 'Two: You're going to donate the product rights to us. And three: You're still not getting any sequel rights.' This I do remember: There was a great board meeting where management said, 'We have to give George the rights to his characters.' But we had a bunch of lawyers who said, 'You can't simply give away property rights!' We voted, and I think it was a six to five vote, because somebody had made the point that you can't own his children."

The inevitable slate of imitations was quickly planned by other studios, as well. Walt Disney productions began work on two films: *Space Station One* with a $10 million budget, targeted for teens, and *The Cat from Outer Space*, for younger kids. Universal and Paramount joined forces to plan a new version of *When Worlds Collide*. Universal began a remake of *The Thing*. The Doug Trumbull–run special effects house Future General was inundated with work, as were other specialty houses as studios wanted to jump-start any science-fiction film that they had stowed away on their shelves. To this day, Leonard Nimoy credits *Star Wars* with getting the first *Star Trek* film made, while, back in 1977, a new *Star Trek* TV series was announced at a fan convention in Los Angeles.

NO BUSINESS LIKE SHOW BUSINESS

"It won't be here forever," says Greg Myers, who accompanied his eight-year-old daughter and two nephews to the cinema. "I thought I'd better see it [again] while I had the chance."

"I've been hearing about this flick since it opened and I had to see it for myself," Robbit Kitsch of Port Huron, Michigan, says. "I think I'm going to come back with a few friends and guide 'em through and enjoy it all over again."

Indeed, repeat customers were another key to *Star Wars*' first-run box-office longevity. Not only was it good, but tens of thousands of people also felt it warranted at least one more viewing—with some attending more than fifty shows—and, before the advent of consumer videos, people had only one place to see it. Thus, by September 13, in Bend, Oregon, an estimated 50 percent of each audience was repeat viewers.

Even with the film's popularity assured, Twentieth Century-Fox's terms—a guaranteed 12-week run, 90 percent of the profits after overhead, and a guaranteed $65,000 against earnings—kept profit margins thin for theater owners, though no doubt the studio expected them to pad their overhead. The studio also benefited from a U.S. Justice Department ruling in April 1977 that required theater owners to bid for films. Until then movie theatres in the same area would make "split agreements" in which they would join together to divide up the season's first-run films—but that was ruled as being in violation of antitrust laws.

The winning bidder in Rocklander, New York, was the Town Theatre, where the film opened on August 5. With the percentage agreement, as reported by Jan Herman in the *Journal-News*, the theater had paid back the $65,000 guarantee by the third week. By the fourth week, the theater collected $16,000 for overhead and $9,300 profit—the rest of the $82,300 went

to the studio. The second-month revenues of $66,400 provided a profit of $5,040 after overhead to the theater, with $45,360 going to Fox. Third-month profits dropped to $1,570 of $31,700 with the distributor getting $14,130.

By November 27, 1977, 90,000 people had attended Town Theatre's 240 showings of *Star Wars*, that is, roughly one-third of the city's population. Half of Benton County in Oregon—approximately 6,750 people—had seen it by July 29. The film ran for at least 18 weeks at the Cinema II theater in Danbury, Connecticut, where "phenomenal" repeat business was in evidence. In the tiny town of Hamilton, Texas, on November 10, Texan Theatre manager Lem Guthrie reported that *Star Wars* had entered its *second* week—which had never *ever* happened there before (one showing per night, $2 admission).

Across the nation, so many theaters were showing the film so often that new prints had to be made because the first were literally being worn out. Popcorn was sold like never before.

Nevertheless, *Star Wars* had to eventually move aside for new movies, such as *Close Encounters*. On October 20, the film was replaced by *The Last Remake of Beau Geste* after a record-setting 18-week run at Waterloo's Strand Theatre in Cedar Falls, Iowa. It left Mentor, Ohio, on December 22, 1977, replaced by Neil Simon's *The Goodbye Girl*.

Back in San Francisco in November, Fox and Columbia started bickering over which film would play the Coronet, *Star Wars* or *Close Encounters of the Third Kind*. "The Coronet has been established as the *Star Wars* theater in San Francisco," Kurtz says. "It's still doing $55,000 a week, which is amazing." The Spielberg film went to the Northpoint. In Denver, Colorado, a press conference was convened in mid-December where it was announced that, to avoid problems, *Star Wars* would move from the Cooper to the Continental Theatre to make way for *Close Encounters*.

THE FIRST TRILOGY:
THX 1138, AMERICAN GRAFFITI, AND *STAR WARS*

Star Wars has probably generated at least one critic for every hundred fans. Lucas himself joked, when he received the American Film Institute Life Achievement Award in 2005, that he was the "King of Wooden Dialogue."

Many consider him only a master of special effects, now known as visual effects (*special effects* referring in contemporary vernacular to those created on the sets, mainly pyrotechnics). But the fact remains that while Lucas was amazed that no one had done a film like *Star Wars* before him, only a few have done one since. And that's because, as the story of the film's creation shows, it's nowhere near as simple as it might look to the casual observer.

Moreover, what comes out in several interviews is that the actual techniques used by ILM were not completely groundbreaking, or all that effective. Before the Dykstraflex was the Trumbullflex; Dennis Muren thinks they could've done better; Lucas certainly found the effects disappointing; and at the film's release several experts didn't find anything revolutionary in it at that level.

One only has to look at Disney's *The Black Hole* (formerly *Space Station One*) to see that if effects and funny robots were the key, then there would be hundreds of *Star Wars*. That 1979 film, which also had beautiful matte paintings by Harrison Ellenshaw, is in fact the film Twentieth Century-Fox was afraid they were getting from Lucas: robots with eyes painted on them, cardboard characters, slight themes, and corny special effects. *The Black Hole* is not that bad a movie—particularly the end montage of hell—but in its attempts to copy *Star Wars*, right down to the opening shot, Lucas's uniqueness of vision becomes clear by contrast.

Joe Johnston was impressed at the time by Lucas's exactness: In each ship's pan, rotation, and bank, there was an incredible eye at work. For what was reviewed as mainstream simplified cinema was actually an amalgam of abstract and cinema verité filmmaking with aspects taken from the work of directors such as Michael Curtiz and John Ford—all enhanced by Lucas's editorial artistry. And for every piece of wooden dialogue, there is solid plotting underneath to support the characters and the themes he is developing.

"THX and Luke are both Buck Rogers," Lucas says. "One is Buck Rogers today and the other is Buck Rogers in fantasy. One is the fantasy and one is the reality. Just two sides of the same coin. It's the same heroism defined in different terms—but they start from the same spot: accepting responsibility for one's actions. That's the one thing I think that ties them together, and which ties them to *American Graffiti*. In a way all three of my movies have been about the same theme. *THX 1138* looked at it from the point of view of a twenty-year-old. *American Graffiti* moved the perspective back to that of a sixteen-year-old. And now *Star Wars* tells the story from a twelve-year-old's point of view.

"It was something I saw in high school and junior college, and it was clearest to me when I was in film school," he explains. "I made seven movies in film school while everybody else was complaining that they couldn't make movies because they didn't have cameras, that they didn't have film. Well, those people are still stuck. They didn't realize that all you have to do is just do it."

While sharing their major theme, *Star Wars* develops what is only hinted at in Lucas's first two features: a more tangible mystical side, a return to the spiritual and perhaps more real self. The arrival of the droids on Tatooine and their purchase by Uncle Owen starts Luke Skywalker on an adventure toward his highest dreams of himself,

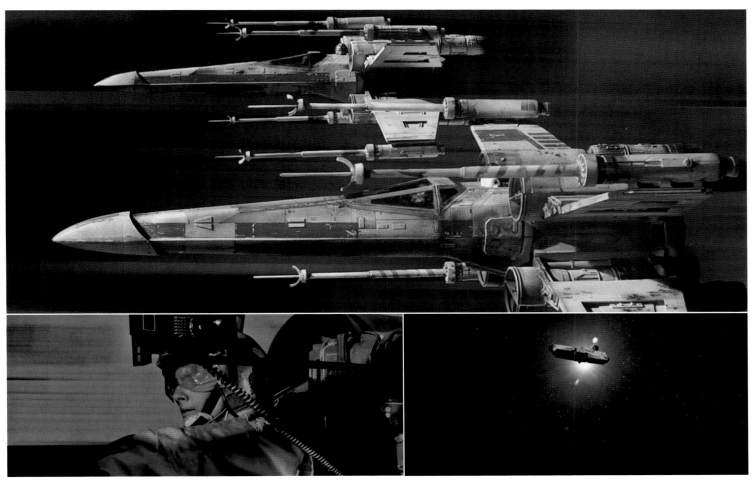

some of which are thrust upon him and some of which he creates. Where he is drifting in the beginning, he is awakened by the end. As is Han Solo, although his transition is often overlooked—but he, too, goes from an ambiguous materialism to an acceptance of responsibility. It's not an accident that Lucas dressed them similarly for the end ceremony.

Psychologically speaking, Luke has to rid himself of his surrogate fathers—Uncle Owen, Darth Vader, and even Obi-Wan—before he can be truly independent. In this sense he also stands with Curt of *Graffiti*, and THX—all three are independent at the end of their films and looking out on the future: Curt from an airplane window, THX at the sun, and Luke from the podium. While Lucas would go on to add many shades of gray to the future saga, *Star Wars* is really the third chapter in the trilogy of his youth. THX is the almost passive rebel who leaves a mindless society behind; Curt is a less passive loner who leaves a small town behind; and Luke is the future and mystical knight-king who leaves his farm behind—but gains a new family in Solo, Leia, Chewbacca, and the droids. Not to mention the Rebel Alliance. He is happily in the world.

MANY FUTURES FOR THE SHOGUN

"Making a movie is very much like constructing a house," Lucas says. "No matter how you plan it, there are adjustments that have to be made along the way, because nobody can envision the finished structure. But that's essentially what filmmaking tries to do, and of course life gets involved in it when you are shooting. Personalities, weather, nature—everything comes into it and adjusts it. As you bring it to life, and the film becomes a real thing, you see it in a different way.

"So I ran the race and I didn't do as good as I should have by a long shot," he adds. "But whether I won or lost, I still ran the race. I couldn't have done it any better because I tried to do it as well as I possibly could. But I certainly fell far short of what I wanted. And nothing will change that. It's really not a matter of being satisfied; I don't think you are ever satisfied. But when I saw the first cut, my only opinion was that I did a terrible job, but it works. It doesn't work very well, but it works. That was reconfirmed when I saw the trailer for the first time. I thought, *This is the movie I set out to make.* Spaceships flying around and monsters and craziness. And then when I finally saw it with an audience for the first time, I realized that no matter how far short I fell, and how far short all the departments fell from what I wanted, the film did work for an audience. I feel a movie is very binary: It either works or it doesn't work. And it did work. The audience did relate to it. They all laughed at the right places and they believed it."

Finally, in the summer and fall of 1977, Lucas took more time off and was able to reflect and relax. He attended a celebratory dinner with the board of directors at Fox, which was held on a sound stage where Lucas was seated next to Princess Grace's daughter Caroline. He also sat down for more interviews with Lippincott, during which he talked about his future plans: "More than anything else, I am interested in seeing the genre of science-fiction adventure become strong, like the Western. I would like to see more high adventures in space. But I don't want to be a slave of technology; I want to be able to have the technology available, and create whatever visions people can come up with. I would like to make it as free as the literary side of the genre, which is asking an awful lot.

"I think science fiction still has a tendency to make itself so pious and serious, which is what I tried to knock out in making *Star Wars*. Kubrick did the strongest thing in film in terms of the rational side of things, and I've tried to do the most in the irrational side of things because I think we need it. I would feel very good if someday they colonize Mars, when I am ninety-three years old or whatever, and the leader of the first colony says: 'I really did it because I was hoping there would be a Wookiee up here.' "

To the press, Lucas stated several times that he was going to retire from directing. Given the experience of the previous four years, he was exhausted. His friends and colleagues were not surprised, as they'd observed his difficulties firsthand. They were also confident that he would remain fundamentally the same. "I don't think you'll see any change," Harrison Ford says. "I don't see any change in George after his success."

In USC's student paper, the *Daily Trojan*, on December 9, 1977, staff writer Rori Benka reported on a visit Lucas made to his alma mater. While the public was still standing in lines to see *Star Wars*, Lucas reiterated in a closed-door presentation how disappointed he was in his film. When asked about his future, he responded, "I'm retired now, I've done it. I have let a lot of distractions into my life, on purpose, because I want to enjoy some things that I've never been able to enjoy before. I can enjoy the success of the film, a nice office to work in, and restoring my house, going on vacations. I've decided to set a year or so aside to enjoy those distractions. Plus, I'm setting up a company and getting the sequels off on the right track."

To create the special effects for the two sequels, Lucas would again employ Industrial Light & Magic—but this time it would be closer to home, as he'd originally envisioned. So those first employees had a choice:

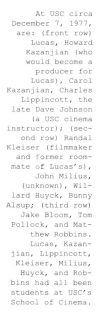

At USC circa December 7, 1977, are: (front row) Lucas, Howard Kazanjian (who would become a producer for Lucas), Carol Kazanjian, Charles Lippincott, the late Dave Johnson (a USC cinema instructor); (second row) Randal Kleiser (filmmaker and former roommate of Lucas's), John Milius, (unknown), Willard Huyck, Bunny Alsup; (third row) Jake Bloom, Tom Pollock, and Matthew Robbins. Lucas, Kazanjian, Lippincott, Kleiser, Milius, Huyck, and Robbins had all been students at USC's School of Cinema.

They could either stay in Southern California or move north to San Rafael.

The ILMers who stayed in the Van Nuys facility changed their name to Apogee. That group included Bob Shepherd, John Dykstra, Richard Alexander, Alvah Miller, Grant McCune, Lorne Peterson, and Richard Edlund—though the latter two would rejoin ILM about a year later. Apogee intended to make a feature film, according to Shepherd, but that never happened. They did do the special effects for *Caddyshack* (1980) and *Firefox* (1982), among several others; the late-1970s TV show *Battlestar Galactica;* and many commercials.

One of those who moved north was Dennis Muren, who was eager to help Lucas advance the capabilities of special effects. "There's no way at the moment that this equipment can do a stop-motion dinosaur," Muren says. "If they eventually can do it, it's going to be great, and we'll be able to have some really neat-looking shots, but that's a long way off." Muren would eventually help bring those dinosaurs to life in Spielberg's *Jurassic Park*, in 1993, at ILM—winning him one of his seven Oscars.

"Of all the people who came here, Joe Johnston is certainly the one who is going to be known and heard from again," Shepherd predicted. "He might art-direct an important movie . . ." Johnston would also make the move to San Rafael, remaining at ILM for a number of years before going off to direct films such as *Honey, I Shrunk the Kids* (1989); *Jurassic Park III* (2001); and *Hidalgo* (2004).

The list of accomplishments later achieved by those who worked on *Star Wars* would fill many pages, even if only measured by awards. Harrison Ford went on to embody Indiana Jones and become a gigantic star, winning the American Film Institute Life Achievement Award in 2000; John Williams continued to write music and win Oscars, most recently for *Schindler's List* in 1994; Paul Hirsch would be nominated for an Academy Award for *Ray* (2004); John Mollo, after working on *Alien*, won for *Gandhi* in 1983; Rick Baker would win six Oscars; Ralph McQuarrie won an Academy Award for *Cocoon* (1986) as did Ken Ralston, who won five others; Ben Burtt received two Oscars, one for Spielberg's *E.T. The Extra-Terrestrial* (1982); John Dykstra received one for *Spider-Man 2* in 2004; Alan Ladd Jr. won an Academy Award for Best Picture in 1996 for *Braveheart;* and of course Lucas was given what is perhaps the industry's most coveted honor, the Irving G. Thalberg Memorial Award, in 1992.

Sadly, John Barry died shortly after making *Star Wars,* while at work on the first of the sequels, on June 1, 1979. And Adam Beckett, who was by all accounts a brilliant animator, died tragically in a fire in 1978. Of course several other *Star Wars* veterans have since passed away.

As for the future of cinema, Lucas's vision of a special effects palette that would allow filmmakers as much freedom of imagination as writers and painters coincided with Dykstra's 1978 prediction: "The next step is digital, because then you can do anything you want."

And while he wouldn't direct again for two decades, Lucas dedicated years of his life and millions of his dollars in pursuit of that digital goal, helping in the process to create digital editing, sound, and cameras, as well as what has become Pixar Animation Studios.

"If one wants to know the future of the film industry, one goes up to San Francisco and visits George," Martin Scorsese says. "It's as simple as that."

"I'm interested in cinema, the psychological process, why certain films work and others don't. Film is magic. *That's all it is. You're sitting there with one hand doing one thing, while you're fooling the audience with the other hand."*
—George Lucas

In 1979 a Japanese poster touted *Star Wars'* Oscars and a sneak preview of *The Empire Strikes Back*, the first sequel (far left); in 1981 a U.S. poster (left) signals another revival—one of many that would continue unabated for decades . . .

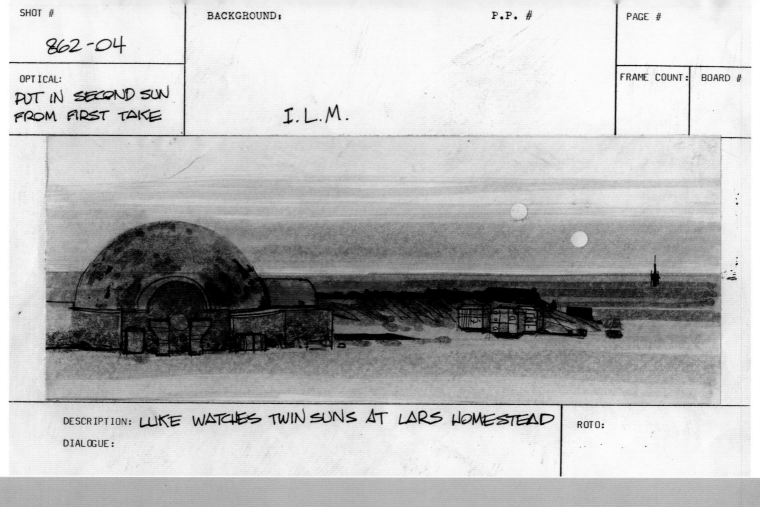

SHOT #	BACKGROUND:		P.P. #		PAGE #
862-04					
OPTICAL:				FRAME COUNT:	BOARD #
PUT IN SECOND SUN FROM FIRST TAKE	I.L.M.				

DESCRIPTION: LUKE WATCHES TWIN SUNS AT LARS HOMESTEAD

DIALOGUE:

ROTO:

GLOSSARY

ANAMORPHIC PROCESS

The technique of fitting a wide-screen image onto a standard, almost-square film frame by optically "squeezing" it. This is accomplished by photographing through a cylindrically shaped lens in addition to a spherical one. When the image is shown, it is "unsqueezed" by projecting it through the same kind of lens. When an anamorphic lens is used on a camera, the developed film image appears squeezed in the horizontal axis, making it half as wide as it should be. A circle becomes an upright oval; a square becomes a rectangle with its top and bottom half the size of its height. These distorted images are particularly difficult to deal with in the creation of optical effects, so the ILM technicians usually use a nonanamorphic camera system (VistaVision) when they composite images.

BI-PACK

Two films that run through a camera or projector at the same time, packed one on top of the other. In special effects work, one usually functions as a matte that will create an unexposed area on the film to be filled in later by some other image; the other may be the fresh, unexposed film or print to be matted. Bi-pack cameras and projectors are commonly used in optical departments and sometimes in special effects or model photography. The matte paintings for the first *Star Wars* film were photographed with a bi-pack camera system. Bi-pack cameras are equipped with twin sets of magazines, one for the unexposed film and the other for the matte. They run through the camera with their emulsions touching. At ILM bi-pack cameras and projectors are frequently used on optical printers and aerial image printers in the creation of elements for traveling mattes.

BLUESCREEN PROCESS

A photographic process that involves filming in front of a brightly illuminated blue screen. After optical rephotography, the process yields film of actors or objects placed against a black background, and also film of their silhouettes against a clear-white background. With these two elements—moving subjects and their identical moving silhouettes—it is possible to place the subjects into any background scene. The silhouette is used to make a moving black space in the background environment, and the image of the actors is inserted into that hole. At ILM the bluescreens are self-lit with fluorescent tubes. The subject in front is lit with white or amber light, and care is taken that no blue from the screen reflects off the subject and none of the light on the subject spills onto the bluescreen. After the film is developed it is rephotographed twice: once with a filter that turns all the blue to black and leaves the subject unaltered, and then with a filter that turns the blue to white and blocks out all other colors, so that the subject becomes the silhouette.

BLUESPILL

Bluescreen requires that an object or actor be photographed in front of a blue screen. When light from this screen illuminates the object and is seen by the camera, it's called bluespill. Uncorrected during photography, these contaminated areas may become transparent during the optical compositing process and create an undesirable matte line wherever the blue light fell on the object. This condition usually occurs when the subject is glossy or white or placed at an undesirable angle to reflect light. Certain lenses are more susceptible to bluespill than others. An experienced bluescreen cinematographer is often able to eliminate or minimize bluespill through special lighting techniques.

FRONT PROJECTION

Also known as the Alekan-Gerard process and the Scotchlite process. A highly reflective screen is placed behind the subject being photographed. A projector is next to the camera with its optical axis at ninety degrees to the camera. A beam splitter reflects the projected image toward the screen while allowing the camera to see through; thus the camera sees the projected image on the highly reflective screen with the subject in front of it. The screen is so reflective, in fact, that only a very dim projection light is used; consequently, the foreground objects do not reflect the projected image.

GARBAGE MATTES

Animated mattes that serve to block out "garbage" in shots, such as unwanted lights, cables, C-stands, and so on. Often there are large areas of the shots in special effects elements that are not used and need to be "plugged up," as it were, with garbage mattes. Usually they are quickly made with pieces of black paper placed above a light box and photographed with an animation camera.

OPTICAL COMPOSITE

A finished special effects shot, made up of two or more images that have been combined on an optical printer. An optical composite can be as simple as a flash of lightning in the sky or as complicated as fifty individual spaceships in a space battle. The most common optical composites place actors, photographed on a stage, into imaginary environments that combine actual live shots with matte paintings.

ROTOSCOPE

A technique in which individual frames of a movie are blown up and traced, one at a time, onto animation cels. Thus live action can be turned into animation (when the cels are rephotographed), ghostly effects can be added to live action, technical marvels can be put into real people's hands (the lightsabers), and so on.

Rebel soldier sketch
by Ralph McQuarrie.

BIBLIOGRAPHY

ADDITIONAL AUDIO/VIDEO INTERVIEWS

1977 (circa): Alec Guinness (audio publicity tape)

1999: Francis Ford Coppola, Fred Roos, Martin Scorsese (Omnibus interviews, Lucasfilm Archives)

2003: Bunny Alsup, Hal Barwood, Steve Gawley, Howard Hammerman, Paul Huston, Lucy Wilson (Lucasfilm History Project, interviews by Pamela Glintenkamp)

2003: Carroll Ballard (interview by Paul Scanlon)

2003: Frank Darabont, Willard Huyck, John Korty, Matthew Robbins (*THX 1138: The Director's Cut* DVD, interviews by Gary Leva); James Cameron, Peter Jackson, Ken Ralston, Norman Reynolds, Ridley Scott, John Singleton, Steven Spielberg, Gareth Wigan (2004 DVD release; Lucasfilm Bonus Disc documentaries)

2004: Charles Lippincott (by Pete Vilmur)

2006: Colin Cantwell (by David Nakabayashi)

CHRONOLOGY INTERVIEWS
(BY J. W. RINZLER)

May 3, 2006: Ralph McQuarrie

May 5, 2006: Lorne Peterson

May 5, May 18, and June 13, 2006: George Lucas

May 31, 2006: Warren Hellman

August 8, 2006: Robert Tong

August 2006: Fred Roos

ADDITIONAL PRINT SOURCES BY SUBJECT

de Aragon, Maria, is quoted from Scott Chernoff, "Bar Room Blitz," *Star Wars Insider,* April–May 1998.

Baker, Kenny, is quoted from Dan Madsen, "The Real R2-D2," *Star Wars Insider,* summer 1994.

Blake, Paul, is quoted from Matt Yeo, "Lounge Room Lizard," *Star Wars: The Official Magazine,* October–November 1998.

Brown, Phil, is quoted from Scott Chernoff, "The Man from Uncle," *Star Wars Insider,* February–March 1998.

Cushing, Peter, is quoted from *Starlog* magazine, July 1985.

Daniels, Anthony, is quoted from Anthony Daniels, "Bonfire of the Utinies," *Star Wars: The Official Magazine,* August–December 1998.

Diamond, Peter, is quoted from Iain Lowson, "The Star Wars Stooges," *Star Wars: The Official Magazine,* April–May 1997.

Fisher, Carrie, is quoted from Judy Stone, "Debbie Reynolds' Daughter Has Grown Up," *San Francisco Chronicle,* January 26, 1977; and Elaine Welles, "*Star Wars* Star Loved Her Role," *Philadelphia Tribune,* June 28, 1977.

Guinness, Sir Alec, is quoted from Philip Oakes, "World Enough and Time," *The Sunday Times,* May 2, 1976; staff writer, *Seattle Post-Intelligencer,* September 25, 1977; and *The New York Times,* January 2, 1978.

Hamill, Mark, is quoted from Harry Tessel, "*Star Wars* Star Is on Cloud Nine," *Long Beach Independent,* June 10, 1977; Pat Berman, "*Star Wars* Lead Was Unexpected," *The Columbia (S.C.) Record,* June 25, 1977; in the *Post-Tribune,* Gary, Indiana, July 3, 1977; and James Van Hise, "An Interview with Mark Hamill," *Rocket's Blast Comic Collector,* October 1977.

Kurtz, Gary, is quoted from Zofia Smardz, "How They Made *Star Wars:* Early Doubts, a Fast Finish," *The Washington Star,* May 30, 1977.

Ladd Jr., Alan, is quoted from Tom Nolan, "He's a Twentieth Century Fox," *Crawdaddy,* May 1978.

Lucas, George, is quoted from Gregg Kilday, *The Boston Phoenix,* June 14, 1977.

Marjdi the elephant is described in Eric Shultz, "The Big Secret Behind *Star Wars* Elephant," *Modern People,* Franklin Park, Ill., December 4, 1977.

Mayhew, Peter, is quoted from Dave Horner, *Asylum,* December 1977; Joe Nazzaro, "Roowarragh!" *Star Wars: The Official Magazine,* December–January 1997–1998.

Mulholland, Declan, is quoted from David Bassom, "The Man Behind the Hutt," *Star Wars: The Official Magazine,* October–November 1997.

Stark, Koo, is quoted from Richard Holliss, "Lost in Space," *Star Wars: The Official Magazine,* February–March 1999.

Taylor, Gilbert, is quoted from Jamie Painter and Chris Gardner, "Taylor-Made," *Star Wars: The Official Magazine,* February–March 1997.

SELECTED BIBLIOGRAPHY

Andrews, Rena. *The Denver Post,* Denver, Colorado. December 14, 1977.

Arnold, Gary. "*Star Wars:* A Spectacular Intergalactic Joyride." *The Washington Post.* May 25, 1977.

Barnes, Harper. *St. Louis-Dispatch,* St. Louis, Missouri. August 14, 1977.

Benka, Rori. "*Star Wars* Writer-Director Says Film Was Disappointment for Him." *Daily Trojan.* December 9, 1977.

Bozereau, Laurent, ed. *Star Wars: The Annotated Screenplays.* New York: Del Rey, 1997.

Canby, Vincent. "Star Wars—A Trip to a Far Galaxy That's Fun and Funny." *The New York Times.* May 26, 1977.

———. "Not Since Flash Gordon Conquers the Universe . . ." *The New York Times.* Sunday, June 5, 1977.

Champlin, Charles. "*Star Wars* Hails the Once and Future Space Western." *Los Angeles Times.* May 22, 1977.

Chuvala, Bob. *News-Times,* Danbury, Connecticut. November 27, 1977.

Cleveland, Jan. *Telegram,* San Bernardino, California. September 6, 1977.

Dodds, Pat. *Record,* Cedar Falls, Iowa. October 20, 1977.

Ford, Stephen. *The Detroit News,* Detroit, Michigan. June 3, 1977.

Gottschalk Jr., Earl C. *Washington Star,* Washington, D.C. July 10, 1977.

The Harvard Crimson. June 1, 1977.

Hearn, Marcus. *The Cinema of George Lucas.* New York: Abrams, 2005.

Herman, Jan. *Journal-News,* Nyack, New York. November 27, 1977.

Hopper, Ila Grant. *Bulletin,* Bend, Oregon. September 15, 1977.

Jones, Steven. *Leaf-Chronicle,* Clarksville, Tennessee. August 21, 1977.

Kauffmann, Stanley. *New Republic.* June 18, 1977.

Morgan, Debbie. *News-Herald,* Willoughby, Ohio. December 21, 1977.

Murf. "*Star Wars* Review," *Daily Variety.* May 20, 1977.

Newsweek. "Fun in Space." May 30, 1977.

Oakland, Mike. *Olympian,* Olympia, Washington. October 18, 1977.

Parks, Jim. *Herald,* Oskaloosa, Iowa. July 30, 1977.

Pennington, Ron. "Movie Review: *Star Wars.*" *The Hollywood Reporter.* May 20, 1977.

Scanlon, Paul. "The Force Behind *Star Wars,*" *Rolling Stone.* May 1977.

Simon, John. "Star Dust." *New York.* June 20, 1977.

Siskel, Gene. "*Star Wars* Flashes with Space Wizardry." *Chicago Tribune.* May 27, 1977.

Solomon, Aubrey. *Twentieth Century-Fox: A Corporate and Financial History.* Metuchen, N.J.: Scarecrow Press, 1988.

Staff writer. *Herald News,* Hamilton, Texas. November 10, 1977.

Staff writer. *Corvallis Gazette-Times,* Corvallis, Oregon. July 29, 1977.

Time. "*Star Wars:* The Year's Best Movie." May 30, 1977.

Titelman, Carol, ed. *The Art of Star Wars.* New York: Ballantine, 1979.

Variety. "20th–Fox Opted for PG Rather than G *Star Wars* Rating." June 2, 1977.

Weitzner, Friedkin. "Galaxy Crisis." *The New Yorker.* May 1977; "Contrasts" (opposing view, anonymous). *The New Yorker.* September 26, 1977.

Note: Artwork dates for Ralph McQuarrie's production illustrations and matte paintings were taken from handwritten (undated) notes by McQuarrie in the Lucasfilm Archives.

INDEX